Y0-AHQ-535

The Ukrainians of Maryland

Stephen Basarab
Paul Fenchak
Wolodymyr C. Sushko
and others

Published by
Ukrainian Education Association of Maryland, Inc.
Baltimore, Maryland
1977

**MARYLAND
BICENTENNIAL
COMMISSION**

This book was published with the cooperation and financial support of the Maryland Bicentennial Commission in its desire to open new vistas of research and to preserve the histories of the peoples of Maryland.

First Edition

© Copyright 1977 by

The Ukrainian Education Association of Maryland, Inc.

Library of Congress Card Number: 77-85157

Ukrainian Education Association of Maryland, Inc.
518 S. Wolfe Street
Baltimore, Maryland 21231

Printed in the United States of America

Contents

1. The European Background
   Stephen Basarab — 1
2. Why Ukrainians Migrated to Maryland/United States
   Wolodymyr C. Sushko — 49
3. Arrivals and Settlements
   Wolodymyr C. Sushko — 71
4. Geography of Ukrainian Population in Maryland
   Hlib S. Hayuk — 121
5. Ukrainian Activities on the Maryland Scene; Interaction with Other Areas and Groups
   Paul Fenchak — 129
6. Ukrainians and Jews in Europe and in Maryland
   Paul Fenchak — 163
7. Religion and Churches
   Stephen Basarab — 185
8. Slavic Studies in Maryland
   Paul Fenchak — 275
9. Ukrainian Heritage Schools
   Wolodymyr C. Sushko — 299
10. Ukrainian Student Life in Maryland
    Areta Kupchyk — 337
11. Ukrainian Foods Becoming a Part of Maryland Traditions
    Lydia M. Sushko — 347
12. *Pysanky*: Ukrainian Easter Eggs
    Sophia Mychajlyshyn — 359
13. Ukrainian Arts and Artists in Maryland
    Wasyl Palijczuk — 371
14. Contributions to Maryland: Military — Sports — Literature — Politics and Government — Music — Professions, Business, and Industry — Organizations
    Editors — 401
15. Bibliography — 499
16. Index — 509

AUTHORS/EDITORS

STEPHEN BASARAB in a manner akin to the Slovenian writer Louis Adamic has diversified experiences in this broad America. Born of Ukrainian immigrant parents in central Pennsylvania, he has worked in stone quarries, coal mines, steel and copper mills, road construction, agriculture, and the United States Civilian Conservation Corps. In 1940 he entered federal service with the Army Department in Washington. Next followed Army duty as a staff sergeant in the Transportation Corps, with roles played in the invasion of Sicily and southern France. He returned from World War II service to the Army Department. After transferring to the Internal Revenue Service his work was interrupted by a second assignment in the Army during the Korean War.

In 1955 he was granted a baccalaureate degree in business administration by Johns Hopkins University, from which school he later received the Master of Liberal Arts degree. Also a certified public accountant, he recently retired as an Internal Revenue agent from the Internal Revenue Service. He is married to the former Wanda Gregorius and the couple has two daughters, Daria and Lisa. A lifelong student of East European affairs, he has held offices for the Ukrainian Congress Committee of America (Baltimore Branch), the Ukrainian Education Association of Maryland, Inc., et al. He is the author of the articles of incorporation for the last mentioned group.

He is a member of the Association for the Study of the Nationalities (USSR and Eastern Europe), Inc., and has participated in many conferences and meetings dealing with the manifold ethnic/cultural groups of Maryland. His industrial and professional experiences in many states have abetted his understandings of grass roots America.

PAUL FENCHAK was graduated from Bigler Township High School, Madera, Pennsylvania (1947), and from Clarion State College (1954). In 1957 he received the Master's degree from Pennsylvania State University and since that time he has completed over 100 more graduate hours in history, philosophy, and theology. He has been the recipient of fellowships from the Newspaper Fund, Inc., in journalism, the American Bar Association in East European studies, and the United Labor Council in the history of American labor. In 1967 he received the Certificate of Competence from the East European Institute of John Carroll University.

Now in his 25th year as an educator he has taught history and English in secondary schools in Pennsylvania, Michigan, New York, and Maryland in addition to having been a principal for seven years. He was a participant in two Conferences on Ethnicity held at the White House in Washington and he serves as secondary school coordinator of the Association for the Study of the Nationalities (USSR and Eastern Europe), Inc. Articles by him have appeared in the *Ukrainian Quarterly, Slovakia, Furdek, International Migration Review*, and various newspapers. For several years he was lecturer in American history at Catonsville Community College and for the past ten years he taught social studies at Pikesville Senior High School.

A former minor league baseball pitcher, he was head baseball coach at Clarion State College in 1953 and is a life member of the Association of

Professional Baseball Players of America in addition to belonging to various academic associations.

He married Ellen Marie Bohachick of Houtzdale, Pennsylvania, and the couple are parents of Judith, Carol, Janice, Marcia, Linda, and Paul G.

WOLODYMYR C. SUSHKO was born on September 3, 1920, in Pidhajchyky, Oblastj Lviv, Ukraine. In 1938 he was graduated from the 8-year secondary school in the city of Peremyshl. His family was displaced from Ukraine by the events of World War Two. He holds the Diploma Engineer of Forestry degree from the Institute of Soil Culture in Vienna, Austria, which is one of the oldest forestry colleges in Europe, (1946). Arriving in the United States in 1949 he lived briefly in Chicago and has resided in Baltimore since 1950.

Presently he is grounds officer of the Baltimore City Schools, physical plant division, in which capacity he has introduced new concepts for the study of nature. He and his brother Jaroslaw have developed two nature study centers — Bragg and Highwood — that are utilized by both elementary and secondary school students of the city. In 1973 he was certified as a Registered Professional Forester by the State of Maryland Department of Licensing and Regulation.

Professionally he belongs to the Society of American Foresters, the Conservation Education Council of Maryland, the Ukrainian Forester Association (OBULID), and the Ukrainian Education Association of Maryland, Inc. His professional achievements have been noted extensively in the Baltimore press and by Baltimore city education officials.

For 14 years he taught in the Ukrainian heritage schools of Baltimore, while also serving as assistant principal. He is the author and/or co-author of several articles appearing in journals and newspapers in both the English and Ukrainian languages.

His wife is the former Olha Charchalis of Yavoriw, Ukraine. Their children are Lydia, Martha, and Zenon.

CONTRIBUTORS

HLIB S. HAYUK was born in Kremynetz, Ukraine, in 1939, the son of Rev. Simon and Alexandra (Zhyglevych) Hayuk. He holds a bachelor's degree from City College of New York and a Master's from the University of Wisconsin (1967). He has been assistant professor of geography and environmental planning at Towson State University since 1969. His wife is the former Zoya Salyk and their children are Yakim and Maya. He served as a member of the Maryland State Bicentennial Commission.

ARETA KUPCHYK completed high school at the Institute of Notre Dame in Baltimore in 1974. She is now a senior at the University of Maryland, Baltimore County Campus, where she is majoring in American studies and media communications. She is active in PLAST (Ukrainian scouts) and in the Ukrainian Student Society of Baltimore in addition to her being editor of her university paper, *The Retriever*, and also serving as a member of the university yearbook staff.

SOPHIA (MULKEWYCZ) MYCHAJLYSHYN was born in Rokobuty, Oblastj Lviv, Ukraine. In 1931 she received a degree in elementary education from Teacher's Seminary in Horlytzi (now Poland). Arriving in the United States in 1949 she became active in Ukrainian women's organizations and since 1953 has been teaching egg painting techniques at the Baltimore Y.W.C.A. In the 1950's she taught at the Ukrainian Saturday School, Baltimore. Her husband Semen and she have a son, Roman, and a daughter, Tatiana.

WASYL PALIJCZUK is chairman of the art department of Western Maryland College where he is also an associate professor. He holds both a bachelor's and master's (1963) degree from the University of Maryland and earned a master of fine arts degree from the University of Maryland (Rinehart School of Sculpture). In 1977 he instituted a new course at Western Maryland College entitled The Ukrainian Experience. His works and biography appear in many professional publications. He is married to Oksana Lesia Lasijczuk. Their twin daughters are Ksenia and Natalka.

LYDIA M. SUSHKO, born in Baltimore in 1954, was graduated from Seton High School, Baltimore, and from Towson State University (1977). A major in history, she is working with the Enoch Pratt Free Library in Baltimore. Lydia has been active in the Ukrainian scouting group (PLAST), in the Ukrainian Student Society of Baltimore, and in promoting the Harvard Ukrainian Studies Fund Committee of Baltimore. She has been an officer of each of the organizations mentioned.

Business Manager

JOHN MALKO, treasurer of the Ukrainian Education Association of Maryland, Inc., served as business manager of the project of compiling this book. Born in Baltimore of the immigrants Mykola and Katherine (Kmyta) Malko, he has been active in Ukrainian affairs in many groups: The Ukrainian National Association, Baltimore Ukrainian National Home, treasurer; Maryland-District of Columbia Fraternal Congress, Resolutions and Credentials Committees; and the Ukrainian Congress Committee of America (Baltimore Branch), among others. He was graduated from Vocational High School and holds a Diploma from the Maryland Institute School of Mechanical Drawing (1937) and a Certificate in Tool Design from McCoy College of Johns Hopkins University. His wife is the former Helen Pise and their son J. Robert, Ph.D. (Purdue University), is chief staff economist for the Wisconsin Public Service Commission. John retired in 1976 from Western Electric Corporation.

Dedication

The Ukrainian Education Association of Maryland, Inc., respectfully dedicates this book to the most accomplished historian of the Ukrainian American experience, Professor Wasyl Halich, whose studied and unimpassioned portrayals of Ukrainians in America, as in *Ukrainians in the United States* (1937), should always be the rule.

Stephen Basarab
Paul Fenchak
Wolodymyr C. Sushko

Acknowledgements

The writers of this book firstly express sincerest thanks to members and employees of the Maryland Bicentennial Commission for their kindness in providing financial assistance and for their patience and exhortation during the several years of research and writing. Without their assistance the magnitude of the project could not have been attained.

Several professional researchers were extremely helpful: Fr. Vincent Eaton, Archivist of St. Mary's Seminary, Baltimore; Dr. Morgan Pritchett, Director of the Maryland Room of the Enoch Pratt Library; and Mr. Henry Bown and Dr. John E. Bodnar, Archivists of the Pennsylvania Historical and Museum Commission, Harrisburg.

To Fr. Casimir Pugevicius, Director of Lithuanian American Catholic Services, gratitude is extended for his encouragement during the planning stages of the book. His departure from Baltimore to New York has left a gap in ethnic creativity in Maryland.

Peter J. Critikos, a Greek American scholar and teacher of social studies at Pikesville High School, was helpful in reading and criticizing several chapters of the book.

Officials of the Baltimore Colts professional football team were most helpful in providing statistics and photographs about several Colt performers of Ukrainian heritage.

To an All-American group, the wives of the editors (Wanda, a Polish-Lithuanian American; Ellen, a Slovak American; and Olha, a Ukrainian American), deepest gratitude is extended for patience and assistance beyond normal expectations. *Mnohaya Lita!*

Particular appreciation is extended to Wanda Basarab for her having compiled the index of the book.

To all persons, Ukrainians and others, who helped in any way — photographs, interviews, articles, commentaries, suggestions, monetary contributions, etc. — heartfelt thanks are extended.

Stephen Basarab
Paul Fenchak
Wolodymyr C. Sushko

Donors

The individuals, firms or institutions listed below contributed financially toward the publication of *The Ukrainians of Maryland*. Without their kind assistance a profusely illustrated book of 500 pages could not have been realized. Their contributions are recognized with deep gratitude by the Ukrainian Education Association of Maryland, Inc.

Amstar Corporation
American Bank of Maryland (Highland-Canton Office)
Baltimore Chapter — League of Ukrainian Catholics of America
Mr. and Mrs. Oleh A. Bendiuk
Mr. and Mrs. Thomas C. Blocknia
Baltimore Federal Savings and Loan Association
Bond Federal Savings and Loan Association
Mr. and Mrs. Anatole Bulawka
Carling National Breweries, Inc.
Mr. and Mrs. Taras Charchalis
Chesapeake Federal Savings and Loan Association
Mr. and Mrs. Andrij Chornodolsky
Coca-Cola Bottling Company of Baltimore
Mr. and Mrs. Mykola Czeczulin
Bernard Dabrowski and Son Funeral Home
Walter G. Dabrowski — Graceland Park Funeral Chapel
Dr. Emil Derey
The Dippel Brothers, Inc., Funeral Homes
Dr. Irvin I. Donick
Philip C. Dypsky — Turn of the Century Museum-Bar
Mr. and Mrs. George Evanowicz
The Equitable Trust Company
First National Bank of Maryland
Mr. Charles H. and Mrs. Natasha S. Flanders — United Credit Bureau of America
Mr. and Mrs. Yale Gordon
Mr. and Mrs. Hlib S. Hayuk
Mr. Roman Herasymowycz
Highland Federal Savings and Loan Association
Dr. and Mrs. Victor R. Hrehorovich
Mr. Eliot P. Hurd
Jack's Corned Beef House, Baltimore
Mr. and Mrs. Casimer Jarema
Mr. John Kaczor
Raymond L. Kaczorowski Funeral Home
Dr. and Mrs. Nicholas Kohut
Mr. George Koneyak
Dr. and Mrs. Demetrius Kostrubiak
Mr. and Mrs. George Kotyk
Mr. and Mrs. John I. Korz
Dr. and Mrs. George N. Krywolap
Dr. and Mrs. Nicolas Lasijczuk
Dr. and Mrs. Andrew Lemischka
Lilly and Zeiler, Inc., Funeral Home
Loyola Federal Savings and Loan Association
Mr. and Mrs. John Malko
Mr. and Mrs. Joseph Marmash

McCully Funeral Homes
Mercantile-Safe Deposit and Trust Company
Congresswoman Barbara A. Mikulski
Mr. Theodore Nykula
Organization for the Defense of the Four Freedoms for Ukraine, Inc., Branch #14, Baltimore
Frank Petro, Esquire
Plast, Inc., Ukrainian Youth Organization, Baltimore Chapter
Mr. and Mrs. George Podhorniak
Mr. Lee Poist
Mr. and Mrs. Orest S. Poliszczuk
Leon A. Podolak and Associates
Providence Association of Ukrainian Catholics in America — Baltimore Branch #66
Provident Savings Bank
St. Michael's Ukrainian Catholic Church of the Byzantine Rite — Rev. Ivan Dornic, Pastor
St. Michael's Ukrainian Orthodox Church of the United States, Baltimore
SS. Peter and Paul Ukrainian Catholic Church
M.F. Sawdowski and Son Funeral Home
The Savings Bank of Baltimore
Mr. and Mrs. Michael Senkiw
Messrs. John and Theodore Shulka
Mr. and Mrs. John G. Smorhun
Hon. and Mrs. Joseph Staszak
Stephan Travel Agency — Paul Kowzan, Proprietor
Mr. and Mrs. W. Curtis Stith
Dr. and Mrs. Irving J. Taylor
Mrs. Mary Miskiw Thompson

Mr. and Mrs. Alexander W. Traska
Dr. and Mrs. Stephan Tymkiw
Alexander P. Ratych Associates, Inc.
Senator and Mrs. Paul S. Sarbanes
Leonard V. Ruck, Inc. Funeral Home
Ukrainian-American Association - Self Reliance, Inc., Baltimore Chapter
Ukrainian-American Bicentennial Committee of Maryland
Ukrainian-American Sport Club — "Dnipro"
Ukrainian-American Youth Association — Baltimore Branch
Ukrainian Congress Committee of America, Inc. — Baltimore Branch
Ukrainian National Association, Inc., Jersey City
Ukrainian National Association — Maryland and D.C. Branches Nos. 15, 55, 81, 148, 290, 320 and 337
Ukrainian National Home, Baltimore
Ukrainian National Women's League of America — Baltimore Branch # 59
Ukrainian Workingmen's Association, Branch #65, Baltimore
George A. Weber Funeral Home
Mr. and Mrs. John Yarema — Maryland Line Inn and Yarema's Lake
Mr. and Mrs. Carl J. Yarema — Ridgely Liquors
Charles S. Zeiler Funeral Homes
Kozub and Herold Families
Mr. and Mrs. George Prodanchek
Ukrainian Congress Committee of America, Inc., New York City

Preface

In his book, *Send These to Me*, Prof. John Higham of Johns Hopkins University states that ethnic diversity is a profoundly important fact of American life, but not always a desirable condition. After noting that ethnic differences can be either constructive or destructive, Prof. Higham suggests that American society has the task of modulating forces towards their constructive potentialities. He concludes his point by stating, "This is an unfinished, perhaps an endless task, which requires new strategies as times change."

To some degree the thinking indicated above expresses the challenge accepted by the Ukrainian Education Association of Maryland Inc., in writing this book, *The Ukrainians of Maryland*. The strategy of the Association was to publish a book *now* lest educators, governmental officials, curriculum planners, and librarians continue certain stances of "selective inattention" about Ukrainians and other East Europeans in American studies.

How well the writers have handled the acid test of history, i.e., penetrating situations and mentalities remote from their own, remains the judgment of readers. Yet certain facts stand: 1. This is the first in-depth study of any Slavic group in the history of Maryland. When it is remembered that the Czech (Bohemian) community is noticeably older in its settlement and when it is recalled that both the Czech and Polish communities are considerably larger than the Ukrainian settlements, it becomes apparent that gaps in Maryland history are greater than many educators realize. 2. Although East Europeans in Maryland constitute a minimum of 15% of the population, existing historical literature about Maryland is very deficient in the coverage of East Europeans. 3. Incorrect nomenclature exists in many histories and periodicals which tends to make Russians out of Lithuanians, Byelorussians, Estonians, Latvians, Poles, Ukrainians, et al.

Ethnic scholars might well begin their new strategies with examinations of other historiographies. To that end most chapters of this book have been closely documented and an extensive bibliography is included to help the researcher locate more data about Ukrainians in both the Maryland and general American sociologies.

Stephen Basarab
Paul Fenchak
Wolodymyr C. Sushko

The Ukrainians of Maryland

MAP OF UKRAINE

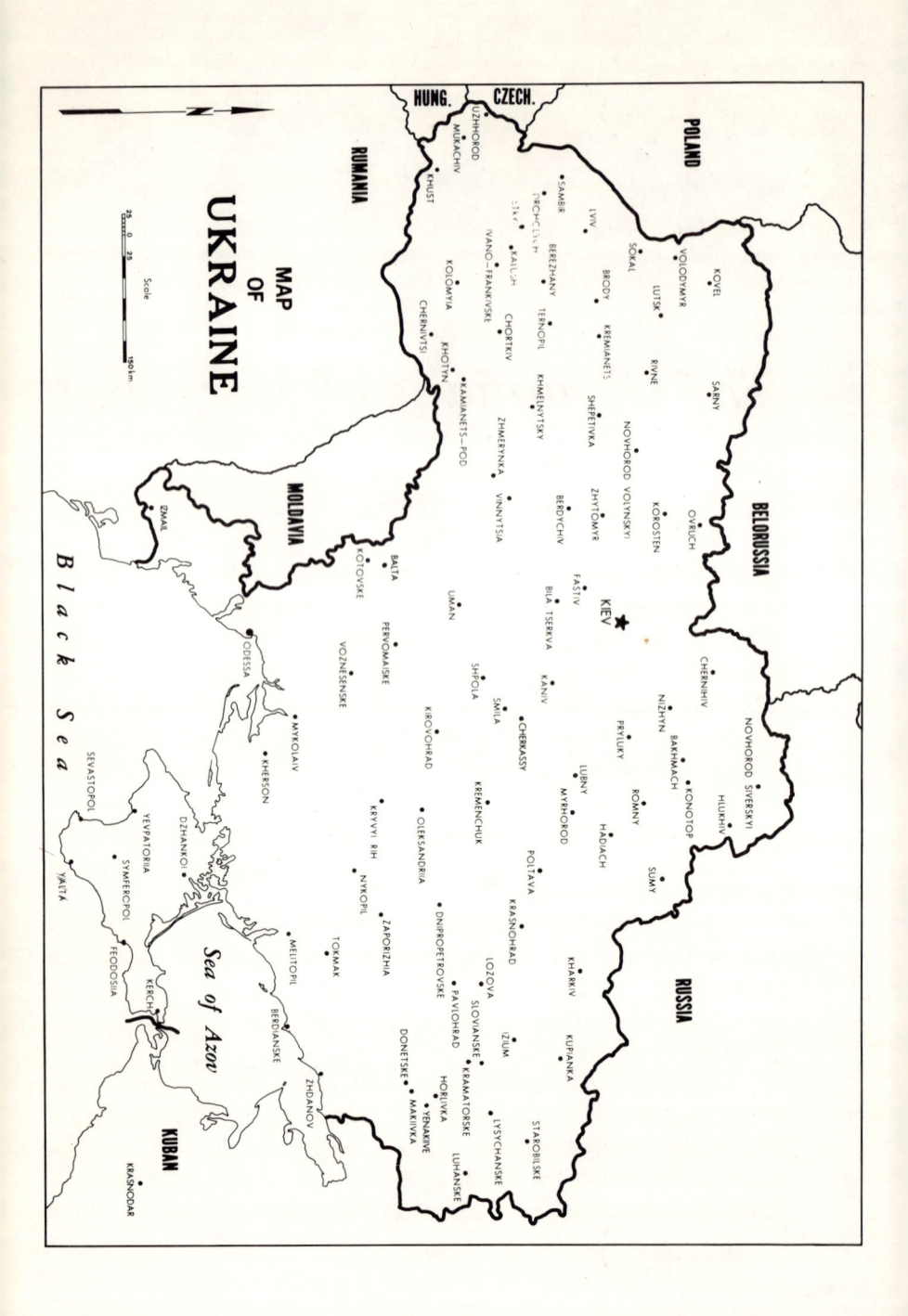

Chapter One
The European Background
Stephen Basarab

LOCATION AND AREA

Ukraine occupies the southeastern portion of Europe. The southern boundary of the Republic extends from the mouth of the Danube River eastward along the shores of the Black Sea and the Sea of Azov. On the west, Ukraine is touched by Romania, the Moldavian Soviet Socialist Republic, Hungary, Slovakia, and Poland. North of Ukraine are the Byelorussian Soviet Socialist Republic and the Russian Soviet Federated Socialist Republic. To the east Ukraine is bordered by the huge Russian Soviet Federated Socialist Republic. The Ukrainian Republic territory lies between 44°20′ and 52°20′ north latitude and 22°5′ and 40°15′ east longitude and encompasses an area of 232,000 square miles.

Ukrainian ethnic lands comprising 56,000 square miles extend beyond the boundaries of the Republic, into the present governments of Byelorussia, Russia, Romania, Slovakia, and Poland. About 80% of this area is in the Russian Federation.

Ethnically mixed territory with substantial numbers of Ukrainians but near areas of Ukrainian predominance embraces 76,000 square miles, with about 90% in the Russian Federation. Most of this land is near the Kuban River and toward the Caucasus Mountains.

GEOGRAPHICAL FEATURES

Most of Ukraine consists of steppes or plains, flanked on the west by the Carpathian Mountains and breached in the south by the Crimean Mountains. The highest peak in Ukraine is Heverlia in the Carpathians, rising to 6800 feet. More than 2/3 of Ukraine is less than 1000 feet in altitude. In the northwest, Ukraine is dotted with lakes and marshlands and contains much forest. Trees also cover the Carpathians and extend into areas to the north of Lviv and Kiev.

The Sian and Buh Rivers flow from the northern slopes of the Carpathians toward the Vistula in Poland. The Prut, Dniester, Boh, and Dnipro flow toward the east and south and empty into the Black Sea. The chief river is the Dnipro which begins in Russia and goes through the middle of Ukraine for a total length of 1420 miles. The Don, only part of which is in Ukrainian ethnic territory, runs into the Sea of Azov. Its leading tributary, the Donets, is almost entirely inside Ukraine.

Some of the world's richest soils, the chornozems or black earth, are found in Ukraine. They extend through Ukraine from the Prut River on the west to the Don River on the east and between the forests of the north and the steppes of the south. A lighter soil and with somewhat less humus is the "Dry Steppe" chornozem to the south which stretches from the lower Danube, north of the Crimean peninsula to the shores of the Sea of Azov.

CLIMATE

Ukraine lies within the temperate zone. In the southern part of Crimea, a milder, Mediterranean climate prevails. Along the Black Sea and toward the Sea of Azov there is a semi-arid belt suitable for grain production. The coldest temperatures occur in the northwest and in the western mountains, while average annual rainfall decreases from west to southeast, 27.5 inches to 11 inches. In the Carpathian Mountains, the average precipitation is 59 inches. Rain blown by winds from the Atlantic falls in greater amounts in the summer, this being favorable to agriculture.

POPULATION

The Ukrainian Republic, according to Soviet population estimates, had 48,100,000 persons on January 1, 1972. Ukrainians constituted 77% and Russians 17%, with the remaining 6% consisting of various peoples: Jews (1,025,800), Poles, Germans, Greeks, Bulgarians, Romanians and Tatars. In addition, Ukrainians living outside Ukrainian ethnic territory amount to 7,500,000 persons.

The majority of the population is of the Orthodox faith, 76.0%; Catholics of the Eastern Rite make up 13.5%; Jews, 2.3%; and Protestants, Baptists, Mennonites, and Moslems, 8.2%.

About half of the Ukrainians still live in rural areas. Kiev, the historic and present capital, is the largest city and cultural center and has a population of over 1,887,000. Other large cities are Kharkiv, the "Pittsburgh" of Ukraine; Odessa, the large seaport; Dnipropetrovsk and Zaporizhia, industrial and electric power centers on the lower Dnipro; Donetske, 1,000,000 population, in the Donbas and noted for metal-smelting and heavy equipment manufacture; Makiyivka, neighbor of Donetske and metal producer; Lviv, capital of Western Ukraine, important communications center and producer of buses, mining and gas equipment, instruments and farm machinery.

PRODUCTS

According to official Ukrainian Republic statistics of January 8, 1974, Ukraine "surpassed the biggest capitalist countries of Europe in most important branches of production, such as: pig-iron, steel, rolled metals, iron ore, natural gas, diesel locomotives, sugar."[1] Articles produced by the Ukrainian Republic include "Planes and ocean liners, locomotives and carriages, tractors and combines, excavators and cars, as well as up-to-date lathes and instruments, electronic microscopes and TV sets, computers and synthetic diamonds." Among its exports, in addition to the foregoing items, are electricity, sulphur, cement, coke-chemical products, coal, manganese, mercury, and mineral fertilizers.

Ukraine is famous for its wheat production, at one time being known as the "bread basket of Europe." It also produces corn, potatoes, sugar beets, sunflowers, and tobacco.

FACTORS AFFECTING UKRAINIAN HISTORY

The Ukrainians through their thousand-year history as a separate Slavonic people have been buffeted and molded by many conditions and forces, often paying a heavy price—and over extended periods—in suffering, deportations, and casualties but mysteriously reviving and confounding again those who had said that Ukrainians do not exist and that the Ukrainian problem is a myth. But they live and write again! Volodimir the Great, Yaroslav the Wise, Bohdan Khmelnitsky, Ivan Mazepa, Mykola Hohol (Gogol), Taras Shevchenko, Mykola Hrushevsky, Semeon Petliura, Taras Chuprynka, and Stepan Bandera have appeared and will reappear in writings about Europe and Ukraine. Many other Ukrainians, lost among the pages of history and literature of other nations, will come forth heralding the truth which sets all free. And a more accurate background of several millions of Americans will become a part of the knowledge of hundreds of millions of Americans, including those in the "Free State" of Maryland.

The influences working on the Ukrainians were many, some of the primary ones being: their geographic position between the two different cultural and political systems of Asia and Central Europe; the relatively level mobility-inviting prairies or steppes; a climate more temperate than that of most of their neighbors; a very rich agricultural land and bounteous natural resources; the generally longitudinal flow of the rivers, providing connecting links and trade routes as well as military access between the Baltic and Black Seas; the political institutions and methods of government fostered by occupying elements which favored large land owners and denied peasants anything more than a precarious existence under a system of harsh, personal regimentation; and the religious differences as Christians of the East not fully acceptable on an equal level by the West.

Under this assortment of conditions survival required a series of alerts, accommodations and unity to thwart the forces arrayed against them: the powerful covetous neighboring rulers and dynasties; the swift, marauding and wandering hordes; the conquerors from the south and east seeking pastures, slaves, converts or control of trade routes and the Black Sea; the Christian "missions" enraptured with divine aims and accompanied with requisite force for the salvation of souls from the Western and Russian Orthodox stance. It is no wonder that Ukraine had been tagged as the frontier or "border" land, as the country or *krai* where all enemies could enter to occupy its stategic position and partake of its luscius fruits. Many historians to this day legitimize and objectify incursions with their deceptive concepts of an empty wasteland or a "wild west" and backward peoples to the detriment of the Ukrainians. They dangle before the reader a borderland ripe for the taking, and not of a centuries-old *krai* or country—Ukraina—in which dwell the Ukrainian people.[2]

This category of historians has spread justification for aggression under such palliative slogans as "the gathering of the Russian lands," and "restoration of an historical Poland." Moreover, this was said against a land often thickly settled and whose civilization was highly developed and refreshed from Constantinople and beyond, but frequently despoiled and its population cut down by the very invaders who would become the masters.

With these many elements confronting them and creating an uncertain atmosphere, the Ukrainians were compelled to become fighters and defenders of their land, families, homes, and basic rights. The most precious values could be enjoyed only under certain minimum standards of freedom. Throughout many centuries they heeded the call of their princes or hetmans to battle against the oncoming "barbaric" hordes from the east, north and south and the "civilized" forces of Christian rulers from the west. With a thunderous roar of horses' hooves, the drawn sabres and lances of valiant Rus knights and daring Kozaks responded in a thousand skirmishes and battles, shaking the very earth and causing mighty warriors to tremble and monarchs to fall. For centuries when rulers in Muscovy, Poland, or the Ottoman Empire planned, they had to consider the hetmans and their Kozak fighters before venturing forth onto foreign terrain.

EARLY ORIGINS

Eastern Slavic tribes had been dwelling east of the Carpathian Mountains in Europe since before the Christian era. In the second century, A.D., the Antae, Slavonic ancestors of the Ukrainians, already had their own political organization, which lasted into the seventh century. The Antae, according to Jordanis, a writer of the sixth century, were the bravest of the Slavs, for they vigorously opposed the Goths and together with the Huns, destroyed the Gothic Empire in 375 A.D.[3]

In the eighth and ninth centuries seven Slavic tribes merged to form the Kievan state. Kyiv or Kiev was named after Prince Kyi of the Poliani, the tribe which occupied that area. The Greeks and Asian peoples in the eighth century commonly referred to the Kievan state as Rus. This was before the coming of the Scandinavians who later furnished the dynastic rulers for Rus.

The name Rus had been attributed to one of these rulers, Rurik, but this origin is now becoming less and less supportable. Professor Riasonovsky rejects the Norman theory of the origin of Kiev or Rus, saying it cannot be traced to the Vikings because Rus had a written literature, written law, coin stamping, and higher cultural level than the lands of the Vikings, and Scandinavian elements in Rus literature, law, religion, customs, and dress are practically nil. He reasons that the origin of the Kievan state is very closely connected to a group, tribe, or people known as the Rus.[4]

Nicholas Fr.-Chirovsky, another historian, also disagrees with the Norman origins of Rus, indicating that the name "Rus" or Ruce or Rhos in Greek was derived either from the River Ros in the land of the Poliani or from the historical Slavic tribe, the Roxolanians.[5] But there now is general agreement that the beginnings of Rus may be credited to the Poliani with the appearance of the Kievan state in the eighth century.

Spurred by their association with the Vikings, the Rus developed trade relationships over wider and wider domains as they expanded their influence. Kiev, as the trade and administrative center, grew and prospered so that by the ninth century it occupied a commanding position in eastern Europe, with the means, if properly led and united, to hold sway over a vast territory extending almost from the Baltic to the Black Seas.

KIEVAN RUS

The Kievan Rus period of Ukrainian history existed from the early years of the ninth century to 1349 when most of Ukraine came under Polish and Lithuanian rule. The members of the Rurikides dynasty, after much fighting, succeeded to the throne at Kiev. They extended their domains by military expeditions, particularly during the reign of Sviatoslav (964-972), son of Prince Ihor and Princess Olha. Ihor subdued many provinces and tribes and in 944 entered into an important commercial treaty with the Greeks. Olha, while regent for her minor son, Sviatoslav, ruled a peaceful and prosperous state while embracing Christianity.

Sviatoslav, a dynamic and resourceful man, spent his time campaigning in the east and south against the Khazars and Asian tribes and to the west against the Bulgars and Greeks. At its peak, the territory controlled by Sviatoslav extended from the Caspian Sea to the Danube River. But the Greeks and Bulgarians united and drove Sviatoslav out of Bulgaria. While homeward bound, he was attacked by a great horde of Pechenegs in a battle near the Dnipro rapids and killed.[6]

A period of consolidation was needed to stabilize the vast Realm of Rus. Fortunately, Volodimir, an able man, became the sole ruler in 980 with the aid of the Varangians (Normans). Although he was the head of a pagan faction he soon realized that the Christian influences were in the ascendancy and that the state needed better administration and protection. Volodimir acquired and fortified the areas in northwest Ukraine and brought the revolting tribes to the north back to Rus control. He then decided to accept the Christian faith for himself and his nation, being baptized in 988, after which he was permitted to marry Princess Anna, sister of the Byzantine Emperor.

There already were Byzantine Slavonic churches in Ukraine and over a century before apostles of the Slavs, SS. Cyril and Methodius, had translated the Bible and liturgical books into the Slavic language. The officially-established religion grew fast, aided by missionaries from Bulgaria, and greatly helped in uniting the people. Volodimir brought in artisans and built many churches in Kiev and throughout Rus, including the most beautiful one, the Desiatynna, or Blessed Virgin Mary. By the time of his death in 1015, Kiev was a great city with many churches, and was said to rival Constantinople.[7] Volodimir abolished capital punishment, established schools next to the churches for the children of the boyars (nobles), and adopted a separate statute for regulating the Church. Because of his many charitable deeds, Volodimir, after his death, was canonized and many writers referred to him as "The Great."

Yaroslav the Wise, who ruled from 1019 to 1050, is noted for his contributions to internal development. He built St. Sophia Cathedral in Kiev, and founded Ukraine's first institution of learning and research, where books were translated from foreign languages into Slavonic and original works were written. The monasteries of St. George and of St. Irene were founded by him. He became famous for the introduction of the first code of laws in the entire Slavic world: *Ruskaia Pravda* (Rus Law). This Code of Law was in force in Ukraine for many centuries.

In Yaroslav's reign, the first Metropolitan, a Greek,

was installed in Kiev with St. Sophia as the Cathedral church. But Yaroslav preferred a deeply religious and learned monk, Ilarion, whom he at a Synod of all Ukrainian bishops selected to replace the banished Greek.

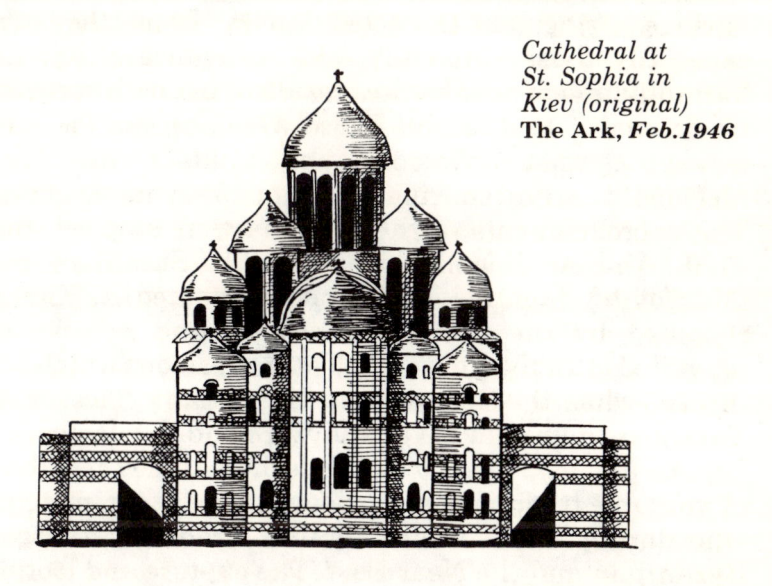

Cathedral at St. Sophia in Kiev (original)
The Ark, *Feb.1946*

Yaroslav was an incessant reader and a good friend of the monks and clergy. He maintained contacts with the west, having friendly relations with the German Emperors and with the royal families of Sweden, Norway, and France. His wife Irene was the daughter of the Swedish King, while his daughters Elizabeth married Harold, King of Norway, and Anna, the King of France.

After Yaroslav's death, Kievan center of Rus power weakened and ended amidst the struggles for control. The laws of succession provided for joint sovereigns and apportionments of the various principalities in order of seniority, with the oldest becoming the Grand Prince of Kiev. Constant transfers of princes from lesser to major principalities made stability difficult. Each prince maneuvered for position and allies on whom he could rely for support. Finally, the dynastic system was discontinued and a Diet of Princes was agreed upon in 1097 to settle common problems and oppose the Cumans (Polovtsi) who invaded from the east. Thus, Rus no longer came under the rule of a Grand Prince of Kiev.

Further disintegration of the Realm of Rus followed the death of Mstyslav I, Prince of Kiev. More and more the various principalities acted apart from the others, especially those ethnically and economically unrelated. Virtually independent states resulted, but with some of the traditions of Rus intact. There were appeals for united action against invasion, unity under the Kievan Metropolitan, and sharing of a common dynastic ancestry. The encroachments of the Cumans were stopped. But in 1169, Andrew Bogoliubsky with his Suzdalian troops (Muscovite) captured Kiev and devastated it. Kiev was regained by the Ukrainian princes and relative calm prevailed until the time of the Tatar invasions which began in 1223 when the Cumans and Ukrainian princes met the Tatars at the Kalka River and were badly defeated.

An important factor in the decline of Kiev was the loss of valuable trade routes, particularly to Italian merchants who during the Crusades obtained trading privileges in Byzantium and the Near East. The capture and looting of Constantinople in 1204 by the Fourth Crusade of western Christians enriched the nobles, who established a Latin empire with a Flemish noble as Emperor and a Venetian as the new Patriarch. Trading concessions gained by the Venetian merchants were not abrogated until the Turks took Constantinople in 1453.[8]

GALICIA AND VOLYNIA

With the downfall of Kiev, Volynia assumed primary importance in the Rus realm early in the 13th century. It was merged with another principality, Halich (Galicia) which had a separate existence for over a century. Galicia, with its capital at Halich, engaged in active commerce down the Dniester River to the Black Sea and carried on an overland trade in salt with Kiev.

Volodimirko (1124-52) united all of the Galician areas inhabited by the Rus and transferred his capital from Peremyshl to the new city of Halich on the Dniester River in 1141.

Yaroslav Osmomysl (1153-87) expanded Galicia during his reign to its greatest power. Galati, on the lower Danube, in what is now Romania, was built as a "Little" Halich.[9] With the dying out of the Rurikides in Galicia, the Volynian Prince Roman took control of both principalities, about 1199, uniting them into a single state. This new Ukrainian state after Roman's death in 1205 in battle was beset with dynastic claims and problems created by rebellious boyars who preferred a weak ruler or the Hungarian king. Finally, in 1245, Daniel, son of Roman, regained Galicia-Volynia, but by this time all of Ukraine had been invaded by the thundering Tatar horsemen.

In 1240 the Tatars took besieged Kiev, which was defended by one of Daniel's governors, and ruined it. The Tatars continued across the Carpathians and into Hungary, leaving destruction along the great trade routes and in fortified cities. By 1241 they reached as far as Silesia in Poland, but they then returned to their western capital on the lower Volga. Henceforth, the Ukrainian princes in the Galicia-Volynian state had to recognize the authority of the Khan, although this part of Rus was not occupied. Daniel died in 1264 without gaining full independence from the Tatars. He and his brother Vasylko who worked closely with him were popular with the townspeople and peasants. In 1253, the Pope had granted Daniel the crown as King of Rus.

Leo (1264-1301) lived at peace with the Tatars and participated in their campaigns when called. He expanded his realm to take in more Rus territory in the west toward Lublin. Under Leo, the capital was transferred to Lviv, which today is the leading city in Western Ukraine.

The Galicia-Volynian state continued under the male line of the Rurikides with George I (1301-15) and Andrew and Leo II (1315-23) in control. But the Tatars attacked this western Ukrainian nation in 1316 and again in 1323, apparently because of close cooperation and trading by the Ukrainians with their western and northern neighbors. The joint rulers perished in the second attack. Boleslaw, a Polish prince and son of the sister of Andrew and Leo, was accepted as King George II. But the boyars were suspicious of him, a Latin rite Christian who had joined the Eastern Church, and had him poisoned in 1340. In the meantime various rulers from Poland, Lithuania and Hungary were laying claims to the Ukrainian lands. Hungary and Poland agreed in 1349 on Polish occupation of Galicia and Kholm, while the Lithuanian Federation acquired Volynia, and later, after the defeat of the Tatars in the 1360's, central and eastern parts of Ukraine.[10]

At the height of Tatar power the Galicia-Volynian state protected central Europe for over a century. Their princes resisted Tatar domination and because of the battles that followed the country was weakened, making it easier for Poland, Lithuania and Hungary to plan its dismemberment. King Casimir justified his aggressions with ideological preparations, creating an opinion in the west that east of the Polish borders there existed "Tatars and other infidels and schismatics . . . who are our deadly enemies."[11]

The Ukrainian boyars, had they upheld their princes and acted in unison, could have saved the western Rus state and halted its decline. But in the Lithuanian Commonwealth of which many had become a part, the princes, whether of Lithuanian, Byelorussian, or Ukrainian origin, were related by blood, faith, language, etc. and they felt at home, as in their own country. It was only when Polish designs and plans were exercised that it became apparent to Ukrainians that they were relegated to second class citizenship, deprived of previously-enjoyed powers and rights and dispossessed of many of their churches.

UKRAINE UNDER LITHUANIA AND POLAND

Early in the 14th century, the Lithuanian princes moved into Byelorussia and Ukraine. During his reign (1316-41), Gedimin gained control of Volynia and Brest, and went as far as the Kievan region. Byelorussian and Ukrainian culture spread to Lithuania and the Orthodox religion was accepted by Gedimin's children. Olgerd (1345-77) enlarged this new Lithuanian-Rus state, defeating the

Tatars at Syni Vody in 1363. The people readily accepted Lithuanian rule, for they were given protection from the Tatars. Moveover, the Rus language became the official language and Slavic customs were followed in the administration, the courts, law and religion. Lithuania had become a Slavic nation.

Weakened by struggles among Olgerd's heirs and pressed by the Teutonic Order in the west and Muscovites in the east, Lithuania joined Poland at the "Krevo Union" in 1385 when Jagello, the ruler, married Queen Jadviga of Poland. Jagello became King of Poland, but retained the title Grand Prince of Lithuania. He also became a Roman Catholic. Meanwhile in 1387 the Poles took Galicia.

The spread of Catholic influence brought revolt by the Byelorussians and Ukrainians, led by Vitovt, cousin of Jagello. After Vitovt became ruler of Lithuania, he pushed its boundaries to the Black Sea at Odessa and the Donets River in the southeast. His advances were stopped by the Tatars in 1399 as his forces were badly defeated at the river Vorskla. But Vitovt, with help from Jagello, won the important battle of Grunwald in 1410 against the Teutonic Knights, thus disposing of this long-standing threat. In a new agreement between Poland and Lithuania, the Orthodox rights were limited, Roman Catholics only could hold state offices, the most powerful Ukrainian princes were replaced, and power was centralized.

Casimir (1440-92), who was Grand Prince of Lithuania and later King of Poland, considerably reduced the autonomy of the Ukrainian princes and made Volynia and Kiev an ordinary province of Lithuania. Moreover, he was unable to control the Tatars, who from 1482 attacked Ukraine almost yearly. The territories along the Black Sea were lost. Moscow now showing her ambitions for lands to the west encouraged Tatar attacks on Lithuanian-held territory.

The encroachments of Moscow into Ukrainian lands began in earnest under Ivan III in the 1490's, with some assists from Ukrainians and Byelorussians who no longer could stand the trend of events initiated by the now dominant Polish nobility. In 1508 the Ukrainians revolted but were defeated.

UKRAINE AFTER THE UNION OF LUBLIN, 1569

Gradually Lithuanians came under Polish influences in the cultural, religious, economic and political spheres. More and more differences separated them from the Ukrainian and Byelorussian subjects. The Polish pressures on Lithuania were so tremendous that they could not be resisted. Poland seized large sections of Ukrainian territory from Lithuania which finally acceded to the Union of Lublin in 1569. Lithuania and Poland accepted a common sovereign and diet but retained separate armies, administrations and treasuries.[12] Emerging considerably weakened, Lithuania was allotted only one-fourth of the members in the diet while Ukrainians lost a friendly recognition of their traditions and Orthodox religion. For Ukrainians a new chapter of trials and tribulations, similar to those imposed earlier on their kin in Galicia, began with the peasants assigned to an arduous existence and city residents forced out of government and limited in trade and other activities. In Galicia serfdom had been introduced and oppression was so bad that widespread uprising had occurred in 1490.[13]

Muscovy now was in a better position to challenge Poland. It had a ruler with centralized authority, unlike Lithuania whose Grand Princes or Dukes had been weakened by the power exercised by princes and boyars and self-governing towns. Lithuanian princes had granted increasing rights to their subjects and in the end the gentry could act only on a unanimous vote. Whereas lands of Ukraine had been occupied for centuries by the same noble families who were able to restrict the power of the Lithuanian rulers, Muscovy operated on an absolutist principle, and could also pose as the defender of Orthodoxy. The connection with Poland helped to make of Lithuania a land of privileged gentry. In contrast with authoritarian Muscovy, Lithuania had to deal with different peoples and cultures in a federated state with diffused powers.

Ukrainian lands under the Polish Crown after Lublin were divided into provinces. The promised self-government was not granted but the Ukrainian language was still retained as the official language. Polish nobles were given enormous estates in Ukraine. As urban development proceeded in Europe, the landlords supplied grain in larger quantities, becoming very wealthy. They built big palaces and lived in luxury. Polonization increased through marriages and the Catholic schools operated primarily by Jesuits. The peasants no longer owned land and could not move freely from place to place.

On the large estates in southeastern Ukraine life was freer for demands for labor were heavy. As a consequence, many fled from Galicia and Volynia to the free southeast. But here after 20 years they lost their free status, so about half of these peasants fled farther east to the "Wild Field" or what was called "Free Ukraine." Other movements were toward the Dnipro rapids. Thus a large Ukrainian population had become established far from the main centers of habitation and inbued with a determination to enjoy freedom and to right the wrongs which it felt had been unjustly dispensed by the Polish *szlachta* (nobility).

H. H. Fisher in *America and the New Poland* described conditions in Ukraine as follows:

> The rulers of Poland and the rising Muscovite empire recognized the value of the Ukrainian Cossacks as defenders of their open frontiers and the richness of the Black Earth lands on which they lived. This acquisitive interest of powerful neighbors presaged the end of free existence of the Ukrainians. In the Sixteenth Century the Ukrainians of the east — the Don Cossacks — were brought by the Tsar Ivan the Terrible under the rule of Moscow, and the Russian predominance was never seriously challenged in the regions of the Don. It was the Western Ukraine, the land of the Dnieper Cossacks, which became the battle-ground of Polish and Russian ambitions.
>
> Stephen Bathory, Prince of Transylvania and one of the greatest of Polish Kings (1576-86), organized and gave self-government to the Ukrainian communities of the Dnieper. Polish colonization, begun in the time of Casimir the Great and continued by his successors, is responsible for the diffusion of the Polish race among the Ukrainians west of the Dnieper, particularly in the most accessible districts as Eastern Galicia and Volhynia. The Poles, like the Germans in Silesia, where a similar process took place, became the dominant element in the towns and the landlords of the rural

districts. With the Polonized Ukrainian gentry they dominated political and social life; commerce fell largely into the hands of the Jews and Armenians; while the Ukrainians made up the peasant population interspersed with islands of Poles.[14]

THE KOZAK PERIOD

The Kozaks provided Ukrainians a reviving national counsiousness and in the sixteenth and seventeenth centuries what one writer referred to as the "heroic age of Ukrainian history."[15] They fought the Tatars who from their Crimean base made frequent forays into Ukrainian areas, freed themselves from Polish aristocratic rule after many uprisings and battles, and defended themselves against Czarist troops as well as those of Turkish and Moldavian leaders. Their free way of life attracted many adventurers of every rank and their accomplishments assumed legendary proportions.

In the 1540's the Kozaks established a *Sich*, or fortress, on a Dnipro island, Khortytsia, led by Prince Dmytro Vysnevetsky, also called Baida. He conducted many campaigns against the Tatars and Turks and greatly increased the power of the Kozaks without the help of the Lithuanians and Poles who had refused him assistance. The Kozaks were feared because of their strength and daring but they were needed by the nobles and officials to protect them from the Tatars. Many popular songs were sung of Baida and his heroic deeds.

With the increased protection offered by Kozak power, eastern Ukraine attracted more people, many towns and villages being built. Anyone not wanting to submit to the landlords could join the Kozak leaders. The Kozaks made bold raids on the Turks and Tatars, fighting many major battles, and often heeded the call of Polish kings. They were not above attacking and plundering the landlords in Ukraine whose policies weighed heavily on the people. The nobles discovered that Kozak fighting abilities were too great to be ignored.

A series of battles with the Polish forces began in 1596, in which the Kozaks after heavy losses were induced to surrender at Lubny. Kolkiewski's troops then treacherously attacked and slaughtered the defenseless Kozaks and their families.[16] Only a part of the Kozaks escaped to return to their *Sich* below the Dnipro rapids (Zaporozhe). The stories of the brutalities inflicted against the Kozaks and their leader, Nalivaiko, spread through Ukraine and Poland and these tales were deeply carved into the Ukrainian mind.

Kozaks getting ready to sail down the Dnipro
M. S. Gambal, **Story of Ukraine**

With the temporary loss of power the Ukrainian people were again at the full mercy of the Polish gentry, and more of the Ukrainian nobles, to preserve their positions, became Roman Catholics and Poles. The Union of Brest, proclaimed in 1596, in which many Ukrainians and Byelorussians rejoined the Catholic Church, further complicated matters, for the Kozaks saw this as an encroachment by Roman Catholic Poland. They thereupon turned not only against the Roman Catholic Poles but also against the "Uniat" Catholic clergy of the Byzantine Slavonic Rite. The Church Union not only survived but gathered adherents in the west and for centuries furnished the spiritual leadership and promoted national reawakening among the western Ukrainian people.

Their ranks replenished, the Kozaks aided the Polish kings in wars against Sweden, Moldavia, and Muscovy. Thirty thousand Kozaks beseiged the city of Smolensk in 1609. They built boats and sailed against the Turks, destroying their fleet at Ochakiv and sacking Trebizond and Sinope on the southern shores of the Black Sea. In 1615 they attacked Constantinople itself, burning parts of the city, destroying the Turkish fleet, and capturing its admiral. Moving into the Crimea, the Kozaks freed numerous Christian slaves held by the Tatars. In 1616 they invaded Turkey, then defeated the Turkish fleet and sacked Constantinople. This was during a period when all Europe trembled with fear of the terrible Turks.

Hetman Petro Sahaidachny, who came from Galicia, became famous for the exploits of his Kozaks. He was also noted for his support of education, literature, and the Orthodox Church, obtaining in 1620 the ordination of a metropolitan in Kiev and four new bishops. Kiev was reestablished as an important Ukrainian center. Hetman Sahaidachny, with over 40,000 Kozaks, joined the Polish army in attacking and defeating the Turks at Khotyn, but there he received a mortal wound, dying April 10, 1622.

The most famous Kozak, Bohdan Khmelnitsky, is said to have begun his plans against the Poles because of the king's failure to punish officials who had burned his estate, beat up his son, and kidnapped his housekeeper. Elected Hetman in 1648, Khmelnitsky organized the Kozaks with the idea of freeing Ukraine from the oppressive landlords. The Polish armies sent to destroy him met disaster, the advance cavalry at Zhovti Vodi (Yellow Waters) on May 6, 1648, and the main forces at Korsun, in which all of the surviving officers were captured. The Poles were left without an army, but Khmelnitsky was in a concilatory mood, dispatching ambassadors to the King and requesting restoration of full rights to the Kozak Host. Uprisings spread throughout Ukraine, and the people drove out the landlords and their servants. A new army organized by the Poles was defeated in September at Pilavtsi in the north. Khmelnitsky then besieged Lviv, collected a ransom, and moved toward Warsaw. Rather than attacking the city, he left after the newly-elected King Casimir agreed to his terms for peace, including full autonomy for the Kozaks.

Hetman Petro Sahaidachny, greatly outnumbered by the Turks, defeated them at the Battle of Khotyn in 1621. The Turkish threat now gone, Poland, unappreciative, limited Kozak rights.
From The Story of Ukraine, **by M. S. Gambal**

But the next year the spared Polish King assembled three separate forces and marched into Galicia to meet the Kozaks and their Tatar allies. Khmelnitsky defeated one part of the Polish army, but the Tatar Khan was bribed by the King into negotiating a settlement. In the Treaty of Zboriv, effective August 18, 1649, eastern Ukraine was made independent, the Kievan Metropolitan (Orthodox) was allowed a seat in the Senate in Warsaw, and a general amnesty applied to all nobles and common people. These terms aroused considerable resentment among the Ukrainians. Many landlords upon their return to Ukraine punished their peasants. Furthermore, the Hetman lost the support of Greek Catholic Ukrainians in union with Rome when he insisted on dissolution of the Church Union. Despite his recent experiences he entered into a new alliance with the Khan, which placed him in support of infidels and against the Church, according to feeling in the west which ran high against the Turkish Moslems who were then threatening central Europe.

In June 1651 an army of over 100,000, with over 20,000 German mercenaries, under King Casimir set out to destroy the Kozak force of 100,000 including 30,000 Tatars. At Berestechko on July 1 the treachery of the Khan whose troops were ordered not to fight and who held Khmelnitsky in their camp, turned the tide of battle decisively toward the Poles. Defeated but not stopped, Bohdan marshalled new forces and in September crushed the combined Polish-Lithuanian armies at Bila Tserkva. The following year in July at Batih he destroyed another Polish army sent against him.

After numerous violations, it was apparent that the Poles would not respect any agreement as to Ukrainian rights. The Ukrainians could not depend on the Tatars who held the balance of power and used it to further their own interests, desiring neither a strong Poland nor a united Ukrainian neighbor. Bohdan turned to Moscow which wished to regain territories lost to the Poles. The Treaty of Pereyaslav, entered into in 1654, established a military alliance of mutual assistance between the Kozak State and the Muscovite Czar. Historians offer many interpretations of this agreement, but since Moscow amended and broke it at will its original terms offered little of its true or actual intent.

The Czar's troops and 20,000 Kozaks struck hard and fast when Poland refused to reinstate Kozak rights. They captured all of Byelorussia and most of Lithuania. The Poles countered, in union with the Tatars, by marching into Podilia, setting towns and churches on fire and allowing the Tatars to take over 100,000 prisoners as slaves to be sold in Crimea and Turkey. While Moscow gained in the north, Ukraine was devastated and depopulated in the southwest.

The "Eternal Alliance" with Transylvania was entered into by Bohdan in September of 1656, followed by another with Sweden. The Transylvanians marched into Poland January 1657, joined by a Ukrainian army, they defeating the Poles at Zamostia and taking Lublin. The Swedes took Cracow and Warsaw, but in turn were attacked by Muscovy and Denmark and forced to withdraw. The Austrians and Tatars went to the assistance of Poland, making it necessary for the Kozaks to retreat. After these failures and while facing many problems, Khmelnitsky was felled by a stroke, dying in August of 1657.

Ukraine was not free, but Poland too had suffered grievous wounds, it being now obvious that Poland lacked the political and social system required to meet the needs and approval of her various peoples. Khmelnitsky organized the Ukrainian Kozaks into powerful military forces and provided for administration and discipline in areas long neglected. Former serfs felt the spark of liberty and responded with heroic efforts in the struggles of a whole people for freedom for their country. The free spirit of the common man had been kindled in Ukraine where it still exists though suppressed and from where it spread to many foreign countries.

Jeremiah Curtin, authorized translator of the works of Henryk Sienkiewicz, the famous Polish author, in the introduction to *With Fire and Sword*, writes of the Kozaks:

> But the Cossack war was of world-wide importance in view of the issues. The triumph of Poland would have brought the utter subjection of the Cossacks and the people, with the extinction of Eastern Orthodoxy not only in Russia but in other lands; for the triumph of Poland would have left no place for Moscow on earth but a place of subjection. The triumph of the Cossacks would have brought a mixed government, with religious toleration and a king having means to curb the all-powerful nobles. This was what Hmelnitski sought; this was the dream of Ossolinski the Chancellor (of Poland); this, if realized, might possibly have saved the Commonwealth, and made it a constitutional government instead of an association of irresponsible magnates.[17]

Bohdan Khmelnitsky, greatest Kozak Hetman.
From an engraving by Wilhelm Hondius in 1651.
Svoboda 1959

A Polish historian, L. Kubala, measuring the abilities of Khmelnitsky, compared him with Cromwell, a contemporary:

> We must recognize that Khmelnytsky's task was by far the more difficult; his country did not have any natural frontiers and it was open on all sides. Compared to Cromwell, Khmelnytsky did not have at his disposal experienced statesmen or an old, powerful national organization. The Army, finance, administration, nation-

al economy, relations with foreign powers, and all things were made by him, provided for by him, and in his care. He had to find men, train them, and look after the smallest details. If his army was not starving, if he had enough arms, munitions, and clever intelligence agents — it was all his own work. From every point of view, he was an extraordinary and very talented man. Of him we can say that he was born to rule; knowing how to conceal his intentions, he was not one to ever hesitate in a critical moment. By his hand of iron and his powerful will he brought everyone to submission. There was no situation from which he was not able to derive some advantage.[18]

The Kozaks elected Bohdan's teen-age son as the new Hetman but the Kozak Officers Council ruled that he was too young under the precarious conditions and chose with the approval of the Kozaks the General Secretary, Ivan Vyhovsky, to act as Hetman. The new Hetman strove to maintain peace, but Muscovy invaded several sections of Ukraine and through its intrigues among some of the Kozaks induced a rebellion against Vyhovsky. This rebellion was crushed at great cost and all relations with the Czar were broken. A new treaty was signed with the Poles September 16, 1658. It was known as the Union of Hadiach, and under it Ukraine agreed to join the Polish-Lithuanian Commonwealth as an autonomous "Grand Duchy of Rus." The Grand-Duchy was to be ruled by a Hetman elected by the entire population of Ukraine.[19]

The Muscovite Czar objected, called the Hetman a traitor and urged Ukrainians to rebel. In the spring of 1659 the Czar sent an army of 100,000 men into Ukraine. A valiant stand at Nizin by 5000 Kozaks gave Vyhovsky time to organize his forces and obtain the help of the Crimean Khan. These troops advanced to Konotop where on June 28 and 29 they completely destroyed the Muscovite invaders. Hetman Vyhovsky could not continue on to Moscow, for internal problems again confronted him. Rebellious Kozaks, opposed to the treaty with the Poles, at the General Council removed Vyhovsky from office.

The Kozaks became unwitting tools of Muscovy. Yuriy Khmelnitsky (Bohdan's son), the new Hetman, agreed to revisions of the Treaty of Pereyaslav which greatly favored Muscovy. The able Ivan Vyhovsky had to flee to Poland, while his three brothers were tortured to death by the

Muscovites. Yuriy, unable to cope with the Kozaks who were now badly disunited, resigned to enter a monastery in 1663.[20] Separate hetmans for the Left Bank (east of the Dnipro River) and Right Bank of Ukraine were selected, but none inspired the confidence of the masses.

Worse still for Ukraine, Poland and Muscovy signed a treaty on January 13, 1667, at Andrusowo to divide Ukraine, under which Muscovy was to rule the Left Bank territories and Kiev, and Poland the Right Bank territories, with both countries keeping the Kozaks under control. The Tatars held sway over the sparsely-populated southern Ukrainian areas.

In August of 1665 the Left Bank Ukrainians elected Petro Doroshenko Hetman. An alliance was then entered into with the Turks, among whose subjects were the Crimean Tatars and Moldavians. To unify Ukraine, Doroshenko had to fight the Poles who invaded Podilia with a large army in the fall of 1671. The Turkish Sultan moved in with 150,000 men and together with the Kozaks besieged Lviv. The Poles sued for peace, signing the Treaty of Buchach in October, renouncing all claims to Right Bank Ukraine and allowing the Sultan to be its protector. In March of 1674 the Turks and Tatars again came into Ukraine to assist Doroshenko, captured Uman which was held by a pro-Polish Kozak, and slaughtered the inhabitants. In 1675 Doroshenko was attacked and his few remaining followers overpowered by the Left Bank Hetman, Samoylovich, at Bohdan's capital, Chihiryn. In August 1677 the Turks and Tatars laid siege to Chihiryn, but retreated to return a year later at which time the defenders set it on fire before leaving. The almost yearly invasions by the Turks and Tatars left this part of Ukraine in ruin, the people fleeing to Left Bank areas.[21]

The ominous threat of the powerful Sultan and the devastations led to another agreement between the Poles and Muscovites defining their spheres of control. The Polish King took steps to revive the Kozaks and invite resettlement of the Right Bank. Fortunately for Europe this was done in time, for when the Turks attacked Vienna in 1683 the Polish King, Jan Sobiesky, was reinforced by detachments of Kozaks under the command of Hetman Mohyla and able to defeat the Turks.

After Samoylovich's removal as Hetman of the Left Bank Ukraine, on August 4, 1687, Ivan Mazepa was elected to succeed him. Muscovy was becoming so strong that a policy "of least resistance and appeasement" was adopted toward the Czar. But the Czar had different ideas. He granted large estates to Kozak officers and opened a wide breach between them and the people. They thus became the new nobility. Mazepa gained the confidence of the new Czar, Peter I. Being wealthy, Mazepa built many beautiful churches and monasteries, rebuilt old ones and founded schools and encouraged cultural works. However, many Kozaks still distrusted him. Petro Ivanenko attempted to stir the Zaporozhian Kozaks, with help from the Tatars, to depose Mazepa, but without success. Another threat to Mazepa was the uprising of Semen Paliy of the Right Bank who, by driving Polish landlords out of Ukraine, was becoming a national hero. Mazepa was fearful that premature revolt would spread eastward. Czar Peter, at war with the Swedes and Tatars, demanded troops from Mazepa. Discontent arose among the Kozaks because of these levies. Mazepa quieted the rebellion on the Right Bank by capturing Paliy and appointing a new deputy-hetman, thus gaining control of nearly all of Ukraine.

Mazepa still had a suspicious Czar to outmaneuver. He carried on secret negotiations (known only to a few of his staff) with the Polish King. When in 1708 Charles XII of Sweden was in Byelorussia fighting Peter, agreement was obtained with Charles for assistance in freeing Ukraine and defending her against all of her enemies. Later Mazepa informed the Council of Officers of the treaty, it then being formally approved. But the Czar discovered the alliance before Mazepa's proclamations could be publicly announced and while his troops were fighting far away, giving Peter the chance to take many Ukrainian towns and cities and capture Mazepa's capital and critical supplies before the Kozak forces could be mobilized. By then even the Orthodox hierarchy who were the beneficiaries of Mazepa's donations believed the scurrilous attacks made by Peter

Churches built by Mazepa, engraving I. Mihura 1706
Svoboda 1959

Hetman Ivan Mazepa
National Museum, Stockholm, Svoboda 1959

and denounced Mazepa as a traitor. The Russian Orthodox Church until 1917 held a special ceremony on the first Sunday of Lent excommunicating Mazepa, demonstrating its submission to Czarist political control.[22] Mazepa's calls to action by the people brought little response under such conditions, for they had for a long time believed Mazepa, because of his close connections, to be a friend of Peter. Hesitation of the part of the Kozaks made it easy for the Czar to move against Charles' army. Only a few Kozak detachments helped the 31,000 Swedish forces, poorly armed with artillery, at the battle of Poltava on July 8, 1709. In defeat Mazepa and Charles escaped into Moldavia, where Mazepa died in September.

Poltava was one of the decisive battles of the world because it brought tightened Muscovite control of Ukraine and heralded Russia's emergence as a world power. After completing the takeover of the Baltic shores, given recognition in the Treaty of Nystadt of 1721, Peter had opened the "Window to Europe" and had become "Emperor" of what was now the "Russian Empire," a far different political model than the Grand Duchy of Muscovy.[23] Since Peter's edict of 1713, when Muscovy was renamed "Russia," foreigners have been persuaded to think of "Russia" as a successor of Rus.

The Ukrainians in 1710 elected a new Hetman, Philip Orlik, a close friend of Mazepa, and proclaimed a new constitution, "Pacts and Constitution of Rights and Liberties of the Zaporozhian Army," in which an assembly, composed of officers, representatives of the Kozaks, and deputies from Zaporozhia were to make the laws. Kozak officers could not use Kozaks and peasants as serfs on their estates. This was the first liberal constitution of the European mainland.[24]

Left Bank Ukraine while nominally independent received more and more attention, but Poland clung to its rigid policies on the Right Bank. In 1722 an ukaze by the Czar formed the "Little Russian Board" of six Muscovite officers to oversee the operations of Hetman Skoropadsky and for the "protection of the common people against the abuses of the Kozak officers." Czar Peter referred to all hetmans from 1654 as traitors. In effect the hetmancy had been abolished in favor of this Board, for little power now resided in the hetman. After Elizabeth succeeded to power in 1741 she restored many of the Kozak rights. A new Hetman, Kyrylo Rozumowsky, was elected in 1750, but he spent so much time in St. Petersburg that the Kozak Officers Council actually governed Ukraine. The notorious Catherine II put an end to these liberal policies, introduced serfdom and brought in colonists from Greece, Germany and Serbia "to add to the diversity of the racial pattern" in Ukraine.[25] Shifting of peoples is a well-known part of the Russification policy of the Red Czars of recent times. While the Kozaks were fighting in Podilia, Catherine secretly captured the Zaporozhian *Sich* in 1775 and destroyed it, sending the leader, Kalynyshevsky, to the cold north where he was locked in a small cell for 25 years. The Left Bank Kozaks, unused to slavery, moved into Turkish or Austrian areas and unsettled parts of the empire to escape the harsh terms of their "Orthodox elder brothers."[26]

West of the Dnipro, again and again the land magnates sent their detachments to restore quiet among the peasantry who were reduced to the level of serfs. The frequent insurrections, often with assistance from bands from other countries or east of the Dnipro, took on serious proportions in 1750 when large groups of Ukrainians, referred to as Haidamaks, drove many of the landlords out. In 1768 Maxim Zalizniak, fighting under the banner of Orthodoxy, led a peasant uprising that covered nearly all of Right Bank Ukraine. He had proclaimed himself Hetman, but Catherine II, who had supported Zalizniak but was now in one of her perfidious moods, ordered his capture, after which he was sent to Siberia while his associate was delivered to the Poles to be executed. Her troops occupied parts of Polish Ukraine. In 1772, the first partition of Poland occurred, with Austria taking most of her former Halich-Volynian lands. The second partition, in 1792, gave Muscovy the provinces of Kiev, Podilia, and part of Volynia. In the third distribution, in 1795, Poland disappeared as a separate nation. With Poland's fall, the practical possibility of freeing Ukraine from Muscovite rule diminished, for the severe methods of Russian absolutism suppressed all political and cultural development. Under Austrian control, a new ray of hope broke through the black clouds that had hovered over a long-suppressed people.

UKRAINIANS IN THE RUSSIAN EMPIRE

With the absorption of the greatest part of Ukraine into the Russian Empire came relative peace and decrease in raids by Tatars and Turks, allowing for settlement south to the shores of the Black Sea. The Ukrainian nobles in defending their prerogatives at the same time were protecting a separateness of national ideals. Literary works and histories appeared in the Ukrainian language, reminding the people of their heritage. Ivan Kotlyarevsky's travesty on the *Aenid* and his operetta *Natalka Poltavka*, kept the people's minds on the dispersed Kozaks and their national customs and traditions. The rich store of folk songs and legends saved Ukrainian culture from the Polish and Russian influences which were strong among the gentry.[27]

In 1838 the population of the Right Bank Ukraine consisted of 4,200,000 Ukrainian peasants and 100,000 Poles. Two-thirds of the latter were petty gentry with little or no land who served on the estates of the great landowners. Poles occupied almost all the posts in the court system and in the local government. After suppression by Russia of the Polish revolts of 1831-2, use of the Polish language was barred in the administration and courts. A policy of Russification began. Another consequence of the revolt was Orthodoxy's becoming "one of the pillars of secular power" with the Church being "Autocracy's political tool, obedient to lay authorities."[28] In furtherance of this philosophy, and also to weaken the still strong hold the Polish aristocracy had in Ukrainian areas, Eastern Rite Catholic Churches were forced into Russian Orthodoxy in Volynia in 1839 and in Pidliashe and Kholmschina in 1875.

Because of the pressures of the nobility over 50 uprisings of the peasants occurred in 1845-8. During the Crimean War, to quell peasant unrest in the Kiev area, the use of military force was required.

In 1840 the works of Taras Shevchenko, Ukraine's greatest national figure, honored and revered throughout the world, started to appear, producing an immense effect on the Ukrainian national movement. In his poems Shevchenko pictured Ukraine's past, contrasting it to the oppressed Ukraine of his day. At a time of European empires and harsh absolutism Shevchenko wrote boldly and with deep feeling for national independence, human equality, and social justice. But the reactionary regime of Nicholas I arrested Shevchenko, the former serf, and sent him as a private to a remote garrison for ten years where he was specifically forbidden to write or paint. Shevchenko had joined the Society of Saints Cyril and Methodius of Kiev, organized January 1846 by Nicholas Kostomarov and including Panteleimon Kulish and other intellectuals interested in freeing the serfs and advancing Ukrainian nationalism through a Slavic federation.[29]

The debasing of the Ukrainian people proceeded under the Czars, with the solutions proposed for the "Ukrainian problem" following the outlines of Nicholas I: "Orthodoxy, autocracy, and nationality." These chauvinistic words also form the basic core for the supernationalism of the Russians in their Soviet Empire. A German traveler, Johann George Kohl, who visited Ukraine in the 1830's, gives a good account of the feelings he encountered:

> Such is the aversion of the people of Little to those of Great Russia that it may fairly be described as a national hatred, and the feeling has rather strengthened than diminished since the seventeenth century, when the country was annexed to the Moscovite empire.... Before their subjection, all the Malorossians (Ukrainians) were freemen, and serfdom, they maintain, had never been known among them. It was the Russians, they say, that reduced one-half of the people to slavery. During the first century after the union, Little Russia continued to have her own hetmans, and retained much of her ancient constitution and privileges, but all these have been swept away by the retrograde reforms of the last and present century . . . To this day, the battle of Poltava is remembered throughout Little Russia with feelings similar to those with which the battle of White Mountain is remembered in Bohemia.... Should the colossal empire of Russia fall to pieces, there is little doubt that the Malorossians will form a separate state. They have their own language, their own historical recollections, seldom mingle with the Moscovite rulers, and are in number already more than 10,000,000.[30]

When serfdom was officially abolished in the manifesto of February 19, 1861, hope sprang for release from not only economic hardship but also for the allowance of greater individual and national freedom. Local peasants revolted in the 1860's and 1870's, for they were still tied to the land and the exactions made on them were onerous. Land allotments were very small, and with an increasing population, for each male individual the parcels averaging by the year 1900 less than half the former allotment. Many Ukrainian peasants settled in Siberia, Turkestan, and the Kuban and Don regions. The nobles that could not afford to hire free labor sold their holdings to merchants and rich peasants. Over 25,000,000 acres were thus sold between 1861 and 1914 in Ukraine.[31]

Changes took place in the economy, with railroads being built and mines opened. Grain, such as wheat and barley, sown increased greatly, with Ukraine becoming the chief exporter in the world by 1900. Sugar beet cultivation made tremendous strides, accompanied by the building of large refineries. Metal industries, utilizing the plentiful coal, iron, and manganese deposits of Ukraine, were established near what is now Donetske. The Donbas as an important coal and iron center grew rapidly.

Official policy of the Russians was to exploit the agricultural and raw material resources indigenous to Ukraine, while prohibiting industries in Ukraine that could be established in Russia proper. Outside capital furnished the impetus for Ukrainian development, since the Russians allowed only half of self-generated profits to be utilized in Ukraine.

For a short time under Alexander II in the 1860's Ukrainian cultural activities progressed, the various communities sponsoring interest in history, literature and language. A welcome awakening was that of young Poles, whose ancestors were originally Ukrainian, they following Volodimir Antonovich, who became a noted historian, in rejoining the Ukrainian people. The Polish nobility dubbed them "khlopamany" or peasant lovers.

When Poland again revolted, in 1863, Count Peter Valuev, Minister of the Interior, associated the Ukrainian revival with "Polish intrigues" and issued an edict:

> The majority of the Little Russians themselves thoroughly prove that there has not been, is not, and never can be any Little Russian language, and that their dialect, used by the common people, is the same Russian language, but corrupted by the influence upon it by Poland; that the general Russian language is comprehensible to the Little Russians and even more understandable than the so-called Ukrainian language now being formed for them by some Little Russians, and especially by Poles, the circle of those persons who try to prove the opposite are accused by the majority of Little Russians themselves of having separatist plans, hostile to Russia and disastrous for Little Russia.[32]

Valuev ordered the censors "to allow to be printed in the Little Russian language only such works as belong in the realm of belles-lettres; and to ban the publication of books in the Little Russian language, both religious and educational, and books generally intended for elementary reading by the people." The impact and significance of this edict spread far and wide, to the schools and universities and publishers and are visible today in the daily press, in textbooks, in maps printed by great societies, in reference works, etc. where the succumbing to Russification is readily discernible.

In June of 1876, Czar Alexander II signed the secret Ems Ukaze which forbade printing in the Ukrainian language and importation of Ukrainian publications and theatrical or musical performances. The elimination of the Ukrainian language from the schools, libraries, and publications introduced a high rate of illiteracy among Ukrainians.

The revolution of 1905 following Russian defeat by Japan brought concessions to the people of the Empire. Ukrainian publications appeared, Prosvita (Enlightenment) societies were formed, Shevchenko's *Kobzar* was printed, lectures in Ukrainian began, a scientific society was founded in Kiev, Ukrainian political parties were organized and many of the intellectuals who had fled to Austrian-held Galicia now returned to eastern Ukraine. Repressive measures were not long in returning, with many of these developments curtailed or destroyed. But despite the Russian government's prohibition of

Shevchenko 100th anniversary celebrations in 1914, they took place throughout all of Ukraine.

WESTERN UKRAINE

The Ukrainian areas in the Austro-Hungarian Empire were located in the provinces of Galicia, Bukovina, and Transcarpathia (Carpatho-Ukraine). The Austrian government provided a theological seminary for Ukrainian Catholics in Vienna, and Ruthenian studies began at Lviv University in 1787, but the studies were discontinued in 1805. A serious obstacle to progress and learning was instruction given in the dead language of the books (Church Slavonic) rather than the Ukrainian language of the people.[33] The Greek Catholic clergy, long in a lowly official status within the Catholic Church but now guided by a Metropolitan in Lviv, led Ukrainian national revival. After the 1848 revolution, the Supreme Ruthenian Council was set up in Lviv. It called for the break-up of Galicia into a Ukrainian and into a Polish province, and union of Carpatho-Ukraine with Galicia. A chair in Ukrainian language and literature was established at Lviv University and the first Ukrainian newspaper in Galicia, *Galician Star*, was published May 15, 1848. A semi-sovereign status was sought by Ukrainian delegates to the Parliament.

In 1851 absolutism was re-established and the Supreme Ruthenian Rada disbanded. Actual rule over Galicia was taken over by the Poles. A new constitution, decreed in 1860, set up a federal parliament and provincial assemblies. Ukrainians elected only 49 out of 150 delegates to the Galician diet in 1861 despite their numerical majority in the population. Later, under more restrictions, the Ukrainian percentage was much lower. Polish landowners dominated the province, the Austrian government in 1867 giving Poles control of the administration, the courts, and counties. Instead of German, Polish became the official language of this Ukrainian part of a German-controlled Empire. With few exceptions the secondary and technical schools and Lviv University became Polish. Average peasant holdings went down from 5 hectares in 1859 to 3 in 1880, and 2.5 in

1900. To survive peasants had to work for the Polish lords or *pans*.

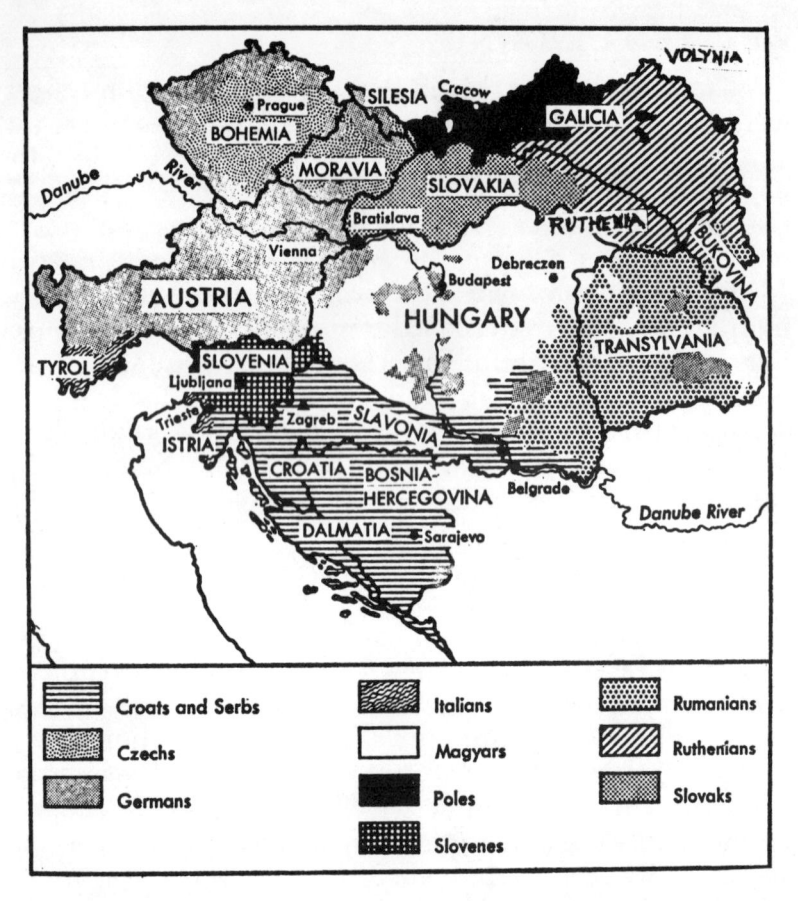

Nationalities in the Austro-Hungarian Empire

The Clergy, largely conservative, was unable to induce the Austrian government to ameliorate the condition of the Ukrainian people and many priests turned increasingly toward Russia. But a populist movement composed of youthful elements in contact with Ukrainians under Russia began in 1860, following the ideals of Shevchenko. Lviv became a center of Ukrainian publications for Ukrainians in Austria and in Russia, where printing in Ukrainian was forbidden. *Pravda*, a monthly, called for Ukrainian unity. Many Ukrainian societies were formed throughout Galicia for furthering education, culture and political awareness. Polish attempts to introduce the Latin alphabet to replace the Cyrillic of the Ukrainians were fought vigorously.

A new National Council (*Narodna Rada*) was formed in 1885, guided by the principles of populism, liberalism, democracy, and progress. Its influence and membership expanded in the 1890's under new leadership. In 1894 Michaylo Hrushevsky became head of east European history at Lviv University. The Ukrainian Radical Party, formed in 1891, defended the peasants and in 1895 called for political independence. This forced other Ukrainian parties to follow suit. The Austrian government adopted terrorist tactics, but could not halt the spread of Ukrainian nationalism. In 1899 the populists formed the National Democratic Party, which also included right wing elements of the Radical Party. On January 5, 1900, the National Democratic Party proclaimed as its goal establishment of an independent Ukraine "where all parts of our nation would unite in one modern cultural state," with the immediate aim of a separate Ukrainian province in Austria.[34]

Before World War I Ukrainian national and social consciousness had risen perceptibly. The Ukrainian Catholics now had a great leader in Metropolitan Andrew Sheptitsky. Ukrainians confronted the authorities with a program that called for equality for the Ukrainian language in public institutions and schools, a Ukrainian university, universal suffrage, and social equality. In 1902 600 Ukrainian students withdrew from Lviv University and the peasants struck successfully against the low wages paid by the nobles and hindrances placed on immigration to America and Prussia. To dilute Ukrainian opposition the Poles supported pro-Russian elements. The Austrian government countered with greater aid and recognition of Ukrainian cultural, educational, political, and economic rights. The tremendous growth that followed included the establishment of elementary and secondary schools, libraries, cooperatives, mutual credit associations, economic and trade associations, an insurance company, and a Land Loan Bank. Contacts between Ukrainians under Russia were very close, and because of Russian restrictive policies against Ukrainians, Ukrainian leaders in Galicia were strongly favoring Austria prior to the outbreak of World War I.

BUKOVINA

Bukovina had been under the rule of Ukrainian princes from the end of the 13th century, when it came under Tatar domination, followed in mid-century by annexation to Moldavia. At the beginning of the 16th century it was included in the Ottoman Empire and in September of 1774 it was occupied by the Austrian armies. Austria attached Bukovina to Galicia. The northern and western parts of Bukovina were inhabited by Ukrainians and the southern by Romanians. During Austrian rule many Germans settled in the capital city, Chernivtsi.[35]

After the peasant uprisings in 1842-5 and 1848-9 Bukovina became a separate crown land within Austria. About the time of Galician populist revival the Ukrainian intellectuals turned away from the Old Slavonic language and began using the language of the people. The Bukovinian writer, Joseph Fedkovich, in 1885 began editing the journal *Bukovina* in the Ukrainian language. Fewer of the educated were becoming Germanized or Romanianized. Stephen Smal-Stotsky, a professor at the University of Chernivtsi, was a leading figure in Ukrainian progress. Ukrainians strove for cultural autonomy and division of the Orthodox Church into two dioceses, Romanian and Ukrainian. Cultural autonomy was finally obtained and the supremacy of the conservative boyars and the Romanian hierarchy was weakened.

The relatively small 300,000 Ukrainian population in Bukovina prior to World War I had a greater share of the administration in Bukovina than did the Ukrainians have in Galicia. The same can be said for schools and cultural and educational institutions. But German influences in Bukovina were strong.

TRANSCARPATHIAN UKRAINE

After the death of Volodimir the Great in 1015 this part of Ukraine across the Carpathian Mountains fell under the control of the Hungarian king. The king's son ran the province as "Duke of the Ruthenians." Slav and Orthodox nobility dominated the region until the 15th century. Prince Theodore Koriatovich from Podilia became lord of Mukachiv (1393-1414). Popular tradition credits him with establishing many national institutions and with bringing in Ukrainian settlers. St. Nicholas Monastery at Monks Hill near Mukachiv and St. Michael at Hrushiv were the centers of Ukrainian religious life. National ties with the Ukrainians across the mountains were maintained through their religious contacts and the flow of the same books and manuscripts. The bishops of Peremyshl in Galicia exerted their influence in the Carpathians.

Hrushevsky, the eminent Ukrainian historian, writes of the early centuries of life:

> The Ukrainian masses found themselves in the role of serfs, and the same was true even of the village priests, who were forced to perform feudal services, being taken from the altar to do manual labor on the estates of feudal landlords and flogged in the same manner as other serfs. Those who elevated themselves above the common masses did so at the price of denationalization and joined the ranks of the Hungarian nobility.[36]

Carpatho-Ukraine became a battleground for contesting Habsburgs and Transylvanians in the 17th and 18th centuries, adding to the suffering of the people. In 1649 the "Union of Uzhorod" placed a western segment of the clergy in union with Rome, but with the Eastern Rites unchanged. It was not until Habsburg control was firmly established that the Greek Catholic Church superseded Orthodoxy in all of Carpatho-Ukraine. Empress Maria Theresa (1740-80) raised the status of the Greek Catholic clergy on an equal level to that of the Latin clergy and removed Mukachiv from the control of the Latin Archbishop of Eger by establishing it as an independent diocese in 1771. In 1780 the diocesan center was transferred to Uzhorod, and in 1816 the western part was made into a new diocese of Priashiv. Under the enlightened measures of the Habsburg rulers the landowners lost some of their exploitative powers over the peasants.

Carpatho-Ukrainians reaching prominence as scholars or literary figures included Ivan Zaikan who was tutor to Peter II of Russia (1727-30); Michael Baludiansky (1769-1847) who taught political economy at St. Petersburg and was the first Rector, University of St. Petersburg; Rev. I. Bazilovich (1742-1821) who wrote a 6-volume history of the Ruthenian Catholic Church which stressed its relations with Kievan Rus; Peter Lodi (1764-1829), who taught philosophy at the Universities of Krakow and St. Petersburg; Michael Luchkai-Pop (1789-1843), who in 1830 prepared a grammar, *Grammatica Slavo-Ruthena*.[37]

When the Hungarian revolution of 1848-9 brought Russian armies into Carpatho-Ukraine to assist Austria, the soldiers were amazed to find "their own" people and similar churches across the Carpathians. The chief Ukrainian leaders, Rev. Alexander Dukhnovich, writer and educator, and Adolph I. Dobriansky, popular writer and political activist, were hostile to Hungary. Rev. Dukhnovich wrote the national hymn of the Carpatho Ruthenians, "I Was, Am and Will Be a Ruthenian," and authored many readers and religious works for use in schools and churches.

The limited autonomy gained by Carpatho-Ruthenia was lost in 1867, after the Ausgleich or formation of the dual monarchy (Austria-Hungary). With Hungary now controlling the area the condition of the people became worse. The Greek Catholic Church and clergy came under increasing pressures of Magyarization. Ukrainian parochial schools and newspapers almost disappeared. The masses of people were further removed from the clergy and their leaders. Little industry existed, making the peasants dependent on the owners of vast estates. Because of the rough terrain, only 18% of the land could be cultivated. Under such adverse conditions large numbers of peasants began to emigrate to the United States in the 1880's, especially from the counties of Sharish, Zemplin, and Uzh. A vivid portrait of conditions is painted by Henry Baerlein who visited Carpatho-Ukraine after World War I:

"So now," said the old schoolmaster, "you want to hear about the schools. This province, which is called Ruthenia or Pod Karpatska Rus — that is, in English, Sub-Carpathian Russia — is inhabited by Little Russians, the descendents of a race which came across the mountains. For a long time, centuries in fact, they languished under the Hungarians, the Magyars; one can see this by the Magyar policy regarding schools. They only paid attention to the towns, where the Hungarians lived; the country places were neglected. Of course, the province had far more Ruthene inhabitants than Hungarians, and yet in those days out of 634 schools the language of instruction in 553 was Hungarian. So the Government hoped to turn these Slavs into Magyars, and in many cases they succeeded. When a boy had gone through the Hungarian school he looked upon himself as a Hungarian and was apt to despise his own people."[38]

In 1902 and 1907 the Hungarian language was introduced in all parochial schools and in 1912 a new diocese of Hayduderog chipped off portions of the Greek Catholic dioceses and Hungarian substituted as the church language. In 1916 the Latin alphabet with Hungarian spelling was forced upon all Ukrainian publications. But Carpatho-Ukrainian writers maintained contact with their brethren in other areas and the strongly-rooted traditions of the peasants, hidden in deep valleys and high mountains, were not to be extinguished. The ruling Hungarian caste, feudal and arrogant in its ways, was not very concerned about the rights and living conditions of the lower classes of its own race, much less of the second and third rank minorities. Pre-World War I Hungary was one of the most reactionary states in Europe.

UKRAINE THROUGH WORLD WAR I

When the Great War began in August 1914 Ukrainian lands of Galicia, Bukovina, and Carpatho-Ruthenia were in the way of Russian armies moving toward their Austro-Hungarian enemies. Russia occupied Galicia within a few months and was not pushed back until late spring of 1915. Ukrainian leaders in Vienna organized a General Ukrainian Council which called for liberation of Russian Ukraine and autonomy in Austria and assisted Ukrainian refugees. When the Council demanded the right of self-determination for Ukrainians in Austria they received for the first time, in May 1917, a cabinet appointment.[39] Polish troops continued to occupy Ukrainian districts taken from Russia and all pleas for Ukrainian units to protect Ukrainians went unheeded. After the Russian Empire collapsed in March of 1917, Ukrainians were ready with demands for autonomy in Austria-Hungary or in the alternative for union with the eastern Ukrainians. On the signing of the peace treaty between the Ukrainian Republic and the Central Powers at Brest-Litovsk on February 9, 1918, Ukrainian Galicia and Bukovina were granted autonomy and Russian Ukraine was acknowledged as an independent nation. A Constituent Assembly decided on October 18, 1918, to proclaim a Ukrainian state for all Ukrainian lands in the now crumbling Austrian Empire. On November 1, 1918, amidst the unsettled conditions and approaching dangers, a government was established in Lviv.

Meanwhile the Central Rada in Kiev, at first led by the prominent historian, Michael Hrushevsky, was faced with the task of organizing the Ukrainian people after the fall of Czarism. The Provisional Russian Government had accepted the idea of federation, but in fact the entrenched Russian administrative apparatus in the large cities and elsewhere opposed it. The Bolshevik Revolution of November 1917 promoted chaos in Ukraine, for now the old administration and military control collapsed. Better armed and more numerous and well-prepared with propaganda promising land to the peasants, the Bolsheviks invaded Ukraine even before the Ukrainians had declared their full independence. On January 22, 1918, the Central Rada said in its proclamation: "From now on the Ukrainian National Republic becomes the independent, free and sovereign state of the Ukrainian people."

On January 22, 1919, the Western Ukrainian National Republic, which was in desperate combat with the Allied-supported invading Poles, issued its Act of Union with the Ukrainian National Republic. In Odessa, the French armies assisted the White Russian forces under Denikin. Blockades by the British and French prevented foreign supplies from reaching Ukrainian troops. When in late 1919

Ukrainian forces were attacked by Denikin they were forced to retreat, for by that time they were severely weakened and reduced to less than one-third of their former strength by a quick-spreading typhus epidemic. With many fronts to cover and without access to medicines, munitions, arms and other materials it is a wonder that Ukrainian units fought on until near the end of 1920.

Semeon Petliura, commander of Ukrainian military forces during the war for independence and Chairman of The Directorate. His forces could not withstand those of the Bolsheviks and the Allied-supported Poles and Russian monarchists. But he gave Ukrainian hopes for statehood a big lift. Unwanted masters are not comfortable in Ukraine, and Ukrainians let the world know how they feel.

Two Ukrainian divisions joined the Poles in fighting the Bolsheviks and entered Kiev on May 7, 1920, only to be pressed back toward Poland. The Poles and Ukrainians counter attacked, driving deep into Ukrainian territory before the Bolsheviks agreed to an armistice on October 18, 1920. The Ukrainians fought on until November 21 but were forced to return into the newly-formed Polish state. However, guerrilla warfare went on until 1924. The main part of Ukraine was incorporated into the Union of Soviet Socialist Republics on December 30, 1922.

In the Treaty of Riga, Poland acquired the Ukrainian areas of Kholm, Pidliashie, western Volynia, and western Polisia. Galicia became a test for the principles of self-determination expounded by the victorious allies, who settled for autonomy for the Ukrainians and certain guarantees. History shows these were nothing more than promises of weak men. Colonel Stephen Bonsal, interpreter for President Wilson at Paris in 1918-1919, wrote on May 3, 1919:

> Today there is undeniably a crisis in our archives. There simply isn't any more room in our safe for the countless memoranda that I have drawn up and the innumerable statements that I have taken down from the authorized Ukrainian delegates and from the free-lance volunteers who also abound. I will not assert that what they have said has gone entirely unheeded by the commissioners, but it has not been as carefully weighed as in my opinion it should have been. In my judgment, if we are to bring the blessing of peace to Eastern Europe, forty million of its inhabitants should not be ignored....
>
> Fortunately an hour ago a "directive" came from Captain Patterson, the "executive officer" of our ship, the *Crillon*...."Take your papers down to the cellar personally," he urges, "and stand by the furnace until they are incinerated."
>
> Well, I obeyed Captain "Dick's" injunction. I took the papers down to the cellar and placed them with my own hands into the furnace that was red hot; then a surprising thing happened. The Ukrainian dossier did not go up in flames — it simply curled up and smoked and smouldered. When I reported this to the Colonel, he said, "I hope that is not prophetic." And so do I, but I have my doubts. The pleas and supplications of forty million people have been, to put it mildly, disregarded; they will smoulder on and some day, perhaps at a moment even more inopportune than the present, they may break out in flames that will spread. I hope the League will do better by the problem and the opportunity than we have done.[40]

Poland was awarded Eastern Galicia by the "Great Powers," Carpatho-Ukraine chose to become a part of a new Czechoslovakia, and Romania occupied Bukovina and Bessarabia. The Peace Conference had failed the acid test of President Wilson: the treatment of the submerged and the oppressed nationalities.

UKRAINE AFTER WORLD WAR I

In the earlier years of the first decade of Russian Bolshevik rule of Soviet Ukraine the Ukrainians were allowed a measure of cultural and economic freedom. But this was to last only until the Bolsheviks got "on their feet." By 1930 the farmers were being forcibly induced to give up their economic and political independence and were herded into collective farms. There they could be more easily watched and the state assured of a greater share of the product of the farmers' labor. The highest priorities of the planners required diversion of the farm products to the workers in the Russian cities and for payments for the machines needed in the new industrial goals. Marxian theory placed progress on a materialist base, so Ukraine became the laboratory for dispossessing the farmers who remained on the lowest rung of the economic ladder for half a century. Ukraine's resources of coal, iron and water power became the means of building huge industrial complexes. Such ambitious plans made regimentation and dictatorial methods, accompanied by maximum austerity, the ordinary way of life.

The high production quotas and the methods of enforcement were resisted. In 1932-3 over 5,000,000 Ukrainian farmers were starved in a man-made famine.[41] Grain was taken away without regard to the needs of the populace. To crush Ukrainian opposition attacks were made on educational institutions, cultural organizations, and political activities and organizations. A curtain descended on Ukraine, with foreign correspondents under orders to stay out of Ukraine and to submit all news stories for censorship. Walter Duranty of the New York Times was persuaded to report on September 18, 1933, "all talk of famine now is ridiculous."[42] The United States and the free world remained silent and inactive, pliant victims of the Soviet Russian propaganda network. The harsh realities of Russian communist methods aroused some belief in a few years during the purge trials and confessions, and later when it became known that practically the entire Ukrainian political leadership and intellectual class had been eliminated in the process of destroying "bourgeois nationalism." Ukrainians and other nationalities would no longer glorify their past, but had to be grateful to the Russians for the "help" and "protection" they were receiving from their "elder brother."[43] The all-powerful concept of the dictatorship of the proletariat had to be respected, with the Russians at the helm. The lowly peasants were to be ruled. National loyalties made way for Russian direction under Stalin, who adopted purges, executions and deportations of millions as standard methods. So devastating were Russian policies under the Bolshevik regime that in 1939 the population in Ukraine was only slightly greater than it had been in 1917.[44]

When World War II came to the Soviet Union in June of 1941 the disenchantment with Russian policies was reflected by the ease with which Hitler's armies marched through Ukraine and Byelorussia, for millions refused to defend a homeland in which they had been overworked, bled, tortured, and starved, where children were taught they had to inform on their parents, and where religion was suppressed as the opiate of the people. Hitler displayed his super race theories by imprisoning Ukrainian leaders and making slave laborers out of the peasants. The Ukrainians responded by warring on all fronts, fighting as a guerrilla army against the Germans and their allies as well as the Russians and their supporters.

When Poland and Romania were broken in 1939 and 1940, 8 million more Ukrainians were added to the Russian Red Empire where they were quickly given a taste of the potions concocted by the Red Czar in removing "imperialist," "nationalist," and religious tendencies among the Soviet citizens. The Russians were interrupted by the German, Hungarian, and Italian onslaughts in June of 1941. Those Ukrainians who managed to escape by being forced into slave labor in Germany or who had time to flee before the Russians returned on Hitler's collapse in 1944 and 1945 still had to contend with misguided English, French, and American military commanders. To the shame of the western democracies the bayonet was used to force many unwilling Ukrainian and other refugees to Soviet execution, slave labor, or resettlement. There are

Ukrainians in Maryland now who came to the United States not from Ukraine but from the harsh, frosty Siberian "educational" climate.

Some recognition was given to the initiatives for freedom exercised during the war by the Ukrainian people when Joseph Stalin, Soviet Dictator, insisted that Ukraine (also Byelorussia) be included as a founding member of the United Nations.[45]

The fact that Eastern Galicia, Bukovina, and Carpatho-Ukraine had never before been under Russian rule subjected these areas to rapid methods of Sovietization, including transfers of the population to other parts of the Soviet Union and the bringing in of Russian administrators and technical personnel.[46] Carpatho-Ukraine, when in Czechoslovakia, had enjoyed considerable progress. After Hitler had bitten off western parts of Czechoslovakia, a portion of Carpatho-Ukraine with its capital at Hust, was granted autonomy and Monsignor Augustine Voloshyn became president on October 26, 1938. Germany allowed the Hungarians in March 1939 to take the remainder of Carpatho-Ukraine. The unexpected opposition of the small Ukrainian forces of infantry were no match for the heavy armor of the invaders. This not only marked the first engagement of World War II but also disclosed Russo-German agreement to dismember Poland, bringing on total war.[47]

The humanization trend following Stalin's death reduced the large-scale cruelties and deportations, but it left relatively untouched the centralized controls by Moscow and Russification. The "friendly Russian brothers" forced Ukrainians to accept overseers in the local Communist party units and in government administration. They provided programs on radio and television which were Russian in language or in content and asked Ukrainians to endure the disgrace of watching their intellectuals be consigned to prisons and mental institutions. The Soviet Russian super race destroyed historical evidence by burning Ukraine's leading library, desecrated and removed monuments, closed or put into nonconforming use churches, and intruded its presence into Ukraine in such a way as to leave no doubt as to the results expected. These behaviors conform to centuries of absolutist training.

The voices of Ukrainian protestors such as Moroz, Chornovil, and Masyutko do not stand alone,[48] for now they are joined by prominent Russians of the stature of Sakharov and Solzhenitsyn and by Jewish leaders who object to being melted into the new Soviet man. Glowing accounts of a wonderful life in a communist paradise, or government by the big lie, have been superseded by the sobering realism spawned by revolutionary voices coming out of Ukraine for human rights and the dignity of man.[49]

NOTES TO CHAPTER ONE

[1] Yuriy V. Bohaevsky, *Ukrainian S.S.R., A Brief Reference*, Kiev, Polihrafkniha. 1974. p. 37.

[2] "Ukraine," *Slavonic Encyclopedia*, New York, Philosophical Library, 1949, p. 1325.

[3] Rev. Isadore Nahayewsky, *History of Ukraine*, 2nd ed., Philadelphia, "America" Publishing House, 1975, p. 10.

[4] Nicholas V. Riasanovsky, *A History of Russia*, New York, Oxford University Press, 1968, p. 25.

[5] Nicholas Fr.-Chirovsky, *An Introduction to Russian History*, New York, Philosophical Library, 1967, p. 20.

[6] Nahayewsky, p. 68.

[7] Nahayewsky, p. 74.

[8] John B. Harrison and Richard E. Sullivan, *A Short History of Western Civilization*, 2nd ed., New York, Alfred A. Knopf, 1969, p. 268.

[9] "Medieval History of Ukraine, Galicia, and Volhynia," *Ukraine, a Concise Encyclopedia*, Toronto, University of Toronto Press, 1963, I, 604.

[10] *Ukraine, a Concise Encyclopedia*, I, 611.

[11] Nahayewsky, p. 110.

[12] Riasanovsky, p. 151.

[13] *Ukraine, A Concise Encyclopedia*, I, 625-627.

[14] H. H. Fisher, *America and the New Poland*, New York, The Macmillan Company, 1928, p. 9.

[15] William Henry Chamberlain, *THE UKRAINE A Submerged Nation*, New York, The Macmillan Company, 1944, p. 11.

[16] Michael Hrushevsky, *A History of UKRAINE*, New Haven, Yale University Press, 1943, p. 185.

[17] Jeremiah Curtin, "Introduction," in *With Fire and Sword* by Henryk Sinkiewicz, Boston, Little, Brown and Company, 1898, p. xvi.

[18] Nahayewsky, p. 185.

[19] Hrushevsky, p. 313.

[20] Nahayewsky, p. 192-193.

[21] Hrushevsky, p. 337.

[22] Nahayewsky, p. 212.

[23] Chirovsky, p. 64-68.

[24] Nahayewsky, p. 213.

[25] Chamberlin, p. 9.

[26] Nahayewsky, p. 218.

[27] Chamberlin, p. 28.

[28] Michael A. Florinsky, *Russia, A History and an Interpretation*, New York, The Macmillan Company, 1953, II, 797.

[29] Florinsky, II, 811.

[30] Ivan L. Rudnytsky, "Reply," *Slavic Review*, XXII-2, June 1963, p. 527-529.

[31] *Ukraine, A Concise Encyclopedia*, I, 679.

[32] *Ukraine, A Concise Encyclopedia*, I, 682.

[33] Hrushevsky, p. 469.

[34] *Ukraine, A Concise Encyclopedia*, I, 704.

[35] *Ukraine, A Concise Encyclopedia*, I, 707.

[36] Hrushevsky, p. 429.

[37] "Carpatho-Ruthenia (Ukraine)" *Slovanic Encyclopedia*, pp. 132-6.

[38] Henry Baerlein, *Over the Hills of Ruthenia*, New York, Boni & Liveright, 1925, p. 103.

[39] *Ukraine, A Concise Encyclopedia*, I, 716.

[40] Stephen Bonsal, *Suitors and Suppliants*, New York, Prentice Hall, 1946, p. 140.

[41] Dmytro Solovey, "On the 30th Anniversary of the Great Man-Made Famine in Ukraine," *The Ukrainian Quarterly*, XIX, 3 and 4, 1963.

[42] Clarence A. Manning, *Ukraine Under the Soviets*, New York, Bookman Associates, 1953, pp. 103-7.

[43] Joseph M. Bochenski and Gerhart Niemeyer, editors, *Handbook On Communism*, New York, Frederick A. Praeger, Inc., 1962, pp. 256-260.

[44] Chamberlin, p. 73.

[45] Yaroslav Bilinsky, *The Second Soviet Republic*, New Brunswick, Rutgers University Press, 1964, pp. 264-278.

[46] Abraham A. Hurwicz, director, *Aspects of Contemporary Ukraine*, New Haven, Human Relations Area Files, 1955, p. 216.

[47] Chamberlin, p. 69.

[48] Michael Browne, editor, *Ferment in the Ukraine*, New York, Praeger Publishers, 1971.

[49] Slava Stetsko, editor, *Revolutionary Voices*, 2nd ed., Munich, Press Bureau of the Anti-Bolshevik Bloc of Nations, 1971.

Chapter Two
Why Ukrainians Migrated To Maryland/United States
Wolodymyr C. Sushko

It is one thing to talk in terms of figures about Ukrainian or any other immigration to the United States and it is another matter to present the story clearly in human terms. The subject leads to the important question of why people migrated from Ukraine to Maryland or to other areas in America.

It is difficult to answer the question succinctly. Students of emigration list five reasons for settling in a new land: economic, political, military, commercial, and religious. In the case of America three main forces influenced people to migrate to these shores: economic hardship, religious persecution, and political oppression. By coming to the United States people were responding in their own ways, according to John F. Kennedy, to the pledge of the Declaration of Independence to seek "life, liberty, and the pursuit of happiness."[1]

The reasons for immigration rested deeply in the mind of each individual. As people migrated, they moved not as pawns in a chess game but as individuals who made judgements in light of their understandings of the world.[2] In each case it was a very personal decision preceded by thorough self-search which led to actions which, as a surgeon's knife, cut athwart the participant's way of life. The decision involved breaking away from the customs of ancestors, leaving a paternal home, and departing from the treasured hills and valleys where the history of ancestors centered.

A good example of the attachment of a Ukrainian emigrant to the land where he was born and lived is found in a novel written by Wasyl Stefanyk in Ukraine in 1900, *The Stone Cross*. The story is about the family of Iwan Diduch, who before leaving his village erected a stone cross on the hill where he spent his life and where he once was injured. Iwan engraved his and his wife's names on the stone cross. When the day arrived to leave for the train, Iwan cried before the whole village, saying, "I yearn for this hill like a baby for its mother's breast. If at all possible, I would like to put it in my coat and take it with me into the world. Leaving in the village the smallest item, the smallest child, causes me to suffer but I shall never overcome the grief for this hill."[3] Stories of Ukrainian immigrants to America in the last decades of the 19th century and the first decades of the 20th century are replete with such examples that involve conflicting forces in the mind of the emigrant. Upon arriving in America shocks often again were experienced in adjusting to a new society and to a new environment.

MIGRATION OF SLAVS TO AMERICA

Ukrainians are a Slavic group and the time when Ukrainians started to arrive *en masse* in America falls within the first immigration tide of Slavs in America. This immigration became noticeable in the last three decades of the 19th century and it lasted until the outbreak of World War I in 1914. This period encompassed one of the most remarkable Atlantic migrations in the annals of American history. Peoples of northern and western Europe, who up to this time held first place in migration totals, yielded their places to Slavic immigrants with startling suddenness. As peoples from eastern and southeastern Europe came to America in large numbers, nations within the Austro-Hungarian and Russian Empires became, against the desires of their rulers, the main contributors of manpower to the United States. At about the same time Italy and

Greece were other countries from which large numbers of people emigrated to America. The noted American social historian, Carl N. Degler, comments as follows on the immigration after 1870:

> The great majority of the immigrants came to the United States in the prime of life — in the working years between fourteen and forty-five. For example, four-fifths of the immigrants in 1900 fell within this age range, though less than three fifths of the native population did. Nor were Americans blind to the economic value of this age grouping. "Thus, immigration brings to us a population of working ages unhampered by unproductive mouths to feed," commented economist John R. Commons in 1906. "Their home countries have borne the expense of rearing them up to the industrial period of their lives," he thriftily pointed out, "and then America, without that heavy expense, reaps whatever profits there are on the investment." Europe was a kind of labor "farm" where workers were conveniently and cheaply raised to full size before they entered American industry.[4]

According to the census of 1850 peoples from eastern and southeastern Europe constituted less than 1/3 of one percent of all foreign-born persons in the United States; in 1870, about 2%; in 1880, 4%; in 1890, 8.9%; and in 1900 they increased to 18.1%.[5] In 1907, the all-time peak of its immigration history, America received 1,200,000 people from Europe. Out of this figure the British Isles, Germany, and Scandinavia combined sent slightly more than 200,000. Austria-Hungary sent a third of a million; Italy, nearly 286,000; and Russia, a quarter of a million.

People who were strikingly different in languages, customs, cultures, and standards of living suddenly began to fill American cities and towns. Baltimore, New York, Philadelphia, Chicago and other cities in the East during this period were like modern Babels of tongues. America stood in awe and amazement before a phenomenon which still today makes historians ponder. Frank J. Warne likens the Slav immigration to an invasion but he calls it a peaceful and quiet invasion. . . . "They came as steerage passengers with all their worldly goods in the small bundle strapped to their backs and shoulders. . . . as peacefully and quietly they distributed themselves into places where they would receive food, clothing, and shelter for their labour, and where they hoped to find freedom and happiness."[6]

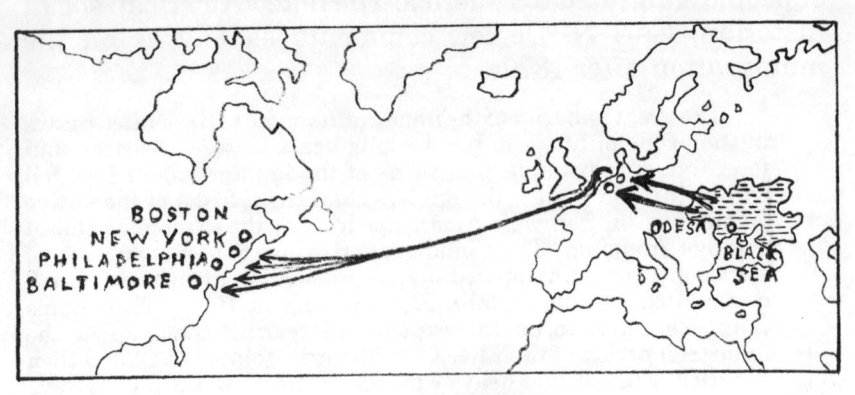

◄—*Emigration
Routes from Ukraine*

*Ukrainian
Ethnographic Territory*

The Slavic migration to America of the period mentioned is the product of both chaotic economic conditions in Europe and of the industrialization process in America. The migration developed from somewhat of a mixture of Europe's discontented people and America's economic and social opportunities. Large expanses of land in the United States were still free and unsettled. New inventions sparked industrial growth. Cheap labor was needed to meet industrial demands. American manufacturers advertized in European newspapers and agents were combing the countrysides of Europe to induce people to come to America. The offer of better opportunities was too great to resist.

EMIGRATION AT WORK IN UKRAINE

When the word about America spread throughout Ukrainian lands it found eager listeners at early times in the western territories which prior to World War I were within the Austro-Hungarian Empire.

A case-study of why Ukrainians left for America is found in the experiences of an elderly Ukrainian immigrant to America, now a resident of Baltimore, Theodore Nykula, who recalls the following:

> I am now eighty two years old. I am from the village of Stremin

in the district of Zhovkva, which is about twenty miles north of Lviv, the major city of western Ukraine. I finished four years of elementary education in the village school in 1908 and helped my father in the field. There were six brothers besides me and one sister. One of my brothers was already in the United States for three years. I remember the letters he wrote home telling us that he was earning one dollar and sometimes two dollars a day. In Austrian currency it meant five crowns to one dollar. Occasionally, when I was lucky to be called, I worked for a local large land-holder in Stremin on a hops plantation. I received ten Austrian cents for a day's work. I could not believe that a man could earn 100 times more in America. In a radius of one kilometer there were three more villages besides Stremin and everywhere work opportunities were scarce. I saw no future for myself and decided to leave for America. My father tried to persuade me to postpone my leaving, saying that I was too young and should complete military service first. But when my brother asked to let me go my father yielded to my request. He borrowed 200 crowns to pay for my travel and in June of 1912 I left for the city of Lviv. My cousin Wasyl Wladyka and another youngster from Stremin, Iwan Peniuk, were going, too. The latter's older brother, Dmytro, took us to Lviv to the office of the steamship company, the Hamburg-America Linie. People were talking more and more about a possible war and the Austrian authorities were not letting young men leave the country. Dmytro Peniuk already seemed to know the steamship agent in Lviv. At that time my older brother, Wolodymyr, was in Moravia on seasonal work. Moravia was a province in the western part of the Austro-Hungarian Empire. The steamship agent persuaded us to tell everybody that we were bound for Moravia to join my brother in the seasonal work. In order not to give rise to any doubts, he took all our documents and money, promising that we would get everything back in Hamburg once we reported to their agency there. He showed us the cap of the Hamburg-America Linie which he was wearing and instructed us to contact any man with such a cap once we arrived in Hamburg. We were on our own how to get to Hamburg. It involved crossing the frontier from Austria to Germany at the railroad station at Oswiencim. We arrived without any difficulty in Oswiencim. I looked out from the window and some 50 or 60 feet from where our train stopped was the German train bound for Hamburg. But how to get to the train? The area between the trains was patrolled by an Austrian gendarme who paced regularly back and forth. We took the moment when the officer walked behind a huge pillar which supported the station roof to run over and board the train. Once inside we felt relieved. It was no trouble to find another agent with the same cap in Hamburg. All our documents and money waited for us there. Three days later we were on a cargo ship, *The Prince Oskar*. There were some 1,500 people on the ship bound for the United States, including many Jews and Hungarians. The Ukrainian emigrants numbered 80 or more. About 30 of the Ukrainians were from eastern Ukraine, then under Russian rule. These Ukrainians had crossed the border into Austria and had worked their way to Hamburg as we did. When asked why they were leaving Russian domination they replied, "The war is imminent. For whom shall we fight?" This answer caused me to reflect for a while as those of us from areas under Austrian rule did not feel the national oppression as strongly as those in eastern Ukraine did. The strongly entrenched Russian government did not permit national aspirations to surface as did the Austro-Hungarian government.

After fourteen and a half days on the water I arrived in the United States at the port of Philadelphia on June 7, 1912. From there I went to Monessen, Pennsylvania, where I worked for U. S. Steel for eight years before coming to Baltimore in 1920 to work for Bethlehem Steel at Sparrows Point.[7]

AMERICAN EMIGRANT COMPANY,

Chartered for the purpose of procuring and assisting Emigrants from Foreign Countries to settle in the United States.

Incorporated with an authorized Capital of $1,000,000.

PAID UP CAPITAL, $540,000.

PRESIDENT—A. G. HAMMOND, President of Exchange Bank, Hartford, Conn. VICE-PRESIDENT—FRANCIS GILLETTE, late Senator in Congress from Connecticut. DIRECTORS—A. G. HAMMOND, Hartford, Conn.; F. CHAMBERLIN, Hartford, Conn.; H. K. WELCH, Hartford, Conn.; JOHN HOOKER, Hartford, Conn.; S. P. LYMAN, New York; JOHN WILLIAMS, New York; CHARLES HULBERT, Boston; JAMES C. SAVERY, Des Moines, Iowa. BANKERS—Bank of New York, 48 Wall Street, New York. TREASURER AND SECRETARY—JOHN HOOKER, Hartford, Conn. GENERAL AGENT FOR EMIGRATION—JOHN WILLIAMS, Office No. 3 Bowling Green, New York.

The object of the American Emigrant Company is to meet the urgent and increasing necessity which is felt for the organization and direction of the labor of the immense multitudes of immigrants arriving in this country; and for this purpose arrangements of the most complete and effective character have been made for the distribution of those persons—South as well as West—immediately on their landing here. The mode of operation is the following:—Agencies have been established in Liverpool, Gothenburg, Hamburg, and Havre, through which information on all American subjects of interest to the emigrant is circulated by means of sub-agencies employed throughout Great Britain, Sweden, Norway, Denmark, Austria, Prussia, Germany, Belgium, Switzerland, and France. Employment in advance is provided for workingmen of every nationality and of every kind of employment, and emigrants coming under the auspices of the Company are in all cases directed to the localities where their services are most required and are best paid.

In addition to this, accurate and reliable information is afforded to all emigrating from Europe with the view of settling upon land, and by this means they are instructed carefully and fully as to the condition and circumstances of any special place they may desire to settle in, and full information to guide them in the judicious choice of a locality for their residence is placed at their disposal. The value of such an agency in Europe, commanding—as the American Emigrant Company does—the respect and confidence of the people coming from Europe to America, and its power to stimulate and direct the flow of emigration, will be manifest. A central office is located at New York, with branch offices in the principal cities of the West and South. By means of this thoroughly organized and widely ramified system of agencies through all sections of the United States, the following ends are gained: 1. Information is afforded gratuitously to every emigrant arriving in New York or Boston, as to the most desirable locality, South, West, or East, for him to select, according to his special object. 2: Employment is secured in the Southern and Western States, in advance, for emigrants arriving, and in many cases the means of traveling to reach it are supplied. 3. Workmen—mechanical, mining, and

REPRODUCTION OF AN ADVERTISEMENT OF THE AMERICAN EMIGRANT COMPANY, ca.1865. Austria and Prussia are cited in the advertisement.
Smithsonian Collection of Business Americana

And so the new tide of immigration to America included more and more Ukrainians among the Slavic peoples coming here.

Pictured at the left is the newly arrived immigrant to America, Theodore Nykula, who has just become a member of the Ukrainian Brass Band of Monessen, Pennsylvania.
U.E.A.M. Collection

HISTORICAL USE OF NAMES AND IMMIGRATION

It is not easy to ascertain when and how many Ukrainians arrived in America. There are special difficulties involved in dealing with Ukrainian immigration. On one side the immigrants used various names to identify themselves, and on the other side, the immigration census data for many years did not differentiate between real Russians, Austrians, Hungarians, or Poles and such submerged nations who were under their rule, as Ukrainians, Byelorussians, Jews, etc.

In order to understand the reasons which were behind the use of those various names, one must go back into the history of their homeland in Europe.

In medieval times, Ukrainians called themselves *Rusyny* (Rusins, Ruteni, Rutheni) and their land was known as Rus'. The application of this name is frequently found in the historic sources of medieval Europe, designating clearly the present Ukrainian territory. Today Rusyn (Ruthenian) is an ancient Ukrainian name. Its application became narrowed to the mountainous western Ukrainian territories of Galicia, Bukovina, and Transcarpathian Ukraine where it was in frequent use until recently, especially in villages. The well-known American observer, novelist Erskine Caldwell, during his stay in 1936 in the Carpathian Mountains, had the opportunity to observe these people. The impression he got was that these people who were known as being Ruthenians were probably closer to being authentic Ukrainians.[8] People in these territories suffered much from economic hardships. A large number of them were illiterate. A very large portion of early Ukrainian mass migration to the United States came from these territories. Here they continued to call themselves "Rusins" (Ruthenians). This group still today survives in the USA, mainly as a religious splinter from the Ukrainian Catholic Church. Around the turn of this century, the Russian Orthodox Church succeeded in propagandizing many of these Rusins into believing they were "Russians." It was fairly easy, considering the illiteracy of many of these immigrants and similarity of Rusin to the word Russian. It has been estimated that about 80% of the members of the Russian Orthodox Church in the United States is made up of former Ukrainian (Rusin) Catholics.[9] Today Rusins in the United States form a rather regional group which is primarily made up of Ukrainians who almost a century ago came from the Transcarpathian Province of Ukraine. Professor Walter Warzeski of the Department of History at Kutztown State College has studied the history of these people, and from his study it is evident that by language, culture, and race the Rusins are a part of the Ukrainian nation.[10]

In the second half of the sixteenth century, the name Rus' started to be identified with a new designation *Kozaks* (Cossacks). Ukrainians on both sides of the Dnipro River came to be known in the seventeenth and eighteenth centuries to the rest of Europe as a Kozak nation, and they formed a Kozak-Hetman State. With the total annihilation of the Ukrainian Kozak Independence in 1764, Russia launched a course aimed at eradicating all the remnants of the Ukrainian Kozak separateness. Tsardom of Muscovy, having earlier appropriated itself Ukraine's very name of Rus', proclaimed that Rus' was Russia, and a brute process of russification of the land began. Ukraine was given the official name of Malo-Russia — "Little-Russia," and it was degraded to a state of province of Russia. Kozak military units were included in the Russian tsarist army, and with time, they lost their national identity. Ukrainian Kozak nobles had to emigrate to other countries. The others were exiled to Siberia, and from there many of them found their way across the Bering Strait to the American side. It can be assumed that they were among the first white settlers in Alaska and California. Eskimos in Alaska still today refer to these white settlers as "our gussuk friends." Gussuk, the Eskimo word for white man, is a corruption of "Kozak." The word Kozak in the Turkish language is gazag. Names like Harry Havrilack are not uncommon among the descendents of white pioneer settlers in Alaska, and they strongly indicate their Ukrainian origin.[11] Many other Kozak nobles are believed to have served in the Revolutionary War. In reviewing the names of the officers in George Washington's military staff, we find such Ukrainian names as Nemyrych, Sadowsky, Hrabowsky, and others.[12]

Some scholars attribute Ukrainian ancestry to an English physician, Dr. Lawrence Bohun, because he may have had the same family origin as the famous Ukrainian Kozak colonel at the time of Chmelnycky, Ivan Bohun. Both Ukrainian and English families of Bohun are said to have originated in St. Georges of Bohon in the southeast corner of the Cherbourg peninsula in France.[13] Dr. Lawrence Bohun came in 1610 with Lord Delaware to Virginia and became the first surgeon-general of the Virginia colony. Another famous Ukrainian Kozak figure is Brigadier-General John Basil Turchin — a hero of battles at Chicamauga and Missionary Ridge from the Civil War time. He was born in the Don River area of Ukraine, and because of his opposition to the despotic tsarist rule, he emigrated to the United States. General Turchin was a very efficient officer, and for his daring attacks, he became known as the "Wild Kozak." The others called him "Terrible Kozak." For a brief time during the Civil War, he was in command of troops at Baltimore in Maryland.[14] Still another educated Ukrainian in America was a Kozak clergyman and political refugee from Russian oppression in Ukraine, Agapius Honcharenko. In 1867-72, he became a noted public figure in California while working for the Government as a consultant on Alaska and edited a semimonthly "Alaska Herald" in which he popularized facts about Ukraine and Ukrainians.

In the meantime in Ukraine, in the face of the official tsarist political terminology Russia imposed upon the land, it is small wonder that in order to counteract the russification drive, the people themselves turned more and more to their other old name — *Ukraine*. Ukraine is as old as the name Rus', and it was in wide use by the people, as their folk songs, Kozak Chronicles, and maps indicate. But it did not gain its modern meaning as a national territory until this very overt attempt on the part of Moscow to destroy the Ukrainian nation. The proclamations of the Ukrainian Republic of 1917 and 1918 officially confirmed the name Ukraina — "Ukraine" in both internal and international usage. This is now the term that denotes the Ukrainian nation and all those who came from that nation.

The other difficulty involved in dealing with Ukrainian immigration is in the statistical records of the U.S. Bureau of Immigration as well as those of U. S. Census. Before 1899, Ukrainians were recorded by the country from which they came. American census officials did not foresee a place for a stateless nation such as Ukraine, or Ruthenia, as it was often termed then. It is only in 1899 that immigration officials began also recording people by their ethnic origin. But even this situation actually did not improve much because immigration clerks frequently continued to record Ukrainian immigrants only according to the country specified on their passports. The prevailing illiteracy of many of the early immigrants, the lack of knowledge of English, and even the fear of revealing their names because of difficulties they had experienced in their homeland, without any doubt contributed much to this unfortunate situation. It was not until 1910 that the United States Census introduced the name "Ruthenians," and not until 1930 that besides "Ruthenians," the term "Ukrainians" was added. The censuses of 1940 and 1950 finally eliminated the term "Ruthenians," leaving only "Ukrainians."

By JOHN ROSOLOWICZ, ("ROSOL")

Ukrainian National Association

Due to these problems thousands of Ukrainian as well as Byelorussian immigrants, during the first stages of emigration, became lost forever in the immigration records and were listed as Austrians, Russians, Hungarians, or Poles. Emily G. Balch in her study *Our Slavic Fellow Citizens* makes reference to this, saying:

> ...and those who are called Russians in the United States are in a large proportion of cases properly Little Russians.[15]

Other scholars make reference to this problem too. Clark Witke reports that by 1920 there were 3,000,000 of Polish parentage in the United States...but he adds that

> ...here again it must be remembered that the Poles were not always sharply distinguished for statistical purposes from the Ruthenians and similar groups.[16]

Perhaps Professor Bohdan P. Procko summarized the problem most succinctly in his chapter of the book *The Ethnic Experience in Pennsylvania*:

> Any attempt to write about the Ukrainian immigration to the United States must constitute only a rough written outline, for neither the United States immigration records nor the immigrants themselves provide complete data for a thorough history.[18]

CAUSES OF UKRAINIAN ARRIVALS

For convenience in discussing the causes which influenced the large-scale coming of Ukrainians to the United States/Maryland, the immigration is divided into three main periods:

First Period — 1870-1914

Some of the principal causes which influenced immigration during this period were overpopulation and fragmentation of land in Ukraine along with the demand for labor in America which was accompanied by a reasonable ease of entering the United States. Mass migration came from the western Ukrainian territories of Galicia, Bukowina, and Carpatho-Ukraine. In these areas population was rising rapidly. As there was almost no modern industry the populace in the main depended on land. As the population grew the fragmentation of land became more and more evident causing great economic hardships for many Ukrainians.

Two huts in the village of Zarwanycja indicate thriftiness but also marginal economic conditions.
U.E.A.M. Collection

Land fragmentation was most prevalent in Galicia. Philip Taylor records: "...In 1900 only some 1,500 holdings exceeded 50 acres; half a million were 7½; 600,000 were between 2½ and 7½; and more than 200,000 were smaller still. Such holdings, except perhaps in vineyard districts, could not sustain a family..."[19] Accordingly, this first period is known as a time of economic mass movement to America. There were other causes for emigration, such as the desire of some men to escape military service in armies alien to Ukrainians and the adverse political conditions in the homeland caused by a reawakening of national consciousness by Ukrainians and the concomitant government reactions to Ukrainian emergence. The dominant factor promoting immigration was simply the matter of economic hardship.

So lured by the enticements of better opportunities in America's growing economy, Ukrainian tillers of the soil left to become workers in coal mines in Pennsylvania, Maryland, and West Virginia or to become laborers in the steel mills of Baltimore, Pittsburgh, Cleveland, or Buffalo.

Warwara Pise estimates that at least 25 people left her village of Wolycja, near Zhovkwa, and came to Baltimore between 1899 and 1914. She herself left Wolycja in 1907 to join her uncle, Oleksa Marmash, who was already in Baltimore, having arrived in Maryland in 1899. In the year 1912 alone, 25 young females and 9 males left the village of Siniawa, near Yaroslaw in the westernmost part of Ukraine. More than 130 kilometers east of Siniawa is the village of Stremin, from which there were 30 young male emigrants. The village of Zarwanycja, located in easternmost Galicia near the Austrian-Russian border sent close to 20 people to America in the years 1910-1914. Nine of these persons settled in the Baltimore area of Maryland.[20]

Painting of a village in the Podilian Highlands of Ukraine.
Mr. and Mrs. Petro Wojtowycz

The Austrian and Hungarian governments attempted to prevent emigration in order that large land holders might retain needed labor in the villages. At times instructions aimed at opposing American attempts to recruit workers were issued to local officials. Emily Balch mentions a Ukrainian priest whom she met while travelling in Galicia. The priest related that in 1880 the Austrian government tried to make priests read a proclamation against going to America but many priests held a conference at which they pledged as a group to ignore the order. The priest Emily Balch encountered had himself destroyed the proclamation given to him.[21] Nothing could stop the increasing mass movement to America. Strangely facilitating the emigration process was the fact that Austria-Hungary and Russia at the time were the only countries in Europe that did not have any emigration laws. Intentions to enact such a law in Austria were hinted by the government in 1897, 1901, and again in 1907, but the law never materialized.[22] The exodus soared until it reached a peak Ukrainian immigration of 36,527 in 1914. Of this number 178 came to Maryland.[23]

Second Period — 1918-1939

The several new immigration laws enacted by the Congress of the United States after World War I drastically reduced the number of Ukrainians coming to America. Emigration from what is now Soviet Ukraine almost ceased. Emigration from Poland, Czecho-Slovakia, and Rumania, which countries ruled territories formerly belonging to the Ukrainian Republic, was severely limited by the national quotas established. Myron Kuropas estimates that no more than 40,000 Ukrainians came to America during this second period.[24] Economic hardship continued to be a factor promulgating emigration. Many individuals left, too, to avoid the political repression inherent with the downfall of the Ukrainian Republic by the year of 1922. Ukrainian political leaders received very harsh treatment in several notorious prisons.

During this period another migration process, the interior migration of Ukrainians among the states in America, is worth mentioning. The movement was caused by a search for better employment and improved living conditions and in many cases, due to the severity of the Depression, the search for employment of any kind. Between 1920 and 1932 a number of Ukrainians moved from Pennsylvania, New Jersey, and New York to Maryland. The modern facilities of the Bethlehem Steel Company, formerly the Maryland Steel Company, attracted many workers from the steel mill and mining areas around Pittsburgh and Johnstown, Pennsylvania. Theodore Nykula states that about 30 families moved to Baltimore from Monessen, Butler, and New Kensington in Pennsylvania. Most workers readily found employment with the Bethlehem Steel Company.[25] Others such as Alex Zuk moved to Baltimore with their plants when the firms transferred to Baltimore from New York. [26] During the days of the Civilian Conservation Corps numerous Ukrainian-Americans worked in C.C.C. projects in western Maryland — planting trees, clearing forests, building dams, etc. Likewise, Ukrainians have helped to staff many of the Maryland military bases.

An interesting observation about Ukrainian settlement in Maryland is that a number of people were atracted to Maryland from the Pittsburgh area by the excellent quality of the drinking water in the Baltimore area. Drinking water in mining areas frequently contained amounts of sulphur which was offensive to people accustomed to using pure water.

Interaction between Maryland and Pennsylvania Ukrainians was increased by the activities of the Baltimore and Ohio Railroad. The firm operated a large railroad repair shop in DuBois, Pennsylvania, and Ukrainians, Lithuanians, Poles, and other East Europeans frequently "followed the tracks" in obtaining work with the railroad or with mining or steel mill operations. The Baltimore and Ohio Railroad served many communities in Pennsylvania and western Maryland where Ukrainians were numerous.

There was frequent movement among miners from town to town and this action included the relocation of some miners from state to state, involving Maryland, Pennsylvania, and West Virginia. Today a number of Ukrainian-Americans hold managerial positions with mining companies and with the United Mine Workers Union.

Third Period — 1946 to Present

The end of World War II found some 250,000 Ukrainians in western Europe. These people, along with thousands of other East Europeans, refused to return to their Russian-dominated homelands. During the war a large number of these Ukrainians had been forcefully taken by the Germans to work in the labor camps of the Third Reich. The larger number of the Ukrainian refugees in Germany were fleeing the oncoming Red Russian armies because they did not want to live under communism. For all of these people it was a long and dangerous journey which had begun in the rolling plains of Ukraine. The exodus proceeded by all possible means of transportation and ended in the World War II labor or detention camps. After the war they gathered in the Allied displaced persons camps.

This photograph shows Mrs. Eleanor Roosevelt visiting a Ukrainian Displaced Persons Camp at Stuttgart-Zuffenhausen, Germany.
U.E.A.M. Collection

This third emigration was considerably different from the first two as it was politically and religiously motivated. These people resisted the Russian oppression of Ukraine and adherents of both the Ukrainian Catholic and Ukrainian Orthodox Churches had been exposed to severe religious persecution which included the destruction of church facilities and the killing of the Ukrainian clergy.

For all these victims of the war there was only one desire: to find freedom somewhere in the world.

Typical of the lot which these people experienced is the story of Lubomyr Janycky as reported in the *Baltimore Sun* of August 5, 1949. Lubomyr Janycky was the eighteen-year-

A JOYFUL DAY. These Ukrainian refugees are leaving the camp at Stuttgart-Zuffenhausen, Germany, by truck to board a ship for the United States.

Mrs. Maria Charchalis

These refugees are bound for America in July, 1949, aboard the United States Army Transport Ship, The General Muir.

Mrs. Sophia Lishchynsky

old son of Wolodymyr Janycky, who upon arriving in Maryland was employed at Rosewood State Training School near Baltimore. Lubomyr's story is as follows:

> I can remember when the Germans and the Russians divided up our country. Our part of Ukraine was taken over by Russia. They spoke of their free life, but it was just like slavery. Even though I was a small child I can remember because it made a great impression.
>
> Living under Russian rule was worse than under the Nazis later. The Russians sent my uncle, aunt and cousin to Siberia in 1940. I think they did this because he was a business man and had some money. The Russians... they have special reasons to send you away...
>
> The Germans came to my village in 1941 and they took us to Vienna in 1943 to work in the forest. It took us two weeks to make the trip in a railroad cattle car. There were too many people — all that time most older people were standing up but the children could sit down sometimes.
>
> At least two dead people were taken from the car by the SS men...
>
> My family was lucky for we all stayed together when we went to the concentration camp. We were at the Leinzer Tiergarten camp (near Vienna) until 1944.
>
> The Germans told us they were going to take us to Salzburg to be shot. I forget the name of that camp. I don't remember anything until I heard somebody shout that the Americans were in the town.[27]

Ukrainians knew well from past experiences that the Soviets, under the pretext of eliminating enemies of communism, were intent upon destroying the Ukrainian national movement — name, language, religion, and culture. These facets of heritage were precious to Ukrainians so they chose to remain in the West under Allied control, hoping to find freedom somewhere in the world. Many have found that freedom in America.

NOTES TO CHAPTER TWO

[1] John F. Kennedy, *A Nation of Immigrants*, New York, 1964, p. 24.

[2] Philip Taylor, *The Distant Magnet*, London, 1971, p. 42.

[3] Wasyl Stefanyk, *The Works*, Regensburg, 1948, p. 107.

[4] Carl N. Degler, *Out of Our Past — The Forces that Shaped America*, New York, 1959, p. 279.

[5] Frank J. Warne, *The Slav Invasion and the Mine Workers*, Philadelphia and London, 1904, p. 42.

[6] Frank J. Warne, *The Immigrant Invasion*, New York, 1913, p. 9.

[7] Oral story told to the writer by Theodore Nykula, Baltimore, Maryland, on October 25, 1975.

[8] Letter from Erskine Caldwell to Paul Fenchak, Baltimore, Maryland, February 10, 1976.

[9] Joseph S. Roucek, *Slavonic Encyclopedia*, Vol. 3, New York, 1949, p. 1099.

[10] John E. Bodnar (Editor), *The Ethnic Experience in Pennsylvania*, Lewisburg, 1973, pp. 175-215.

[11] Keith Tryck, "Rafting Down the Yukon," *National Geographic*, Vol. 148, No. 6, December 1975, pp. 851-859.

[12] Wasyl Luciw, PhD, & Theodore Luciw, M.A., *Ahapius Honcharenko and The Alaska Herald*, Toronto, 1963, p. 64.

[13] Theodore Luciw, *Father Agapius Honcharenko: First Ukrainian Priest in America*, New York, 1970, p. 8.

[14] *Harpel Scrapbook*, p. 98, February 6, 1886, from the Collections in the Library of the Chicago Historical Society.

[15] Emile Greene Balch, *Our Slavic Fellow Citizens*, New York, 1910, p. 126.

[16] Carl Witke, *We Who Built America*, New York, 1939, p. 424.

[17] Julian Bachinsky, *Ukrainian Immigration to the United States of America*, Lviv, 1914, pp. 103-104.

[18] See 10 — p. 216.

[19] See 2 — p. 53.

[20] Oral Statements by Warwara Pise, Baltimore, Maryland, November 2, 1975; Theodore Nykula, Baltimore, Maryland, October 25, 1975; Mychajlyna Evanuk, Baltimore, Maryland, November 13, 1975; Alex Zuk, Baltimore, Maryland, October 28, 1975.

[21] Emily G. Balch, *Our Slavic Fellow Citizens*, New York, 1910, p. 136.

[22] See 17 — p. 10.

[23] Wasyl Halich, *Ukrainians in the United States*, Chicago, 1937, p. 150.

[24] Myron Kuropas, *The Ukrainians in America*, Minneapolis, 1972, p. 43.

[25]See 7 — Oral Statement by Theodore Nykula, Baltimore, Maryland.

[26]See 11 — Statement by Alex Zuk, Personal Interview, Baltimore, Maryland.

[27]"Thirteen Ukrainian Refugees Help at State Mental Institution," *The Sun*, Baltimore, Maryland, August 5, 1949, p. 26.

Chapter Three
Arrivals and Settlements In Maryland
Wolodymyr C. Sushko

The mass migration movement of Ukrainians to the United States did not begin until about 1870 and did not take noticeable proportions until about 1890. This movement increased in numbers each year until World War I put a stop to it in 1914. The largest number of Ukrainian immigrants went to Pennsylvania and other northern states. Maryland was also the recipient of some of these people although in proportionately smaller numbers.

Wasyl Halich quotes the statistical data taken from the annual reports of the Commissioner of Immigration that between 1899 and 1914 a total of 1,133 Ukrainians arrived in Maryland. The largest group, containing 263, arrived in 1907, with the next largest group arriving in 1914. The smallest group came in 1900 when only 11 Ukrainians gave Maryland as their destination.[1] The foregoing figures must not be considered complete as many Ukrainians entered this country and became registered as Poles, Russians, and Austrians. It is fair to assume that the actual number of Ukrainian arrivals in Maryland in the period mentioned must have been much larger.

BALTIMORE AND STEERAGE

For many Ukrainians, the same as for Poles, Germans, Italians, and others, Baltimore was the port of entry to America. In the second half of the 19th century and up to the first World War, Baltimore was a bustling city. This was a period of flourishing commerce between America and Europe. American products, among them tobacco from Maryland and Virginia, were finding good markets in Europe. In return Europe provided America with a source of much needed labor. This led to the development of a steerage business for steamship companies. Steerage required no special accommodations and services and only minimal facilities. The emigrants who hardly had enough money to pay for their tickets to America were packed together in the lower portions of a ship where they stayed during their long and dreaded journey. The transportation of steerage immigrants became a vast and lucrative business for steamship companies. Their cargo ships were bringing immigrants to America and on the way back to Europe were transporting goods. Eastern American as well as European ports profited from this business. Baltimore, being a shipping point for Maryland and Virginia tobacco, became the natural destination of ships from Bremen. The North German Lloyd Line ships, *Braunschweig*, *Bremen*, *Baltimore*, *Ohio*, and others, brought human cargo to Baltimore. On their return voyage to Bremen their holds were filled with tobacco which in turn was processed in Germany and sold with great popularity throughout Europe. The ship company operated under an arrangement with the Baltimore and Ohio railroad which built and maintained a terminal at Locust Point where passengers disembarked. The ships of the Lloyd Line made regular crossings between Bremen and Baltimore. Some 600,000 European immigrants were deposited at Locust Point between 1870 and 1900. Immigrant traffic to Baltimore continued up to World War I. The majority of Ukrainians arrived at the Baltimore Port between the years of 1900 and 1914. Among some early arrivals were Antin Pise (1904), Alexander Shandrowsky (1908), Wasyl Burko and Wasyl Wladyka (1909). Baltimore became the home of Antin Pise and Alexander Shandrowsky while the others boarded trains for Monessen, Pennsylvania, and Youngstown, Ohio. Many more Ukrainians arrived in 1910, among them two sisters Mychajlyna and Maria Stelmach who made Baltimore their home.

Immigrants cover a deck of the Bremen, *docked at Locust Point about 1900.*

Peale Museum

VOYAGE OF A STEERAGE

The journey across the ocean was not easy for many of the steerage passengers. The journey in a cargo ship lasted from two to three weeks. Passengers were exposed to all the evils of the cargo system. They were directed down deep stairways to the lower decks usually below the water level. Theodore Nykula recalls his deck's being level with the water. The sleeping compartments consisted of three rows of berths arranged one above the other. Bathing facilities were next to none. Most men slept in their clothes. Many steerage travellers, especially single males, stayed in one and the same garment during the whole journey and their personal cleanliness left much to be desired. Women were usually first to effect some action at remedying these unsanitary conditions. They washed their clothes right on deck, and readily washed the clothes of those male passengers who asked them. Nykula recalls many single male immigrants sitting on their berths covered with blankets while their garments were being washed for they had no other clothes to put on. More than 64 years since he arrived in America, Theodore Nykula still relates many of the experiences he had on the vessel *en route* to America. In many matters steerage passengers themselves had to assume the duty of regulation. With a sense of humor he relives in his reminiscences how one day they caught their rations chief cheating them on their meal rations:

> We ate in our berths. We were organized in groups, and one man from each group was appointed to go with a pot to the dining room to receive the meals. It was usually soup and stew. The turn came for this particular fellow from our group. There were four of us Ukrainians and we naturally were together. We saw the others receiving plenty of meat, and our ration was nothing but a thin watery soup. This was enough to make us suspicious. The next day we sneaked behind this fellow. In order to get to the dining room one had to go through a long corridor. On his way back this man used to take the meat out of the pot with his hand and eat it. We really yelled when we saw this. We demanded to see the captain, not giving up. Finally the captain responded. With whatever English and German we knew and gesticulating we explained what had happened. The whole incident had a happy ending because the captain gave the four of us a separate pot, and for the rest of the journey we went after our own meals . . .[2]

COMING TO STAY

As was the case with most other steerage arrivals, it was predominantly the younger and single Ukrainians who ventured to the United States before World War I. Some were coming with the single hope of earning money and returning to Ukraine. Some did return. The majority, however, stayed, and they became the nucleus of Ukrainian settlements in Maryland.

SETTLEMENTS IN BALTIMORE

The first and oldest Ukrainian settlement in Maryland was in Baltimore. Today Baltimore is still known as a city of hidden charms. One of these charms has always been the ethnic composition of the city. Some twenty-five nationality groups live in Baltimore in somewhat isolated ethnic colonies. Germans, Irish, Italians, Poles, Greeks, Czechs, Slovaks, Ukrainians, and many others, formed immigrant neighborhoods upon their arrival, first along the waterfront not far from where they landed, and then later in other sections of the city. Unlike most other American cities where waves of new settlers moved in to mix with the old, Baltimore's village-neighborhoods remained astoundingly unaffected and unchanged through generations.[3] One today can yet experience this subtle ethnic charm when visiting the old section of Baltimore in Little Italy, Fells Point, Canton, Highlandtown or further south across the harbor waters in Locust Point and Curtis Bay. It was in this city's Ethnic Haven or, as Stuart S. Taylor, Jr., calls it, "The Mysterious East,"[4] that the Ukrainians put their first roots into the Maryland soil.

The influx of Ukrainians into Baltimore began in the late 1890's, later than that of some other immigrant groups. Unlike the other nationalities who upon arrival in Baltimore could count on some help from many of their countrymen already occupying positions of power and influence here, the first Ukrainians had no one to look to for help. Not understanding English, they had nobody to turn to for advice.

The experience of many of the early Ukrainians contains some of the basic elements of that of the early pioneers. They did not despair. They came with a stubborn willingness to work, and many of them often walked miles upon miles of strange roads and places in search of work. Perhaps, also, they hoped to find someone to whom they could speak in their own language. The most explicit story here about those early Ukrainians in Baltimore is the one the late Petro Marmash, who was one of the first Ukrainian residents of Baltimore, told Theodore Nykula back in the 1920's. Theodore Nykula repeated the episode to the author:

> ... Baltimore at all times was one of those few cities where one could always find a job. Our people were coming to Baltimore from other places in search of jobs. There were few Ukrainians in those early years here, and most of them did not know each other for there was not an established Ukrainian community as such yet. Over there where you now see huge oil storage tanks near O'Donnell and Dundalk Avenues, there used to be large farm fields. There were no streets. And if there was public transportation, this one man could not know it. He was walking to Baltimore to find a job. He walked straight across the fields in the direction of the City. He was tired. A soft, breathless stillness of the air and surrounding green fields reminded him so much of his village fields in Ukraine... But he was here in Baltimore stranded in the field not knowing his way. He needed somebody to direct him how to get to the city. He sees there is somebody working in the field. Without thinking twice he approaches this man. He takes off his hat and greets him in Ukrainian as he used to do in the old country, saying... Daj Bozhe Shtchastja ("May Lord Give You Luck")... and this man replies to him as if nothing has happened, also in Ukrainian ... Daj Bozhe i Wam, Djakuju za Dobre Slowo ("May Lord Give You, Too, Thank You For Your Good Word")... For a moment both of them could not believe their ears... and then they ran to each other and with tears in their eyes embraced one another...[5]

One of the first Ukrainians to arrive in Baltimore was Oleksa Marmash. He came in 1899 and settled in East Baltimore. But it was not until the middle 1900's that Ukrainian life in the city began to shape itself in small but well-defined Ukrainian neighborhoods.

From the beginning two Ukrainian neighborhoods developed in Baltimore — one of them in East Baltimore and another in Curtis Bay. The East Baltimore colony in 1922 numbered approximately 500 while in Curtis Bay there were from 250 to 300 Ukrainians.[6] Employment in the

A typical Ukrainian Wedding Scene, this photo shows the marriage of Anastasia Stodolny to Petro Marmash in Baltimore, 1910.

Mr. and Mrs. Joseph Marmash

East Baltimore and Curtis Bay factories was for the most part the reason why Ukrainians settled there. Also, a sizeable Polish community may have had some influence on their settling. Not knowing English, many of these Ukrainians at least could communicate with Poles with some reasonable ease. Furthermore, being deeply religious people, they attended Sunday services in the Polish churches of St. Stanislaw, St. Casimir, and St. Athanasius, until they built their own churches.

Because of the distance between East Baltimore and Curtis Bay, from the early days both Ukrainian communities went their own ways, having little to do with each other as if they were in two separate towns. With the establishment of their churches in 1911 in Curtis Bay and in 1913 in East Baltimore they became even more confined within the borders of their respective parishes.

Of the Ukrainians in Baltimore the greater number always lived in East Baltimore. Within this colony they formed two distinctive groups, one of them concentrating around Wolfe Street and the other in the Canton area. Chronologically, the first settlement is that around Wolfe Street. Here in the narrow streets near the waterfront where still memories of the bygone era of the steerage migration linger, sometime in the 1890's a group of Ukrainians, or as they called themselves, Rusyns (Rusniaks), established their first homes. Most of them came to this country from the impoverished westernmost Lemko region of the Carpathian Mountains in Ukraine. One of the first arrivals from that group is believed to be Makarij Tyrpak who came to Baltimore in the early 1890's and settled at 1605 Lancaster Street. He worked as a stevedore at Locust Point. At about the same time came John Batryn and Ignatius Ladna, and they resided in the 800 block of South Bond Street. Estimates place the number of that group at 100 or more having been present here in 1907. In that year they were already established as a community group and were organized in a local lodge of a fraternal organization called *Sojedynenije* (Union). Ignatius Ladna, John Batryn, and Makarij Tyrpak were much instrumental in establishing this lodge. They also served in the executive branch of that lodge for many years. *Sojedynenije* or Greek Catholic Union of the U.S.A., was formed by Ukrainian priests in 1892. It is the oldest fraternal organization of immigrants from Ukraine in the United States, with headquarters in Pittsburgh, and originally most Ukrainian immigrants belonged to this Union. However, because of conflicts over the localism of leadership in 1894 the members from Galicia and a large segment of those from the Priashiv region left the *Sojedynenije* and formed the Ukrainian National Association which now is the largest Ukrainian fraternal organization in the Free World.[7] Today *Sojedynenije* consists mostly of those immigrants from Ukraine who continue to call themselves Rusins. Also Slovaks and Hungarians who are of Eastern Catholic Rite are members of this organization. With the formation in 1912 of the first branch of the Ukrainian National Association in East Baltimore many from the Wolfe Street group left *Sojedynenije* and joined the Ukrainian National Association.

The Makarij Tyrpak Family, ca. 1908. Mr. Tyrpak was one of the founders of Baltimore's *Sojedynenije*.

Mr. and Mrs. John Boyko

Among the more active pioneer members from the Wolfe Street group were Ignatius Ladna, Lucas Turyk, John Batryn, Josyf Capak, Makarij Tyrpak, Iwan Warga, and many others. They were very instrumental in establishing the present St. Michael's Ukrainian Catholic Church on Wolfe Street. Many of them spent considerable time travelling each year between 1908 and 1914 from town to town throughout the eastern United States where Ukrainians lived and solicited donations for the church building fund.[9] Theodore Nykula recalls that in 1914 while still in Monessen, Pennsylvania, he gave one dollar to the church building fund in Baltimore. One dollar in those days was equivalent to one day's work. 'Nobody asked questions," said Nykula. "Everybody gave according to his means . . . and I made my donation although I never dreamed that a few years later I would be in Baltimore . . ."

The other source of funds for the church building fund were theatrical performances and concerts. John Boyko who came to Baltimore in 1912, had much to do with these cultural activities. With the help of Reverend Zacharij Orun, the first Catholic priest for Ukrainians in Baltimore, in 1913 he established a Ukrainian amateur dramatic group and a church choir. Theatrical plays, songs and dances at St. Michael's hall enjoyed great success throughout the 1920's.

Some of the other early settlers of the Wolfe Street group were the families of Josyf Durdela, Danylo Kernyckyj, Iwan Szpatura, Petro Bodnar, Petro Balko, Semen Kuzyk, Mychajlo Kluchnyk, Theodore Zacharchuk, Petro Miskiw, Jacob Poliszuk, Philimon Zacharko, Semen Saplywyj, Iwan Kusyk, Joseph Davis, Stephan Topolnicki, and many others.

The Canton group centered around O'Donnell Street and Ellwood Avenue but individual families scattered among other ethnic groups over a vast area from Patterson Park in the west through Canton and Highlandtown to Dundalk in the east. The steel mills of Sparrows Point and the lumber yards and other factories of East Baltimore for the most part claimed the working hours of those Ukrainians. A majority of them came to Baltimore from the

Podillan Highlands of Ukraine. They were hard working people. Warwara Pise recalls with nostalgia the harmonious association which was characteristic of the lives of many of these families in their first years here:

> ... there was a lumber yard near the water, I don't remember the place, on Decker Street or somewhere near ... It was a quiet isolated place ... On Sunday afternoons many of us would walk there and sit on the water's edge and talk ... And we all sang our songs like we used to do in our villages in Ukraine ...[10]

Warwara Pise came to Baltimore in 1907.

More Ukrainians settled among this group in the twenties. These were people who moved to Baltimore from other states in search of jobs. Theodore Nykula estimates that a total of 171 Ukrainians came here between 1920 and 1932. Eighty-eight of these came from Monessen, Pennsylvania, alone. Some of these people were Josyf Olyniach, Theodore Taras, Josyf Fall, Andrij Peltz, Andrij Opar, Les'ko Remeniuk, Iwan Perezuk, Mychajlo Blama, Dmytro Karbanyk, Alex Zuk, Theodore Nykula, Kasimir and John Jarema, George Evanowich, Theodore Lucyshyn, Mychajlo Kryz, Dmytro Fall, and others.

A distinct trait of many of the Canton Ukrainians has always been their pride in being of Ukrainian nativity. They were proud of their culture and wanted their children to learn about it. In 1929 a group of them, among whom were Theodore Nykula, Petro Marmash, Andrij Peltz and the Semenkiw brothers, met and formed the Ukrainian-American Citizens Club. They acquired a building at the corner of O'Donnell Street and Ellwood Avenue which became the Ukrainian National Home. Petro Marmash and Theodore Nykula, among others, served on the executive board. Thanks to their unceasing efforts throughout the thirties this home was a busy center of cultural activities of all kinds. These activities also reached out to a wider Baltimore audience. The Ukrainian National Choir under direction of Josyf Swobodjan gave singing performances over the WCBM and WFBR radio stations and at the Peabody Music Conservatory on several occasions during the years 1936-1938. The Ukrainian Dancing Club, led by its 23-year-old director, Mychajlo Korchynskyj, performed

"MNOHAJA LITA" — "MANY HAPPY YEARS" resulted from the marriage of Warwara Marmash to Antin Pise in Baltimore, ca. 1907.

Mr. and Mrs. John Malko

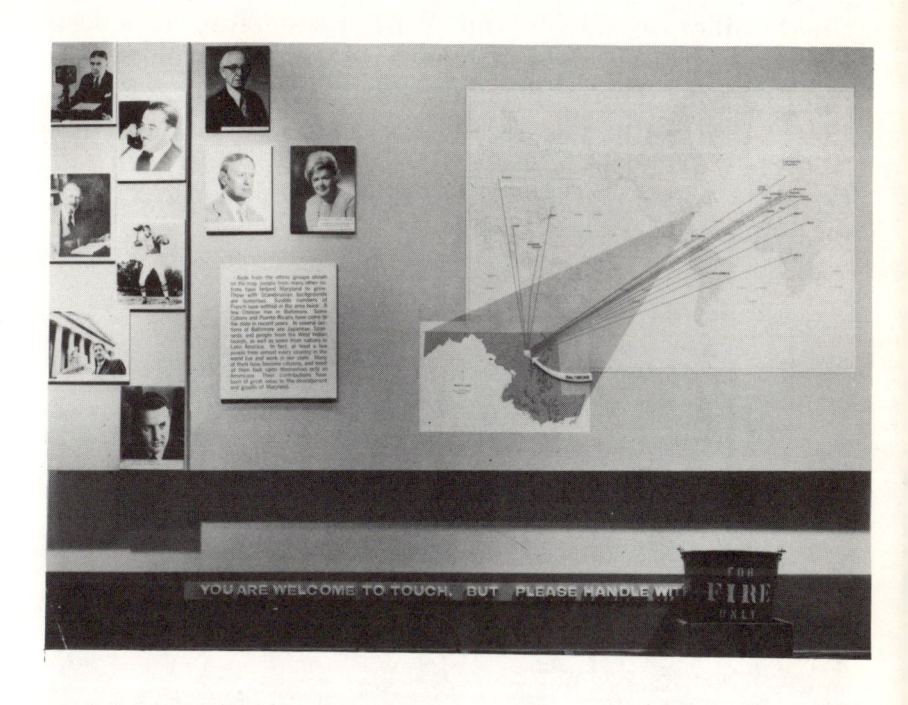

This exhibit at the Maryland Historical Society depicts the many homelands of Maryland's peoples. Prof. William Zuk (to left of the only lady) is the son of Ukrainian immigrants.

Mr. Steve Knox

at the International Center of the Y.W.C.A. These concerts and dance performances gave Baltimoreans a new perspective on the activities of the little know Ukrainian group in their city. Carole Boone Stolba, an American of German and Irish parentage, lived in the 1940's with her parents on Elliott Street not far from the Ukrainian National Home. She attended many of the cultural events at this Home. "I was not a Ukrainian, and they did not have to let me in but they did . . . they were willing to share a part of their culture and customs with other ethnic groups, which resulted in better relationships among all members of the community," says Carole Stolba.[11] Among some of the younger active members during those years were

Joseph Marmash and John Malko. Both are still active in the Ukrainian life of Baltimore in 1977.

Some of the early residents of the Canton group were the families of Jacob and Petro Semenkiw, Theodore Chorney, Iwan Bilobran, Petro Marmash, Wolodymyr Evanowich, Petro Emche, Josyf Pryjmak, Pawlo Petryshak, Antin Pise, Mykola Malko, George and Nick Shulka, Mychajlo Dmytriw, Theodore Kaszak, Iwan Gewera, Alexander Iwachiw, George Podhorniak, and many others.

AN OLD KOZAK GLORY LIVES AGAIN. The Sword (Zaporozhets') dance performed by the Ukrainian Dancing Club of Baltimore, ca 1938.
U.E.A.M. Collection

The beginning of the Ukrainian neighborhood at Curtis Bay dates back to about the year of 1900. It is a much smaller community and it has always centered around Church Street where the SS Peter and Paul Ukrainian Catholic Church is located. Actually, the church developed because the neighborhood was already established and the people wanted to have a center which would hold them together. Here on the hillside above Pennington Avenue overlooking the waters of Curtis Bay one will find small residences where Ukrainian families live. Few of them such as Michael Budahazy came from the western region of Carpathian Mountains. A good many, however, originated from the interior of the Podilla Highlands of Ukraine, especially from the Zarwanycja area.

They were morally and physically healthy people and from the first years they started to plan their future in the new homeland. The first Baltimore branch of the Ukrainian National Association fraternal organization was established here in 1903 by Josyf Kulczycky, Mykola Durdela and Michael Budahazy. It had 17 members that year.[12] It was through the efforts of this organization that in 1909 a lot was purchased at Prudence and Church Streets and soon a small wooden church was built. They were rather poor folk but extremely thrifty. Men worked in railroad shops and other factories down the hill on the waterfront, but the eight dollars they received a week could not support their families. Wives came to the rescue. Usually they supplemented the income by going in harvest time to the nearby farms and picking strawberries, beans, and tomatoes. In those days, where Ritchie Highway and the Baltimore-Washington Airport are now located, there were large produce farms. Many wives also travelled with their children to the Eastern Shore of Maryland and Delaware and lived through the summer in the barracks right on the farm while working there.[13] Conditions improved somewhat with the outbreak of World War I which created better paying jobs. A few of these people ventured into commercial enterprises. One of them deserves special mention. Alexander Shandrowsky arrived at Locust Point in Baltimore in 1908. He opened a shoe repair store on Curtis Avenue but did not remain in that venture because he started a cement block business which was located on his lot where water and sand were available. Building construction was booming all around and his little business prospered. Shandrowsky was also a socially-minded member of his little community. It was a time when the church was going to be built and funds were needed; he and three other parishioners, Damian Lubunetz, Nykola

Shandrowsky, and Pawlo Woytowycz, got an idea. They bought peanuts from local farmers who usually sold them in large sacks, broke the sacks down into pound bags and resold them with good profit. Profits went to the church fund. Shandrowsky himself was very fond of canaries. He raised the birds by the hundreds and sold them. Profits again went into the church fund.[14]

Preserving the Ukrainian theatrical heritage in Curtis Bay, ca. 1914. Second from left (rear) is Reverend Zacharij Orun — the first Ukrainian Catholic pastor in Baltimore, Maryland.
Mrs. Mychajlyna Evanuk

Some of the other early residents of their Curtis Bay community were Iwan Walega, Antin Tchyketa, Iwan

Bakalyk, Stephen Kostiw, Oleska Lishchynskyj, Nykola Durdela, Iwan Ivanuk and others. It is interesting to note here about Iwan Ivanuk. He originated from the village of Stebrowo near Brest-Litowsk in the Polisja region of the then Russian-dominated part of Ukraine. His father was a prosperous farmer in Stebrowo, but the son did not want to remain on the farm. In 1911 he travelled to England and from there emigrated to Argentina. Disappointed, he left Argentina in 1914 for Baltimore and settled in Curtis Bay.

Still other residents in those days were Iwan Horniatko, Petro Bukata, Antin Cyketa, Pawlo Rajca, Iwan Cehaniuk, Stephan Demczak, Iwan Bakalik, Nick Nahnybida, Pawlo and Antin Bartoch and many more.

CHESAPEAKE CITY — MARYLAND'S "LITTLE UKRAINE"

In the study of immigrants to Maryland the Ukrainian community of Chesapeake City is unique in its character and history from all other Ukrainian settlements in the state. Here in the shadow of a tall bridge on US 213, which overspans the Maryland section of the Chesapeake and Delaware Canal, some forty Ukrainian families live their quiet rural life seemingly unconcerned with the heavy modern traffic high above on the bridge. But Maryland's "Little Ukraine" actually begins before one reaches the bridge coming from Elkton. Farm lands of the Ukrainian Catholic Orphanage run along both sides of the highway before the bridge. The Orphanage itself is situated in a small grove of trees at the top of the gently raising farm land. From here one can see down across the open fields the white dwellings of the city bunched together at the canal. Nearby is the bridge suspended high in the air dwarfing everything below it.

A white dog at the Orphanage barked at the approaching visitors. Sister Augustina greeted the visitors with a traditional Christmas Greeting, "Chrystos Razdajetsja" (Christ is Born). From the way she spoke in Ukrainian one would hardly believe that she never lived in Ukraine and was born in this country of a Polish-

75-year-old Yurko Breza (standing) introduces Edward Falcone whose mother was Ukrainian, to the intricacies of a farm tractor. Both spent their whole life-times at the Orphanage.

U.E.A.M. Collection

A HISTORIC DAY. His Beatitude Patriarch Josyf Slipyj during His visit to the Chesapeake City Orphanage in 1968. To His left is Bishop Joseph Schmondiuk of Stamford, Connecticut, and to the right Sister Augustina of the Orphanage.

Convent of St. Basil the Great

Ukrainian family of economically struggling miners in Pennsylvania. The Ukrainian settlers in Chesapeake City, the Orphanage and some 125 acres of surrounding orphanage land are her companions and home. During more than 60 years spent here her family consisted of countless foster children. Some children grew to become prominent figures among Ukrainian-Americans, such as, Bishop Joseph Schmondiuk of Stamford, Connecticut, Monsignor Sylvester Hladky of Warren, Ohio, Joseph Hanusey, music store owner in Philadelphia, and countless others. Sister Augustina has no desire for any other world. The feeling of belonging here is so strong that even an offer by the Patriarch of the Ukrainian Catholic Church, Josyf Cardinal Slipyj, during His visit to the Orphanage in 1968 to come to work at the Ukrainian Catholic Church Center in Rome could not convince her to change locations.

The beginning of the Orphanage and the little Ukrainian community of Chesapeake City dates back 66 years when in 1910 the first Ukrainian Catholic Bishop in the United States, Stephan Ortynsky of Philadelphia, bought a tract of land on the Chesapeake and Delaware Canal for the purpose of establishing a farm, which would produce food for the rectory and convent of St. Basil in Philadelphia, and also would serve as a summer site for the Diocesan orphanage. A corporation was formed and registered in accordance with the laws of the State of Maryland on June 29, 1912, under the name of Convent of Saint Basil the Great. Sisters of the Order of St. Basil took the land into possession. They cultivated the fields and raised corn, wheat, oats, and barley. At times they had as many as 60 cows and 300 chickens. There were many mouths to feed in 1914, therefore, they established an orphanage for Ukrainian infant children up to the age of six. When the children reached the age of 6 years, they were transferred to the orphanage for older children at Philadelphia. In 1916 the sisters took care of as many as 36 infant children.[15]

At the same time the convent was established, Bishop Ortynsky also purchased 700 acres around Hog Gut and encouraged his people throughout the country to settle on

Charter of Incorporation of St. Basil's Convent, 1912.

First group of little girls in Nursery at Chesapeake — 1914.
   Convent of St. Basil the Great

Enjoying the early spring.
   Convent of St. Basil the Great

Tract of Land Purchased by Bishop Ortynsky in Chesapeake City.

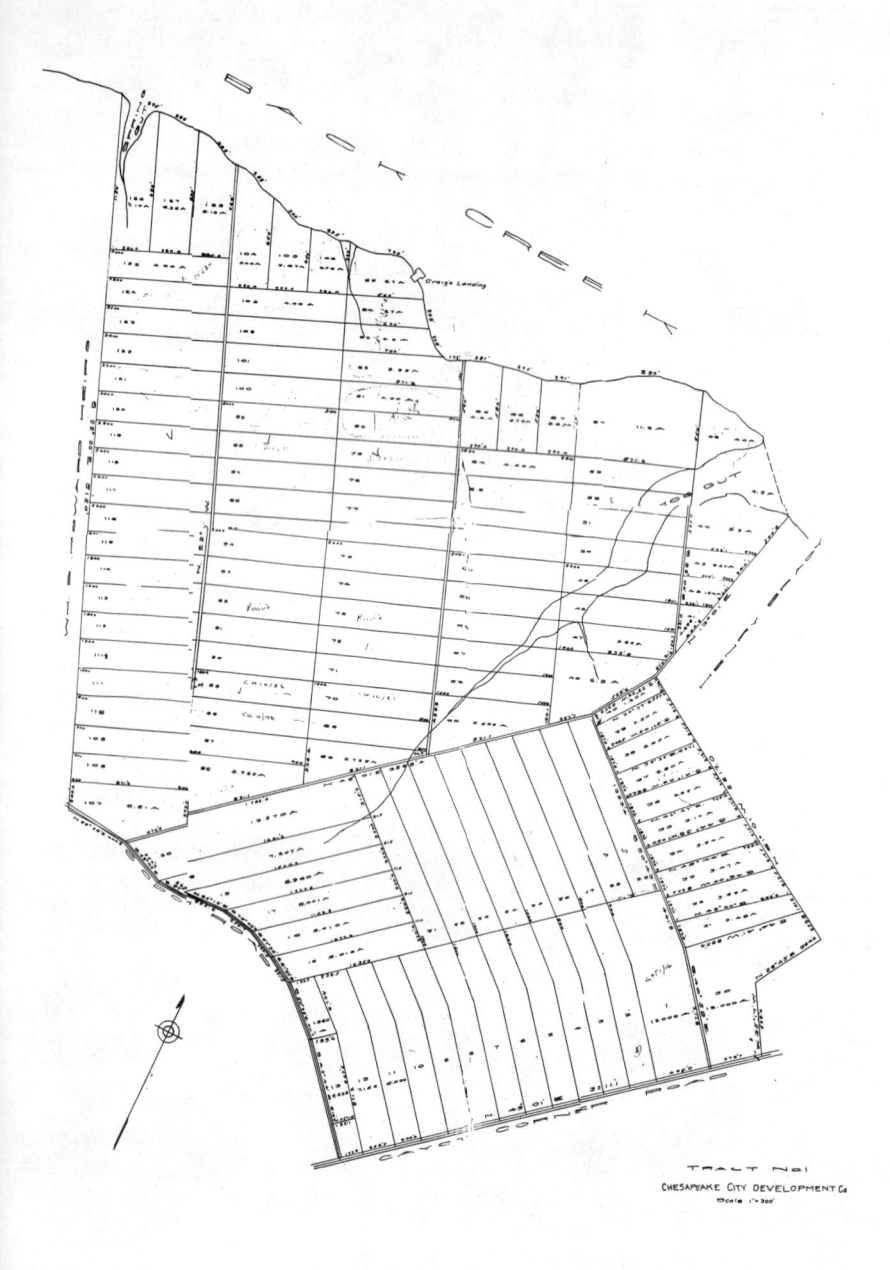

the Maryland land. He placed his brother Joseph Ortynsky in charge of the project to establish a Ukrainian community at Chesapeake City. Many Ukrainian immigrants arriving in the United States had fared poorly economically in Ukraine. Arriving in America without any resources they were forced to secure quick jobs in the cities or in coal mines in order to earn a livelihood. Life in strange cities, however, confused many of them, and deep in their hearts they wished again for fields and woods. Many of these immigrants, maladjusted in urban life, had one strong desire — to own land again. When word reached them urging them to buy a tract of the Maryland land and establish homes, they went. Originally forty families settled and their number increased every year till in 1925 it reached the high point of seventy families.[16] Most of these people came from the coal mines, especially from Wilkes-Barre, St. Clair, and Scranton areas, and from the city of Philadelphia.

The story of Ukrainian settlers in Chesapeake City recalls a saga of early pioneers in America. The land was nothing more than swamp and brush. They had to convert this wilderness of scrubland into a prosperous farmland. It was not an easy task. But no force could turn them back to the cities and coal mines they just left. Harry Haller relates a story which is typical of the lot of these people upon arrival at Chesapeake City:

> One of the first newcomers recalls an arrival at 2:00 A.M. by train at Elkton. The newcomer walked until dawn brought him to Ortinsky's house and he was directed to the plot of land he had purchased. It was one plot among many in a broad expanse of rocks and mud and trees. He took off his coat and started to clear a space to put up a shack. The next week his young wife arrived and the settlers purchased a horse and began to clear the land in earnest. The wife worked beside her husband, chopping tall trees to the ground, clearing away the rocks and digging the underbrush away with bare hands.[17]

Each year more families arrived. Bill Krochak recalls that while working in the coal mine he heard that they needed someone in Chesapeake City who would know how to build fences. So he sold everything he had in Pennsylvania, came here and settled.[18]

The Ukrainian newcomers to Chesapeake City had to overcome not only nature but also initial resentfulness exhibited by native residents. The soil here was rather poor requiring much money for suitable fertilizer. The natives were earnestly convinced that the unknown foreigners would not be able to make a living from their little acreages. They feared that Ukrainians would steal their poultry and livestock. "There is scarcely enough here for us to live on," they said. "The foreigners will starve if they don't steal."[19] They underestimated the Ukrainians and their determination to make a living even from the small farms.

Although not many of these Ukrainians had seen each other before, from the first day they were united in their common bond to get ahead in their new surroundings. Men worked during the day in various jobs: government work such as building streets, laborers with the Chesapeake and Delaware Canal, or bakers who commuted daily to Wilmington to work in the bakeries. Evenings were spent clearing the land. Quite often proper tools were lacking as was a knowledge of how to fertilize the soil. They received invaluable assistance from LeRoy Foard who owned a farming supply store in Chesapeake City. Many Ukrainians today recall how willingly he permitted them to use his tools and how he carefully advised concerning their crops. People usually came to him late in the evening after work, and this kind-hearted merchant always helped them with their problems. The newcomers worked together helping each other with their individual skills. There were cobblers, carpenters, well diggers, welders and other tradesmen among them. They helped each other in times of need. Emil Chicosky recalls that during a flu epidemic his father went outside in the morning to look at the neighbors' chimneys. If smoke was rising, he knew they were still alive, and he would go find out if anybody needed anything.[20]

From a wilderness of scrubland the Chesapeake City Ukrainians slowly developed a little self-sufficient community. Most of the farms they owned were under 30 acres. Anything that went on the table was grown in their fields. The principal food supplies they had to buy were coffee, sugar, salt, and molasses. Most farm work was done by the women because many men held other jobs.

The Hotra Family Home in Chesapeake City.
U.E.A.M. Collection

Wives tended the livestock, plowed fields and painted barns. In this work they had an industrious example in the sisters at the St. Basil's Convent who likewise drove the horses out into the fields and tilled the soil at th orphanage.

With their own Ukrainian Catholic St. Basil's Church built in 1920, the Ukrainian community at Chesapeake City became well established. The foreigners whom the non Ukrainian residents were ready to write off, became respected members of the community. "Our people have high morals and they never caused scandals here," said Sister Augustina. Sister Augustina's statement held true throughout the 66 years of Ukrainian presence in Chesapeake City as the Ukrainians conducted themselves well, supporting their families and Church without aid from the Government. During the depression other people in Chesapeake City went on relief, but not the Ukrainians. Nothing was ever wasted. Even feed bags were used to make bed clothes or sometimes even clothes for people.

What future lies before the Chesapeake City Ukrainian community? The Malinowsky family is a typical example: Two of their four children now reside in Philadelphia, Pennsylvania; two others, a son Iwan and a daughter Maria, reside in Chesapeake City. Kathryn Malinowsky, who came to Chesapeake City with her late husband Wasyl in 1916, proudly points up the hill to a neat brick house where the Waclawsky family lives. "We gave our daughter, whose husband is also from Chesapeake City, a five acre tract of land. Many young people who sold the land they got from their parents are now sorry," says the 93-year-old Kathryn Malinowsky. Across the road from the

Kathryn Malinowsky standing in front of her neatly kept flower garden.
U.E.A.M. Collection

Malinowsky residence is the Hotra family farm. The late Alex Hotra came to Chesapeake City in the early 1920's. One of his sons, Stephen, is now a priest of the Philadelphia Ukrainian Catholic Diocese which includes the state of Maryland. The youngest son, Joseph, remained on the farm and now resides with his family on the homestead.

The legacy which the pioneer families of Wasylczuk, Luzetsky, Hrabec, Shostak, Malinowsky, Waclawsky, Terpeluk, Shwaika, Tymko, Hotra, and many others established for themselves in this corner of Maryland has long won respect and recognition from Marylanders. It highly reflects on Ukrainians. To quote Harry Haller, the Ukrainian community at Chesapeake City is truly "Maryland's Little Ukraine."

WESTERN MARYLAND

National origins of all inhabitants of coal mining areas of Allegheny and Garrett counties in Western Maryland show that in 1910 there were 247 Russian and 248 Hungarian born residents in those counties.[21] When one remembers that the majority of Ukrainians during that period were recorded as Russians, Austrians, or Hungarians, it is only logical to assume that a number of these "Russians" and "Hungarians" might have been Ukrainians. This contention seems to find backing in the records of the Russian Orthodox Church in America. The 1974 Directory of the Altoona-Johnstown Deanery of the Archdiocese of Pittsburgh and West Virginia records many Ukrainian names. According to this Directory, most parishes were organized by Galicians and Carpatho-Russians from Austria-Hungary, known as Little Russians.[22] The subject of Galicians, Carpatho-Russians and Little Russians has been studied by many scholars, and objective students by now know that these people were in fact Ukrainians, and not Russians.

Ukrainian miners lived in mining communities in Pennsylvania. In West Virginia approximately six thousand Ukrainians lived in Wheeling and adjacent mining communities.[23] Obviously, Ukrainians as well as Lithuanians, Poles, Slovaks, et al., were employed in coal mines of Allegheny and Garrett Counties, Maryland. Names like Vesely, listed on the wall of St. Mary's Annunciation Catholic Church in Lonaconing, strongly suggest Ukrainian origin. As the coal industry declined, many miners left for cities to work in factories. Probably some descendents of Ukrainians may be found scattered in former coal-mining towns in the George's Creek Valley of Allegheny County as well as in Garrett County.[24] The coal region of George's Creek ranks as the most important coal centre in Maryland. An occasional coal tipple and dark-

Ukrainians researching in Moscow (Maryland). Janice Fenchak and Wolodymyr Sushko are pictured in the mining town of Moscow in Western Maryland.

U.E.A.M. Collection

A coal mining house in Lonaconing, Maryland, of the type immigrants lived in.

U.E.A.M. Collection

grey hills along the road are all that remain of the booming past in this valley.

Besides those persons engaged in coal mining, there are other Ukrainian families scattered throughout Western Maryland. They settled here for a variety of reasons such as job transfers, marriage, etc. They live in comparatively isolated situations away from the main stream of their culture, yet proudly preserve the heritage of their parents. Caroline Markovchik came from Hazelton, Pennsylvania, to Washington, D.C., in 1948 to work with the United States Marine Corps. Her father was the president of the Church Council of St. Mary's Ukrainian Catholic Church. In 1958 she met her husband, James Clark, and settled in Cumberland. Mary Clark is fond of the Ukrainian Christmas customs which are part of the heritage shared with her husband and children. Another Ukrainian, Mary Kotyk Gladysiewski, moved to Cumberland from Ford City, Pennsylvania, in 1956. As a child she attended the Ukrainian Evening School in Ford City. She proudly shows the Ukrainian Reader which she used in school. Her husband is of Polish parentage. In their home the Ukrainian and Polish heritages are well preserved. A plate with Ukrainian Easter eggs in their living room draws the attention of a visitor. This is the work of their children, Tamara, Damian, Clement, and Felicia. "The whole family is dyeing Easter eggs," says Mary Gladysiewski with a note of pride in her voice. At Westernport on the Potomac, a Slovak-Ukrainian, John Miklusek, tenderly speaks of his mother who was a Ukrainian by the name of Hlushko from Uniontown, Pennsylvania. To emphasize his Ukrainian ties, he cheerfully bids us a farewell on a cold Sunday morning in January in front of St. Peter's Catholic Church in Westernport, saying "Na Zdorowlja" (Stay Healthy). Yet another Ukrainian, Peter Solonish, is a Pennsylvanian from Hyndman just across the Maryland State line. He commutes every day to Cumberland, where he works with Kelley Springfield Tire Company. His grandparents came from Carpatho-Ukraine in the late 1890's. When work in coal mines declined, many miners went to Cleveland, New Jersey, Baltimore, and Pittsburgh. Solonish and his family remained. "A very sad thing happened with our generation," says Peter Solonish. "Parents spoke Slavish when they did not want us to understand. The result is we know so little about our past." He recalls his parents referring to themselves as Carpatho-Rusins. "It is coming back, in Johnstown at the church hall they now teach Ukrainian dances, songs." "I call myself Ukrainian," he declares[25]. A similar situation repeats itself in Washington County. Families like those of John Daviduk, John Senuta, Joseph Prisak, all of Hagerstown, live in their isolated community, yet remain conscious of their background.

THE DISPLACED PERSONS ACT

After World War II in the years 1949-1951 came an unprecedented wave of new immigrants into the United States. Contracted by the International Refugee Organization, the *SS Marine Marlin, USAT General Muir, SS Marine Flasher, USAT Harry Taylor* and other former United States military transport ships made several crossings between Europe and America, each time bringing thousands of new immigrants into this country.

These were the victims of World War II, coming principally from Ukraine, Poland, Estonia, Latvia, Lithuania, Yugoslavia, and in smaller numbers from Czechoslovakia, Hungary, and Rumania. They were the innocent peoples who were uprooted from their homes and livelihoods by totalitarian aggression, and who, after the war, turned down repatriation to their native lands because they refused to live under a reign of Communist terror. After the war they were classified as "Displaced Persons" and "Refugees." They remained under the care of the International Refugee Organization, a temporary agency created by the Allied Nations for the purpose of solving the refugee problem in Western Europe. A majority of these people were men and women of culture and skill.

These refugees lived primarily in displaced persons camps and centers situated for the most part in the American, British, and French zones of Germany and Austria and in Italy. In December of 1948, three years after the war, their numbers in those countries totalled 769,300.[27]

Ukrainians were one of the largest groups of refugees. The records of the United Ukrainian American Relief Committee indicate that on June 30, 1948, there were 138,000 Ukrainian displaced persons and refugees in Germany and Austria who were awaiting resettlement. This number was in addition to some 37,745 Ukrainian refugees who already were relocated in various free countries, such as England, which took the largest number, 25,721. The United States by 1948 had admitted only 917 Ukrainian refugees, these being the immigrants who under the existing Immigration Act had received personal affidavits from their relatives and friends in the United States.[28]

The year 1948 brought many changes in immigration history. In June, 1948, the Congress of the United States passed the Displaced Persons Act. In reality, the Act was an amendment to the existing Immigration Act. The Displaced Persons Act stated that beyond the scope of regular quotas, there would be admitted 205,000 displaced persons who might establish permanent residence in America. In passing this Act, the United States joined more than 40 other countries in the free world that offered resettlement opportunities and new lives to victims of the authoritarianism and brutalities that both preceded and were parts of World War II.

From its beginning the Displaced Persons Law encountered difficulties. Problems stemmed from the unworkability of the pattern of restrictions, limitations, preferences, and priorities established by the law. The Act provided three categories for the entering refugees: First, those persons engaged in agricultural pursuits who would be employed in the United States on farms or who would follow other agricultural pursuits. This group merited preferential treatment. The second group consisted of persons having specific skills, such as clothing workers, household workers, or any professional workers. The third group consisted of persons who were to come at the request of relatives in America.

Unlike other countries whose programs for receiving refugees were based on the feasibility of "labor recruitment," the American program, in addition to usual immigration requirements, necessitated individual assurances for housing, employment, and inland transportation before prospective persons or families could be considered for admission. Briefly, the Displaced Persons Act of 1948, endowed with good intentions, was complicated and in many ways discriminatory. References to difficulties can be found in the Second Semi-Annual Report of the Displaced Persons Commission to the President and the Congress wherein the Commission warned that joint efforts of all agencies — public, private, and Commission endeavors — might fail to meet the goals established by the Act unless amendments to the 1948 legislation were forthcoming.[29] Pragmatically, the Displaced Persons Act raised new hopes in the hearts of many victims of tyrannies who were living lives of despair and hopelessness in refugee camps in Austria and Germany.

COOPERATIVE ACTION FOR RESETTLEMENT

Helping displaced persons to become settled and adjusted in America required close cooperation between public and private agencies.

The administration of the Displaced Persons Act was vested in the Federal Displaced Persons Commission. Of great assistance to the Federal commission were state commissions, various agencies accredited by the Federal Government as voluntary organizations, e.g., the United Ukrainian-American Relief Committee of Philadelphia, branches of national fraternal and mutual assistance groups, and benevolent citizens.

In Maryland a State Committee for Displaced Persons was established in 1948 by Governor W. Preston Lane, Jr., with Judge William F. Laukaitis as chairman. The Maryland Committee was composed of representatives of all ethnic groups that were eligible for resettlement under the Act. The Ukrainian member of this Committee, Joseph

Marmash, was appointed a member of the Committee by Governor Lane on September 30, 1948.[30]

The Baltimore Ukrainian Relief Committee. First from the right (sitting) is Joseph Marmash, the Ukrainian member of the Maryland State Committee for Displaced Persons.

U.E.A.M. Collection

Among the many nationally active groups which performed much charitable work in behalf of displaced persons was the Baltimore branch of the United Ukrainian-American Relief Committee. This Baltimore Ukrainian Relief Committee was organized on February 6, 1949, with Mrs. Julia Maniosky as president. Some of the other members were Harry Kany, Joseph Prymak, Alex Zuk, Joseph Marmash, John Malko, and Olha Szpatura. The Committee devoted great effort to finding sponsors for the Ukrainian refugees in order to speed up their emigration under the Act. Assistance was provided for the newcomers during their first days after having arrived in Baltimore. A large percentage of Ukrainian displaced persons came to Maryland as farm workers. Baltimore was a distribution center. After arriving in Baltimore, displaced persons were often housed at the Fifth Regiment Armory for a brief

Bread and Salt: Yesterday an old Ukrainian ceremony welcomed Maryland's 44 newest citizens.
Baltimore Sunpapers

period. While housed at the Armory, members of the Baltimore Ukrainian Relief Committee prepared hot meals for the refugees, often featuring Ukrainian Borshch (beet soup). Members of the Committee also served as interpreters in addition to performing various humanitarian functions to engender feelings of belonging and happiness in minds of the newcomers. The arrivals received traditional Ukrainian greetings. The manner in which the Ukrainian Relief Committee of Baltimore met the first group of 44 Ukrainian displaced persons upon their arrival at the Fifth Regiment Armory on January 18, 1949, is illustrated by the following:

> Holding a large round loaf of wheat bread, which she had baked especially for the occasion, Mrs. Julia Maniosky of 524 South Wolfe Street, broke off small pieces, sprinkled them liberally with salt and passed them to each of the 44 persons. The loaf was carried in a gaily decorated shawl in the traditional Ukrainian fashion. The short welcoming ceremonial is an old Ukrainian custom, and the refugees plainly showed their appreciation. . . .[31]

Many non-Ukrainian Marylanders contributed greatly to the resettlement of displaced persons and generously assisted the refugees when they arrived. Franklin Hastings of Berlin, Worcester County, was the owner of a prosperous poultry business in 1949. Next to his plant he built ten one-family dwellings which were completely furnished and which he leased on favorable terms to families of displaced persons whom he had sponsored. For months refugee families were permitted to occupy these dwellings with no rental fees. Families paid only for the furnishings. In 1950 when Mr. Hastings closed his business he saw to it that all males who had worked for his firm procured new jobs with a local construction company.[32]

The Very Reverend Monsignor Eugene Stout of Salisbury, Wicomico County, became personally acquainted with more than 150 Ukrainian Catholic refugees who settled in areas served by his parish in 1949. His pastorate of St. Francis de Sales in Salisbury and the mission churches in Crisfield, Pocomoke City, and Ocean City were most helpful in ministering to the spiritual needs of Ukrainian Catholics, whose Eastern (Byzantine) rite differed from the Roman Catholic rite. Reverend Wasyl Sushko, a displaced person, served as a missionary priest to his Ukrainians immediately after his arrival in the United States in 1949. His assignments included many areas in Maryland as well as the environs of Gettysburg, Pennsylvania. A modern circuit rider, as the Baltimore *Sun* described him, Father Sushko travelled by bus to his many missions.[33] Most of the ecclesiastical stations where he conducted Ukrainian liturgies were on the Eastern

Reverend Wasyl Sushko (to the right of the Sister of the Order of St. Basil) on the way to one of his missionary stations.
U.E.A.M. Collection

Shore. The great success of his spiritual and social work on the Eastern Shore of Maryland in those years was greatly the result of the support he always received from Monsignor Eugene Stout. Through Father Sushko's untiring efforts and with the assistance offered by Monsignor Stout and his assistant priest, Reverend Couming, many Ukrainian displaced families were spared hardships and were able to change sponsors when it was found that employers tried to take advantage of the people.[34] On many occasions Monsignor Stout's church buses gathered the Ukrainian newcomers who worked in Berlin and the surrounding area and transported them to the Catholic Church in Ocean City where Father Sushko both held Holy Liturgy in the Ukrainian Rite and otherwise assisted them in their spiritual and cultural needs.

Teofil Popowycz of Baltimore, together with his wife, came to Maryland through the personal efforts of Louis O'Donnell, Assistant to the Governor of Maryland in 1949. In order to assist the World War II victims in Europe, Louis O'Donnell secured 30 job assurances for nurses and other hospital personnel in Maryland State hospitals and personally came to await the train bringing those families to Maryland. Twenty-three of these positions were in the Rosewood State Training School near Pikesville in Baltimore County. They were filled by Ukrainians. "They came at a time we were having difficulty getting attendants in all the mental hospitals," said Dr. George A. Johns, Superintendent of the School. "When I first saw them I said I would take them all. I was quite certain from the first that they would do well. They are a decent, wholesome sort, and have taken a great interest in their work."[35]

Many Ukrainian displaced persons of Baltimore still feel kind words of gratitude and appreciation to Richard A. Lidinsky, Administrative Assistant to the Mayor of Baltimore from 1947 to 1959, for the invaluable assistance given to them in their first years of living in a new strange city. There were always many problems of technical and administrative nature, including jobs, with which they were unfamiliar. Richard A. Lidinsky's always ready advice and help made their problems much easier.

THE MARYLAND PLAN AND ITS FAILURE

Since the Displaced Persons Act gave first preference to farm workers, and Maryland farmers continued to be in need of labor, the Maryland State Committee For The Resettlement Of Displaced Persons came up with a plan to resettle some of Europe's refugees on Maryland farms. This Maryland Plan became the first of its kind in the Nation. The State Committee, recognizing the effective work on behalf of the refugees in Europe of the United Ukrainian American Relief Committee of Philadelphia, Pennsylvania, had enlisted the services of the Ukrainian group. At the instigation of the State Committee and the Ukrainian Relief Committee 402 families, consisting of 1,196 persons, most of them Ukrainians, found jobs and living accommodations in Maryland in 1949. Of this group, 394 families were farm workers, included also were eight nurses. Each county in the State received its share of these families, the majority going to Baltimore, Carroll, Queen Annes, Harford, Howard, Talbot and Wicomico Counties.

Maryland's "Farm Labor" plan operated satisfactorily in the early part of 1949, but it bogged down miserably by 1950. The reason for this was the tendency among displaced persons to desert their tenant farmers after they worked on the farms for several months, and move to the cities. This attitude naturally created a genuine dissatisfaction among farmers with the displaced persons program. Richard K. Tucker studied this problem, and explained in the Baltimore *Evening Sun*:

> In Howard County there was a young Ukrainian woman named Anna who used to cry at night even after a kindly farm family had taken her to a movie or to the hairdresser. Adam, her husband, would look at the farmer and explain in faltering English — lonely — lonely.
>
> The files of Joseph Marmash, Maryland D.P. Committeeman and father-confessor to newly arrived Ukrainian immigrants, contains many grateful letters. There is one that reads: "We are living quite comfortably and the farmer is good to us. Our only problem is that we are lonesome for our own people."
>
> Another letter states: "I managed a large department store in Europe and never in my life have worked on a farm. I would like to be among my own Ukrainian people if possible."
>
> In another County, where a farmer was not so kind, a man and his son were getting a total of $10 a month, a Maryland D. P. Committeeman said bitterly: "He must have thought he was getting serfs."
>
> One farmer would be paying $50 a month and another $120. News of this got around among the D. P.'s: a man might rightly wonder why his farm work was worth less than half of an others . . . .[36]

Language barriers, cases of bad pay or bad housing, unfamiliar work, loneliness, and the fact that many of the displaced persons hired as farm laborers were not farmers at all, were the reasons that many D. P.'s left the farms.

The primary cause for the failure of the Maryland "farm labor" plan was the very Federal Displaced Persons Act that overemphasized farm labor. As a result, two human natures conflicted with each other: homeless victims of Soviet aggression, cultured and productive, yearned for new lives in a free country, while farmers in Maryland were interested in primarily one matter — farm labor. The fact that both the United States Senate and House of Representatives belatedly agreed that establishing priority for displaced "farmers" was a mistake and should be discontinued, the considerations came too late as the Maryland farm labor program failed.

Work in progress in a tobacco-stripping room. Shown here are (from left) Charles Johnson, Mr. Watkins, Mrs. Maria Shepet, a displaced person from Ukraine, and her children.

Baltimore **Sunpapers**

Good things also came out of the Maryland Farm Labor Program. Some families did remain, but they were few of the many hundreds. Alex Rybak arrived in Maryland in February, 1949, as a gardener bound for the farm of Dr. Amos Hutchins in Arnold, Anne Arundel County. He had worked around flowers all his life in Ukraine, helping his brother-in-law, a florist, in Pacykiw, near Stanyslawiw (now Novo-Frankivsk). There he developed a love for gardening, which he chose to continue in Maryland. Alex

Rybak now lives in Harwood, Anne Arundel County, where he manages one of the farms of Richard E. Lankford, former United States Congressman from the Fifth District of Maryland. The congressman's appreciation of Rybak's talents is stated:

> There is no way we can thank you for all you do for us and mean to us. Each day I am more grateful for all my rich blessings and the Rybak family are a big part of my many blessings....[37]

Alex Rybak shows his magnolia nursery to Jaroslaw G. Sushko, another Ukrainian displaced person and now a horticulturist with the City of Baltimore.
U.E.A.M. Collection

INCREASE IN SIZE OF BALTIMORE COMMUNITY

As the result of the influx of new immigrants, particularly the displaced persons, the Ukrainian communities in East Baltimore and Curtis Bay increased considerably. The communities more than doubled. The registrar of the Baltimore Branch of the Ukrainian Congress Committee of America for the year of 1975 cites 606 families in the Baltimore area.[38] There are, however, many other families living in the area of Greater Baltimore who do not identify with community organizations, but who nonetheless consider themselves Ukrainians. Few, if

The house at 2223 E. Pratt Street is a landmark partly because of its iron railing. Its new owners, Emmanuel and Anna Prytula, proudly preserve one of Baltimore's charming features.

U.E.A.M. Collection

any, of the displaced Ukrainians joined the Ukrainian community in Chesapeake City, due probably to limited employment opportunities in that locale of Cecil County.

As a result of the newcomers to Baltimore, community activities intensified. Today the Ukrainians of Baltimore are known as one of the most active and scintillating groups in Baltimore's ethnic mosaic.

NEW SETTLEMENTS

The recent immigrants also gave impetus to the establishing of two sizeable Ukrainian settlements in the state — the suburban Washington community and the farming community on the lower Eastern Shore.

WASHINGTON, D.C., AND ITS MARYLAND SUBURBS

Prior to World War II there were few Ukrainian families living in the Nation's Capital. Among the first community leaders were Julian and Priscilla Tymm (Tymchyshyn) who moved from Detroit, Michigan, to

> The
> **MARYLAND BICENTENNIAL COMMISSION**
> for the
> Commemoration of the American Revolution
> **Recognizes**
> the activities of
>
> Ukrainian Student Society of Baltimore
> for their Participation in the
> Tree Planting Program in the
> Ukrainian Neighborhood, Patterson Park

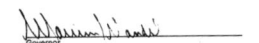

Washington in 1934. In the absence of Ukrainian Catholic divine liturgies in Washington the Tymm family attended services at St. Michael's Ukrainian Catholic Church in Baltimore, 40 miles from Washington.[39] The community grew considerably in the late 1930's and early 1940's with the arrival of Ukrainians from other states, notably Pennsylvania and New York, to work for the federal government. Stephen Basarab who came to Washington in October, 1940, estimates that at that time there were over 30 families living in the District of Columbia.[40] They were organized in the American-Ukrainian Society which convened in the Young Women's Christian Association Building at 17th and K Streets, N.W. Some of the more active members of the Society were Gregory Shlopak,

Theodore Carpin, Steve Marenka, Eugene Skotzko, and Ann Dudiak. Their cultural activities included Ukrainian choral programs and dances. Religious life centered around the Carmelite Chapel at 2131 Lincoln Road, N. E. Religious services were offered by the priests of St. Josaphat's Ukrainian Catholic Seminary. At this time all parishioners resided in the District of Columbia.

The group increased significantly in the 1950's when Ukrainian scientists, both American-born and European-born, obtained employment in various federal agencies, including the Library of Congress and the Ukrainian division of Voice of America. These arrivals strengthened significantly the community in Washington and its environs in Maryland. The current records of the Holy Family Ukrainian Catholic Church, 4817 Blagden Avenue, N. W., and of St. Andrew's Ukrainian Orthodox Church, 16th and Blagden Avenue, N. W., indicate that the churches have membership totals of 295 and 275, respectively.[41]

During the 1960's more than half of the newcomers moved to suburbs in Maryland and Virginia where they purchased homes. Suburbs in Maryland include an estimated 256 Ukrainian residents, distributed as follows: Silver Spring, 38; Avondale, 23; Hyattsville, 21; Rockville, 16; Adelphi, 11; Bethesda, 10; College Park, 10; and the balance being distributed in several other localities. Though the Ukrainian community in Metropolitan Washington does not consist of well-defined neighborhoods and is much more widely scattered than communities in East Baltimore, Curtis Bay and Chesapeake City, the Ukrainians are cohesive in their organizations. Their lives center around their two churches, the Ukrainian School of Studies where their children master the Ukrainian language and related subjects, and various centers for cultural and social activities. Language classes are held in the Forest Grove Elementary School of the Montgomery County Public Schools. St. Josaphat's Seminary and the recently established branch of St. Clement the Pope Ukrainian Catholic University of Rome, Italy, provide centers for spiritual and philosophical development.

THE FARMING COMMUNITY ON THE LOWER EASTERN SHORE

The family of Stephen Sisak in Willards, Wicomico County, has lived and farmed on the Eastern Shore for many years. Most Ukrainians on the Eastern Shore, however, arrived in conjunction with the Maryland Farm Labor Plan of 1949.

Several Ukrainian refugee families arrived on the lower Eastern Shore in 1949 as farm or factory workers. Falling in love with the countryside and the Shore's way of life, they decided to establish themselves there. Wasyl Macuk is an example of one of the modern-day Ukrainian homesteaders. He arrived in Berlin, Worcester County, in 1949 to work on the poultry farm of Franklin Hastings. In 1950 the farm was purchased by Bowen E. Quillin, who recognized Mr. Macuk's talents and requested him to remain. Today the Macuks are also proud owners of a poultry farm (20 acres) not far from the farm where Mr. Macuk began his labors after arriving from Europe. Some of his impressions of his experiences follow:

> Living on a farm after the terrible war years and hopeless staying as refugees in Displaced Persons' camps seemed to do good to us and our nerves. Being close to Ocean City we could afford to enjoy the beach and the sun. In addition, the chicken farm does not require extensive machinery or large outlays of money...[42]

Other Ukrainians seemed to reason in a manner similar to that of Mr. Macuk. Some of the families who left the farms on the Eastern Shore for employment in factories in Philadelphia and Cleveland returned in the mid-1950's and purchased poultry farms with their savings. 32 Ukrainian families now own farms on the Eastern Shore. Most of the farms are located in Wicomico, Worcester, and Somerset counties, with a single farm being found near Easton in Talbot County.

In size the farms range from 10 to 100 acres, with 20- to 50-acre farms predominating. One family owns a farm of 350 acres. Nearly all the farms are poultry farms, except for several whereon blueberries are grown. The production of poultry ranges from 8,000 to as many as 70,000 a season,

A PROUD HOMESTEADER. Wasyl Macuk in front of one of his chicken houses. Mr. and Mrs. Macuk were among the 33 honored as outstanding 1976 poultry and hatching egg producers during this Year's Delmarva Poultry Industry's poultry booster banquet.
U.E.A.M. Collection

with most farms producing between 10,000 and 30,000.[43] Robert Miller, agricultural agent of Wicomico County, states that the immigrant farmers

> . . .Have made out very well. . .Some older members of the families speak very little English and remain independent of state or Federal agencies that offer assistance to farmers. . .Their children, however, are as active in school activities and 4-H clubs as any other farm children. . .[44]

In addition to the 32 farming families approximately a dozen other families have settled in Salisbury, Berlin, and Pocomoke City. Some operate businesses such as auto body shops while others are employed in various industries. Dr. Stephen Tymkiw, a pathologist, is a resident and instructor at Wicomico County Hospital in Salisbury.

Distances of between 5 to 25 miles separate the farm households of many of the Ukrainians on the Eastern Shore, but as is customary in rural communities, social activities often center at the churches. Ukrainian Orthodox religious adherents organized a parish in Whaleysville in Worcester County. Their church and parish home and

A center for the Ukrainian Orthodox community on the Lower Eastern Shore.
U.E.A.M. Collection

St. Francis de Sales Catholic Church in Salisbury, Wicomico County, has unique Rome-Eastern role. Standing (in the picture) is Mr. Paul Fenchak, President of the Ukrainian Education Association of Maryland, Inc.
U.E.A.M. Collection

picnic grounds were established on the former property of a Presbyterian congregation. The facilities were transformed to Ukrainian Orthodox traditions. Reverend Walter Chuhaj, formerly of Milwaukee, is the present pastor.

The Ukrainian Catholics, who are a minority on the Shore, continue to hold religious services in hospitable St. Francis de Sales Roman Catholic Church in Salisbury, where more than twenty-five years ago Rev. Wasyl Sushko, a displaced priest from Ukraine, first celebrated the divine liturgy for them. The missionary work at Salisbury is now continued by the pastor of Saints Peter and Paul Ukrainian Catholic Church in Curtis Bay, Maryland.

NOTES TO CHAPTER THREE

[1] Wasyl Halich, *Ukrainians in the United States*, New York, 1970, p. 151.

[2] Statement by Theodore Nykula, Baltimore, Maryland, personal interview, December 27, 1975.

[3] William Bray, "The Hidden Charms of Baltimore," *The Sun Magazine*, Baltimore, Maryland, June 15, 1975, p. 15.

[4] Stuart S. Taylor, Jr., "The Mysterious East: City's Ethnic Haven," *The Evening Sun*, Baltimore, Maryland, p. C1.

[5] Statement by Theodore Nykula, Baltimore, Maryland, personal interview, October 25, 1975.

[6] "Little Towns Within City Walls — Their Inhabitants Have Helped Build a Greater Baltimore," *The Sun*, Baltimore, Maryland, November 12, 1922.

[7] Volodymyr Kubijovyc, *Ukrainians Abroad, Offprint from Ukraine: A Concise Encyclopedia*, Toronto, 1971, p. 31.

[8] Statement by Warwara Pise, Baltimore, Maryland, personal interview, November 2, 1975.

[9] See 8 — Statement by Warwara Pise.

[10] See 8 — Statement by Warwara Pise.

[11] Statement by Carole Boone Stolba, Baltimore, Maryland, personal interview, February 10, 1977.

[12] Dr. Luke Myshuha, *Jubilee Book of the Ukrainian National Association*, Jersey City, 1936, p. 554.

[13] Statement by Mychajlyna Evanuk, Baltimore, Maryland, personal interview, November 13, 1975.

[14] Statement by Maria Shandrowsky, Baltimore, Maryland, interview by Petro Mudryj, November 4, 1975.

[15] Opinion expressed by Sister Augustina of Convent of St. Basil the Great, Chesapeake City, Maryland, in a personal interview, December 30, 1975.

[16] See 15 — Opinion by Sister Augustina.

[17] Harry Haller, "Maryland's Little Ukraine," *Baltimore Sun*, Baltimore, Maryland, May 16, 1937, p. 4.

[18] Statement told by Bill Krochak to Edward Falcone, both of Chesapeake City, ca. 1955; repeated by Edward Falcone to the writer on January 30, 1976.

[19] See 17 — Harry Haller, "Maryland's Little Ukraine."

[20] Geraldine Garrett, "Memories of the Ukraine," *The Sun Magazine*, Baltimore, Maryland, April 2, 1972, p. 21.

[21] Katherine A. Harvey, *The Best-Dressed Miners — Life and Labor in the Maryland Coal Region, 1835-1910*, Ithaca, 1969, Table 2.

[22] *Directory, Altoona-Johnstown Deanery*, Archdiocese of Pittsburgh and West Virginia, Orthodox Church in America, 1974, p. 1-38.

[23] See 1 — Wasyl Halich, *Ukrainians in the United States*, p. 30.

[24] Opinion expressed by Walter Romanovsky, Baltimore, Maryland, March 19, 1976.

[25] Statements by Caroline Markovchik Clark, Cumberland, Maryland, Mary Kotyk Gladysiewski, Cumberland, Maryland, and Peter Solonish, Hyndman, Pennsylvania, personal interviews, January 19, 1976.

[26] Written information received by Paul Fenchak, Lutherville, Maryland, from Arnold Skalsky, Ijamsville, Maryland, March 1, 1976.

[27] The Displaced Persons Commission, *Second Semiannual Report to the President and Congress*, August 1, 1949, Washington, 1949, p. 4.

[28] *Report* of the United Ukrainian American Relief Committee, Inc., June 30, 1948, Home Office: Philadelphia, Pennsylvania; European Headquarters: Munich-Pasing, U.S. Zone, Germany, p. 9.

[29] See 27 — The Displaced Persons Commission, *Report*, p. 44.

[30] Letter from W. Preston Lane, Jr., Governor, Executive Department, Annapolis, Maryland, to Joseph Marmash, Dundalk, Maryland, September 30, 1948.

[31] "44 'Displaced' Ukrainians Know They Are In Right Place," *The Sun*, Baltimore, Maryland, January 19, 1949.

[32] Written information received by the writer from Wasyl Macuk, Berlin, Maryland, January 10, 1976.

[33] "Rev. Basil Sushko Dies Unexpectedly," *The Evening Sun*, Baltimore, Maryland, November 26, 1958.

[34] Rev. Wasyl Sushko, *Memoirs About Missionary Work in Maryland in 1949*, unpublished document in possession of the writer.

[35] John W. Ball, "D.P.s Please State at Rosewood School," *The Washington Post*, March 5, 1950, p. 8M.

[36] Richard K. Tucker, "Loneliness Drives D.P.s to Cities for Work," *The Evening Sun*, Baltimore, Maryland, May 16, 1950.

[37] Letter from the Lankfords to Alex Rybak, Weston Farms, Harwood, Maryland, 20776, January 15, 1976.

[38] *Register* of the Baltimore Branch of the Ukrainian Congress Committee of America for Year 1975, compiled by Bohdan Salamacha, Baltimore, Maryland.

[39] Ukrainian Catholic Shrine of the Holy Family, Washington, D.C., *The Memorial Book*, Washington, D.C., 1975, p. 26.

[40] Statement by Stephen Basarab, Baltimore, Maryland, personal interview, May 29, 1976.

[41] Statements by Rev. Stephen J. Shawel, CSSR, Pastor of the Holy Family Ukrainian Catholic Church, Washington, D.C., and by Marie Koby, Secretary of the St. Andrew's Ukrainian Orthodox Church Council, Washington, D.C., joint interviews with Paul Fenchak, Lutherville, Maryland, December 29, 1975.

[42] See 32 — Written information from Wasyl Macuk.

[43] See 32 — Written information from Wasyl Macuk.

[44] Mary Corddry, "Russians file claim to Wicomico farm," *The Sun*, Baltimore, Maryland, March 14, 1976, p. A18.

ETHNIC ORIGINS

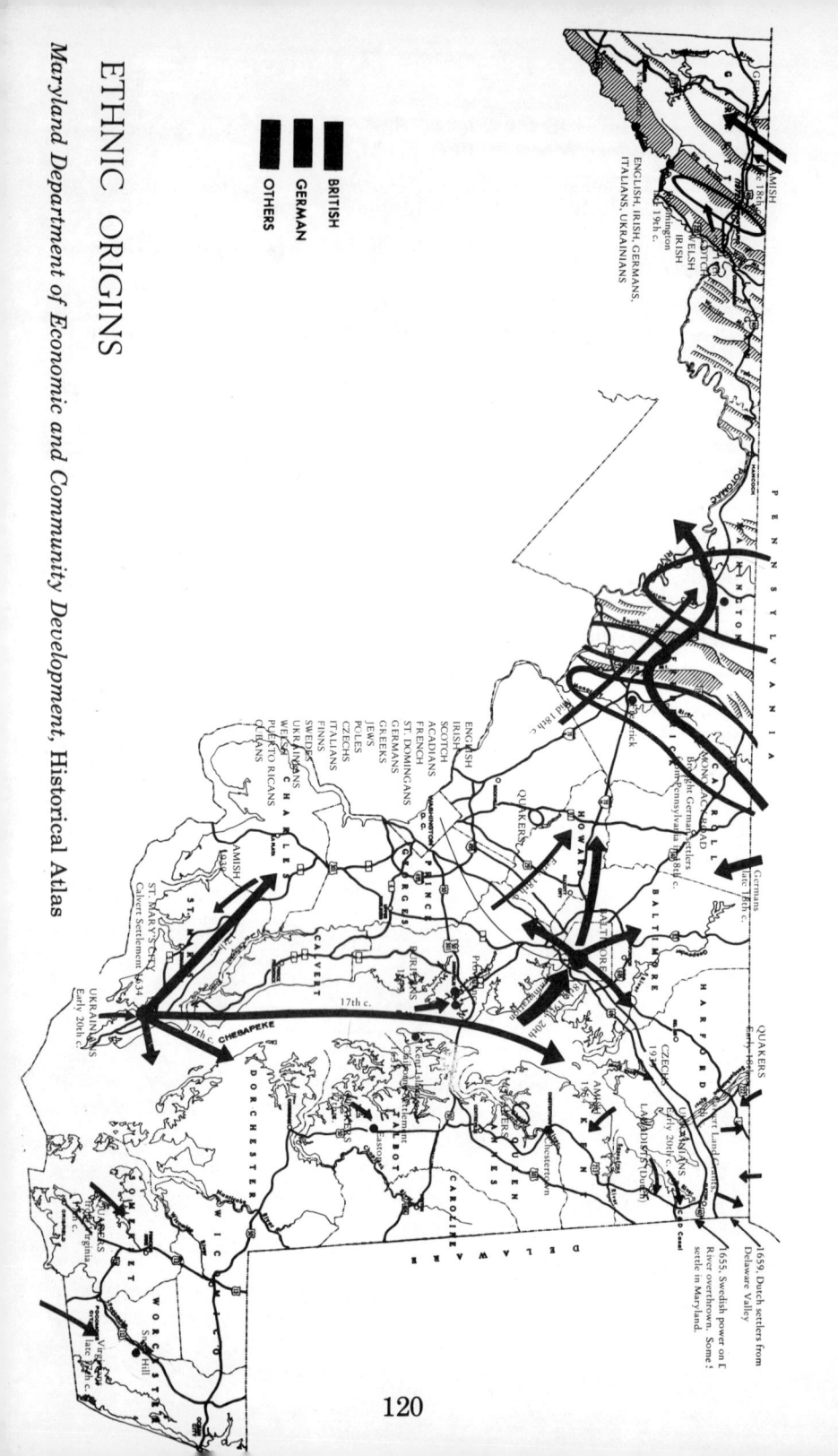

Maryland Department of Economic and Community Development, Historical Atlas

Chapter Four
Geography of Ukrainian Population in Maryland
Hlib S. Hayuk

The early pioneers who arrived in small numbers from 1620 to the 1870's settled widely throughout the United States from Jamestown, Virginia, to California, Alaska, and Hawaii. It seems that no section of the country held a special attraction for Ukrainians. As a result there was no definite geographical concentration of Ukrainians anywhere in the United States at this time.

Beginning about 1877, when the first mass migration of Ukrainians took place, they tended to settle in the northeastern part of the United States. These immigrants were attracted by jobs and economic opportunities which were available in the industrial and urbanized northeast. The geographical sketch established by the first mass wave created the pattern of settlement for the other waves that followed. The only major exception to the rule was the post World War II influx of political refugees who, although tending to follow the previous settlement outline, inclined to diverge considerably and moved in large numbers to the south, southwest, and the west coast of the United States.

Immigration records maintained between 1899 and 1930 showed that for every 100 Ukrainians 43% indicated Pennsylvania as their destination, drawn primarily by employment openings in coal mines and steel mills of that state. An additional 23% listed New York and 11% New Jersey, led there chiefly by various jobs in industry and transportation and secondarily by farm land available in the Mohawk Valley of New York and the coastal plain of New Jersey. As thus officially recorded three quarters of all Ukrainians during this time settled in three northeastern states. Of the others, 4% listed Ohio, 4% Illinois, 3% Connecticut, 3% Massachusetts, 2% Michigan and 7% seven different states, including Maryland.

Today the vast majority of Ukrainians is found in the same places. During and following World War II and accelerating in the 1960's, an internal movement of Ukrainians in the United States occurred. Thousands moved outside of the original northeast states, establishing Ukrainian communities in the south; in cities like Miami, Atlanta, Richmond and Arlington; in the southwest, in Houston, Denver, and Phoenix; and on the west coast, in Los Angeles, Hollywood, San Francisco and Seattle.

The post World War II internal movement of Ukrainians is partially due to second and third generation Ukrainians leaving the northeast for better economic opportunities and partially because of the thousands of professionals who entered the country during the 1947 to 1955 period and accepted employment wherever it was available. Pockets and clusters of Ukrainians today can be found in practically every American city. Many Ukrainians stay in touch with their *kraiani* (countrymen) through the ethnic press, fraternal organizations, various associations, youth camps and even common vacation areas for young and old such as Kerhonkson and Hunter in New York, or Wildwood Crest in New Jersey, just to name several out of many.

Geographical space is no longer looked upon as an insurmountable obstacle for maintaining contact with the community. Likewise, what may appear to be geographically isolated pockets or small communities may not feel small at all because they are in constant touch with other communities all over the state of Maryland or even other parts of the country.

Based upon church records, rosters of various organizations and extensive field work by the authors of this book, it is felt that there are approximately 20,000 Marylanders of Ukrainian extraction living in the state.

The figure of 20,000 Ukrainians for the state of Maryland is not at all exorbitant. If it is considered that there are between 1.2 and 1.5 million Ukrainians in the United States (and perhaps over 2 million according to some authorities), and that the vast majority is located in the northeastern states with Maryland's neighbor, Pennsylvania, being the most populous, then a figure of 20,000 for Maryland may be rather conservative. This figure would mean that about 1-2% of all Ukrainians in the United States are found in Maryland, indicating again that this may be a moderate estimate.

The present geographical distribution of Ukrainians in the State of Maryland is the result of various periods of Ukrainian settlement in the state. It is also a reflection, to a large degree, of the general distribution of the whole state population.

Although small groups of Marylanders of Ukrainian descent may be found practically in every town and county in the state, the majority or about 85% is concentrated in and around the Baltimore-Washington metropolitan areas and the corridor between these two cities. The remaining 15% is scattered throughout the state, exhibiting smaller concentrations in the eastern shore counties and in western Maryland.

More than two-thirds of all Ukrainians in the state are found in and around the Baltimore metropolitan area. Of this number, about half reside within the city limits of Baltimore. (See map of Ukrainians in Baltimore.)

Within the city approximately half live in East Baltimore, especially around Patterson Park. This is the single largest and one of the oldest Ukrainian neighborhoods in the state. East Baltimore is the location of a youth home, a sports club, a federal credit union, professional offices and businesses as well as several churches. This neighborhood stretches roughly in an east-west direction along Patterson Park and Eastern Avenue and spills over the city boundary into Baltimore county, especially into Essex. The East Baltimore Ukrainian neighborhood experienced a large influx of people after World War II. Today the neighborhood is decreasing in size

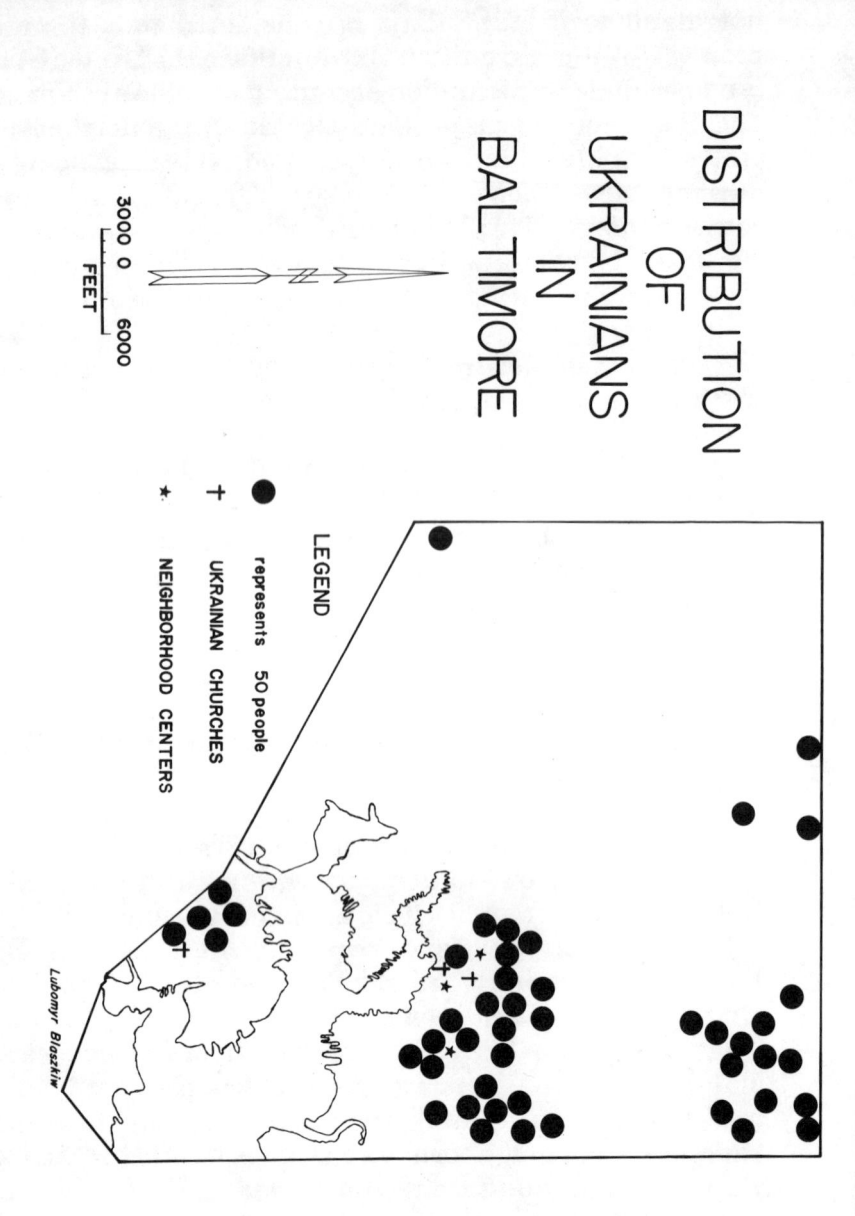

DISTRIBUTION OF UKRAINIANS IN BALTIMORE

LEGEND

● represents 50 people
+ UKRAINIAN CHURCHES
* NEIGHBORHOOD CENTERS

Distribution of Ukrainians in Baltimore   *Cartography by Lubomyr Blaszkiw*

and in geographical area as the first and second generation Maryland-born Ukrainians acquire better education and more gainful employment, many of whom then move into the suburbs, especially into the southern part of Baltimore County but also to new communities such as Columbia in Howard County, between Baltimore and Washington.

The second, less distinct and less compact, Ukrainian neighborhood is found in the northeastern corner of the city, popularly referred to as Hamilton. Quite a few post World War II Ukrainians have purchased homes in this area running along Harford and Bel Air Roads to reinforce the already considerable number of Ukrainians already settled there. This neighborhood spreads into southern Baltimore County into Perry Hall and Parkville communities.

The third very distinct but smaller Ukrainian neighborhood is located in the southern part of the city known as Curtis Bay. It extends into adjacent Anne Arundel County.

The fourth area of Ukrainian residence in the city is found along north Charles and north York roads blending into southern Baltimore County in the Towson and Ruxton communities. This area is inhabited by the more affluent and some professionals. A few Ukrainian families are also found in the southwestern part of the city which merges into Catonsville in the southwestern part of Baltimore County and into Ellicott City in adjacent Howard County.

Outside of Baltimore city there is a heavy concentration of Ukrainians in Baltimore County, especially in Towson, Lutherville, Parkville, Perry Hall and Essex communities. Smaller numbers are found in Timonium, northern Baltimore County, Pikesville, Randallstown, Reisterstown and Catonsville.

In Howard County there are many Ukrainian professionals and a few farmers, especially of the post World War II category, who have settled in Columbia and Ellicott City.

Outside of the Baltimore metropolitan area the next highest gathering of Ukrainians is found in the

Washington metropolitan area in southern Montgomery County and adjacent northern part of Prince George's County. This is the second most populous cluster of Ukrainians in the state. Most of the inhabitants here are federal employees working in and around Washington, D.C., although some are professionals and a few are in business. The inhabitants of this Washington cluster consist of mostly post World War II arrivals but also of many second and third generation Ukrainians predominantly those born in Pennsylvania but including significant numbers from other states and even Canada. The Washington Ukrainian community is well organized, maintaining several churches and supporting many organizations, including an exemplarily conducted elementary school of Ukrainian studies. This community is growing constantly as new arrivals, comprised mostly of young couples, obtain government jobs.

The third Ukrainian cluster is found on the eastern shore around Whaleysville in Worcester County and Salisbury in Wicomico County. Several Ukrainian families live near Pocomoke City in Worcester County. Practically all of these people are involved in farming although a few are in business activities related to Ocean City, Maryland. Some of the residents are already second and third generation Marylanders, although many are post World War II settlers and recent retirees.

The fourth Ukrainian cluster is found in the eastern part of Cecil County centered on Chesapeake City where there is a Ukrainian orphanage and a church. All of these people are second and third generation Marylanders and are involved in farming or work in nearby Elkton, on the Chesapeake-Delaware Canal, or in Wilmington or Newark in Delaware.

The fifth and last Ukrainian cluster is found in western Maryland in Allegheny and Garrett Counties. Many of these people came here when coal mining was an important activity. Today the community is decreasing in size as the second and third generation people pass away or move from the area because of the lack of economic opportunities. A few post World War II Ukrainians, who originally settled in

Distribution of Ukrainians in Maryland

the Baltimore area, have bought property in the area and intend to retire in the vicinity, especially near Round Lake.

There are also some Ukrainian families near the Pennsylvania border in Washington, Frederick, Carroll and Harford Counties. Most of these people are second, third, and fourth generation Ukrainians from Pennsylvania who turned away from coal mining to factory work or farming in Maryland.

Today geographical dispersal is influencing all Ukrainian neighborhoods and communities. Scattering of members of cohesive groups, made possible by the automobile, is generally increasing everywhere in the state, diluting the Ukrainian neighborhoods and clusters. Perhaps the only exception to the rule is the Washington oriented Ukrainian community which is attracting people from various sections of the state as well as from other parts of the United States and Canada.

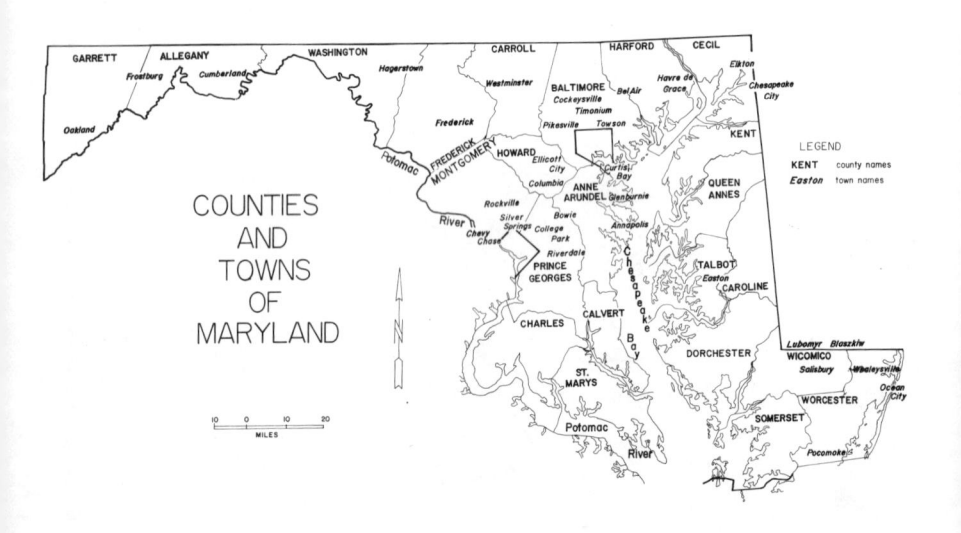

COUNTIES AND TOWNS OF MARYLAND

Chapter Five

Ukrainian Activities On the Maryland Scene; Interaction with Other Areas And Groups

Paul Fenchak

As ethnic studies increase throughout the United States, the state of Maryland merits greater academic analyses than it has received in the past. Whereas New York and Pennsylvania have received a great amount of attention in the story of Ukrainian immigration to America, the port of Baltimore was also busy receiving immigrants of many backgrounds. The Locust Point Immigration Center in the harbor of Baltimore was the fourth largest immigration post in the United States and with the Baltimore and Ohio Railroad's being a route of access to many farming, mining, lumbering, and mill centers, thousands of newcomers funnelled through Maryland via the railroads, general overland travel, or by the Potomac or Susquehanna river systems.

Early in the history of the development of railroads in the United States, Baron von Krudener, the Russian ambassador at Washington, came to Baltimore in 1830 to study the potential of railroads with officials of the Baltimore and Ohio Company. Philip E. Thomas, first president of the Baltimore and Ohio Railroad, mentioned Ukrainian areas along the Dnieper (Dnipro) River and the Black Sea in his reply to Baron von Krudener:

> Would the Emperor (Nicholas I) introduce railroads into Russia it would not be many years before a railway would be constructed between the Baltic and Black Seas, along the rivers Dwina and Dnieper, and such a road would enable Russia to encircle in her arms not only the northern but also the eastern frontier of Europe, and thus greatly extend her power and influence.[1]

To all of this, the Baron Krudener replied with a fine diplomatic naivete:

> My dear sir, you cannot suppose that Russia has any ambition, or that she desires either to increase her power or influence! On these points she will remain content with her present position.[2]

Yet presently Ross Winans was sent for, to go to St. Petersburg to superintend the mechanical installations of the Russian railroads.[3] Ross Winans built a locomotive and sent his son Thomas to the Imperial Court to demonstrate its operation. With Winans went Major George Washington Whistler, a West Point-trained engineer, whose son was James McNeill Whistler, the great American artist. Winans and Whistler lived in the Russian Empire for some years and Winans returned a very wealthy man — his total wealth being about $2,000,000. The chronicler states, "He went abroad a mechanic and returned a millionaire." Returning to Baltimore, Thomas Winans rebuilt a palatial mansion he called *Alexandroffsky* in memory of his success in the Russian Empire. Razed in 1927, *Alexandroffsky* was located on a tract of several acres, bounded by Baltimore, Hollins, and Callender Streets and Fremont Avenue. Alexandroffsky (Oleksandrivske in Ukrainian) is the former name of the city of Zaporozhye (Zaporizia) in Ukraine.

Winans named his summer home *Crimea* after the pleasant peninsula in southern Ukraine. *Crimea*, located on an estate of nearly 1,000 acres, still stands today in what is now Baltimore's Leakin Park near the western boundary of the city.

Other Ukrainian influences came upon Winans as he and George Gillingham built a railroad engine, the *Mazeppa*, that entered Baltimore and Ohio service in October, 1838. Apparently named after Hetman Ivan Mazep(p)a (1644-1709) of Ukraine, the engine bears a name highly respected by Ukrainians as Hetman Mazeppa (ruled 1687-1709) succeeded in obtaining freedom for Ukraine from the Czarist Empire of Peter I (called "The Great") with the result that Mazeppa was perhaps the strongest individual personality in the heroic Kozak (Cossak) period

ALEXANDROFFSKY was developed by Thomas D. Winans with funds paid him for bringing railroad technology to the Russian Empire in 1830's.

Maryland Department of Enoch Pratt Free Library

of Ukrainian history. The Kozak period of Ukrainian independence extended from the middle of the 17th century to the end of the 18th century. It is worth noting that a town named Mazeppa exists in Pennsylvania located several miles west of Lewisburg in territory served by the Baltimore and Susquehanna Railroad before the line was incorporated in the Pennsylvania Railroad system. Towns named Mazeppa also exist in Minnesota and North Carolina. George Gordon Lord Byron, noted English romantic writer, commemorated the spirit for independence held by Mazeppa in a poem written in 1819, "Mazeppa." Even as Mazeppa loved freedom, so did Byron who died of exposure in Greece in 1824 while fighting for Greek independence from the Ottoman Empire.

CRIMEAN WAR — BALTIMORE STYLE. *The dummy fort pictured was constructed at the time of the Civil War on the grounds of "Crimea," summer home of Thomas D. Winans, a Southern sympathizer who had the 'fortress' built to deter Union troops.*
Baltimore News-Post

The *Mazeppa* engine was followed by the *Cossack* in Baltimore and Ohio service in 1848; later in 1849 came the *Tartar*, which name in the Ukrainian language reflects the Mongols who ravaged Ukraine from the east in the 13th century.

Perhaps the *Sandusky* which was proudly exhibited at Halethorpe, Maryland, at the Baltimore and Ohio Centenary, "The Fair of the Iron Horse," in 1927 also presents Ukrainian terminology as it is posited that Sandusky, Ohio, and other places bearing the name may have been named after an early Ukrainian in America James (Jacob) Sadovsky (Sadowsky), whose name was rendered in the English language as "Sandusky."

Bearing the Ukrainian name, THE MAZEPPA, this engine was built by the Baldwin Locomotive Works and entered B. & O. service in 1838.
U.E.A.M. Collection

Claimed by several Slavic groups, THE SANDUSKY, appeared at the B. & O.'s Centenary Exhibition, The Fair of the Iron Horse, at Halethorpe, Md., in 1927.
U.E.A.M. Collection

"Sandusky" served in the army of George Washington during the Revolutionary War.[4] He helped George Rogers Clark conquer the Northwest.

How coincidental it was that the engines mentioned above should have drawn cars of coal mined by Ukrainian miners in Pennsylvania, Maryland, West Virginia, or other states.

Certainly Maryland had influenced areas of Ukraine by the 1850's. According to Katherine Harvey in her thorough history of coal mining in Maryland, *The Best-Dressed Miners — Life and Labor in the Maryland Coal Region, 1835-1910*, the mining industry was not prospering in 1855:

> The curtailment of orders for Maryland coal in 1855 was attributed to depression in the iron industry, to suspension of the operations by several manufacturing establishments, and to the loss of the bunkering trade occasioned by the withdrawal of Atlantic steamers to supply troops and munitions for the war in the Crimea.[5]

In addition to mentioning the loss of the coal trade for purposes of fighting the war in the Crimean province of Ukraine, the Crimean War (1853-1856), Katherine Harvey refers to an upsurge of the industry in Western Maryland that enticed enterprising Americans:

> Warren Delano, maternal grandfather of Franklin Delano Roosevelt, was a trustee for two pieces of coal property transferred to the Consolidation Coal Company in 1871. He was also a director of the Consolidation Coal Company from 1864 to 1875, and one of the first directors of the Cumberland and Pennsylvania Railroad. Franklin Roosevelt's father, James, was a director of the Consolidation Coal Company from 1868 to 1875.[6]

The state of Maryland was closely interrelated with industrial endeavors in Pennsylvania, the focal point of Ukrainian immigration to America. The interrelation is attested to by nomenclature that is historical to both Maryland and Pennsylvania, e.g., the mining and lumbering community of Karthaus in Clearfield County, Pennsylvania, was owned by and received its name from Peter Karthaus, a wealthy Baltimore merchant. Lumber and coal were shipped down both the West and North branches of the Susquehanna River, arriving in Baltimore.

The Baltimore and Ohio Railroad, the Cumberland and Pennsylvania Railroad, the Baltimore and Susquehanna Railroad, the Pennsylvania Railroad, and the Western Maryland Railroad, among others, served industries of Pennsylvania as well as other states, with the port of Baltimore being a terminus.

Of importance is the fact that the first national highway (the Cumberland Road or U.S. Route 40) extended from Cumberland, Maryland, in its first section to Wheeling, West Virginia, on the Ohio River, after winding through western Pennsylvania. Ukrainians settled in large numbers in the many mining communities in southwestern Pennsylvania as well as in Wheeling and other communities in West Virginia. Cumberland was not only a division point of the Baltimore and Ohio Railroad but it was also the western terminus of the Chesapeake and Ohio Canal. The importance of historic Cumberland to the development of our nation is described by Frederick Gutheim in the book, *The Potomac*:

> The effect of the railroad on the countryside through which it passed was phenomenal. It had helped boom Harper's Ferry from an arsenal town to an important junction point. The population of Cumberland had been trebled, and that mountain city became by far the most important center between salt water and the Ohio. The values of many farms on either side had skyrocketed, and the prices the farmer obtained for his crops made dramatic increases as the ease of getting them to market grew... Abundant natural resources, heretofore worthless, became wealth.
>
> After the last spike had been driven at Rosby's Rock on Christmas Eve, 1852, the feverish looting of forest and mine in the virgin territory beyond Cumberland made fortunes for fifty years. Sawmills were built and coal mines opened on lands which the railroad had made accessible.[7]

These several accounts of industrial interaction are of great import as they set the stage for the westward migration of immigrants from various ports. In 1828 the first shipment of bituminous coal reached Philadelphia, to which it had been transported by ark from Karthaus, Pennsylvania, to Port Deposit, Maryland, located at the head of Chesapeake Bay (near Chesapeake City), and then to Philadelphia. Also, in 1828 the first shipment of coal was carried via the Susquehanna River from Karthaus to

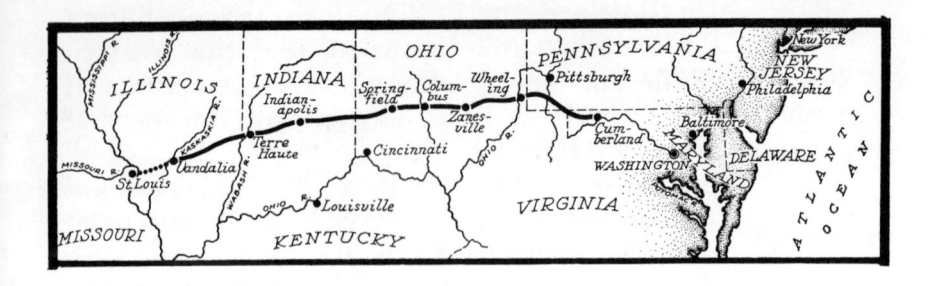

Work on the Cumberland Road, the first National Highway, began in 1806, westward from Cumberland. By 1811 the road reached Wheeling going through areas where many Ukrainians now live.

Baltimore. It was in the same county where Karthaus is located, Clearfield, that one of the oldest Ukrainian Catholic churches in the United States was founded in 1889, viz., St. Mary's Nativity in Osceola Mills. In 1893 the church became apostate through the incitement of Fr. Alexis Toth and entered Russian Orthodox membership. Nearby in Clearfield County at Ramey a much larger Ukrainian Catholic Church, St. Mary's Annunciation, was founded in 1893.

Mrs. Olga Worrall, for years a resident of Towson, Maryland, states in one of her books that her father, a Russian Orthodox priest in Europe, was ordered by the Russian Czar in the early 1900's "to go to America to organize Russian Orthodox parishes throughout the Eastern United States."[8] As time passes it is possible to discern a gradual return to Ukrainian circles by many Ukrainian families that were proselytized by Russian organizers. It must be remembered that difficulties in transportation induced many Ukrainians in scattered communities to join conveniently located 'Russian' organizations, which according to the eminent Czech sociologist, Joseph S. Roucek, were over 80% Ukrainian in composition.

If Vladimir Wertsman is correct in stating in his book, *The Ukrainians in America — 1608-1975* (p. 1), that Ivan Bohdan was the first Ukrainian in America, it is then possible that the same Ivan Bohdan may have accompanied Captain John Smith when Smith was the first white man to explore the mouth of the Susquehanna River in Maryland in 1608. A Slavic-American engineer, Charles Trcziyulny, was engaged during the term of Governor J. Andrew Shulze of Pennsylvania to study 'The River Susquehanna' and on March 8, 1827, he presented an extensive report of his surveys to Governor Shulze and the Senate and House of the Commonwealth of Pennsylvania. The grave of Charles Trcziyulny is in Bellefonte, Pennsylvania, and there is a Trcziyulny Street in Osceola Mills, Pennsylvania.

It is the central-western area of Pennsylvania, so much influenced by Maryland, that commands additional study about Ukrainians in America. In the early days of the forming of the Knights of Labor, the United Mine Workers of America, and the American Federation of Labor, mine workers in the present District Two (U.M.W.) of Pennsylvania were in constant interaction with those of Maryland's George's Creek region. The primary leaders in union endeavors served both regions in the two states. Michael Demchak, an effective leader in District Two, was very highly rated by John Brophy, one-time president of the district and a challenger to John L. Lewis for the presidency of the United Mine Workers Union. Brophy's keen sense for understanding the need for educated union leadership was shown in his having placed Michael Demchak as a student at Brookwood College, the leadership school he started in New York state.

An early account of life in America written by a Ukrainian in the diplomatic service of the Russian Empire is found in a book by Petro Poleticka (Poletyka). Poleticka (1778-1849) was the son of Ivan Poleticka, a physician and professor who had studied at Kiev University, Kiel University, and the University of Leiden. Petro Poleticka entered Russian foreign service in St. Petersburg in 1798; later he held several diplomatic posts and from 1817 to 1822 was both special envoy and Russian minister to the United States.

In 1826 E. J. Coale of Baltimore printed Poleticka's interesting book, *A Sketch of the Internal Condition of the*

United States of America and of their Political Relations with Europe. In researching for the book Poleticka spent a number of weeks in Baltimore, where he was particularly impressed by the then incompleted Washington Monument. Translated from the French, the book, *a la* Alexis DeTocqueville's *Democracy in America* which followed in 1835, is a lively commentary on American life in which Poleticka discussed topics such as General Considerations, The Army, The Navy, Finances, Political Relations, Administration of Justice, and Penitentiaries. Somewhat of a precursor of "detente" in foreign policy, Poleticka observed:

> It may be said, that the disposition of the government and the American nation in regard to Russia, is generally amicable. The name of the Emperor Alexander is revered in the United States. This is owing to the moderation with which the imperial government always treated the interests of America, at a time when they came into collision with those of all the other maritime powers of Europe. Russia, formidable as she is, inspires no fear in that country. They even reckon on her support in any difficulty in which they may be hereafter involved with any European powers, whose dispositions are less favorable to them.[9]

PERPLEXED IMMIGRANTS AT THE LOCUST POINT IMMIGRATION CENTER

Attitudes towards immigrants from the Austro-Hungarian Empire are interestingly revealed in the following article that appeared in the *Baltimore Sun* on August 23, 1901:

> **AUSTRIANS ALLOWED TO GO; SUSPECTED STEEL WORKERS RELEASED FROM HOUSE OF DETENTION**
>
> The 120 Austrian immigrants who arrived at this port (Baltimore) on Wednesday afternoon on the North German Lloyd Steamer *Hannover* from Bremen and who were suspected of coming here to work in steel mills in violation of the Contract Labor Law were released from the House of Detention at Locust Point yesterday by Immigration Inspector Headquarters, no evidence of a nature to detain them being found.
>
> In the afternoon a board of 5 officers connected with the Immigration Bureau went to Locust Point to investigate the case. About 25 of the men were rigidly examined. They were asked why they had come to this country, who had given them the money to pay for their passage, what they intended to do and a number of other questions. Almost all the men are natives of Austria

A SKETCH

OF THE

INTERNAL CONDITION

OF THE

UNITED STATES OF AMERICA,

AND OF THEIR

POLITICAL RELATIONS WITH EUROPE.

BY A RUSSIAN.

TRANSLATED FROM THE FRENCH,
BY AN AMERICAN,
WITH NOTES.

Baltimore:
PUBLISHED BY E. J. COALE.
B. EDES, PRINTER.
1826.

Petro Poleticka, a Ukrainian in the diplomatic service of the Russian Empire, wrote the interesting book whose title page is shown above.
U.E.A.M. Collection

and had tickets to Pittsburgh, Cleveland, Steelton, and other places near the big steel mills. This led the authorities to suspect that they had been imported here to take the places of strikers in the steel mills in violation of the law. The closest questioning, however, failed to elicit from any of the immigrants the fact that money had been given them to buy their tickets or that any inducement had been offered by anyone for them to come to this country.

Most of the men examined said they had come here because they understood a man could make good wages in this country. Each asserted that he had himself saved the money for his passage here, although one man stated that in his own country his wages amounted to 25 cents a day in American money and upon this sum he supported his family. Most of the men claimed to be laborers, and almost everyone had the name of a friend in this country who would aid him in case he failed to get work.

No evidence sufficient to justify the authorities ordering the return of the men to Bremen was found and they were released about 4:00 o'clock. Their progress through the country will be watched by the immigration inspectors as it is possible to send them back any time before the end of a year.

The immigrants will be taken to their different destinations as speedily as possible.[10]

The article suggests that apprehension smacking of nativism continued for some Marylanders at the turn of the century, recalling the fact that in the presidential election of 1856 the Native-American, or Know-Nothing, presidential candidate, Millard Fillmore, was successful in winning the electoral votes of one state: Maryland. It is logical to assume that some of the 'Austrians' mentioned were really Ukrainians when it is remembered that a steady stream of Ukrainians left the Austro-Hungarian Empire via Bremen in Germany and that many did venture to Pittsburgh and Cleveland here in America. Examinations of naturalization records indicate that Ukrainians were often regarded as Austrians. In the year of 1902 a total of 55,802 immigrants arrived in Baltimore and according to statistics issued in 1912 the number of immigrants had decreased to 23,771 by 1911. Yet records indicate that numerous Ukrainians were coming to the United States in the immigration wave that ended with the advent of World War I in 1914. George F. Will maintains that in 1911 two steamship lines had more than 5,000 ticket agents in Galicia, Austro-Hungary.[11] As a result of recruitment of

THE BALTIMORE SUN ALMANAC, 1914.   201

IMMIGRATION TO BALTIMORE 1913.

Total number of immigrants admitted at the Port of Baltimore, for the calendar year 1913, shown by countries:

Austria	6,456	Switzerland	16
Hungary	7,930	Turkey in Europe	23
Belgium	2	England	5
Bulgarian, Servian and Montenegrin	54	Ireland	1
Denmark	2	Scotland	4
German Empire	2,075	Other Europe	1
Greece	8	Turkey in Asia	1
Italy, including Sicily and Sardinia	19	Other Asia	1
Netherlands	11	Africa	2
Norway	78	South America	3
Russian Empire and Finland	24,965	West Indies	31
Spain, including Canary and Balearic Islands	1		
Sweden	5	**Total**	**41,693**

IMMIGRATION TO MARYLAND 1913.

Immigrants arriving at the Port of Baltimore, January 1st to December 31st, 1913, giving Maryland as their final destination and admitted—shown by race:

African	13	Ruthenian (Russniak)	159
Bohemian and Moravian (Czech)	150	Scandinavian, (Norwegians, Danes and Swedes)	1
Bulgarian, Servian and Montenegrin	15		
Croatian and Slovenian	37	Scotch	4
Dalmatian, Bosnian and Herzegovinian	5	Slovak	10
Dutch and Flemish	1	Spanish	1
English	13	Turkish	1
German	688	Other peoples	1
Hebrew	1,379		
Irish	1	**Total**	**4,784**
Lithuanian	301		
Magyar	16		
Polish	1,064	Non-immigrant aliens admitted during year	804
Roumanian	19		
Russian	905	Aliens deported from Baltimore	322

Ukrainian (Ruthenian in chart above) arrivals in Baltimore in 1913 totalled 159.

Baltimore Sunpapers

immigrants, the number of immigrants arriving at the Port of Baltimore in 1913 was nearly double the number that arrived in 1911, totalling 41,693, most of whom did not have Maryland as their final destination. Figures from *The Baltimore Sun Almanac, 1914,* show that 159 Ukrainians (Ruthenians, Russniaks), settled in Maryland in 1913.[12]

After the Civil War John W. Garrett, president of the Baltimore and Ohio Railroad, initiated transatlantic steamship service in and out of the port of Baltimore by purchasing three wooden propellors from the United States government. Naming these steamships after the Maryland counties of *Somerset, Carroll,* and *Worcester,* the Baltimore and Ohio-owned ships began service in September of 1865. Having little success with this venture, transatlantic operations were discontinued in 1868.

Baltimore and Ohio appetites were whetted, though, and in 1867 a working agreement between the Baltimore and Ohio and the North German Lloyd Steamship Company was signed. To accommodate the German ships, a splendid passenger and freight wharf, with exchange and banking facilities and provisions for passenger trains, was built at Locust Point. It was such endeavors that lured many immigrants to arrive in Baltimore.

BUSINESS, BALTIMORE, AND ODESSA

The same as railroads, the steamship lines needed business other than passengers, so Maryland's "fast" steamers were pointed in many directions. A notable victory for American enterprise and dollar diplomacy was won in 1899, when the Czarist government of St. Petersburg awarded to the Maryland Steel Company (acquired by Bethlehem Steel Corporation in 1916) of Sparrows Point the contract for 80,000 tons of steel rails for the Chinese Eastern Railway. The United States had managed to elbow out European competitors only after lively representations by the Department of State.[13] The Sparrows Point plant imported high quality iron ore from Cuba, Chile, and Venezuela, and received shipments of coal and limestone via railroad from Pennsylvania. A fully integrated steel works beginning with the ore and producing finished steel products, including ships, the plant has continued to grow until it is now the largest single industry in Baltimore and the world's largest tidewater steel plant. That Ukrainian sinews added to the growth of this industry is bespoken by the fact that countless Ukrainian-Americans mined the coal and manned the open hearths used by Bethlehem Steel operations.

In 1956 the Maryland Port Authority was established to guide the development of the port. In recent years new copper refining and chemical plants have been opened in the harbor. Though shipbuilding continues, the pattern has been to trade in bulk cargo — the export of steel goods, coal, and grain, and the import of iron ore, copper ore, chemicals, and oil.

AN AGREEMENT ON FRIENDLY RELATIONS BETWEEN

THE CITY OF
BALTIMORE, MARYLAND, U.S.A.

AND

THE CITY OF
ODESSA, U.S.S.R.

WHEREAS, it is recognized that the establishment of friendship between the Cities of Odessa and Baltimore will contribute toward international peace, mutual understanding, the development of friendly relations, and cultural exchanges; and

WHEREAS, the exchange of delegations of representatives of these Cities, including specialists in the various fields of city life, science, technology, culture, tourism, and the performing arts has been initiated by the visit to Baltimore of a delegation headed by the Chairman of the Executive Committee of the Odessa City Council of Workers Deputies; and

WHEREAS, these two Cities have a mutual interest in international maritime commerce through their two great ports; and

WHEREAS, the exchange of information about the life of our citizens and the activities of our local governments will be of mutual help derived from our experiences in such areas as culture, education, health care, social welfare, tourism, arts, and sports.

NOW, THEREFORE, BE IT AGREED, THAT:

1. The Mayor of Baltimore and the Chairman of the Executive Committee of the Odessa City Council of Workers Deputies, on behalf of the people of their respective Cities, enter into a Sister City affiliation for the purpose of creating greater mutual understanding between their Cities and between their Nations; and

2. The Mayor of Baltimore and the Chairman of the Executive Committee of the Odessa City Council of Workers Deputies hereby officially authorize representatives of their respective Cities to carry out these ties of mutual friendship and cultural exchange, and to lay plans for future collaboration; and

3. Copies of this AGREEMENT will be provided to the Mayor of Baltimore and the Chairman of the Executive Committee of the Odessa City Council of Workers Deputies, to the town Affiliation Association of the U.S., Inc., and to the Embassy of the U.S.S.R. at Washington, D.C., U.S.A.

THIS AGREEMENT (in Russian and in English), has been signed on September 18, 1975, and its provisions shall remain in effect indefinitely.

Mayor

Chairman

On behalf of the
City of
Baltimore,
William Donald
Schaefer, Mayor,
City of
Baltimore,
Maryland, U.S.A.

On behalf of the
City of Odessa,
Vladimir Shurko,
Chairman,
Executive
Committee, Odessa
City Council of
Workers Deputies

In recent years the port of Baltimore has been a center for the shipment of grain to the Soviet Union, much of the grain arriving in the Ukrainian city of Odessa. Perhaps this "bear market" in grain, which has aided several American railroads financially and has induced them to increase their rolling stock is one of the reasons for the signing of AN AGREEMENT ON FRIENDLY RELATIONS BETWEEN THE CITY OF BALTIMORE, MARYLAND, U.S.A. AND THE CITY OF ODESSA, U.S.S.R. on September 18, 1975. The writer of this article is somewhat suspect of the agreement mentioned as the agreement makes no reference to trade *per se*. Standard flowery phrases — international peace, mutual understanding, friendly relations, cultural exchanges, etc. — are mentioned, yet data obtained from the Maryland Port Administration indicate that the Soviet regime may be hankering most for an increase in trade with Baltimore. The number of short tons exported from the port of Baltimore to the Soviet Union in 1974 was 48,450; in 1975 it was 364,321. Imports from the Soviet Union in 1974 totalled 86,927 short tons, in 1975 there was a drop to 4,611 short tons. Corn or maize totalled 318,762 of the tonnage exported to the U.S.S.R. in 1975. Imports were mostly in ores and fuel oil.

As the Jewish populace of Maryland watches the Baltimore-Odessa agreement, so do the Ukrainians, the principal ethnic group of Odessa, although the city at one time had a population which may have been as high as one-third of Jewish stock.

To trade or not to trade? Ukrainians ponder over the question of precisely what is being traded. Remembering the man-made famine in Ukraine in 1932-33 when upwards of 5,000,000 Ukrainians were starved in strengthening Bolshevik domination, Ukrainians reflect in the way the Jews remember Nazism when they see ships such as the *Salvador Allende*, with its Marxist connotations, docked in the port of Baltimore. As Ukrainians recall the mountains of bodies and rivers of blood shed in behalf of their Orthodox and Catholic churches, the philosophical question becomes, "Should a nation trade with cannibals?"

The Soviet ship, SALVADOR ALLENDE, is pictured being loaded in the harbor of Baltimore.

Baltimore Sunpapers

On December 14, 1975, a display of photographs of the Ukrainian city of Odessa and a copy of the "Sister City" agreement for friendly and cultural exchanges between Baltimore and Odessa began at the Maryland Historical

Society. Also on display was a collection of news articles, stories, and other materials dealing with the development of the Ukrainian community in Maryland since the 1800's. Wasyl Palijczuk, an eminent Maryland artist, arranged the exhibit showing the contributions of Ukrainian-Americans to the cultural life of Maryland.

In 1956 President Dwight Eisenhower initiated the People-to-People program at the White House. Out of this grew Sister Cities International which has assisted more than 560 American cities to establish affiliations with over 710 cities in 75 nations around the world.

In addition to being a sister city of Baltimore, Odessa also has special relations with the French port of Marseilles and the Japanese port of Yokohama. It is interesting to note that near to the Ukrainian communities around Whaleysville on the Eastern Shore of Maryland is the town of Odessa, Delaware, which supposedly is called Odessa because of the similarity of the harbor in Delaware to that of Odessa, Ukraine.

OUR SLAVIC COUSINS AND RELIGIOUS DEVELOPMENTS

Maryland's role in the immigration movements is felt keenly in the area of religious development. Early Slavic religious leaders who served in Maryland include Fr. Demetrius Gallitzin, the third seminarian to be ordained a priest in the United States at St. Mary's Seminary in Baltimore and the first priest to have received all of his theological training in America. He was ordained in 1795 by Archbishop John Carroll, founder of the American Catholic hierarchy, who received his secondary education at Bohemia Manor, Maryland, at an academy situated on an immense tract of land granted to the Czech map maker, Augustine Hermann.

Fr. Demetrius Gallitzin, a Russian prince, whose name suggests accretions from Galicia, served several communities in Maryland and later became the "Apostle of the Alleghenies." It was he who expanded Catholicism into Cambria, Clearfield, and other counties in Pennsylvania. Near the town of Gallitzin, Pennsylvania, is the town of

Carrolltown, named after Archbishop John Carroll. In this area Ukrainians are very numerous with churches and other organizations being located in Barnesboro, Altoona, Nanty-Glo, Johnstown, et al. The colleague-biographer of Fr. Gallitzin, Fr. Peter Lemke, stated that Fr. Gallitzin may have been a descendant of the Lithuanian King Gediminas (1316-41) who proudly called himself "King of Lithuania and Many Ruthenians." The use of the word "Ruthenians" is most interesting as it includes Ukrainians and Byelorussians whose identities during the reign of Gediminas were clearly not "Muscovite," or of the people near Muscovy (present-day Moscow). The grave of Fr. Gallitzin is in Loretto, Pennsylvania, on the campus of St. Francis College.

Blessed John Nepomucene Neumann, born in 1811 in Prachatice, Bohemia, now Czecho-Slovakia, came to the United States in 1835. He helped in the spread of Catholicism to western Maryland, serving in the mining communities of Lonaconing, Westernport, and Cumberland in the early 1840's, prior to his becoming the fourth Bishop of Philadelphia in 1852 in Consecration services held at St. Alphonsus' Church, Baltimore, on March 28. Blessed John Nepomucene Neumann, who will be canonized a saint in the Catholic church on June 19, 1977, dedicated himself to the care of immigrants. He spoke at least eight languages. He was the first Bishop in the United States to establish a church for the special and exclusive use of Italian Catholics.[14]

The first cleric to become a member of the Redemptorist Order in America, Blessed John Neumann professed his vows in St. James' Church, Baltimore, in 1842 to the Very Reverend Alexander Czvitkovicz. Though the surname of Rev. Czvitkovicz is Slavic in nature, the Redemptorist scholar, Rev. John F. Byrne, refers to Rev. Czvitkovicz as a Hungarian who on March 11, 1841, arrived at Baltimore as Superior of the American mission.[15] It seems to the present writer that the name Czvitkovicz might well indicate one of the Slavic nationalities of Austria-Hungary and might not be Hungarian *per se*.

Saint John Nepomucene Neumann (left) was an ardent missionary from Bohemia who in 1843 offered services in the Old Stone House in Lonaconing, Md.

U.E.A.M. Collection

When as Bishop of Philadelphia, Blessed John Nepomucene Neumann experienced problems of competition among the nationality parishes of his diocese, he is quoted as having stated, "Thank God I'm not a German; I'm a Bohemian."[16] That his mother, Agnes Lebis Neumann, was a Czech is a fact and that he was fluent in Slavic languages is also established by his biographers.

In the development of St. Wenceslaus Bohemian Church in Baltimore the nephew of Blessed Neumann, Father John N. Berger, was of great service in the 1870's. Numerous Slavic priests assisted in this parish which also served Poles, Slovaks, and Lithuanians. The brother of Blessed Neumann, Wenceslaus, was a lay Redemptorist who died in New Orleans in 1896, while his sister in Bohemia, Sister Mary Caroline, was a Sister of Charity of St. Charles Borromeo.

The very first Redemptorist Seminary in America was established in Cumberland, Maryland, operating from 1851 to 1866, and later serving as the novitiate. Referred to at times as a "German" Order, the Redemptorists of Maryland have had many Slavic religious laboring in their communities. Numerous Ukrainian priests are Redemptorists in the United States, Canada, and Europe and several have served Ukrainian parishes in Chesapeake City and Baltimore.

Similarly, Slavic religious have been numerous in Maryland in the Jesuit, Franciscan, Benedictine, and Basilian Orders, among others, as well as in the various orders of sisters. The case is the same among Orthodox groups.

INTERACTION OF UKRAINIANS WITH BLACKS AND INDIANS

According to an article that appeared in the *Baltimore Afro-American* on February 11, 1976,

> John Abramovitch Hannibal, the son of Abraham Hannibal, a man who was brought straight from Africa as a boy and adopted by Peter the Great, Tzar of Russia, was appointed by Empress Catherine the Great of Russia to build a fortress in the Ukraine province of the country in 1778.[17]

The article continues that the fortress built by Hannibal helped in the development of Kherson, Ukraine, today a city of great importance to Soviet commerce and industry. Another account maintains that the fort was supervised in construction by Potemkin, the favourite of Catherine the Great, in 1778.

In any event Kherson, which had been a center for Greeks starting in the 5th century B.C., has left its influence in the naming of grains of America, as have other Ukrainian places:

> "Kubanka," "Crimean," and "Kharkov" are well known kinds of Ukrainian wheat, used now on American plains. Kherson oats,

some Ukrainian kinds of rye, buckwheat, alfalfa, sunflowers and millet are extensively planted by American farmers.[18]

An admirable case of comraderie and concern for freedom for oppressed peoples began on December 30, 1859, when the great Black American Shakesperian actor, Ira Aldridge (ca. 1807–1867), met the Ukrainian poet-artist, Taras Shevchenko (1814–1861), in the salon of Count and Countess Fjodor Tolstoy in St. Petersburg. The rapport that ensued in the meeting of the two humanitarians is well-described by Prof. Roman Smal-Stocki:

> For Shevchenko, who was well acquainted by Russian translations with the works of Shakespeare, Byron, Dickens, and Scott, Aldridge became the phonetical herald of the Anglo-American living sounds — both words and language — and a living part of America where Negroes had a fate similar to that of the Ukrainian peasants in Russia.[19]

Additional material about the friendship between Aldridge and Shevchenko appears in the writings of Marie Trommer-Trembicka and Herbert Marshall and Mildred Stock. Marie Trommer-Trembicka relates:

> They began to meet regularly. Shevchenko used to come in early. He was engaged in drawing a portrait of Aldridge, and while waiting would sharpen his pencils and arrange his lighting effects. Aldridge was always late. He would rush in, take off his cloak, and inquire: "Is the artist here?" Shevchenko, anxious to see his model, used to reprimand him for being late. Feeling guilty, Aldridge would assume the required pose with no comment. He could not keep his pose very long though.
>
> Aldridge would begin to fidget and grimace and Shevchenko would swear good-naturedly in the Ukrainian language, "Oh, you child of the devil!"
>
> Aldridge, seeing his friend's displeasure, would jump up and begin to chant Negro slave songs, to dance Negro dances, to present scenes from his beloved Shakespeare. Shevchenko would leave his drawing board and join in the chanting. Then both would dance. Suddenly they would kiss and cry. Long quiet conversations would take place between them. They used to speak of the similarities of their fate.
>
> Aldridge spoke about the Negro slavery and Shevchenko about the peasants in Russia. They spoke of the large sums of money Aldridge was sending to America to alleviate the suffering of his brethren, and Shevchenko told of doing his bit by giving to the Ukrainian serfs as much as he could spare from his small earnings as a poet.

IRA ALDRIDGE. This portrait was drawn by the Ukrainian poet, **Taras** *Shevchenko, with black and white pencils.*

TARAS SHEVCHENKO did this self-portrait (pencil) in 1845.

... At other times they would be joined by the artist Mikeshin. Aldridge, enchanted by Russian and especially Ukrainian melodies, used to participate in the singing. Later, he would burst into singing poetical English romances still unknown in Eastern Europe.

... On February 28, 1861, the two friends parted forever. For Shevchenko died on that day, his health having been undermined by lifelong privations. He was buried in Ukraine on a hill above the Dnieper River.

... In 1861 ... The itinerary of Ira Aldridge took him to Ukraine, to the country that Shevchenko had cried and sang about. And, Aldridge wept over the grave of his friend, the grave which towered on the hill above the Dnieper.

Ira Aldridge lived six years longer than Shevchenko. He died while on his second Russian tour of 1867.[20]

Aldridge was given a state funeral and was buried in Lodz, Poland, near Warsaw. He had played in many Ukrainian cities — Kiev, Odessa, Zhitomir, Kharkov, Simferopol, Stavropol, Dykanka, et al. — and had received enthusiastic receptions at his performances. In Zhitomir the tragedy *The Merchant of Venice* was repeated three times. *Othello* was given twice. One newspaper account in Zhitomir told of a procession of Jews headed by the Rabbi visiting the theatre to thank Aldridge for his interpretation of Shylock. Shakespeare's Jew had become a human being in Aldridge's productions.[21]

The grandson of a Senegal tribal chieftan who had been slain by his tribesmen because he had ruled that prisoners of war should not be sold into slavery, Ira Aldridge, born in Bel Air, Maryland, was not accepted by the theatrical profession in America, so his was the fate of having to play on distant strands. His comradeship with Shevchenko ranks as a companion story: two kindred souls, two slaves from distant countries, who managed to escape into the cultural realms in order to dream of what might have been. Perhaps Shevchenko mused of such thoughts when he wrote

Wretched is the fettered captive
Dying, and a slave
But more wretched he that, living
Sleeps, as in a grave,

Till he falls asleep forever
Leaving not a sign
That there faded into darkness
Something once divine.

For a number of years now the Ira Aldridge Players have represented dramatic endeavors at Morgan State University in Baltimore. Though Ira Aldridge rests in Lodz, Poland, his spirit permeates the hearts of freedom-loving Blacks in Maryland, even as the fervor of Shevchenko inspires his Ukrainian kinsmen in Maryland. Ukrainian groups in Maryland regularly commemorate the birth of Shevchenko and Ukrainians in America have commemorated Shevchenko with an impressive monument in Washington, D.C. Black bands participated in the dedication ceremonies.

Contrary to the present policy in the Soviet Union racial antagonism against Africans was unknown in the Russian Empire. Hannibal, the Ethiopian slave mentioned above in the article in the *Baltimore Afro-American*, married a woman of the Russian aristocracy and since that time a small amount of African ancestry exists in numerous Russian aristocratic families who are proud of the matter. The national poet of the Muscovites, Alexander Pushkin, was the great-grandson of Hannibal.

In an article in the book, *Race — Individual and Collective Behavior*, Walter Kolarz, using the word 'Russian' freely as though it includes Byelorussians and Ukrainians, maintains that

> Absence of racial pride and prejudice is thus for Russia not a revolutionary principle, but is both the natural prerequisite of the growth of the Russian Empire and the natural outcome of centuries of racial intermixture. A conservative Russian nobleman would have been as proud of being a descendent of Genghis Khan as of the most highly-born Slavonic ancestry. The Soviet regime may have transformed antiracialism into a dogmatic principle, it may have formulated this principle legally and politically, but Russian antiracialism is no Bolshevik creation, it is a component part of Russian history.[22]

Ukrainians have shown consistent interest in broadening the base of ethnic studies in the state of

"When shall we get ourselves a Washington
To promulgate his new and righteous law?
But someday we shall surely find the man!"

TARAS SHEVCHENKO—1848

„Коли діждемось Вашінгтона
З новим і праведним законом?
А діждемось таки колись!"

Reproduction of a postal card commemorating the unveiling of the Taras Shevchenko Monument in Washington, D.C., on June 27, 1964. Location: 22nd and P Streets, N.W.

Shevchenko Memorial Committee

> DEDICATED
> TO THE LIBERATION,
> FREEDOM AND INDEPENDENCE
> OF ALL CAPTIVE NATIONS
>
> THIS MONUMENT OF TARAS SHEVCHENKO, 19TH CENTURY UKRAINIAN POET AND FIGHTER FOR THE INDEPENDENCE OF UKRAINE AND THE FREEDOM OF ALL MANKIND, WHO UNDER FOREIGN RUSSIAN IMPERIALIST TYRANNY AND COLONIAL RULE APPEALED FOR "THE NEW AND RIGHTEOUS LAW OF WASHINGTON," WAS UNVEILED ON JUNE 27, 1964. THIS HISTORIC EVENT COMMEMORATED THE 150TH ANNIVERSARY OF SHEVCHENKO'S BIRTH. THE MEMORIAL WAS AUTHORIZED BY THE 86TH CONGRESS OF THE UNITED STATES OF AMERICA ON AUGUST 31, 1960, AND SIGNED INTO PUBLIC LAW 86-749 BY DWIGHT D. EISENHOWER, THE 34TH PRESIDENT OF THE UNITED STATES OF AMERICA ON SEPTEMBER 13, 1960. THE STATUE WAS ERECTED BY AMERICANS OF UKRAINIAN ANCESTRY AND FRIENDS.

The love of freedom shared by both Taras Shevchenko and Ira Aldridge radiates from the inscription on the Shevchenko Monument in Washington, D.C.

Shevchenko Memorial Committee

Maryland. On February 7, 1974, a Black educator, Garland A. Brown of the School of Urban Affairs of the Community College of Baltimore, presented an address at the Ukrainian Youth Center. Sponsored by the Ukrainian Education Association of Maryland, the lecture, "Politics: What Ethnics Need to *Do*," was attended by other East European groups as well as the general public. Mr. Brown identified some similarities in problems faced by both Ukrainians and Blacks in America and closed his address with a strong exhortation that ethnics need to key in on matters of economics, that culture, art, music, and freedom are corollaries of economic successes.

In subsequent discussions Mr. Brown maintained that Blacks and ethnics are frequently matched against each other by the power elite or prime movers in American society, with the result that Blacks and Ukrainians become

Garland A. Brown

debilitated at times because of animosities toward each other that were caused by Machiavellian moves by those who have historically wielded a disproportionate share of influence in America.

Referring to the American public schools, Blacks, Ukrainians, et al., Mr. Brown cited the following contention of Prof. Mildred Dickeman:

> American schools are racist by design. Their racism is part of a larger philosophy, an ethnocentric dedication to the remodelling of citizens to conform to a single homogenous acceptable model. That dedication, that definition of the function of schools, was formed in the period from 1830 to 1880, during which a modern, industrial class-stratified society was emerging, in which the ethnic diversity of this country was considerably increased by the immigration of large numbers of Europeans who formed a new mass of urban poor ... It was the influx of a large laboring class of diverse languages, religions and values into the growing urban centers which created a problem for the emerging White power structure ... If that elite does not provide enough members to replace itself, the upper castes and classes must be drawn from the lower ranks. The school's function was, then, to select those few, as needed, who possessed adequate loyalty and sufficient conformity in attitudes, values, behavior, and appearance, to be adopted into the expanding middle class.[23]

Ukrainian groups have endeavored to provide programs and educational materials for Blacks in Maryland when requested. At a Ukrainian Festival in Hopkins Plaza in Baltimore in 1973 a request came from a Black elementary school teacher to have Ukrainian participation in an Ethnic Fair at Westside Elementary

In top photo, left to right, Hattie Seward, Bernardine H. Johnson, and Luba Rad prepare a program at Westside Elementary School and the students later (bottom photo) learn about the Ukrainian language.
Westside Elementary School

School (No. 24), Fulton Street, of Baltimore City Schools. In a short while Mrs. Luba Rad and Mrs. Pauline Schneider organized a delegation from St. Michael's Ukrainian Catholic Church that participated in the school's ethnic festival. The more than generous gratitude of the students was shown when a contribution of $15.00 was received from the teacher of the sponsoring class, Bernardine H. Johnson. In her letter to the Ukrainian Education Association, Mrs. Johnson spoke of the "heartfelt thanks" expressed by her students and how the students "wanted to show their sincere appreciation" for the kindness shown by the Ukrainians when they travelled by bus to the school on Fulton Street to share their songs, costumes, food, etc., with the Black students. The writer of this article is pressed to find finer examples of spontaneity in ethnic relations — a request by a Black teacher, a visitation by a Ukrainian group, and, most importantly, the sincere expression of thanks by a group of Black youngsters who gave what they could even though nothing was asked, monetarily.

Perhaps the visitation of the Ukrainians served to reinforce the idea that a homogenous elite is not needed to establish policies for America's public schools. Agencies whose functions are the indoctrination and control of all by the reliable elite hardly find time, or have the desire, to help "poor" groups to exchange viewpoints. Rather, "Third Forces" such as Ukrainians, who have possibly no entries in the *Baltimore Social Register*, might rather be pitted against Blacks by the power elite, or *vice versa*.

Billy Tayac, Tribal Leader of the Piscataway Indians of Maryland, is quoted, "Indians always had good relations with the Slavic peoples . . . there were no problems with them in Maryland."[24] Again, this Piscataway Tribal Leader, whose tribal hospitality dates back to at least 1639 in which year Andrew White, a Jesuit missionary, who was greeted ". . . in the palace of the king, whom they call Tayac, at Piscataway"[25] spoke of the empire-building craze of the English. In injuries developed Blacks and Indians suffered alike. It is entirely plausible to conjecture that Ukrainians, because of the many injustices inflicted upon them in having their lands expropriated, can at once communicate with both Blacks and Indians in a language undefiled by contrived pleasantries. Garland Brown of the Community College of Baltimore maintains that minorities in America are not at each other's throats by accident, rather they are pitted against one another in order that their energies become dissipated, leaving them debilitated and unable to attain common interests.

Matthew Josephson mentions the commonalities of Negroes and Slavic immigrants during an exploitive era in the American meat packing industry:

> ... Thereafter laborers hung the carcasses by wire around the legs to a moving trolley-line, cut, bled, dressed, and classified them. The operations of the laborers, chiefly Negroes and Slav immigrants, gathered in mighty armies, was thoroughly and shrewdly regimented and driven at top speed throughout the process. Finally every by-product, every species of animal raw material, was put to use so that tremendous economies were gained on every hand in a hundred different ways.[26]

In Maryland ideas similar to those reflected by Josephson appeared in an article by Mary Carter Smith, "Oppression Makes People Kindred," in the Baltimore *Afro-American* after several members of the Ukrainian Education Association of Maryland, Inc., had visited with Mary Carter Smith and Elizabeth Murphy Oliver of the *Afro-American* staff. The article reveals how the father of Joseph Marmash often told his children that he found Black people willing to give information and help when he did not know where to turn. Other peoples turned away from the distress of the immigrant Ukrainians.

"Having lived in coal-mining towns of Pennsylvania, West Virginia, and Kentucky," states Ms. Smith, "I can remember and my aunt, Mrs. Sally Coleman tells me, of the warm friendships between the coal miners from the Ukraine and the Black coal miners from Alabama. People who have suffered recognize each other. Suffering is a bond that unites people regardless of differences and ethnic backgrounds."[27]

Two Ukrainian brothers employed by the Baltimore City Board of Education, Wolodymyr C. Sushko and Jaroslaw G. Sushko, worked long hours "to transform old

FREEDOM SHRINE. Left to right, Glascoe Ryales, Wolodymyr Sushko, Jaroslaw Sushko, Elizabeth Murphy Oliver of Afro-American, Joseph Marmash, John Malko, and Stephen Basarab are shown on a visit to Orchard Street Church on January 28, 1977.

Baltimore Afro-American

Orchard Street Church into a building of beauty for the celebration for January 11, 1976, when a celebration was held marking the placing of the church on the National Register of Historic Places." Skilled in the artistry of flowers and plants, the Sushko brothers gave many hours of their own time to make the huge permanent wreath that decorates the entrance to the slave tunnel by the Orchard Street Church. At this same Orchard Street Church Harriet Tubman helped slaves escape to freedom via the "underground railroad," according to popular accounts.

To give time is charitable indeed; to provide money is equally, if not more, so. Evidence of Ukrainian concern for assisting American Indians can be found in the annals of the Ukrainian Self-Reliance Federal Credit Union, which has been operating at 239 S. Broadway Street, Baltimore, since 1956. Self-Reliance (Samopomich) has helped Indians with loans for about 10 years. Earl Brooks, an Indian realtor, who helped finance the neighboring American Indian Center has been involved with the Ukrainian firm on several occasions in obtaining loans for individuals or groups. Officers of Samopomich have found Indians to be diligent in matters of business.

The entire matter of Indians, the first Americans, borrowing from Ukrainians, who essentially are counted among the new immigration, is indeed a paradox. Perhaps a kind of "Indian essence" permeates the hearts of Ukrainians, who, as the Indians, have also walked as strangers in their own land.

NOTES TO CHAPTER FIVE

[1] Edward Hungerford, *The Story of the Baltimore and Ohio Railroad — 1827-1927* (2 vols.), New York, G. P. Putnam's Sons, 1928, p. 81 of Vol 1.

[2] *Ibid.*, p. 81.

[3] *Ibid.*, p. 81.

[4] Wasyl Halich, *Ukrainians in the United States*, Chicago, University of Chicago Press, 1937, p. 19.

[5] Katherine A. Harvey, *The Best-Dressed Miners — Life and Labor in the Maryland Coal Region, 1835-1910*, Ithaca, Cornell University Press, 1969, p. 145.

[6] *Ibid.*, p. 11.

[7] Frederick Gutheim, *The Potomac*, New York, Holt, Rinehart, and Winston, 1949, pp. 287-288.

[8] Ambrose A. Worrall and Olga N. Worrall, *The Gift of Healing*, New York, Harper and Row, 1965, p. 86.

[9] Petro Poleticka, *A Sketch of the Internal Condition of the United States of America and of Their Political Relations with Europe*, Baltimore, E. J. Coale, 1826, p. 72.

[10] "Austrians Allowed to Go; Suspected Steel Workers Released from House of Detention," *Baltimore Sun*, August 23, 1901.

[11]George F. Will, "We Wanted Immigrants... Once," *Baltimore Sun*, May 8, 1975.

[12]*The Baltimore Sun Almanac*, 1914, p. 201.

[13]Thomas A. Bailey, *America Faces Russia — Russian-American Relations from Early Times to Our Day*, Ithaca, Cornell University Press, 1950, p. 172.

[14]John F. Byrne, C.SS.R., *The Redemptorist Centenaries — 1732: Founding of The Congregation of the Most Holy Redeemer; 1832: Establishment in the United States*, Philadelphia, The Dolphin Press, 1932, p. 303.

[15]*Ibid.*, pp. 298–299.

[16]Tom Langan, *Harvester of Souls — John Neumann*, Huntington, Our Sunday Visitor, Inc., 1976, p. 114.

[17]"Black Citizens Were Founders of Many Major Cities," *Baltimore Afro-American*, February 11, 1976.

[18]Jaroslav J. Chyz, *The Ukrainian Immigrants in the United States*, Scranton, Ukrainian Workingmen's Association, 1939, p. 27.

[19]Roman Smal-Stocki, *Shevchenko Meets America*, Milwaukee, Slavic Institute of Marquette University, p. 20.

[20]Marie Trommer-Trembicka, "Ira Aldridge, American Negro, and Taras Shevchenko, Poet of Ukraine," *Svoboda Ukrainian Weekly*, April 18, 22, 29, 1961.

[21]Herbert Marshall and Mildred Stock, *Ira Aldridge — The Negro Tragedian*, New York, Macmillan Co., 1958, pp. 287–288.

[22]Walter Kolarz, "Soviet Russia," in Edgar T. Thompson and Everett C. Hughes (Eds.), *Race — Individual and Collective Behavior*, New York, The Free Press, 1958, pp. 96–98.

[23]Mildred Dickeman, "Teaching Cultural Pluralism," in James A. Banks (Ed.), *Teaching Ethnic Studies — Concepts and Strategies*, Washington, National Council for the Social Studies, 1973, pp. 5–6.

[24]Statement by Billy Tayac, Tribal Leader of Piscataway Indians, at program dealing with Ethnic Youth in Maryland at Maryland Science Center on November 17, 1976. After the program his statements were expanded in conversing with Wolodymyr C. Sushko, Peter J. Critikos, a Greek-American historian, and Paul Fenchak.

[25]Rev. William P. Treacy, *Old Catholic Maryland and Its Early Jesuit Missionaries*, Swedesboro, N.J., (Publisher Unknown), 1889, pp. 35, 167.

[26]Matthew Josephson, *The Robber Barons — The Great American Capitalists, 1861–1901*, New York, Harcourt, Brace and World, Inc., 1934, p. 285.

[27]Mary Carter Smith, "Oppression Makes People Kindred," *Baltimore Afro-American*, 1977. (Exact publication date unknown when this chapter went to press.)

Chapter Six
Ukrainians and Jews In Europe and in Maryland
Paul Fenchak

In discussing the backgrounds of the Jews of Maryland or of other states exchanges such as the following have occurred and facets mentioned deserve close scrutiny for understanding relationships between Ukrainians and Jews:

"But I thought I was a Russian Jew..." states a bright scholar of the Minority Experience unit at Pikesville High School, which is over 85% Jewish in the composition of the student body.

"So might your undertaker," replies the student's instructor.

"How does my undertaker-to-be enter the matter?"

"It's a long story but let's first examine the following article from the Baltimore *Evening Sun* of July 13, 1964:

> RUSSIANS LEAD STATE 'FOREIGN-STOCK'
>
> Maryland's largest single "foreign stock" population — immigrants from abroad and their children — is Russian.
>
> The 45, 887 Marylanders from Russia — and their children — outnumber by a slim margin the 45,048 Marylanders who hail from Italy...."

"Again, what does this article have to do with my undertaker?"

"If you don't search your roots you might believe such messages and spend the rest of your life thinking you are a Russian Jew and the undertaker might forward an obituary to *The Sun*, or *News-American,* or *Jewish Times* that reads

ADAM J. JANOFSKY died on January 1, 2037. The renowned artist was the son of Abraham and Ruth Janofsky, both of whose parents immigrated to the United States from Kiev, Russia (or Vilnius, Russia; or Minsk, Russia; or Riga, Russia; or Tallin, Russia) . . . ."

"I'm confused," says Adam.

"Don't feel badly . . . so are the morticians and many journalists. For you there is hope. The morticians may go to their graves never knowing the difference and some journalists may keep writing in such confusing ways, as some historians and clergymen may, also."

"Please explain."

"A knowledgeable person would say that Kiev is in Ukraine, Vilnius in Lithuania, Minsk in Byelorussia, Riga in Latvia, and Tallin in Estonia. To say otherwise is as wrong as to say Edinburg is in England and London is in Scotland when telling about the United Kingdom."

"Do journalists misplace cities?"

"If an American president (Gerald Ford) can arbitrarily free Poland and other East European nations, journalists can relocate cities and rivers with ease. Examine this statement from the *New York Times* of July 11, 1954: Danube Flood Damages Linz and Prague."

"So what's wrong."

"The Danube River is at least 125 miles from Prague."

"Ethnicity can be complicated."

"Not when candid writers such as Earl Arnett help us."

"Earl who?"

"Arnett . . . He's a feature writer for the *Sunpapers*." Examine one of his studied articles:

THE SUN
BALTIMORE, FRIDAY, FEBRUARY 16, 1973

Anglo-Saxon arrogance

The press is always goofing on the ethnics

By EARL ARNETT

The Scene: A local restaurant.

The Players: Andrij W. Chornodolsky of the Baltimore branch of the Ukranian Congress Committee; Professor Hlib S. Hayuk of Towson State College and member of the Ukranian Education Association of Maryland; Paul Fenchak, teacher at Pikesville High School and secondary school coordinator for the Association for the Study of Nationalities, Inc.; John G. Shmorhun, Ukrainian-American and member of the Republican State Nationalities Council of Maryland; the Rev. Casimir Pugevicius, priest at St. Vincent's Catholic Church and member of the Baltimore Lithuanian community; Kes Chesonis of the Lithuanian-American community in Baltimore; Dr. Joseph Pauco, national secretary of the Slovak League of America; and Walter Melianovich of the Byelorussian-American Association.

The Situation: All eight men have agreed, at the instigation of Mr. Fenchak, to meet with a reporter to talk about questions of ethnic consciousness he raised in a recent newspaper article. Some seemed particularly upset that City Councilwoman Barbara Mikulski (D., 1st) had been quoted as a spokeswoman for the diverse ethnic groups that make up a vital, but frequently hidden contribution to this country's cultural heritage.

Pugevicius: The media frequently make mistakes in identifying ethnic groups; there are so many. There's a basic American ignorance about Eastern European history.

Melianovich: We saw that in the reporting on the Olympics in Munich. The American reporters labeled everyone on the Soviet team "Russian," even though some team members insisted they were not. They were Ukranian or Beylorussian or another nationality among the many now included in the Soviet Union. But the American press doesn't make these distinctions. When they label everything "Russian," they contribute to the Soviet myth of unity. The fault is really the educational system of the United States, which teaches only one part of the history, that of imperial Russia. Unless Americans start dying somewhere, they don't really care about other parts of the world.

Shmorhum: Americans look at the Soviet Union as they do the United States, as divided into states like Pennsylvania and Ohio. But that's not true as far as many European countries are concerned. There are states with distinctive cultures which have been struggling for a long time to achieve independence.

Hayuk: This attitude is a carry-over from the British imperial empire, which was prejudiced against nationalisms. But there are various forms of nationalism. There's destructive nationalism, the Russian kind; the Soviet Union is the only nonliquidating empire, but they work hard to keep the contrary myth alive. And there's also a constructive, liberating nationalism.

Reporter: I've often wondered if the Anglo-Saxon cultural tradition doesn't include a built-in arrogance against other groups, a prejudice that every minority group in this country has had to endure and resist.

Pugevicius: I don't think you can blame the Anglo-Saxon culture particularly. This is a phenomenon associated with any predominant majority. If another group had been in the majority in this country, it would have discriminated against the minorities. It's a human failing, what we call original sin.

Fenchak: What we're talking about, ethnic activity or contribution, ethnic presence is not new. There may be a new awareness of ethnic groups. We were just omitted from the standardized textbooks.

Pugevicius: One of the problems here is that we don't talk among each other. I have discovered that the more I appreciate my own ethnicity, my own Lithuanian heritage, the more I appreciate somebody else's.

Shmorhun: That's true, and as a result, we have probably a deeper, better appreciation for the colored man's struggle than most people.

Chornodolsky: The Ukrainians, Slocaks and Poles were the niggers of Pennsylvania. The Irish of Cumberland, Md., were completely ghettoized.

Pauco: I was born and raised in Slovakia; 900,000 people, or about a third of the county, moved to the United States before World War I. What did we give to this country? (He named Slovak personalities who achieved prominent positions.) We feel it's not correct if someone calls us Czechs. Czechs are not Slovaks, and Slovaks are not Czechs. The United states was created by many nationalities; more than 40 million people in the country are of ethnic origin. Identify us by our right names. We are what we are.

Shmorhun: The problem of ethnicity is a greater problem; it's broader than Eastern Europe. Everyone belongs to an ethnic group, not just people with names that are difficult to pronounce.

What is necessary, they agreed, is for all of us to understand and appreciate this diversity, to call people by their right names and to be knowledgeable of past histories and present cultures. Knowledge of your own cultural identity leads to appreciation and understanding of the next man's. And that leads to the kind of practical brotherhood we all need.

Some journalists are better analysts than others."
"Even about my ethnicity?"
"Certainly. Look at several points covered in an article in *The Sun* of February 13, 1967, "Russian Community Loyal to Churches." Author Harold D. Piper quotes Anthony K. Uchuck:

"There are probably not more than five or six families of true Russians in Baltimore," says one man who is a "true Russian," born in the city of Kazan, where Ivan the Terrible defeated the Tartars.

Notice how different this concept is from the one expressed in the article entitled "Russians Lead State 'Foreign Stock'."

The following paragraph also from the article by Harold D. Piper shows some of the strange arithmetic used by census officials and reporters in befuddling the nationalities of some Marylanders:

> Most of Baltimore's Russians are in fact from the smaller Russian nations — Ukrainian, Galician, Byelorussian or like Mr. Lisowsky's mother, Carpatho-Russian. They consider themselves Russian by heritage, but they speak slightly varying dialects, and their lands have twisted histories of alternating domination, independence and domination by some other country.

This statement is a masterpiece of confusion, both about languages and political control. Good scholars know that the development of Cyrillic characters in Slavic languages was a south-to-north movement, with development coming first in Bulgaria, later in Ukraine, and lastly in *Imperium Muscoviticum*, which is how western cartographers labelled Russia proper or Muscovy. Concerning Carpatho-Russians (Rusyns), how could this have been a Russian area when Muscovite control did not exist there at any time in history until 1944?

Of course there have been other discerning writers locally in addition to Earl Arnett. In an article that appeared in the *Baltimore Sun* on December 4, 1935, R. P. Harris in "All Others" stated, "The official census for Baltimore is a curious intensely interesting document, both for what it reveals and for what it leaves out. It lists some 14,000 non-existent Russians and contains vague hints of a polygenous percentage which it does not bother to define... Officially there are 1,637 Hungarians in Baltimore, 1,441 Rumanians, and no Ukrainians, no Serbs." Some of these identity problems that confused matters for Ukrainians also complicated issues regarding Jews from Ukraine. As mentioned, it's a long story . . ."

"Mr. Fenchak, your course sounds to be some undertaking."

"Oh well, Adam, we'll progress together. I hope we never reach the condition of being both confused and destroyed as related in the famous short story, "By the Waters of Babylon." "

UKRAINIANS AND JEWS IN EUROPE

As Ukrainians were frequently not masters in their land it is simply naive to think that they were policy formulators throughout centuries of rule by various captors. As political minorities Ukrainians and Jews in Ukrainian lands frequently danced to similar tunes called by their masters.

Without delving into the activities of the Khazars, the largest group that ever converted to Judaism, and the Karaites on Ukrainian ethnographic territory and without trying to recount the earliest settlements in Ukraine by Sephardic or Ashkenazic or whatever Jews, the writer would refer to analysis of the most accomplished scholar of East European Jewry, Prof. Bernard D. Weinryb of Dropsie College and Harvard University:

> Our analysis has shown that most of the theories about the origin of east-European Jewry succumb to searching criticism in the absence of factual information. . . . Most of the theories and hypotheses concerning the beginnings of east-European Jewry are no more than fiction.[1]

In accepting the 1974 Bernard H. Marks Award for Jewish History presented by the Jewish Book Council for his book *The Jews of Poland — A Social and Economic History of the Jewish Community in Poland from 1100-1800*, Weinryb stated that facts and events in history have to be interpreted through patterns, general notions, categories, and classifications. In examining literature dealing with Ukrainians and Jews in the European setting, both groups seem to fall under a caution issued by Weinryb:

> . . . Minorities and small nations, whose history is so badly neglected in general historical works have also the tendency, probably to a greater degree than larger nations, to hanker for status, to emphasize or overemphasize their importance in the

BERNARD D. WEINRYB, winner of the 1974 Bernard H. Marks Award for Jewish History, delineates carefully among Ukrainians, Poles, Byelorussians, Russians, Lithuanians, et al., in his analyses.

world. In historiography this manifests itself by attempts to overstate the link in the group's past with worldwide or global historical events (great wars, large-scale developments, trade, science, the arts, literature, communications, etc.) by stressing "participation," and inflating minor facts out of proportion to their true value and their historical perspective.[2]

Evidences of such overplay are numerous in both Slavic and Jewish sources, with one topic being the extent of brutality that Bohdan Khmelnitsky (Khmelnytsky, Chmielnicki, et al.) and his Kozaks inflicted upon the Jews of Ukraine during the Kozak rebellion against Poland in 1648. At this time *ca.* 500,000 Jews were killed by Khmelnitsky's forces according to older books by Jewish authors, with many of these unstudied analyses having been based upon accounts presented in Nathan Hanover's *Abyss of Despair. Encyclopedia Judaica* describes Hanover's work as unresearched and Prof. Bernard Weinryb in an address delivered to the national convention of the American Association for the Advancement of Slavic Studies on April 20, 1973, is quoted that Kozaks "may have killed 2,000 or 3,000 Jews."[3] An immediate question in examining the *ca.* 500,000 figure is, Were there 500,000 Jews in Ukrainian lands in the mid-1600's?

In discussing the Khmelnitsky era, Weinryb avers:

The chronicles and stories dealing with the events of those years in which any sort of interpretation of the historical facts is given ... are written from a pro-Polish viewpoint. When they report the miserable lot of the Ukrainian peasants, whose exploitation by the nobles contributed to the uprising, they do not seem to be condemning the Polish nobility and the state. They tend to put almost all the blame on the Ukrainians.[4]

Of importance to understanding subsequent Ukrainian-Jewish relations under tsarist rule (when a popular tsarist slogan was "Kill the Jews and save Russia") is that the Pale of Settlement instituted by Catherine II in 1791 proscribed Jews from living in Russia proper. Jews were restricted to living in a triangular area extending from Lithuania on the Baltic southward and eastward to Ukraine and the Black Sea and from there westward to Poland. According to the *McGraw-Hill Encyclopedia of Russia and the Soviet Union,*

> It was the desire of all the rulers of Russia to convert the Jews from their religion to Christianity and from the "parasitic" occupation of commerce to "useful" toil. This endeavor pursued fitfully and with clumsy ruthlessness bore no fruit; and the recalcitrant people was kept in appropriate subjection.[5]

Also kept in subjection were the Ukrainians who were frequently pitted against Jews by masters of both groups. The renowned Ukrainian poet, Taras Shevchenko, in 1858 signed a statement, at great risk, in which he defended the rights of Jews in the Russian Empire. He was joined in this protest by Marko Vovchok, Pantelemion Kulish, and Mykola Kostamarov.[6]

Once Ukraine became independent in the World War I era, the treatment of Jews by Ukrainians is weighed by Frederick M. Schweitzer in *A History of the Jews — Since the First Century A.D.*:

> The Lvov-Kerensky government that came into power in March, 1917, took at last the momentous step of Emancipation (of Jews), as did some of the newly established states, particularly Ukraine, where Jews were granted full equality.[7]

The equality saw Dr. Arnold M. Margolin, whose daughter Lubov A. Margolena Hansen now resides in Washington, D.C., serve first as a member of the Supreme

אוניווערסאל

פֿון דער אוקראאינער צענטראלער ראדע.

אוקראאינער פאלק און אלע פעלקער פון אוקראאינע!
א ביטערע-שווערע צייט לעבט איבער די הסלענדער רעפובליק. אין צפון זיין די חיפוס-שטעט קעט
שאר א בלוטינער ברודער-קאמף. קיין צענטראלע מאכט איז ניטא און איבער דער גאנצער מלוכה האקסט
אנארכיע און צעהרודינג.
אונזער קאנט איז אויך אין געפאר. אהן א מאכט א שטארקער, איינהייטליכער, פון א פאלקס-מאכט
וועט אויך אוקראאינע געווארן וועין אין אפגרונט פון בלוטיגן ברודער קריג און פון פולן אונטער-
גאנג.
פאלק פון אוקראאינע, דו האסט אונז צוזאמען מיט אלע ברידערליכע פעלקער פון אוקראאינע אויפ-
געשטעלט אפגעזונדערטן די רעכט פאר דיינעם פעלקים ארבעטן, געוואהרן דורך קאמף, וו זאל ארדענונג און גרעכ-
טיגן לעבן אויף אונזער ערד. און מיר, די אוקראאינער צענטראלע ראדע, ערפולענדיג דיין
ווילען, לשם דער ארדנונג אין אונזער קאנט, לשם דער רעטונג פון גאנץ רוסלאנד, ערקלערן:
פון היינט אן וועט אוקראאינע זיין אן אוקראאינער פאלקס-רעפובליק.

On November 20, 1917, the Ukrainian Central Rada issued its Third
Universal by which the Ukrainian National Republic was proclaimed.
This facsimile is part of the Universal in Hebrew.
           Ukrainian Congress Committee of America

The Jewish people of Ukraine received recognition on this 1917 currency
issue for 100 karbovantsiv, along with Poles and Russians. Hebraic
characters are under the number 100.

Court of the Ukrainian People's Republic, and later as Deputy Minister of Foreign Affairs of the Republic. In 1926 Margolin defended the honor of Semeon Petliura, Ukrainian national leader, who had been labelled as anti-Jewish by Bolshevist supporters. In 1919 an interesting booklet appeared in Washington, D.C., entitled *The Jewish Pogroms in Ukraine*. As one of the contributors, along with Israel Zangwill author of the play, "The Melting Pot," among others, Margolin stated:

> At the time of the proclamation of Ukrainian independence, the Jews were divided into two camps. On the one side were the Jewish assimilators, who had been brought up in an All-Russian political atmosphere, and who adopted a negative attitude towards the formation of the Ukrainian State. This party, which numerically was not important, was supported by a number of Jewish refugees from old Russia. On the other side were ranged the National Jews, the Zionists, Itoists, and Jewish Socialist parties, who took up a favourable attitude. Those Jews who had national aspirations of their own could not but view with favour similar strivings on the part of a people which had hitherto lived in a position of tutelage.[8]

Dr. Solomon I. Goldeman, one of the leaders of the Jewish Party "Poalei Zion" who worked in Ukraine during the whole period of the Ukrainian Peoples' Republic and cooperated with authorities of the Republic, stated, "If not for the catastrophic outcome of the Ukrainian National Revolution, the constructive forces within the Ukrainian community would have mastered the *pogromist* anarchy, and the Jewish national autonomy would have remained as a constituent part of the democratic Ukrainian Republic."[9] Money printed by the Ukrainian Republic included the use of the Yiddish language along with Ukrainian and Polish.

Dr. Solomon I. Goldeman analyzed the subject of Jewish equality in Ukraine in a book entitled *Jewish National Autonomy in Ukraine — 1917-1920*. Another book on the subject of Ukrainian-Jewish relations, published by the Ukrainian Congress Committee of America, Inc., is *Ukrainians and Jews — A Symposium*. This publication of 1966 includes articles, testimonies, letters and official documents dealing with interrelations of Ukrainians and Jews in the past and present. Among the Jewish contributors are Leo Heiman, Dr. Michael Broida, Dr. Judd

Teller and Eugene Sanjour. In the opening article Dr. Matthew Stachiw cites at length from S. M. Dubnow's two-volume *History of the Jews in Russia and Poland.*

THE "RUSSIANS" ARE COMING TO MARYLAND BUT WHERE DID THEY COME FROM?

It is generally accepted that most of the pre-Civil War Jewish immigrants to Maryland came from German areas and that by the 1880's they were fairly well established in Maryland. Jewish immigration from Germany to Maryland was not very numerous after the 1860's.

East European Jews were often called "Russian" Jews as indicated in a chapter entitled "The 'Russians' Are Coming" in Isaac M. Fein's detailed study, *The Making of An American Jewish Community — The History of Baltimore Jewry from 1773 to 1920.* When the East European Jews began to arrive in the post-Civil War period a kind of coolness emanated from the Germans toward the East Europeans who "drew attention to themselves by being so uncouth, so untutored, so ragged, so outlandish in their manners and mannerisms in the eyes of the German Jews."[10] Among these Jews were the Litvaks (from Byelorussia and Lithuania) and the Galitzianers (from Ukraine and southern Poland).

By 1865 there were enough Polish Jews in Baltimore to form a congregation of their own, the Key Street Congregation, where the people who spoke Yiddish wanted to be among their own people, choosing not to join a German congregation. Earlier the Polish Bikur Cholim had been founded and in 1873 the synagogue, B'Nai Israel, was started for Litvaks. The synagogue was known as *Russishe Shul*, Russian synagogue. East European impact on Judaism in Maryland is noted by the fact that by 1899 there were twenty East European synagogues in the city of Baltimore.[11] According to figures cited by Fein, epidemics and famine in Poland and Galicia brought 74,903 Jewish immigrants from these countries to the United States in the 1860's and 1870's. By 1875 there were enough immigrants alone from Bialystok (in Byelorussia) to establish a synagogue of their own, the Ohel Yakov Bialystoker *Shul*.[12]

A. D. GLUSHAKOW: labor leader, author, and promoter of brotherhood in Maryland. He began his career as a reporter for newspapers in Ukraine.
Jerome F. Esterson

This bust of Lesyia Ukrainka, Ukrainian poetess, graces the shelves of Jack's Corned Beef and Delicatessen in Baltimore because the owner's wife was intrigued with the statue.
Roman Hankewycz

Of the East European Jews of Maryland who in present times are labelled by many as Russians — perhaps as a matter of facility in a land where no great number of people know much about Slavic nations and cultures — many Jews came from Ukrainian areas. Among the leading researchers about Jews of Maryland, Professor Isaac M. Fein was born in southwestern Ukraine, while A. D. Glushakow, whose latest book is *Maryland Bicentennial Jewish Book*, was born in Starodub, Ukraine. Jacob Edelman, long-time leader in Jewish activities and current chairman of the Maryland Human Relations Commission, came to the United States from Rivno (Rovno), Ukraine.

The list of Ukrainian Jews in Maryland is endless and would include names of Jews in many walks of life, such as, Lubov Keefer, professor of Russian and music at Johns Hopkins University; Israel Dorman, violinist and businessman from Kiev; the Fedders family from Zhitomir; and the Fradkin family of the Al Fradkin Furniture Company of Baltimore.

One of the finest students of Ukrainians in America has been Joseph L. Lichten, who contributed an outstanding chapter, "Ukrainian Americans," in what has been one of the best books ever compiled about ethnic groups here, *One America*. Another Jewish scholar, Vladimir Wertsman, recently completed *The Ukrainians in America — 1608-1975*. Wertsman's book mentions Ukrainian schools in Baltimore.

In the field of literature many Jewish writers developed their skills in Ukraine, among them Abraham Goldfaden, considered the father of the modern Yiddish theatre, and Boris Tomashevsky, star of the Yiddish stage.

There exist in American libraries countless books that are not definitive enough to adequately explain ethnic, linguistic, and cultural differences of Slavic peoples. The statistical tables of such books as *Beyond the Melting Pot* by Glazer and Moynihan include no data enumerating Jews from Byelorussia, Ukraine, Slovakia, Bulgaria, et al., so such books fall short by ignoring the realities of Jewish life among Slavic, Baltic, Romanian and other peoples.

Ukrainian Jews have strongly identified with the

cause of organized labor in Maryland. A. D. Glushakow was a prominent leader who in 1917 pioneered the movement of "Poale Zion" (Labor Zionist) for a First Jewish Labor Congress. He subsequently held offices in the Cloakmakers Union and the International Ladies Garment Workers Union. Ukrainians and Jews alike profited from the endeavors of A. D. Glushakow as the garment industries of East Baltimore employed both groups in large numbers. Edward K. Muller and Paul A. Groves use imprecise language about clothing workers in an article in *Maryland Historical Magazine*:

> Nationally, the contracting system is reported to have begun in the 1870's. The massive immigration of impoverished and unskilled Russian Jews after 1880 provided the cheap labor force, but large numbers of Bohemians, Austrians, Lithuanians, and later Italians also worked in and ran such workshops.[13]

A map in the aforementioned article adds to the complications as the key to the map indicates numerous

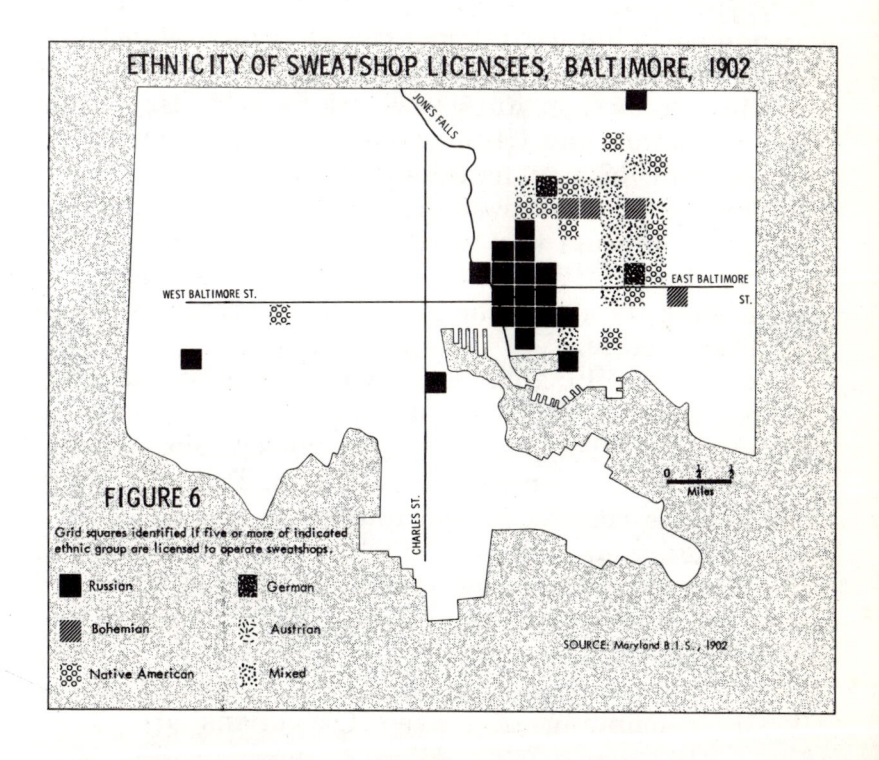

FIGURE 6

ETHNICITY OF SWEATSHOP LICENSEES, BALTIMORE, 1902

Grid squares identified if five or more of indicated ethnic group are licensed to operate sweatshops.

- Russian
- German
- Bohemian
- Austrian
- Native American
- Mixed

SOURCE: Maryland B.I.S., 1902

sweatshop licensees in Baltimore in 1902 to be Russians.[14] One can assume that Russians are meant to be Jews in this instance and that the terms are used interchangably. It seems most questionable that Russians as such were sweatshop licensees in the area of East Baltimore Street in 1902.

In ten years of teaching thousands of Jewish-American students at Pikesville, Md., High School, the writer of this article had many opportunities to glean data about the heritages of Jewish Marylanders. On an optional "Questionnaire for Minority Experience" completed by over 1,000 students, data about family origins overwhelmingly indicated very few cases of families that would be properly termed Russian Jews. Rather, it was most common to observe Ukrainian cities and towns to be the foremost places of family origins: Kiev, Odessa, Kharkov, Kherson, Peremyshl, Rivno, Sanok, Dubno, Zhitomir, Kamenets, et al.

At most one place-name out of a hundred indicated a city or town in Russian ethnographic territory, while Byelorussian places such as Minsk or Bialostok were many times more numerous than Russian locations. Likewise, Lithuanian, Estonian, and Latvian place names were more numerous than Russian, as were Romanian.

Some of the more revealing data gleaned from the questionnaires indicate that there would be a direct conflict between the identities of people living in places mentioned, e.g., Riga, Latvia, and the identities attributed to places, e.g., Riga, Russia.

A definite willingness existed on the part of students to sharpen their definitions and perceive themselves as Lithuanian, Polish, Ukrainian, or Byelorussian Jews — instead of using the misnomer, Russian. This willingness complements current Jewish interest in having liberties secured for their brethren in Eastern Europe, even as Ukrainians, Estonians, Lithuanians, Latvians, Byelorussians, and others have wanted clear identification as they vie for their freedoms.

In Maryland numerous Jewish names are so Ukrainian-sounding that even Ukrainians are fooled.

Several years ago when a member of the Frostburg State College varsity soccer team, Glen Kotelchuck, a Jewish-American alumnus of Pikesville High School, received a questionnaire to complete after he had been named to the Ukrainian All-America soccer team! His ancestors, though, had lived in Ukraine. Many Jewish families have undergone changes of surnames in Maryland, with names such as Kovalsky becoming Smith (a Slavic translation for Kowalsky) and Jablonowsky becoming Appleton.

COMMON INTERESTS OF UKRAINIANS AND JEWS

When Sylva Zalmanson, a Jewish refugee from the Soviet Union, lectured at Baltimore Hebrew College on November 18, 1974, over a dozen Ukrainians were present to hear her report about hardships experienced by Jews, Ukrainians, and other groups in the Soviet realm. Also in attendance were several Jewish families who had recently come to the United States from such Ukrainian cities as Zaporizhia, Odessa, and Kiev.

After the lecture the Jewish emigres and several Ukrainians joined in asking Mrs. Zalmanson questions pertaining to Ukraine. Her keen interest in the rights of Ukrainians was spontaneously indicated by her first remark, "How is Moroz?" — in referring to the plight of the Ukrainian historian who, being incarcerated, stood as a symbol to millions of Ukrainians.[15] This same type of spontaneity was evidenced earlier in Baltimore, too, when Simas Kudirka, the famed Lithuanian sailor who unsuccessfully sought refuge on an American ship, was speaking at the Lithuanian Hall. Having been in the same Soviet prison as Moroz, Kudirka sought to know the latest regarding his plight.

When the Baltimore Committee for Soviet Jewry was being organized at the Jewish Community Center in 1967, the writer of this article and his Slovak wife endorsed the following:

The Baltimore Conference on Soviet Jewry

Suite 1917 Maryland National Bank Building

Baltimore, Maryland 21202

A STATEMENT OF CONSCIENCE

In this 50th anniversary year of the Soviet Revolution, we appeal to Soviet leaders to act upon the promises of national self-determination and religious freedom for all groups, promulgated 50 years ago by Lenin in the Declaration of Rights to the Peoples of Russia and embodied in Soviet law and formal policy statements.

The continuing systematic strangulation of Jewish religious, cultural, and communal life in the Soviet Union should be halted. Maintenance of synagogues, training of Rabbis, Jewish education, and family reunion with relatives in other countries should no longer be impeded by the Soviet government.

NAME_____
        (Please Print)

Address_____

Ukrainian interest in rights for Jews in the Soviet Union was pointedly reflected in a lengthy article that appeared in the *New York Times* on January 29, 1967:

UKRAINIAN CALLS FOR YIDDISH BOOKS
Smolich, A Writer, Demands Publication in Kiev

A Ukrainian writer recently called publicly in Kiev for the publication there of books in the Yiddish language.

The demand was voiced at the recent Ukrainian Writers Congress by the Ukrainian author Yuri Smolich. Mr. Smolich denounced the failure to print books by authors writing in Yiddish and other languages of the Ukraine's minorities. He pointed out that the present situation contrasted unfavorably with that before World War II, when the Ukraine had a special publishing house for issuing books in the languages of the minority peoples living in that Soviet republic.

Excerpts from Mr. Smolich's speech, translated from Ukrainian into English, appear in the latest issue of the Digest of the Soviet Ukrainian Press, published here.

American observers could not recall any other recent instance in which a published speech by a Soviet intellectual or official had touched on the delicate subject of the rarity of Yiddish publications in the Soviet Union. Mr. Smolich's speech originally appeared in the Ukrainian newspaper, Literaturna Ukraina.

Publications of Yiddish books in the Soviet Union was resumed in 1959 after a hiatus of 10 years that followed Stalin's closing of Jewish cultural institutions in 1948-49. However, publication of Yiddish books, limited to no more than half dozen a year, has thus far been restricted to Moscow.

Many of the speeches at the Ukrainian Writers Congress attacked Russification of Soviet minorities during the Khrushchev era. Speakers charged that during the early nineteen-sixties pressure was exerted to win support for the idea that Ukrainian and other minority languages had to disappear quickly and leave the Russian language as the only one used by all the different peoples of the Soviet Union. . . .

Jewish interest in the welfare of Ukrainians is developed in the writings of Anatole Radygin, another former Soviet prisoner, who addressed the Ukrainian community of Baltimore at the Ukrainian Youth Center on June 2, 1974. During Radygin's address the writer of this article, seated near the speaker, reflected at length upon the scars of Radygin's otherwise well-formed face. The obvious conclusion was that the scars were caused by torture, even as the Lithuanian Simas Kudirka was knouted for his having jumped from a Soviet ship. In his book, *A Close Look at Life in a Mordovian Concentration Camp,* as in his lecture in Baltimore, Anatole Radygin described the harsh treatment accorded Ukrainian prisoners, ranging from Valentyn Moroz to Katerina Zaretska, among others, and exhorted Ukrainians to persevere in their quest for freedom.[16] Ukrainians remember how Avraham Shifrin likewise tried to inform Americans about the lack of human rights for both Ukrainians and Jews. Shifrin testified

Anatole Radygin    *Gen. Petro Samutin*

before U. S. Congressional committees on the subject of Soviet atrocities.

Knowing of Ukrainian-Jewish fervor for freedom, the Soviets have used guises in order to obstruct the mutual quests for freedom. Moscow has played the classic game of *divide et impera* (divide and rule) well. It uses anti-Semitism as a powerful weapon against Jews and Christians alike. A clear example was the publication in 1963 in Kiev of *Judaism without Embellishment* by Trofim K. Kichko. Printed under the auspices of the Academy of Sciences of the Ukrainian S. S. R., the book created world-wide indignation and protests because of its condemnation of Jews. Moscow's sinister manipulation managed to bring about severe damage to the Ukrainian name.

A sign on the campus of Beth Tfiloh Synagogue and School speaks of the idea of human rights sought by Jews, Ukrainians, Lithuanians and others.   *U.E.A.M. Collection*

The sustained work of the Ukrainian Catholic Metropolitan Andrew Sheptytsky during World War II in interceding in behalf of Jews endangered by the Nazis is well known. Pinchas Lapide, a former Israeli diplomat, records some of the Metropolitan's actions in behalf of Jews as follows in *Three Popes and the Jews*:

> After the Rohatin massacre, he wrote an indignant letter to Himmler, protesting the employment of Ukrainian police in such actions. But he did not content himself with interventions and pastoral letters. In his cathedral in Lvow he hid fifteen Jewish children and six adults, including Rabbi Dr. David Kahane, who, after the liberation of Poland, was appointed Chief Rabbi of the Polish Army. Twenty-eight others he disguised in monks' cowls in the monastery of St. Basileus. On orders from the Metropolitan, 156 Jews, most of them children, were hidden in convents of the Order of the Studites in Eastern Galicia. Approximately 500 monks and nuns had knowledge of these facts, but in spite of the death penalty for sheltering Jews and financial rewards for all informers, none of the Metropolitan's wards fell into Nazi hands. His ringing appeals must have had some impact on a great many peasants and workmen, clerics and priests. By the end of 1943, some 650 Jewish children in Warsaw were hidden in various municipal, church and social institutions.[17]

A case of Jewish intercession to save the life of a Ukrainian shows in the life of General Petro Samutin of Baltimore. A fighter for Ukraine who was caught between many firing lines, Gen. Samutin served in the armies of five nations. In an interview with Earl Arnett of the Baltimore *Sunpapers*, General Samutin told how his life was spared when a Jewish school mate, who likewise was caught between firing lines in having to serve in the Bolshevik army, saved his life in 1920 by beating General Samutin in moderate amounts with his rifle under the pretense of killing him as Bolsheviks were doing to Ukrainians.[18]

Ukrainian melodies inspired many compositions of George Gershwin, among them the well-known song "Don't Forget Me" from the operetta *Song of the Flame*.[19] Many Jewish scholars have studied the culture of Ukraine, among them the distinguished historian, Hans Kohn, whose seriousness in reflecting upon Ukrainian history might be capsulized by his having quoted the Russian Alexander Hertzen in the best book on the subject, *Pan-Slavism*:

> And if Ukraine wishes to be neither Polish nor Russian? The solution seems to me simple. We have then to recognize Ukraine as a free and independent nation.

Pleasantries of Ukrainian-Jewish relations are recalled by some of the reminiscences of A. D. Glushakow (Hlushakow in Ukrainian) as stated in an interview:

> I remember my childhood in Ukraine. The water was fresh. Everything was good. My father had a store and sold tea, poppy seeds, kerosene, bagels, and beer in a big room to farmers and miners.... I tell you it was the life.... It was so healthy. You should be proud of your heritage and remember that the instigation for some of the problems came from the *tsars*.[20]

And Ukrainians in Baltimore remember the "Good old days" of when they were helped when ill by Dr. Joseph Rosenblatt, of how they enjoyed the delicacies of the Levin Bakery owned by Lewis Levin, of dealing for clothing at the store owned by "Jack" Nettleman Shorarovsky, and of having purchased auto parts from Sam Gold's used parts business. All of the Jews of East Baltimore mentioned above spoke Ukrainian and shared a close comraderie with Ukrainians. The comraderie reached a high point when the individuals mentioned, often accompanied by their wives, joined the Ukrainians whenever they produced cultural programs at the Ukrainian Home on O'Donnell Street in the 1930's and 1940's.

NOTES FOR CHAPTER SIX

[1] Bernard D. Weinryb, *The Beginnings of East European Jewry in Legend and Historiography*, Leiden, E. J. Brill, 1962, pp. 499-500.

[2] *Ibid.*, p. 456.

[3] A paper entitled "Chmelnitsky in the Light of Nathan Hanover's Abyss of Despair" was presented by Bernard D. Weinryb at the Sixth National Convention of the American Association for the Advancement of Slavic Studies, New York, Hotel Roosevelt, April 20, 1973. Weinryb stated that the Kozaks "may have killed 2,000 or 3,000 Jews" during discussion after having read his paper.

[4] Bernard D. Weinryb, *The Jews of Poland — A Social and Economic History of the Jewish Community in Poland from 1000-1800*, Philadelphia, Jewish Publication Society of America, 1973, p. 172.

[5] Michael T. Florinsky (Editor), McGraw-Hill *Encyclopedia of Russia and the Soviet Union*, New York, McGraw-Hill Book Company, Inc., 1961, p. 257.

[6] Ukrainian Congress Committee of America, Inc., *Ukrainians and Jews — Articles, Testimonies, Letters and Official Documents Dealing with Interrelations of Ukrainians and Jews in the Past and Present*, New York, 1966, p. 121.

[7] Frederick M. Schweitzer, *A History of the Jews Since the First Century A. D.*, New York, The Macmillan Company, 1971, p. 243.

[8] Julian Batchinsky, Arnold Margolin, Mark Vishnitzer, Israel Zangwill, *The Jewish Pogroms in Ukraine — Authorative Statements on the Question of Responsibility for Recent Outbreaks Against Jews in Ukraine*, Washington, The Friends of Ukraine, 1919, p. 17.

[9] Cited in *Ukrainians and Jews — Articles . . .*, p. 12.

[10] Isaac M. Fein, *The Making of An American Jewish Community — The History of Baltimore Jewry from 1773 to 1920*, Philadelphia, Jewish Publication Society of America, 1971, p. 144.

[11] *Ibid.*, p. 142.

[12] *Ibid.*, p. 142.

[13] Edward K. Muller and Paul A. Groves, "The Changing Location of the Clothing Industry: A Link to the Social Geography of Baltimore in the Nineteenth Century," *Maryland Historical Magazine*, Vol. 71, No. 3, Fall 1976, p. 411.

[14] *Ibid.*, p. 419.

[15] Statement by Sylva Zalmanson to Wolodymyr C. Sushko, Bohdan Salamacha, and Paul Fenchak at Baltimore Hebrew College on November 18, 1974.

[16] Anatol Radygin, *A Close Look at Life in a Mordovian Concentration Camp* (In Ukrainian language), Munich, Ukrainian Institute for Free Study, 1974.

[17] Pinchas E. Lapide, *Three Popes and the Jews*, New York, Hawthorne Books, Inc., 1967, p. 186.

[18] Interview of General Petro Samutin, Baltimore, at his home by Earl Arnett of Baltimore *Sunpapers* on January 9, 1975. Also present were Hlib S. Hayuk, Bohdan Salamacha, and Paul Fenchak.

[19] Yaroslav J. Chyz and Joseph S. Roucek, "Ukrainian Americans" in Francis J. Brown and Joseph S. Roucek (Editors), *One America*, New York, Prentice-Hall, Inc., 1945, p. 135.

[20] Statements by A. D. Glushakow, Baltimore, to Paul Fenchak in an interview on August 23, 1976.

Chapter Seven

Religion and Churches

Stephen Basarab

Because the early Ukrainian immigrants in Maryland were largely from the Austro-Hungarian Empire, their religious affiliation was usually Catholic. Yet they were different from the Catholics they met upon their arrival in Maryland. And most likely, as elsewhere in the United States, they were greeted not joyfully as coreligionists, but as strangers unqualified to join the flock.[1]

The reasons for the shunting aside of these newcomers are numerous. The Catholics whom the Ukrainians met were of the Latin Rite, while they were of the Byzantine Slavonic Rite, one of the Eastern Rites of the Catholic Church. Although both are under the guidance of the Holy Father, the Pope of Rome, these Greek Catholics (as they were then commonly known) differed in their liturgy, ceremonies, customs, canon law, and language.

In the Latin Rite, a bishop confers the Sacrament of Confirmation at about the age of twelve at which time a middle name is given the recipient. In the Eastern Rites, confirmation is conferred upon the infant immediately after baptism by a priest, and no new name is added. Holy Communion, among Ukrainian Catholics, is administered with a spoon under both species, bread and wine. During the Holy Liturgy, Ukrainians frequently make the Sign of the Cross, using two fingers and the thumb (commemorating the Blessed Trinity), going from the right shoulder to the left and not from left to right as in the Latin

Church. The Ukrainian custom during services includes bowing and making of crosses, rather than genuflection, or bending of the knee, as a gesture of surrender and adoration.[2]

Then, too, instead of seeing statues when entering a Ukrainian Church, one is struck by the many paintings which adorn the walls and ceiling, and especially those making up the iconostasis. This series of icons separates the sanctuary from the body of the church. Father Englert, who refers to this "great picture-screen," continues his glowing description:

> ... On it are icons of Our Lord, Our Lady and many angels and saints. This screen is an object of great veneration to the people, representing in a beautiful and concrete — though imperfect — way, the glory and greatness of the holy citizens of heaven... It is pierced by three doors, all of which are used during the sacred functions of the liturgy, adding great solemnity and pomp to the processions

Msgr. Melnyczuk of St. Michael's giving Holy Communion in the form of bread and wine.

that pass through them, and giving an air of holy mystery to the singing of the clergy behind the eikonostasis. The central doors are opened wide at the important parts of the service — disclosing a vision of priest and altar wrapped in clouds of incense, a vision that appears like some majestic scene from the Apocalypse.[3]

Another noticeable peculiarity of the Ukrainians was their calendar. Holy Days, such as Christmas and Epiphany, did not fall on the same days of the year as those of the Western European or Latin Rite Catholics. These older Americans could not understand why members of the Eastern Rites, or of the Orthodox Church, would celebrate Christmas on a different day, 13 days later, while insisting that their Christmas was on December 25. These "Easterners" retained the Julian Calendar in their services despite the fact that for over a century Holy Days for other American Christians were set according to the Gregorian Calendar (adopted by England and her American colonies in 1752).

A leading point of difference, and one which was probably the primary cause for misunderstanding and opposition, was the noncelibate state of many of the priests of the Greek Catholic Church. In Europe, prior to ordination, a Ukrainian candidate for the priesthood was permitted to marry. However, once a *priest*, a man could not marry. The presence of married priests with families in the United States led to the issuance of directives in 1890 and 1894 by the Vatican (*De Propagande Fide*) instructing the Ukrainian hierarchs to return married priests to Ukraine and placing all Greek Catholic priests in the United States under the jurisdiction of Latin Rite bishops, thus putting in jeopardy or question the agreement under which Ukrainian Catholics for three centuries had been functioning within the Church.[4]

Now, after years of contact and many common endeavors in America, it is more generally known that there are many Eastern Rites, in which by far the most numerous adherents belong to the Byzantine Slavonic Rite. This Rite embraces the Ukrainians and those Carpatho-Ukrainians who still cling to the old name, Rusins or

Ruthenians, Slovaks, Croatians, and Hungarians. In 1936 Ukrainians were the leading group in 577 churches in the United States. Among these churches were 300 Greek Catholic, 194 Russian Orthodox, 65 Ukrainian Orthodox (those that broke away from the Vatican and established themselves independently) and 18 Protestant.[5]

CHRISTIANITY IN UKRAINE

The Ukrainians are said to have accepted Christianity in 988 at the insistence of Volodimir, the ruler of Kievan Rus. But there is evidence that long before this Christianity was widely practiced in Kievan Rus, then a prosperous state which had extensive trade relations with Byzantium.[6] St. Andrew, one of the twelve apostles, travelled northward and founded the Church in Byzantium, a city at what is now Istanbul in Turkey. He then went along the northern shores of the Black Sea, and as far north on the Dnipro River to what is now Kiev, the capital city of Ukraine. Along the way he preached Christianity to the Scythians who inhabited the area. During these wanderings, St. Andrew suffered martyrdom. He was followed about 100 A.D. by St. Clement, the fourth Pope, who had been driven from Rome and who preached in the Crimean area. St. Olha, grandmother of Volodimir, was baptized a Christian about the year 945. One traveler, after visiting Kiev in the year 1018 wrote that Kiev contained 400 churches, 8 market places and "countless numbers of people."[7]

In welcoming the Ukrainians under a new agreement defining their status within the Catholic Church after the separation of many Eastern churches in 1054, in the words of the bull *Magnus Dominus* issued in 1595, Pope Clement VIII wrote: "We permit, we allow, we approve . . . all the Sacred rites and ceremonies used by the Ruthenian Bishops and Clergy in the divine offices, in celebration of Mass, administration of Sacraments, and all other religious functions which were introduced by the Greek Fathers."[8]

SLAVIC NEIGHBORS

Coming to a new land with different customs and a

language which they did not understand, the first immigrants moved into neighborhoods where other Slavic peoples, such as the Poles, Czechs, and Slovaks, lived. The Ukrainians from Eastern Galicia were in contact with the Poles, whose nobility in fact had been permitted by Austria to exercise direct political and administrative control. Moreover, Polish colonies existed in various parts of Eastern Galicia. Because Polish was a kindred Slavic language, communication between Ukrainians and Poles was easily conducted. The Ukrainians south of the Carpathian Mountains were the neighbors of the Slovaks, both of whom were ruled by Hungarians. The Czechs and Slovaks also were Slavs so understandable conversations were readily developed with them by the Ukrainian immigrants. For the Ukrainians in Maryland to settle in significant numbers first in the Baltimore area where there were already large colonies of Slavs near Polish and Czech Catholic Churches, among which were St. Stanislaus, St. Casimir, Holy Rosary, St. Wenceslaus, and St. Athanasius, was more than just a coincidence.

FIRST UKRAINIAN CHURCH IN THE UNITED STATES

The first Ukrainian church in the United States was established in Shenandoah, Pa., through the efforts of Rev. Ivan Volansky, who came from Galicia to the United States in 1884. He was sent by Metropolitan Sylvester Sembratovych, Archbishop of Lviv (Lemberg), Western Ukraine (then under Austrian rule). Not only was the church the vital element in religious life of the people, it was also the center of cultural and educational activity.

When large numbers of Ukrainians began arriving in the northeastern areas of the United States in the mid 1870's and in the 1880's, they felt strongly and incessantly the desire for churches and priests. They wrote often to their relatives and friends in Ukraine, pleading and praying for help. *Svoboda*, a Ukrainian newspaper, estimated that by 1890 there were between 200,000 and 300,000 Ukrainians in the United States, nearly all of them of the Byzantine (Greek) Slavonic Rite of the Catholic Church.

In the early years of immigration, the few priests in the United States, with vast territories to cover, held services in homes of the people, then in halls or larger buildings, and finally in the churches of kindly neighbors. But in 1884, when St. Michael's Ukrainian Greek Catholic Church was built in Shenandoah, Pa., a new wave of architectural form as well as Catholic devotion and worship began in America, their development not then foreseen and their attributes and influence even today not properly gauged or adequately studied. By 1898 there were 51 Ruthenian Greek Catholic Churches in the United States. The official Catholic Directory for 1976 states there are 413 parishes in the two Byzantine Rite Metropolitan Provinces in the United States.

BEGINNINGS IN BALTIMORE

The religious experience of Baltimore's Ukrainians occurred in a series of steps, with services in homes, larger buildings, and finally in churches. More and more immigrants came to work in the factories and railroad yards and shops. By 1893 the Holy Liturgy was being celebrated by itinerant Ukrainian priests or by priests from the not-too-distant hard coal fields from Eastern Pennsylvania or from Philadelphia. St. Stanislaus (Polish) Catholic Church of the Latin Rite at 700 South Ann Street offered its facilities for use of their Slavic brethren of the Eastern Rite. In addition Ukrainians were befriended by an understanding Polish Franciscan priest and pastor of St. Casimir's Church, Father Josaphat Bok, who was fluent in Ukrainian. He was generous in assisting the fledgling group of former village folk and farmers to worship in the only way they knew — according to the Greek Rite in the Old or Church Slavonic language.

By 1910, when Father Zachary Orun had been assigned by Bishop Soter Ortynsky of Philadelphia to Baltimore to minister to the spiritual needs of its Byzantine Slavonic faithful, there were already two significant centers of population in the area: Curtis Bay (which was then a part of Anne Arundel County) and the Fells Point, Canton, and Highlandtown sections of East Baltimore.

On May 16, 1912, St. Michael's Ukrainian Greek Catholic Church (The deeds contain the name St. Michael's Russian Greek Catholic Church, because the name of the immigrants who called themselves *Rusins* was officially improperly translated.) purchased lots, each 20 by 80 feet, at 520 and 522 South Wolfe Street, between Eastern Avenue and Fleet Street, for the purpose of constructing a house of worship.[9] On these lots, costing, according to the deeds, $1,000.00 and $1,590.00, a red brick building soon arose, put up under contract. Much of the interior work was done subsequently by volunteers from among the parishioners.

St. Michael's Ukrainian Catholic Church

U.E.A.M.

For years continuous exertions had been made to collect sufficient funds to begin construction. But Bishop Soter Stephen Ortynsky was able to inspire a number of men to devote some time and energy to this cause. He found an able servant in Ihnaty Ladna, who had in his native land been a gendarme or policeman and who perhaps became more quickly attuned to the American environment than most of his fellow countrymen. His initiative, and that of similar workers, provided the organizational unity and funds to bring the dreams of all of his people for a church into the reality of a House of God. They could now look upon the new edifice as being "our own," like those in their native villages in Ukraine.

After 20 years, in August of 1913, the first Holy Liturgy held for East Baltimoreans in a Greek Catholic Church in the Old Slavonic language was led by Father Zachary Orun. Assisting the parishioners as *dyak* (cantor) and providing the responses in the chanted Holy Liturgy was a young man from the Province of Galicia of Western Ukraine, named John Boyko. He continued in this capacity at both St. Michael's and SS. Peter and Paul's in Curtis Bay for some fifty years. As *dyak*, choir leader, teacher, and advisor to the growing community of Ukrainian immigrants and American-born children, Mr. Boyko helped furnish a firm foundation for religious development within two parishes.

The new parish went through many a turbulent stream and traveled the rocky roads of dissension, economic hardship, and shortages of priests before it reached a plateau where it could forge ahead and move on a smooth and even course. It stood fast and strong when the times called for such displays and survived to serve the spiritual needs of thousands as a bastion of the Eastern Rites south of the Mason and Dixon Line.

The lack of a bishop, since the death on March 26, 1916, of Soter Stephen Ortynsky, Bishop of Philadelphia, left all Ukrainian Catholics in the United States under two administrators: Father Petro Poniatishin for the Galicians and Father Gabriel Martyak for the Trans-carpathians. Added to the local problems were those of a national scale, and even of the Holy Father in Rome who did not act until 1924 to resolve the jurisdictional crisis which confronted the Church.

In 1924 the Holy See instituted two separate eparchies (dioceses) for the Eastern Rites in the United States by establishing a new eparchy in Munhall (Pittsburgh), Pa. Vasyl Takach was appointed the first bishop for this eparchy which was to serve primarily the Transcarpathian Ukrainians, but also included the Croatians, Slovaks, and Hungarians. Constantine Bohachevsky was appointed bishop of the Philadelphia eparchy to serve all of the remaining Ukrainian faithful in parishes in the United States.

The Ukrainian Catholic Church showed dramatic growth in the United States despite the many uncertainties and the early opposition of the Latin rite hierarchy who disliked sharing the Catholic name and jurisdiction with the newcomers and notwithstanding the open subsidy of Russian Orthodoxy by the Russian Czar of pliable and disaffected elements. "The Russian Orthodox Church," according to the *Slavonic Encyclopedia*, "carried on vigorous missionary work in the United States among the Ukrainian Greek Catholics, and succeeded in proselyting many of them. . . . It has been estimated that about 80% of the members of the Russian Orthodox Church in the United States is made up of former Ukrainian Greek Catholics."[10] Such inroads would not have been possible had Ukrainians received more cooperation and understanding as Catholics in full communion with Rome. Pope Benedict XV in 1917 gave heed to these losses by revising church administration and establishing the Sacred Congregation of the Eastern Churches and a Pontifical Institute for Eastern Studies.[11]

There were many positive efforts to help the Ukrainian Catholics in Maryland. Among the earliest friends was Father Paul Sandalgi, of Armenian descent, pastor of St. Athanasius Latin Rite parish in Curtis Bay. He not only assisted the Ukrainian priests and parish members, but because of his language versatility (knowing Polish, Ukrainian, Turkish, French, English) would conduct services in the absence of Ukrainian priests in the

Byzantine Rite in St. Michael's or the Curtis Bay Church of SS. Peter and Paul. At St. Stanislaus the pastors and individual parish members, although of the Latin Rite, adopted a helpful attitude and put it into practice on many occasions and requests.

BALTIMORE AS TRAINING CENTER OF PRIESTS

There was a large, unfilled demand for priests throughout the wide expanse of Ukrainian settlement. In Maryland, the world-renowned St. Mary's Seminary of Baltimore in 1913 was accepting students from the Philadelphia Ukrainian diocese for the study of Theology and Philosophy. Father Dyer, Rector of St. Mary's Seminary, agreed to take four candidates for the priesthood in his letter of September 9, 1913, to Rev. Basil Steciuk, Chancellor, 816 N. Franklin Street, Philadelphia, and he guaranteed him the benefit of one-half burse to each student and that "the Right Reverend (Ortynsky) will not be called upon to pay more than one hundred dollars a year for each or any of these three students." The first student had been granted previously a full McCadden Burse.

There are earlier instances of Ukrainian attendance at Baltimore seminaries. For example, in 1906 Zyhmont Bachinsky, assistant editor of *Svoboda*, resigned his position to enter a "spiritual seminary in Baltimore," according to Mr. Surmach.[12] In 1913, the first Ruthenian Greek Catholic priest, Rev. John Rubynowych, was ordained at St. Mary's Seminary.

Father Dyer, of St. Mary's Seminary, not only enrolled Ukrainian students with less than a full complement of English knowledge or instruction in courses of Theology and Philosophy, but he also replied in the affirmative to the request of Bishop Ortynsky of October 28, 1915, to have Very Reverend Constantine Kuryllo, a Ukrainian, teach the students. Bishop Ortynsky wrote as follows: "My clerics need very badly some knowledge of history, law and discipline of the Oriental Church, as well as of ceremonies, and rituals which are necessary for ordination," and "to give an order to my students that they should do their best to attend them (the lessons)."

BISHOPS CHANCERY OFFICE   **816 N. FRANKLIN STREET**

Philadelphia, Pa., *October 28th, 1915.*

Very Rev. E. R. Dyer, S. S. D. D.,
St. Mary's Seminary's Rector,
Baltimore, Md.

Very Rev. & Dear Father:—

My clerics need very badly some knowledge of history, law and discipline of the Oriental Church, as well as of ceremonies and rituals, which are necessary for ordination. Knowing that in your seminary they can not be thought of all of those, I decided that instead of ritual, ceremonies and cantus of the Roman Catholic Church they should have lessons in that according to our Rite. For that purpose I appointed Very Rev. Constantine Kuryllo of Baltimore, Md., an expert in this line, and beg you, my dear Father, to be so kind to appoint some time for his lessons and to give an order to my students, that they should do their best to attend them. It would be advisable, too, that they should have some practice on Sundays in ceremonies, cathechetic and preaching.

I hope, my dear Father, you will help me in the matter of best possible education of my priests and I thank you in advance for every assistance you will show to Father Kuryllo.

I am,

sincerely yours in Xto.

+ S. S. Ortynsky

Bishop.

195

Baltimore had become an important center in the United States for the training of Ukrainian Catholic priests of the Byzantine Rite. The qualifications of the Ukrainian instructors were high, as is exemplified by the appointment by the Diocesan Administrator, Rev. Petro Poniatishin, in his letter of March 15, 1917, to the Rector of St. Mary's, Very Rev. Edward R. Dyer, D.D.:

> I beg to inform you that I appointed Rev. Dr. John Perepelycia who is pastor of the Ruthenian Catholic Church in Baltimore, to be Lector for the Ruthenian students in your Seminary. Will you kindly permit him to instruct these young men in our Ruthenian Greek Rite and Liturgy: Dr. Perepelycia will arrange with your faculty and the students themselves as to his hours for lectures, etc. He is well equipped for his work, as he has obtained his academical degrees and doctorate in theology from the Austrian University.

At that time Father Perepelycia was residing in the parish house at 518 South Wolfe Street.

The number of Ruthenian boys at the Seminary had been greatly increased from the previously mentioned four. On the opening day of the fall semester, September 20, 1917, nineteen students were enrolled:

Nicholas J. Woloschuk	Michael Rapach	John Kolczun
Andrew Rudakewicz	Joseph Fechko	Stephen Gulyassy
Roman Kaczmarsky	Theodosius M. Wolkay	John Zavalla
Peter Sadlock	John Oleksa	John Taptich
John Loya	Michael Morris	M. Kapiec
Joseph Sklepkowicz	George J. Chegin	George Simchak
Michael Varady		

In his letter of September 18, 1918, Very Rev. Petro Poniatishin requested Very Rev. Edward R. Dyer to admit 17 ecclesiastical students for the coming semester from among his own boys and the 10 selected by the Hungarian (Carpatho-Ruthenian) Administrator, Very Rev. Gabriel Martyak. The students were named as follows:

R. Kaczmarsky	Andrew Kovacs	J. Loya
A. Rudakevich	John Taptich	Gregory Monita
Vladimir Gela	John Zawalla	John Sawulak
John Kowal	George Symchak	Stephen Loya
Stephen Pobucky	J. Feczko	John Kryweniak
Andrew Paulish	M. Rapach	

For the Baltimore Ukrainian parishes, this was an

unexpected blessing. Priests were few in number and had to be sent to areas of Ukrainian population to minister to their spiritual requirements at least sporadically lest they be lost to the Church through neglect amidst the many adverse elements in a strange land. Now the young students could offer some assistance, as well as learn from the practical problems which they had to face at the parish level.

Highly informative and interesting is the letter of January 7th, 1918, of Father Dyer, President of St. Mary's Seminary, to Father Poniatishin, of Newark, N.J., Diocesan Administrator, which states in part:

> I duly received your despatch in regard to the Christmas vacation, etc. of the Greek Ruthenian students in St. Mary's Seminary. I allowed Mr. Kaczmarsky to go to the Ruthenian Church for the midnight service last night and for the services of today. I also allowed Messrs. Simchak, Taptick and Zavalla to accompany him for the greater solemnity of the services. We would have permitted all the students to attend the Christmas day services had there been a priest to celebrate Mass, etc. at the Ruthenian Church.
>
> Upon the request of the parishioners I permitted Mr. Kaczmarsky to remain for the next two days in order to settle up the accounts of the Church, etc.
>
> We could not permit your young men to go home for Christmas, as none of our other students go home at this time.

St. Mary's Seminary continued to receive Ukrainian students in various numbers throughout the years as late as the 1940's. The *Catalogue of St. Mary's Seminary of June 1941* lists the following Ukrainian Greek Catholic seminarians: Nicholas Babak, Constantine Berdar, Basil Charles Borota, Stephen J. Chrepta, Basil Cooper, Walter Dudiak, Samuel Fetzko, Paul Nestor Graskow, Stephen Hotra (of Chesapeake City), Walter Kachmar, Michael Basil Klymko, Peter Leskiw, Michael Nahornia, Bohdan Olesh, John Thomas Panas, Ihor George Pelensky, Theodore Pogar, Basil Onuphrey Sheremeta, John Stock, Andrew Joseph Ulicki, and Nicholas Wolensky. Listed among those who were ordained priests during the academic year of 1940-1941 were Rev. Samuel Fetzko, Rev. Andrew Joseph Ulicki, and Rev. Nicholas Wolensky.

Most Reverend Yaroslav Gabro, Exarch for

Ukrainians of St. Nicholas of Chicago, pursued part of his studies for the priesthood at St. Charles College, Catonsville, studying there during the years 1939 and 1940. His Excellency was ordained a priest on September 27, 1945.

Reverend Onufrey T. Kowalsky, a student at St. Mary's Seminary early in 1917, authored *Ukrainian Folk Songs: A Historical Treatise* (1925). While studying in Baltimore, he frequently assisted at St. Michael's parish.

The year 1940-41 was a transitional one for Ukrainian seminarians as many at this time returned to America from European seminaries with the advent of World War II. On September 8, 1941, Bishop Constantine Bohachevsky rented a building at 2315 Lincoln Road, NE, Washington, for St. Josaphat's Ukrainian Catholic Seminary. With this action Ukrainian seminarians departed from St. Mary's Seminary in Baltimore, except for those sent to St. Mary's for special training in theological disciplines.

St. Mary's facilities served as a bridge between Orthodoxy and Catholicism, for it was here that Vladimir Vladimirof Alexandrof maintained an Eastern Rite Chapel until his death on May 20, 1945. Born in Kherson, Ukraine, in 1871, Archbishop Elect Alexandrof was Russian

U.E.A.M.

Orthodox Synodal member before embracing Catholicism in 1933. He strove for reconciliation through the Eastern Rites as the logical step by which all Orthodox might come again under the spiritual leadership of the Holy Father in Rome.

ST. MICHAEL'S CHARTERED

The legal establishment of St. Michael's Ruthenian Greek Catholic Church is recorded as of December 18, 1913, in Liber 7, Folios 349 through 352, in the Corporation Charter Section of Maryland in Baltimore. The organizational methods and controls provided in the Articles of Incorporation are interesting, for they depict the conditions of the time and the native Western Ukrainian sources from which they come. The first four paragraphs outline the jurisdictional lines of authority:

> WHEREAS, The Right Reverend Soter Stephen Ortynsky, the ordinary of the Ruthenian Greek Catholic Church in the United States of America, a denomination of Christians in communion with the See of Rome, and holding his appointment according to the discipline and practice of the Roman Catholic Church and the rules and regulations thereof relating to the Eastern Catholic Church, deems it advisable to have created a body corporate under the laws of the State of Maryland, for the purposes and with the powers specified herein and by the laws of said State in such cases made and provided; and
>
> WHEREAS, Reverend Zachary Orun of Baltimore City, in the State of Maryland, is for the time being the pastor of said church; and
>
> WHEREAS, The Said Ordinary has designated Reverend John Konstankevich and Ignatius Ladna to be associated with him in the formation of the said corporation; and,
>
> WHEREAS, Lucas Turok and Nicholas Kapustey of Baltimore City, in the State of Maryland, were duly elected by the male parishioners of the said congregation from among their number to be associated in the formation of such corporation; . . .

According to Article III, membership of the corporation shall consist of the Ordinary, the Pastor, two persons designated by the Ordinary, and two persons to be selected by the male parishioners in good standing. These same members, as stated in Article V, constitute The Board of Directors. As indicated in Article VI they shall be the source also of the Officers: President, Vice-President, Treasurer, and Secretary. Thus the organizational structure puts effective control in the Diocese, through its power of appointment of the pastor and two members of the board of directors.

Male members of the parish were deemed to be in good standing if they complied with the laws of the church with reference to their Easter Duties and if they had paid their monthly dues which for married men were fifty cents and for single men, twenty-five cents. All of such members were allowed to vote for directors at the annual meeting, which was to be held "on or about the Sunday next succeeding the first day of January in each year."

The attorney who drew up the charter "Americanized" the names of the incorporators and directors. However, when the incorporators signed the Articles, two of them reverted to the Ukrainian given name:

> Ignatius Ladna — Signature: Ihnaty Ladna
> Lucas Turok — Signature: Luka Turok

These two were already citizens of the United States and apparently were somewhat unsympathetic to the standardization goals and melting processes which were dissolving the immigrants' backgrounds and traditions.

The Articles of Incorporation traveled a circuitous route, from Baltimore to Philadelphia, to Shamokin, Pa., then back to Baltimore. Right Reverend Soter Stephen Ortynsky's signature was notarized on November 11, 1913; Reverend John Konstankevich's, on November 12, 1913; and Reverend Zachary Orun's, Ignatius Ladna's, Lucas Turok's, and Nicholas Kapustey's on November 18, 1913. The Mason and Dixon Line was crossed several times before the successful organization of St. Michael's was accomplished, with Father John Konstankevich, a prominent priest and qualified administrator from Shamokin, representing Bishop Ortynsky.

At about the same time as the incorporating plans were being carried out at St. Michael's, a change in the corporate name on property records was submitted to city officials. The name "Russian" led to confusion with the "Great

Russians" of Muscovy (or *Moskali* as the Baltimore Rusins called them). Many Ukrainians in the United States still adhered to, and preferred to use, their ancient name of "Rusin," particularly those from Carpatho-Ukraine or Ruthenia. In the Austro-Hungarian Empire from where these Catholics came, the government used the name Ruthenian when referring to its Ukrainian population.[13] Thus the native's use of Rusin became Ruthenian in America to conform to the terminology for centuries applied by the Church of Rome and followed by the rulers of the Austro-Hungarian Monarchy.

This clarification was effected on December 30, 1913, with a new deed submitted to the Baltimore City recorder, who recorded it in SCL 2872-447, as a transfer of the church property, covering two lots and the structures thereon, to St. Michael's Ruthenian Greek Catholic Church, Incorporated. Luka Turok, president, signed the instrument.

The Articles of Incorporation were amended belatedly on March 26, 1954, as recorded in F453, page 491, to the current designation, St. Michael's Ukrainian Greek Catholic Church, Inc.

PASTORAL ASSIGNMENTS

The priests assigned to serve the parishioners at St. Michael's were fully-occupied, striving to meet their obligations as pastors toward the members of two parishes until 1950 when a full-time priest was provided for SS. Peter and Paul in Curtis Bay. The assigned priests and their years of service are as follows:

    Rev. Zachary Orun 1910-1914
    Rev. Basil Maniosky 1914-1914
    Rev. Constantine Kuryllo 1914-1916
    Rev. John Dumych 1916-1916
    Rev. John Perepelycia, D.D. 1917-1917
    Rev. Joseph Dzendzora 1917-1918
    Rev. Tymotheus Wasilevich 1918-1918
    Rev. John Zacharkiw 1919-1919
    Rev. Volodymyr Korytowsky 1919-1920
    Rev. Basil Maniosky 1921-1927
    Rev. Michael Lukawsky 1927-1929
    Rev. Michael Koltutsky 1929-1931
    Rev. Volodymyr Tytar 1931-1931

Bishop Constantine Bohachevsky and Reverend Basil Maniosky
Markiewicz Photo

Rev. Basil Maniosky 1931-1956
Rev. Bohdan Volosin 1946-1948 (Assistant Pastor)
Rev. Basil Seredowych 1948-1949 (Assistant Pastor)
Rev. Roman Hanas 1949-1950 (Assistant Pastor)
Rev. Wasyl Sushko 1949-1953 (Assistant Pastor)
Rev. Alex Kobryn 1953-1956
Very Rev. Petro Melnyczuk 1956 to present
Rev. Eustachius Wesolowsky (Assistant Pastor, 1965-Feb. 17, 1976)

The longest record of service was that of Father Maniosky who first came to Baltimore in 1914. Staying only a short time during that year, Father Maniosky returned in 1921 when World War I was over and with his wife and children with whom he had been reunited in 1920 after six long years of separation. Many a husband and father had left his family behind in Ukraine, while attempting to amass sufficient funds for railroad and steamship fares in return for his hard daily labors. Father Maniosky's separation was enforced by the dictates of a cruel war, stretching over four years when sea travel from the Central Powers was impossible because mighty Britannia ruled the waves and had imposed a blockade on all shipping (including American) with Germany. Fortunately for Mrs. Maniosky she was able to leave the battlegrounds of her native land two years after the Great War's "Armistice," and successfully maneuver past new boundaries, outposts, and officials, accompanied by her four small children.

In Baltimore, the small parish and its members had to

Sisterhood of Blessed Virgin Mary, Rev. Maniosky 1938

be developed and expanded, the various families and single persons of the Greek Catholic faith and origin gathered into a functioning unit. For many years, priests had come and gone, hardly a proper atmosphere for planning and establishing a sense of unity and the institutions needed for smooth functioning. A vigorous effort had to be made toward caring for the spiritual responsibilities required by the Greek Slavonic Rite and its revered leader in Lviv, Metropolitan Andrey Sheptitsky.

Father Maniosky systematically worked toward attaining the many urgent goals facing him, in his frugal but determined way, assisted quite often by his able wife. The debt for St. Michael's Church was paid and its interior beautified with religious paintings which are traditional in the Eastern Church. Buildings were purchased, remodeled and enlarged to serve as a school, hall, and cultural center. Now *Swatey Nikolai* (St. Nicholas), in his bishop's garb and mitre, could appear yearly, on December 6, to smile upon and reward the little children for being good and learning their prayers and catechism. This was an important day at St. Michael's, for not only was it reminiscent of the traditions of a faraway land, but the preparations involved months of study and practice on Saturdays or in the evenings on the part of the children, instructed by the pastor, the cantor and many hard-working, dutiful parents and parishioners. Growth of a cohesive community was furthered and there was much joy in the undertaking which preceded the oncoming Christmas Holy Days.

Fortunately for the parish, among its members was a skilled cabinet maker, Nicholas Shurma. He devoted many off-duty hours to the construction of the iconostasis, retaining the beautiful colors of the natural wood. It was completed in the early 1920's. Mr. Shurma subsequently returned to his family which had remained behind in Ukraine.

The third, and longest period of service, lasted from 1931 until Father Maniosky's departure from the earthly sphere on April 28, 1956. After years of teaching by himself, Mrs. Maniosky, and Mr. John Boyko who had been the cantor and choir leader since the church building was

Iconostasis in St. Michael's, Msgr. Melnyczuk, c. 1970.

Iconostasis and altar in St. Michael's, 1930.

erected in 1913, Reverend Maniosky brought two Sisters from the Order of St. Basil the Great in Philadelphia to teach in the parochial evening school. The Basilian Sisters were highly respected as teachers and disciplinarians. Consequently, the parents were more than eager to send their children to the parochial school even though the study day was lengthened beyond the public school hours.

The beauty and sacred character of the church was enhanced by the installation of stained glass windows with biblical scenes in the northern and southern walls of the building. These six inspiring picture windows were added through the generosity of parish members and organizations: Sofia Davis; Ivan and Maria Shulka; Brotherhood of St. Andrew, No. 57; Sisterhood of Saint Anne, *Sojedinenija*; Sisterhood of the Blessed Virgin Mary; and Julia Blama and Elena Bukowska. Large stained glass windows were also donated by Father Basil and Julia Maniosky and by Evhenia and Simeon Kusyk. The somewhat smaller but no less beautiful windows of stained glass at the rear (entrance wall) of the building were installed because of the donations given by Anna Tyrpak, Joseph Prymak, Womens' League Branch 59, Theodore and Anna Chorney, and Nikola Shulka and Ivan Kusyk.

Father Michael Koltutsky served as pastor from 1929 to 1931. During this period administrative and pastoral activities were coordinated and extended with the pastor's engaging personality and diplomatic manners gaining the cooperation and assistance of even apathetic church members. Detailed financial reports were issued in the years 1929 and 1930 for the information of the members. General collections in 1929 were $1,515.60 and in 1930, $1,850.40. Monthly dues paid in 1929 by 98 members were $905.10 and in 1930 by 101 members were $868.75.

An unfortunate interruption in church use occurred in 1929 when fire near the altar damaged the interior. Expenditures in 1929 to restore the church structure and furnishings amounted to $2,354.90.

St. Michael's Ukrainian Catholic Church, having a number of assistant pastors since the oncoming of the new immigrants in 1949 and the early 1950's, became the source

*Greek Catholic Brotherhood of St. Andrew the Apostle, No. 57 (**Markiewicz Studio**)*

St. Michael's Choir and musicians, John Boyko, Director; Rev. Maniosky, 1932 (Markiewicz Studio)

of a missionary effort for serving Ukrainian Catholics scattered throughout Maryland and the Gettysburg area of Pennsylvania. For the past two decades an adequate number of priests sharply contrasted with the shortages of the first three decades of Ukrainian Catholic settlement.

ST. MICHAEL'S CEMETERY

Unfulfilled for many years was the need for a site where all Ukrainian Catholics could be buried and remembered according to their own rites and customs. Through careful practices and good management Father Maniosky was able to save sufficient money from the donations and events held at the church hall to meet part of the cost of 8.67 acres of ground located across the eastern borders of Baltimore City near German Hill Road and 48th Street. This purchase was made by Father Maniosky on September 25, 1940, following the longest and deepest era of financial distress and unemployment in United States history. On October 17, 1940, 4 of these acres were deeded to St. Michael's for $1500.00, while the remaining portion was not transferred until August 18, 1954 for $2000.00 as measured by the documentary stamps.[14]

Little by little improvements were made to the cemetery as more and more of the parish faithful were laid to their final rest. Surveys of the land were conducted by Leon Podolak, followed later by the laying out of plots by Alex Zuk and John Pisok. Under Father Melnyczuk's administration four acres of the cemetery grounds were cleared and landscaped, with trees and shrubs planted, and a hard top road was built. A fence was erected to enclose the plot.

A parcel of land 100 feet by 150 feet abutting into the cemetery tract had been purchased by Joseph and Ksena Prymak on July 7, 1945. Mr. Prymak, seeing that this piece of land was bounded on three sides by the cemetery, viewed this "indentation" as a desirable plot, possibly a good place in an open area where he and Mrs. Prymak could plant and tend a garden, away from the crowded row houses in Baltimore City. But such hopes did not materialize, perhaps

May procession after First Holy Communion in 1969. Monsignor Melnyczuk, pastor.

Visitation of Metropolitan Ambrose Senyshyn to St. Michael's; Rev. Alex Kobryn, pastor.   **Photo by Connie Zuk**

because the leading motive had always been to "straighten out" the cemetery by adding their parcel to it. This was done on January 28, 1960, when a transfer was made to St. Michael's Ukrainian Greek Catholic Church at the buyer's cost.

CALENDAR CHANGE

As the Ukrainian communities centering on the two Catholic parishes in Baltimore became more integrated into American activities, the inconsistency of celebrating legal holidays and events under one calendar and Ukrainian holy days and national holidays under another calendar was more and more apparent. The Julian calendar of the Ukrainians could easily be replaced by the Gregorian calendar in general use so that time loss for missing work and the consequent income penalty for being absent on such days as Christmas (January 7), New Years Day (January 14), etc. would be eliminated. Bishop Bohachevsky had already granted parishes in the United States the right to choose whichever calendar they wished to follow. In 1948, St. Michael's and SS. Peter and Paul's Churches voted to accept the new (Gregorian) calendar. But to this day a number of Ukrainian Catholic and nearly all Orthodox parishes persist in retaining the traditional Julian calendar, fearing that a change would give impetus to the westernization, or disappearance of, their eastern religious practices and eventually a complete assimilation into the predominant American customs, recognizing fully that from an astronomical calculation there is a lag in the Julian calendar.

SISTER MIRIAM TERESA DEMYANOVICH

Sister Miriam Teresa Demyanovich of the Sisters of Charity of St. Elizabeth, Convent Station, N.J., was a member of an order founded by Saint Elizabeth Ann Seton, of Emmitsburg, Maryland, founder of the Sisters of Charity. Sister Miriam, whose parents Alexander and Johanna Suchy Demyanovich were from Bardiov, in the Priashiv Greek Catholic Eparchy, now in Czechoslovakia, is the subject of beatification and cannonization procedures by the Sacred Congregation of the Causes of Saints in Rome. Teresa Demyanovich was baptized and confirmed as a member of Assumption Blessed Virgin Mary Ukrainian Catholic Church in Bayonne, N.J.

Although she lived only from 1901 to 1927, Sister Teresa strove for *Greater Perfection*, by pleasing God which meant doing His will. "We love with the will and not with the feelings," she often said.[15] This young Ruthenian Greek Catholic wrote the conferences (lectures) which were delivered to the novices of the Latin Rite convent and which were used by many other religious orders. Later, Sister Teresa's lectures were assembled in a book, *Greater Perfection*, and read by religious and laity alike.

Children who received First Holy Communion May 31, 1964, from Msgr. Melnyczuk.

SINCE 1956

Very Reverend Monsignor Petro Melnyczuk, who was born in the County of Sniatyn of Galicia, has been pastor of St. Michael's Church since March 26, 1956. While yet a seminarian in Stanislawiw his musical talents were recognized, for he was made choir director and cantor at the seminary. After his ordination in 1928, Msgr. Melnyczuk, in addition to performing his pastoral duties, frequently used his musical abilities to train others and in the conduct of various services.

In 1958 Archbishop Constantine Bohachevsky appointed Father Melnyczuk as Archdiocesan Consultor. Metropolitan-Archbishop Ambrose Senyshyn named Father Melnyczuk dean of a territory which includes Washington, D.C., Maryland, Delaware, Virginia, and Florida. On May 31, 1968, Pope Paul VI awarded Father Melnyczuk honors of Very Reverend Monsignor (*inter suos Cappellanos adle git Reverendum Dominum Petrum Melnyczuk*).

During the 21-year tenure at St. Michael's Church of Father Melnyczuk, the church was repainted, the traditional step for Holy Communion in front of the iconostasis was extended, rugs were placed from the front entrance to the altar and the sanctuary, kneelers in the pews were "softened" with rubber covering, an air conditioner was installed, the hall was repainted and new hardwood flooring laid, and many improvements made to the cemetery.

Plans for erection of a new church near the present one required advance property acquisitions at opportune times and at favorable prices, particularly when the urge to move to Suburbia was guiding many city home owners. Father Melnyczuk bought seven houses adjoining the church properties for parish use and expansion before inflationary prices spread into the area. Although the land and financial bases for much needed physical expansion have already been prepared through Monsignor's management, the question of best location for a new or enlarged parish church has been held in abeyance and remains unresolved. Two locations, four acres adjacent to the cemetery and the present site on Wolfe Street, are available. Each has its advantages, with perhaps the present location with its centralized position in relation to the urban area and city offerings and amenities, better transportation facilities, greater concentration of parishioners, sentimental connections with the past, and inclusion in a historical preservation area of Baltimore outweighing those of open and larger space and greater choice of type of structure only four miles away.

Msgr. Melnyczuk has been a frequent writer for Ukrainian religious publications, usually on church subjects. In addition he has written seven books and is currently preparing a biography of Bishop Hryhoriy Chomyshyn, a victim of Soviet Russian persecution. While still in war-torn Europe, subject to secret police methods

Children who received First Holy Communion May 15, 1966 from Msgr. Melnyczuk.

and not knowing his fate, Father Melnyczuk promised if he survived that he would express his thankfulness at various shrines and write about the Holy Family and the outstanding holy places noted for the miracles which have come to those with abiding faith. One product of this vow is his book *Lourdes, Rome, Fatima, Jerusalem* which was published in 1964.

As an ecumenical leader Monsignor Melnyczuk has been in the forefront among the Ukrainian Catholic clergy. He, individual parishioners, and parish organizations have made contributions in the form of lectures, religious services at various locations as well as at St. Michael's, choral presentations, and Christmas caroling. Peter Marudas of the *Sunpapers* wrote in May of 1963 of St. Michael's ecumenical role: "This combination of Ukrainian nationality, Greek ritual and Roman dogma accounts for St. Michael's lengthy name and the Uniat churches' pivotal

Ukrainian Festival, Sept. 1973, Hopkins Plaza
U.S. Senator Paul Sarbanes, Mayor Schaefer, Msgr. Melnyczuk

position, often described as an 'eccleciastical bridge between East and West.' " In driving toward Christian unity, Father Melnyczuk stressed "it is God's will that His church should be one and holy. Although, we worship Christ in our own particular way, it is our continuing and sincere prayer that we may make a real contribution so that unity will truly be achieved."[16]

St. Michael's under Msgr. Melnyczuk has made a significant impact among the Christians of Central Maryland. The Holy Liturgy, according to the Byzantine Rite, was celebrated and the Rite explained at many high schools and colleges, including St. Mary's Seminary, Woodstock Jesuit Seminary, Notre Dame College, and Loyola College. Father Melnyczuk also lectured to students at Morgan State College, Goucher College, and the Newman Club. The pupils and teachers from over 20 schools have attended Holy Liturgy especially conducted for them at St. Michael's. A notable example was that of the 150 students and 20 teachers of Bryn Mawr School who participated in the Holy Liturgy, then proceeded to the church hall where they had a typical Ukrainian meal and looked at exhibits of Ukrainian easter eggs, embroidery, ceramics and wood carvings. On Saturday, June 19, 1973, the Baltimore Museum of Art in sponsoring an "ethnic tour" filled St. Michael's Church with strangers exploring Ukrainian ways, who were amazed when seeing the ornate iconostasis and hearing the singing during the Holy Liturgy.

St. Michael's Choir, under the direction of Dmytro Kostrubiak, M.D., has also been a goodwill ambassador among Baltimoreans, it having sung Christmas carols at Mr. Vernon Place United Methodist Church on December 23, 1973, as one of four participating choral groups. On Sunday December 14, 1973, St. Michael's Choir sang the traditional Ukrainian Christmas carols in a program under the auspices of the Maryland Historical Society to an overflow crowd in the Society's auditorium.

St. Michael's and SS. Peter and Paul's Ukrainian Catholic Churches, with Father Melnyczuk presiding, honored imprisoned Metropolitan Archbishop Joseph Slipy of Lviv on the 70th anniversary of his birth in a

The Choir of St. Michael's Ukrainian Catholic Church at Maryland Historical Society Dec. 14, 1973. Directed by Dmytro Kostrubiak.

program held in St. Michael's Roman Catholic Church Hall on February 18, 1962. They hoped, prayed and petitioned for Archbishop Slipy's well-being and release from Soviet Russian prisons and slave labor camps where he had been held since April 11, 1945. For refusing to lead his people and Church into Russian Orthodoxy, Metropolitan Slipy had been forced into 18 years of suffering and privation, which ended only when Ukrainian bishops protested the presence of representatives of the Soviet Orthodox Church at the Ecumenical Council at Vatican II while their own Ukrainian Catholic prelate was imprisoned.[17] Released February 10, 1963, his 71st birthday was celebrated in Rome. On February 25, 1965, Archbishop-Major Slipy, primate of the Ukrainian Catholic Church, was consecrated a Cardinal, the fourth Ukrainian to be so ordained.

On the arrival of Father Melnyczuk, Andriy Zacharkiw was church cantor at St. Michael's, he holding this position until the coming of Ivan Senuta in 1957. Mr. Senuta also served as choir director and teacher almost to the date of his death in 1966. He then was succeeded by John Rad, who remains in this capacity as cantor today, while Dmytro Kostrubiak, M.D., is director of the choir.

Assisting the pastor as members of the church committee or trustees have been four parishioners, who for 1977 are: John Rad, Wasyl Werny, Wasyl Stasiuk, and Michaylo Woytowich. In addition a very active and hardworking woman's auxiliary previously led by Mrs. Rosalie Ewachiw and presently by Pauline Schneider has performed numerous tasks such as decorating the church for Christmas and Easter; cooking and serving the annual Christmas and Easter dinners; preparing and selling pyrohi (potato dumplings), holubchi (stuffed cabbage), and typical Ukrainian foods and delicacies for special occasions, distributing religious articles, pamphlets and publications among the parish members; and working with and maintaining contacts with parishioners and other individuals and groups. The efficient operation of the food preparation and distribution processes was made possible through the remodeling performed on rooms adjacent to the hall and installing therein of kitchen equipment and storage and work facilities by John Polisczuk and his son, Walter.

From among St. Michael's parishioners the church has drawn vocations into two religious communities of women. Martha Bayda, now Sister Mary Michael of the Sisters of the Order of Saint Basil the Great (OSBM), was an assistant to Cardinal Slipy in Rome. She started a novitiate in Argentina and is now supervising the building of a convent in Brazil. Sister Natalie Panas is a teacher in Holy Angels Parish of the Latin Rite in Trenton, N.J., as a member of the Sisters of the Third Order of St. Francis. Sister Natalie also edits the Provincial monthly, *The Seedling*. She is the daughter of John and Olga (Stysley) Panas.

Meeting of UCYL members from Baltimore, Chesapeake City, and Washington with His Excellency Ambrose Senyshyn at St. Basil's Academy, Fox Chase, Pa., September, 1954, to assist with plans for National Eucharistic Marian Congress of the Oriental Rites.
16th Annual UCYL Convention Book, 1954

LEAGUE OF UKRAINIAN CATHOLICS (FORMERLY UKRAINIAN CATHOLIC YOUTH LEAGUE)

At the initiative of His Excellency Constantine Bohachevsky of Philadelphia the Ukrainian Catholic Youth League of the United States of America (UCYL), now known as the League of Ukrainian Catholics (LUC), was organized. Since August 19, 1933, when members of the newly-formed chapters met at the Chicago World's Fair, this organization has contributed to Catholic Action and knowledge of the Eastern Slavonic Rite of which its members are a part. Dedicated to God and Country, the League has had a salutary effect, particularly on the youth. The UCYL helped them grow spiritually and develop lofty ideals, at the same time turned their energies to assisting their parishes, seminaries, parochial schools, and the Catholic press and to encouraging vocations as priests and nuns and furthering the Christian life.

It may be said that Ukrainian Catholics have been more insulated from the more rapid changes in the Roman Catholic Church because of the adherence to the traditions of their rite and the purposes for which the League was formed: "To organize and unite all Ukrainian Catholic youth in America into a strong Catholic action group; coordinating their cultural, patriotic and fraternal activities; fostering and preserving devotion to our Byzantine-Slavonic Rite (Ukrainian) and loyalty to the United States of America, its constitution and flag; and combating secularism and all other materialistic isms by associating our youth more closely with the Church."[18]

In 1948, the Baltimore Chapter of the UCYL was formed at St. Michael's, guided by the National Board and Rev. Basil Maniosky, the pastor. Membership grew steadily, so that by June of 1949 it was reported to the national headquarters that 49 members belonged to the Baltimore Chapter. At the time of the annual meeting on December 16, 1949, the treasury balance stood at $185.50, indicating the Chapter was an active one.

One of the early ceremonies participated in by the Branch was the 11th Annual Memorial Field Mass at

Members of League of Ukrainian Catholics in procession to St. Michael's with Stations of Cross presented in 1957.

Arlington National Cemetery sponsored by the Washington General Assembly, Fourth Degree, Knights of Columbus, in May of 1949. Wreaths were placed on the Tomb of the Unknown Soldier by more than 100 national and diocesan Catholic organizations. For many years thereafter the Baltimore UCYL members took part in these field masses as representatives of the national membership of the UCYL.

The Baltimore members provided the impetus for the establishment of the Capital Council (now the St. Christopher Council) of the League of Ukrainian Catholics. This council, the twelfth in the United States, was organized on August 27, 1950, at a meeting held in St. Michael's Church Hall. Representatives from the various parishes in Maryland, Washington and Virginia assembled with national officers to form this council and discuss plans for its operation. Harry Kany, and subsequent council presidents and executive board members, supported an extensive program of action, from holding outings for the orphans at Chesapeake City, dedication of the new St. Josaphat Seminary in Washington on Memorial Day weekend in 1952, and assisting the clergy and lay organizations at their parishes to helping in numerous ways the escapees from the Soviet Union and providing the spark for interesting and fruitful national conventions and special rallies and assemblies. So energetic were the St. Christopher Council officers and members that they were selected by national delegates to staff the National Board for 1953 and 1954 and to host the 16th Annual UCYL Convention in Washington, D. C., on November 11-14, 1954, and the 25th annual LUC Convention at the Lord Baltimore Hotel, Baltimore, on October 24-27, 1963. The theme of the 1954 convention stressed the development of Catholic lay leadership while the 1963 convention appropriately concentrated on the encouragement of vocations to the religious life, both within the primary aims of the League.

In 1957 the St. Christopher Council of the UCYL published a monthly, *The Christopher Council News*, edited by Wanda and Stephen Basarab. *Action*, begun in 1965 as the national publication of the LUC, has been edited for many years by the current editor, Harry Makar, a member of the Baltimore Chapter. The LUC members at St. Michael's devoted many hours to a variety of activities to obtain over $10,000 for their parish and additional amounts for archdiocesan purposes.

SS. PETER AND PAUL UKRAINIAN CATHOLIC CHURCH

The first immigrants in the Curtis Bay area arrived at the turn of the century. In 1901 they were already working at the Baltimore and Ohio Railroad piers and yards. They came from the westernmost parts of Ukraine, from the Turka and Sianik regions in what was then under Austrian rule, and were of the Greek Catholic faith.

As their numbers grew, establishment of their own church became a necessary goal, which attainment became more likely with each passing year for these religion-oriented people. So in May of 1909, a meeting was held at the call of a group of devout faithful to set in motion the plans for organizing a parish and building a house of worship. A lot was purchased on Prudence Street at a cost of $457.75. The visit of Rev. Ivan Sandetsky from Zolotny, a village on the Strypa River, on March 29, 1910, at the invitation of former parishioners now located in Curtis Bay brought further inducement to action. The decision to build a small chapel on Prudence Street was forwarded to Most Reverend Soter Stephen Ortynsky who not long before had arrived in Philadelphia. Meanwhile a church committee began functioning: Mikola Durdela, Oleksa Lischynsky, Joseph Semenkiw, Ivan Hornyatko, Stach Kondrat, Blazey Swirchko, Petro Faryon, Pawlo Kysil, Emilian Shutran, Petro Miskiw, Pawlo Woytowych, Stephan Kostiw and Yakiw Semenkiw. Among the other residents who joined the infant parish were Ivan Fialka, Andriy Budahazy, Ivan Walega, Yakym Semaniuk, Thoma Shandrowsky, Wasyl Fedoronko, Semen Stasiuk, Filimon Zacharko, Sofia

SS. Peter and Paul Church which burned down in 1913.

Chachka, Elysaveta Budahazy, Onufrey Boyko, Ilko Oleksiuk, Petro Myskiw, Antin Cykieta, Oleksa Shandrowsky, Ivan Bakalyk, Antin Petryk.[19]

Construction of the wooden church was completed in 1911. According to the church committee records dated August 15, 1911, the cash expenditures were $975.00. Services were conducted by Father Zachary Orun who at the time was also ministering to the spiritual needs of residents in the Wolfe Street section of Baltimore for whom he conducted services in the basement of St. Stanislaus Roman Catholic Church. Father Orun, who had been secretary at the chancellory in Philadelphia, lived at St. Athanasius Roman Catholic parish house with Rev. Paul Sandalgi, the pastor. The cantor or *dyak* was John Boyko, a young man who had been trained by the Basilian Fathers.

SS. *Peter and Paul Ukrainian Catholic Church in Curtis Bay.*
U.E.A.M.

As *dyak*, Mr. Boyko led the church choir, taught students in the parish school, and was a leader in the cultural activities of the parish. In a similar capacity, he served the east Baltimore residents.

In the autumn of 1913 the small wooden church was destroyed by fire, believed to have been caused by the glowing embers coming from a censer used in burning incense and which was left unemptied after the Sunday vespers. Fortunately for the parish an empty Presbyterian church and a parish house were located only one block away, at Church and Fairhaven Streets. Father Orun, with the help of Father Sandalgi, arrived at an agreement with the Presbyterians to buy both the brick church and the brick parish house for only $4000.00. Alterations were quickly made and the church services were resumed. The first floor of the parish house was made into the parish hall.

Until 1946 SS. Peter and Paul was served by the pastor of St. Michael's on Wolfe Street, who commuted, together with Mr. Boyko, to Curtis Bay. Each Sunday and Holy Day they went twice to SS. Peter and Paul, 8:00 A.M. for the Holy Liturgy, and 3:00 P.M. for Vespers. The times were trying when many of the members barely eked out an existence and when the priest and the *dyak* went unpaid for months. The depression years tested the fortitude and spiritual reserves of a people who previously had experienced much privation in the unfree land of their birth. Then, too, they had to overcome the same forces of disunion which for some time encroached on a national scale, penetrating the area with renewed vigor in the economic doldrums of 1929-1931 and which were bent on weakening the strong sense of Greek Catholic identity which prevailed among the Ukrainian Catholics in the United States. As in the preceding decades of Russian attempts at conversion, the Orthodox persuaders were meticulous in retaining the words "Greek Catholic" when assigning a name to a succumbing parish.

Moreover, to some the idea of an independent church in their new country had a certain measure of democratic appeal whereby there was a loosening of ties from central church authority all the way to Rome, as well as from those

Canonical visitation of Bishop Bohachevsky in 1924, the year he arrived in the United States as the second bishop for Ukrainian Catholics.

American political and economic tyrants who had so abused their positions of power that many values formerly cherished had come into question and were severely battered when exposed to the erosion of material hardship and privation.[20] The Ukrainian Greek Catholics in Curtis Bay withstood the attacks from all quarters, just as in earlier times members of Ukrainian parishes had to meet more powerful and better-financed forays into their ranks as described by Wasyl Halich:

> In the Russian mission the clergymen are, in the majority of cases, without any higher education or distinctive ability. Most of those of the latter group have had probably the equivalent of six grades of an American public school. Their theological course was likewise very abbreviated, consisting of two to six months of private study. In 1914, when Russian armies entered East Galicia, the agents of that government in America used every means possible to make Russian Orthodox out of Ukrainian immigrants. Almost to the end of the World War, any Ukrainian in America with any kind of intelligence and ability to read and write could have become a Russian priest, if he wanted to.[21]

The extent of Czarist Russian government intervention among Ukrainian Catholics who were or had been citizens of Austria-Hungary can be gleaned from the following extracts from *Orthodox America 1794-1976* published by the Orthodox Church in America:

> The American Diocese, being perhaps the largest missionary diocese of the Russian Church, depended heavily upon the Mother Church for financial assistance prior to the October Revolution. In 1916, the American Diocese requested that the allotments made to her be increased, as the previous sums had grown insufficient. Of the $1,000,000 requested by the Diocese, the Holy Synod of Russia alloted $550,000. With the Revolution, however, all funds were cut off permanently, and the North American Diocese was thrown into economic chaos by the sudden and unexpected need to depend on its own resources and communicants for financial support.
>
> The termination of funds from Russia was especially felt by the priests, who were entirely dependent upon the Mother Church for their salaries and pensions. . . .[22]

After World War II, the flow of new immigrants and priests benefitted SS. Peter and Paul. On January 1946, Bohdan Volosin, a newly-ordained priest, arrived from Rome to assist the aged Father Maniosky and to act as pastor of SS. Peter and Paul. Residing in the parish house in Curtis Bay, Father Volosin in his short tenure gave impetus to a new sense of wholeness and nearness to the requirements of the people. A church choir was organized by Yuriy Sabol. New liturgical books were purchased through the generosity of Maria Konrad and ornamentation was added to the altar. Father Volosin's duties also included ministering to the needs of the mission parish of Manassas, Virginia.

On August 20, 1948, Father Basil Seredowych was assigned as the resident pastor and assstant to Reverend Maniosky at St. Michael's parish. He initiated a number of important projects, the chief of which was the painting of the church interior by the famous Ukrainian artist, Sviatoslav Hordynsky. Included in his work were eleven large paintings of saints and religious scenes.

Reverend Roman Hanas was pastor from May 8, 1949, to October 10, 1950. During this period many Ukrainian families moved into the suburban surroundings of the parish, the membership rolls showing a substantial increase.

Archbishop Constantine Bohachevsky as of October 10, 1950, assigned Father Wasyl Solowiy as the first full-time pastor of the now self-sustaining parish. Under Father Solowiy's long pastorship, many imporvements and additions to the church facilities, such as replacement of the heating system, new reflector lights and sidewalk, renovation of two rooms in the rectory attic, were made. A requisite of churches of the Byzantine Slavonic Rite was finally met through the generosity of Anthony and Elizabeth Bartoch who willed their house to the parish for meeting the costs of installing an iconostasis. The wooden designs and intricate carvings were done by William Zahrodnik of New York. The paintings or icons were drawn by Christine Dochwat of Philadelphia. Many parishioners donated sums to cover the costs of the paintings: Bohdan and Hryhoriy Woytowycz, $200, Jesus Christ; Mrs. Stefania Cykieta, $200, Blessed Mother; Mr. and Mrs. Ivan Ilchytyn, $100, St. Michael; anonymous donor, $100, St.

Rev. Wasyl Solowiy and Sisterhood of Immaculate Conception of Blessed Virgin Mary in Curtis Bay

Archdeacon Stephen; Myhailo Smoliak, Bohdan Dudyma, Ivan Olsun and Mr. and Mrs. Bohdan Lasiuk, $50 each for the four evangelists on the Royal Doors. When the Golden Jubilee of the present church, the Sisterhood of the Immaculate Conception of the Blessed Virgin Mary, and the priesthood of Reverend Wasyl Solowiy were celebrated on June 23, 1963, the iconostasis was ready for these simultaneous events. Father Solowiy continued as pastor until April 1971.

Pastors of SS. Peter and Paul thereafter were as follows:

    Rev. Martin Canavan, April 1971-August 1972
    Rev. Oryst M. Balaban, September 1972-February 1973
    Rev. Lev Dorosh, February-June 1973, Assistant Pastor with
        Very Rev. Petro Melnyczuk as Administrator
    Rev. George Markewych, June 1973-August 1975
    Rev. Volodimir Hrabec, September 1975-September 1976
    Right Rev. Walter Paska, September 1976 to present

Current members of the Church Committee are Michaylo Ihnat — treasurer, Michaylo Smoliak — secretary, Michaylo Choma, Adam Cizdyn, Bohdan Woytowycz, Ilko Zaron, Bohdan Lasiuk, Anton Lukianczuk. The parish adult membership numbers over 100, the majority of whom are from among the newer immigrants.

ST. BASIL'S UKRAINIAN CATHOLIC CHURCH

The Ukrainian Catholic community in northeastern Maryland had its beginnings with the plans of Bishop Soter Stephen Ortynsky of Philadelphia for the erection of a convent and orphanage at Chesapeake City. In 1910 land was bought for this purpose, and in 1914 the Sisters of St. Basil the Great were operating their school and orphanage. Bishop Ortynsky had also acquired 700 acres of land on which he encouraged settlement of Ukrainians, with particular appeals to those doing hard, dangerous work in the coal mines and urban mills and factories.

As the population grew, religious services were held more frequently, usually in the homes of parishioners, with an out-of-town priest leading the Holy Liturgy. On October

His Excellency The Most Reverend Soter Stephen Ortynsky, OSBM, D.D., first Ukrainian Catholic Bishop in United States. He arrived in the U.S. August 27, 1907 and died March 24, 1916.

28, 1917, an official meeting was held at the home of Paul Wasylczuk at which time a board of trustees was elected and a name, St. Basil the Great, selected for the parish. The trustees, chosen for one year, were Joseph Ortynsky, Andrew Barahura and Alex Krochak. Joseph Ortynsky donated the trees from one acre of his forest land for cutting into lumber for use in building the church. Wasyl Malinowsky and Peter Tycki volunteered to serve as collectors of funds.

On August 26, 1918, Paul Wasylczuk gave a lot, 60 by 80 feet, as the site for the church. Each family was then assessed $25.00 as its official minimum contribution to the building fund. The trustees elected in 1918 were Wasyl Malinowsky, Nicholas Hrynick and Stephen Motowylak.

At a meeting held on October 30, 1919, building of the church was discussed and steps taken to begin construction. With Reverend Basil Petriwsky in charge, the work began. The carpenters, Alex Korchak, John Hrabec, Michael Breza and Alex Hotra, assisted by every available parish hand, quickly erected the strong frame then skillfully added the roof, siding, flooring and the many other touches and finishes which only their church, they felt, must have. For a number of years they devoted much time to these tasks and the raising of funds to pay off the debts which were incurred. In 1924 the church was expanded and pews were installed. The use of seats at St. Basil's, and at many other Ukrainian Catholic Churches in the United States, was a welcome departure from the hardiness test imposed under the old European custom. The property was landscaped and a fence put up.[23]

Father Basil Petriwsky had served the people of Chesapeake City as a mission community from 1915, holding services in various homes. Divine Liturgy was offered by him at the Chapel of the Basilian Sisters in 1919 until the completion of the new church in 1920. Father

St. Basil's Ukrainian Catholic Church, Chesapeake City (U.E.A.M.)

Petriwsky continued as pastor to the year 1924, with assistance from Fathers John Ortynsky, Basil Korishowsky, D. Jaczkewich, Zachary Orun, Antin Litowich, and Zaharowey. In the following years the pastors were Reverend Oleksy Pelensky and Reverend Paul Protsko.

During all of these years nonresident pastors served the parish, but in 1930 Reverend Stephen Chehansky moved into Chesapeake City to carry out his priestly duties on a full-time basis. Father Chehansky remained at St. Basil's until June 1, 1936, when he was transferred to the pastorship at Hamtramck, Michigan. In 1931, during his administration, a parish hall was constructed.

Reverend Jacob De Boer, a Belgian Redemptorist Father who accepted the Byzantine Slavonic Rite, learned Ukrainian and served in both Ukraine and the United States, became the next pastor. Father De Boer was at St. Basil's until 1941. From May of 1944 until June 1948 he was the rector of St. Josaphat's Ukrainian Catholic Seminary in northeast Washington and also conducted the Holy Liturgy for residents of Washington and the nearby Maryland and Virginia communities. In 1942 and part of 1943 Father Myron Leshchynsky was pastor, followed by Reverend John Zabawa for a few months in 1943. The latter was succeeded by Father Myron Plekon, who organized the parish branch of the Ukrainian Catholic Youth League. This branch of the UCYL became very active in carrying out many tasks of benefit to the local and neighboring parishes.

The names of individuals who became members of St. Basil's Parish during its formative years follow.[24] The families of all members were automatically included as parishioners.

> October 28, 1917: Joseph Ortynsky, Stephen Motowylak, Andrew Barahura, John Hrabec, Elias Shestock, Alex Krochad, Alex Stephaniuk, Nicholas Hrynick, Samuel Chicosky, Harry Arkatin, John Martiniuk, Paul Wasylczuk, Peter Tycki, Nicholas Loburak, John Harasymczuk, Wasyl Malinowsky, Daniel Yonko, Michael Lichowid, Anthony Waclawsky, John Teresczuk, John Losten, Nicholas Swyka, Alex Onufreychuk, Nicholas Pitel.

The most Reverend Basil H. Losten, Apostolic Administrator of the Ukrainian Catholic Archeparchy of Philadelphia. Born May 11, 1930 in Chesapeake City, ordained June 10, 1957, and consecrated May 25, 1971.

Sanctuary and iconostasis in St. Basil's Ukrainian Catholic Church, Chesapeake City.
U.E.A.M.

1918: John Paslawsky, Paul Lysak, Joseph Zaborowsky, John Kutz, Dmytro Ladnick.

1919: John Hrycek, Philip Truch, Nicholas Kurischak, Adam Schreiber, Luke Yedniak, Michael Breza, Alex Hotra, John Irshak.

1921: Luke Korcheba.

1922: Stephen Blendy, Alex Luzetsky, Stephen Boyko, Peter Kmet.

1923: Wasyl Andryshyn, Michael Basalyga, Nicholas Kulyk.

1924: Michael Maksyn, Leon Swyka, Alex Starowsky.

St. Basil's Parish is outstanding in its contribution to religious vocations, having furnished two priests and two sisters to the Ukrainian Catholic Church: Most Reverend Basil Losten, now Apostolic Administrator of the Archeparchy of Philadelphia, ordained June 10, 1957; Reverend Stephen Hotra, ordained 1944; Anna Arkatin, Sister M. Barnarda, Order of St. Basil the Great; Sophia Arkatin, Sister M. Tharcillia, Order of St. Basil the Great.

Father Victor Pospishil, now Very Reverend Monsignor and a recognized authority and writer on canon law, came to the parish in December of 1952, serving the faithful until 1958. Father John Lebedowycz's pastorship which began in 1958 lasted until December 1966, when he suffered a severe heart attack. Reverend Peter Laptuta, a Redemptorist Father from Newark, was then assigned to St. Basil's from January 1967, being the pastor during the Golden Jubilee celebration. In 1972 Father Roman Martyniuk, a native of Pennsylvania and an American-educated priest with 10 years of work in the Midwest, became the spiritual leader of the Chesapeake City congregation. He was succeeded in December of 1972 by Reverend Myron Sozanski of the Redemptorist Fathers. Beginning in 1976, after the illness of Father Sozanski, reverend Roman Dubitsky, pastor of the Wilmington, Delaware, parish, also assumed similar responsibilities for the flock at St. Basil's Ukrainian Catholic Church.

HOLY FAMILY UKRAINIAN CATHOLIC CHURCH

Ukrainian Catholics of the Byzantine Slavonic Rite residing in the Washington Metropolitan Area have, since October 5, 1941, publicly worshipped in their own rite, beginning in rented facilities of the Chapel of the Discalced Carmelite Fathers, 2131 Lincoln Road, N.E. Father Emilian Ananevich, the first rector of St. Josaphat's Seminary and later a member of the Franciscans, led the Divine Liturgy for twenty persons. For eleven years the Carmelite Chapel served as the center of worship for Ukrainian Catholics of Washington and the nearby suburbs. With the purchase on April 21, 1943, of 1.29 acres of land for $20,000 by Bishop Constantine Bohachevsky at 201 Taylor Street, N.E., on which to construct seminary buildings, a resurgent Ukrainian Catholic community was assured in the nation's capital.[25]

The faithful were served by rectors of the seminary, among whom were Father Athanasius Chimy, OSBM, who came November 10, 1941; Father Jacob de Boer, a Redemptorist who arrived May 12, 1944; and Father Stephen Hrynuck who was appointed as of June 28, 1948. On May 24, 1949, Father Wolodymyr Wozniak was assigned by Bishop Bohachevsky to organize a parish, he holding the first Holy Liturgy for the Holy Family parishioners on June 19, 1949, at the Carmelite Chapel. The parish house was in a rented building at 1938 Summit Place, N.E.

Another planned milestone appeared in *The Way* on September 10, 1949, in the form of a sketch of the new major St. Josaphat's Seminary to be built on the plot acquired in 1943. Ground-breaking ceremonies, with Bishop Constantine Bohachevsky celebrating the Divine Liturgy in the crypt of the nearby National Shrine, were held in the presence of 3,000 people on May 28, 1950. The Apostolic Delegate, Amleto G. Cicognani, presided and delivered the sermon. The responses to the Divine Liturgy were sung by the Cathedral Choir from Philadelphia combined with the Dumka Chorus from New York. A banquet attended by 500 persons was held in the Catholic University gymnasium to end the joyous occasion.

A parish committee was approved by Bishop Bohachevsky for the year 1950: Dr. Yuriy Starosolsky, Marvin Gretchen, Michael Kosciw, and Stephen Kistulentz. Father Canon Wolodymyr Pylypec succeeded to the pastorship of Holy Family Parish on November 1, 1950. More space being required for parish use, a house was rented at 3119 12th Street, N.E. To help with rental payments a number of rooms in this building were sublet to university students. The Gregorian calendar was adopted by the parish on December 17, 1950, accompanied by a general consensus of the advantages accruing by concurrent identification with the common Christian feasts and Holy days. The parish was now functioning in many areas typical of Ukrainian Catholic congregations. A choir was singing the responses, hymns, carols, etc., plays and other presentations were made, Easter and Christmas dinners were held, religious and language instructions were given, and many other activities were sponsored. Among the leaders in enlivening participation in parish programs was the local chapter of the Ukrainian Catholic Youth League, which officially formed on January 21, 1951, with Michael Cello as president; Andrew Petruska, vice-president; Marian Cello and Oksana Starosolsky, secretaries; Dr. Wasyl Siokalo, treasurer; and Walter Prokopik, membership director.

A more spacious church, the St. Vincent de Paul Chapel, at 3802 Brookland Avenue, N.E., on the campus of Catholic University was made available on May 4, 1952, to the parish without charge through the approval of Archbishop Patrick O'Boyle. But steps were soon taken to establish a building fund for acquiring or building a church which would be owned by the parish. However, for ten years this ideally-located chapel was the spiritual center for Ukrainians of Metropolitan Washington.

Ukrainians of Washington, Maryland and many sections of the United States took part in the solemn blessing of the completed St. Josaphat's Ukrainian Catholic Seminary, costing $500,000, on Saturday, May 31, 1952. Archbishop Constantine Bohachevsky blessed the seminary and celebrated the Solemn Episcopal Divine

Father Canon Wolodymyr Pylypec began to celebrate Divine Liturgies in St. Vincent de Paul Chapel on Catholic University campus on May 4, 1952.　　　　　　　　　　　　　　　　　　　*Holy Family photo*

Liturgy, assisted by Bishops Ambrose Senyshyn, Niel Savaryn, Andrew Roborecki, and Daniel Ivancho. Presiding and delivering the sermon to over 80 priests and 7,000 faithful was Amleto Cicognani, Apostolic Delegate. A combined choir of 136 voices under the direction of Michael Dobosh from three parishes — the Cathedral and St. Nicholas parishes in Philadelphia, and St. John the Baptist in Newark — sang the responses.

The 16th Annual Convention of the Ukrainian Catholic Youth League was held on November 11-14, 1954, in the Mayflower Hotel in Washington, with the Holy Family Chapter of Washington and the St. Michael's Chapter of Baltimore furnishing the administrative and planning personnel under the direction of Stephen Koslo, chairman.[26] The voices of the Holy Family Choir, directed by Matthew Berko, penetrated throughout the United States to make more joyous the holidays in millions of

Father Athanasius Chimy, OSBM, and seminarian Ihor Pelensky with members of Washington congregation after Holy Liturgy at Carmelite Chapel in 1942. First service was on October 5, 1941.
Holy Family photo

American homes when Ukrainian Christmas carols were sung on a national radio network on December 25, 1954.

Reverend Henry Sagan who replaced Father Pylypec on April 28, 1955, regularly issued a Sunday bulletin which informed parishioners of their religious obligations and contained parish news and events of general interest. On September 7, 1955, he was succeeded by Father John Litwak, under whom on December 19 the parish members and its choir participated in the Second Annual Pageant of Peace on the Ellipse near the White House. This event was televised and broadcast nationally, and the Ukrainian Christmas customs were described by Michael Waris, Jr., and subsequently transmitted over the Voice of America. The pastorial assignment of Reverend Theodore Danusiar began on March 21, 1956, he following the less-than-a-month tenure of Father Paul Harchison, and remaining for

His Excellency
The Most Reverend Ambrose Senyshyn, O.S.B.M., D.D.
Metropolitan-Archbishop of Philadelphia
Spiritual Head of Ukrainian Catholics—U.S.A.

Shrine of the Immaculate Conception near which the Ukrainian Catholic Shrine of the Holy Family is now being built.

11 years. On April 29, 1956, Bishop Ambrose Senyshyn made the first canonical visitation to Holy Family. Shortly thereafter, on June 17, the Metropolitan Andrew Sheptitsky Branch (No. 222) of the Providence Association of Ukrainian Catholics of America was formed. This fraternal organization assists Ukrainian Catholics in time of need and bereavement and provides loans for parish projects and realty purchases.

A new parish residence was acquired at 3900 4th Street, N.W., in June 1956. Parishioners donated sums for purchase of various articles, such as an altar, linens, tabernacle, gospel book, candlesticks, priestly vestments, offertory stands, *plaschanytsia*, etc. for use in the chapel set up in the residence. Beginning January 20, 1957, an early Divine Liturgy at 10:00 A.M. began regularly at this location. The chanted liturgy was continued at 11:00 A.M. in the St. Vincent de Paul Chapel.

A celebration of national importance was organized by Holy Family Parish for November 4, 1956, when commemorative ceremonies were held for the 1000th Anniversary of the Baptism of St. Olha, Grand Princess of Ukraine. The Solemn Divine Liturgy, with Bishop-elect Joseph Schmondiuk as the main celebrant and with Archbishop O'Boyle of Washington presiding, was held in the crypt of the National Shrine with about 2500 persons participating.

Expansion of the parish and acquisition of its own church were recognized as near term goals. In the general meeting of September 28, 1958, a planning committee was elected for pursuing these goals. On February 1, 1959, a fund-raising campaign was launched, with 37 volunteers under the direction of Michael Burda signed to solicit funds. A target of $150,000 was set, with each family asked to pledge a minimum of $300. The Chancery in Philadelphia in a letter of March 21, 1961, placed new restrictions on property purchases by requiring the parish to have on hand 50% of the cost of any realty it desired to buy. Fortunately, an acceptable offer was made for a highly desirable property at 4817 Blagden Avenue, N.W., embracing 0.7 acre and containing a large residence. On September 12, 1961,

Holy Family rectory and chapel at 4817 Blagden Ave., where two Divine Liturgies were begun by Father Danusiar June 10, 1962.

Holy Family photo

the agreement was completed with Albert W. Fox for the transfer at a cost of $50,000. For $17,000 Miroslav D. Nimciv remodeled the veranda and several rooms into a chapel large enough for 200 worshippers. Rooms were furnished for classes in religion and Ukrainian studies and for use as the parish rectory. Parish members donated a new altar, linens, phelonions, pulpit, votive stands, stations of the cross, Christmas crib, chairs and other articles. St. Mary's Church in Crescent, N.Y., contributed the pews. The outdoor church cross was taken from 4th Street and placed at the Blagden Avenue site.[27] On June 10, 1962, Divine Liturgy was celebrated twice, at 9:00 A.M. and 11:00 A.M. at the Blagden Avenue Chapel, the present site of parish worship. Father Danusiar, on May 26 of the next year, marked the 50th Anniversary of the creation of the Ukrainian Catholic Exarchate (diocese) in the U.S.A. by the Apostolic See on May 28, 1913, with a Thanksgiving Solemn Liturgy. And on November 24 Father Danusiar was one of 3 clergymen-chaplains officially taking part in the funeral of President John F. Kennedy.

Holy Family Parish, during the 3-day ceremonies for the unveiling of the Taras Shevchenko Monument while over 100,000 Ukrainians from all over the free world were in Washington, on June 26, 1964, had an all-night vigil with the exposition of the Blessed Sacrament, singing of hymns, candle-light procession, way of the cross, and special prayers for our persecuted Church, bishops, priests, religious and faithful. On Sunday, June 28, four Divine Liturgies attended by thousands were celebrated on the Holy Family grounds. The Holy Name Society, which had been formed the previous year, in September 1966, provided the core for an orchestra led by Eugene Proch. For several years the "Federalists" played at parish festivals, weddings, dances, etc. Father Dmytro Szul, who had served the parish as an assistant pastor since 1950, died on October 28, 1966, after having passed his 85th birthday. The Ladies Society, organized April 7, 1967 and which had an envious success record in its many fund-raising activities, published a 166-page *Ukrainian Cook Book* in 1969 and a 100-page *Ukrainian Easter Egg Book* in 1970.

The Holy Family Parish, at the request of Metropolitan Ambrose Senyshyn, began a new era of pastorial care under the Ukrainian Redemptorist Fathers. Father Wolodymyr Krayewsky, C.SS.R., the new pastor, in the presence of the dean, Father Petro Melnyczuk and Father Theodore Danusiar, signed the agreement for the assumption of this responsibility. Father Myron Sozansky, C.SS.R., became the assistant pastor at the parish.

The Holy Family Chapel on August 2, 1968, was the scene of a Solemn Divine Liturgy concelebrated by His Beatitude the Major Archbishop Cardinal Joseph Slipy, Metrolopitan Ambrose Senyshyn, Bishop Niel Savaryn, Bishop Joseph Schmondiuk and Bishop Jaroslav Gabro. Following the Liturgy at a reception at Catholic University, Cardinal Patrick O'Boyle bestowed upon Cardinal Slipy an honorary doctorate from Catholic University.

A parish library was started in February 1973 at the initiative of Euhenia Sharko, who donated 22 religious books. The importance of this information and study center grew as the number of books increased through donations from parish members and organizations. Caring for the library and promoting circulation were Oksana Starosolsky, Olha Nakonechny, and students such as Maria and Sophia Nakonechny, Mary and Catherine Sokil, and Olena and Larysa Kurylas. A parents' committee serves as a selection and policy-formation unit. After each Holy Liturgy, the student librarians issue and receive books.

Ukrainian Catholics and Orthodox from Baltimore, the Washington area, and various parts of the United States gathered at the Shevchenko Monument to pray and call attention to the starvation of 7,000,000 Ukrainian farmers and villagers during the man-made famine of 1932-33 when the Godless Soviet communist rulers, through the use of force, denied peasants access to food crops they had grown. This Day of National Mourning, May 26, 1973, was held by Ukrainians wherever throughout the free world Ukrainians had been scattered.[28]

An interesting poll was taken by Father S. J. Shawel regarding the location preferred for the building of a new church: 99 chose Washington; 51, Maryland; 20, Virginia; 10, it makes no difference; 7, wherever the majority wants; and 10 did not express an opinion. The preference for a central site, associated with city amenities and accessible to nearly all parishioners, especially by public transportation, is apparent.[29]

A Holy Liturgy, primarily in English, was introduced in the parish, at 9:00 A.M., November 4, 1973. The American-born, now numbering 4 generations, who have little understanding of Ukrainian now could participate in ceremonies of their inherited rite with better grasp of its meaning and some basis of belonging and equality as those experienced or trained in the use of Ukrainian.

On February 28, 1974, Father Michael Hrynchyshyn, Provincial of the Ukrainian Redemptorist Fathers, viewed with Fathers Shawel and Denischuk the 6 building sites which had been investigated by the Parish Building

Committee. In the opinion of the Fathers, the Harewood Road location was preferable and should be purchased if offered at a price within the financial means of the congregation. On June 15, Father General Michael Daniel of the Franciscan Society of The Atonement agreed to sell the property and assigned negotiating tasks to Father Austin Kittredge. On January 29, 1975, a cost of $2.25 per square foot for the plot believed to contain 2.69 acres was accepted. But as surveyed the land area consists of over 3 acres, or 130,717,41 square feet, which at a rate of $2.25 establishes a sales price of $294,114.17.

A campaign executive committee for conducting a funds drive for building the new church was confirmed as follows: General Chairman, Michael Waris, Jr.; Co-Chairmen, Eugene Jarosewich, Ihor Vitkovitsky, and Walter Zadoretzky; Financial Secretaries, Anna Lucille Tymm and Helen Ostrosky. Bishop Basil Losten blessed the building site on July 14, 1975. In less than two years, on May 22, 1977, ground-breaking for construction of the first phase of a church and parish center began, with ceremonies conducted by Bishop Basil H. Losten. The plans provide for a Shrine to Our Lady of Pochayiv and a commemorative cross on the occasion of the 1000th anniversary of the Baptism of Ukraine (1988). Pochayiv, in Volynia, is famous for the many miracles which occurred there since the 13th century, attributed to The Mother of God and since the 16th century emanating through the miraculous Icon of the Mother of God of Pochayiv. Since 1831, when the Russians seized the Pochayiv Monastery, the icon has remained hidden, presumably where placed by and known only to the Basilian Fathers.

Near the Holy Family Church and Shrine is the Polish Chapel in the National Shrine of the Immaculate Conception. In this Polish Chapel, Eastern Rite Catholics may pray before the ancient icon (copy) of the Mother of God of Polotsk (now in Czestochowa) and the mosaic of St. Josaphat Kuntsevich, the Ukrainian Archbishop of Polotsk. In the Sacristy of the National Shrine is a stained glass window of Soter Stephen Ortynsky, first Ukrainian Catholic bishop in America, and on the right side of the

St. Josaphat Kuntsevich, martyred Nov. 13, 1623. Native of Volynian section of Ukraine and member of the Order of St. Basil the Great, he worked for reunion of Byelorussians and Ukrainians with the Catholic Church, retaining the Byzantine Slavonic Ruthenian Rite.

Sanctuary is a mosaic of the Vatican Council II, containing also Cardinal Joseph Slipy, Ukrainian Major Archbishop.[30]

When the Ukrainian Catholic Shrine of the Holy Family is completed, it will be a "monumental church of God" in the capital of Washington and an example and encouragement for the whole Ukrainian community, wrote Metropolitan Ambrose Senyshyn to the Pastor, Very Reverend Stephen Shawel.

PATRONAGE OF THE MOTHER OF GOD BYZANTINE CATHOLIC CHURCH, ARBUTUS

Maryland's first parish of the Passaic, New Jersey, Eparchy of the Byzantine Ruthenian Rite had its beginnings on October 22, 1966, when Reverend John S. Danilak of St. Gregory's in Washington held the Holy Liturgy at St. Joseph's Monastery in Catonsville. Six families attended. Efforts to organize a parish were intensified by a group which included William Rudy. Frank Loya, Nicholas Scochin, and Eugene Kakalec. A Christmas Liturgy was celebrated on December 25, 1966,

Seminarians of St. Josaphat's Seminary, 1963-64, with Metropolitan Ambrose Senyshyn and Fr. Rector Basil Makuch. The Seminary was blessed on May 31, 1952, by Archbishop Constantine Bohachevsky. It is located at 201 Taylor St., N.E. **Holy Family photo**

after which it was announced that Holy Liturgy would be regularly scheduled for each Sunday and Holy Day. Services were transferred to the chapel of the Polish Sisters of St. Joseph's Nursing Home, Catonsville, on June 9, 1968, where more consistent scheduling was possible. In January, 1969, a parish advisory council was formed to assist the priest in administering and expanding activities. The Nursing Home chapel was outgrown, so on June 1, 1969, Our Lady of Perpetual Help Church, Woodlawn, became the third home of the mission parish.

Bishop Michael J. Dudick acceded on February 22, 1969, to the request that the church be named Patronage of the Mother of God. The parishioners responded by working harder, holding dinner dances, picnics, bingos, etc., to provide funds for building their own church. On June 14, 1970, Bishop Dudick made his first canonical visitation, celebrating Divine Liturgy of Thanksgiving that afternoon. Negotiations with the Sulpician Fathers of St. Mary's Seminary for purchase of 2½ acres of land at Maiden Choice Lane, near the Wilkins Avenue Exit of the Beltway, were completed on August 27, 1971. The Passaic Diocese contributed $10,000 for the purchase of this land. In the meantime, Father Lee, rector of St. Mary's Seminary College, permitted the parish to use its chapel on Maiden Choice Lane for the Divine Liturgy, starting on July 3, 1971. Preliminary plans were made for construction of a parish center on the newly-acquired property.[31]

On Tuesday of Holy Week 1972, the parish members discovered that Nativity Lutheran Church in Arbutus was going to be sold. The church building at Linden and Highview Avenues was only 20 years old and it contained a basement suitable for meetings and parish events. In addition, adjacent to the church was a parish house. The consensus of the parishioners was quickly obtained and with the approval of Bishop Dudick contractual arrangements for purchase of Holy Nativity were signed on April 17, 1972. Even before completion of the sale, Reverend Albert E. Bielenberg, pastor of Nativity, invited the Byzantine Rite Christians to use the church for Divine Liturgy. So on June 17, 1972, Patronage Mother of God

Patronage Mother of God Byzantine Catholic Church
U.E.A.M.

Parish and Holy Nativity Lutheran Parish coexisted, utilizing the same edifice until the end of February 1973 when Holy Nativity's new church two blocks away was ready for occupancy. This "ecumenical spirit" drew the favorable attention of the *Arbutus Times*. Legal settlement for the transfer was effected as of January 30, 1973, the consideration amounting to $65,000.

After March 1973 alterations and additions were made to the interior of the church to conform it as nearly as possible to the traditional Byzantine Slavonic architecture and beauty. An *iconostasis* was installed to separate the sanctuary from the large part of the church, the nave. Within the sanctuary an altar with a cover or "baldachino" was erected. Almost every parish member contributed many hours to the work of renovation, so that by October 7, 1973, the solemn blessing and dedication by His Excellency

Sister Miriam Teresa Demyanovich, a Ruthenian Greek Catholic of Bayonne, N.J., 1901-1927, now under beatification and cannonization procedures. **M.M. Conklin Photo.**

Father John S. Danilak, Pastor of Patronage of Mother of God and St. Gregory.

Michael J. Dudick could proceed under the essential design features of the Byzantine Rite. Besides the many hours of planning and labor parishioners gave generously in money to meet the costs of renovation and the articles which were purchased. Specific items for which donations were made in memory of loved ones are as follows:

> Preparation altar — Kakalec Family, Anna Scherbik, and Margaret Pcsolar; vesting altar — Katherine Scochin, Margaret Pcsolar; baptismal font — Mr. and Mrs. John Mikus; chalice — Ruszin family; censer and stand — Joseph Lochte; ciborium — Mr. and Mrs. Walter Kratzen; cruets — Mr. and Mrs. Paul B. Jackanicz; flags — Mr. and Mrs. Ronald Thompson; holy water fonts — Mr. and Mrs. Philip Finnegan; holy water sprinkler — Mr. and Mrs. Joseph Swigar; iconostasis — St. Nicholas: Mr. and Mrs. Daniel Magnes; Mother of God: Mr. and Mrs. Hank Zabka; Christ the Teacher: Mr. and Mrs. Nicholas Scochin; Patronage of the Mother of God: Mr. and Mrs. Paul N. Yackanicz; Dormition: Mr. and Mrs. Arnold Timko; Right Deacon door: Kuchta Family; Last Supper: Mr. and Mrs. Andrew Turian; mirovaniye plates — Susan Pcsolar; nativity set — Mr. and Mrs. William Seck; processional cross — John and Michael Skovran Families; sanctuary chairs — Miss Agnes Napfel and Mrs. John Polaschik; sanctuary lamp — Mrs. Frank Ruszin; tabernacle — Miss Caroline H. Napfel and Mrs. Margaret Rabl; three-branch candelabra — Mr. and Mrs. Frank Bukszar; Christ All-Powerful icon — Mrs. Nicholas Kolesar.[32]

The blessing of the parish center, church cornerstone, and the church on October 7, 1973, was a memorable occasion, with Bishop Dudick as chief celebrant and Bishop Austin J. Murphy, Auxiliary Bishop of Baltimore, presiding. The Holy Ghost Choir from Philadelphia rendered the responses mostly in the English version of the Holy Liturgy of St. John Chrysostom rather than in the Church Slavonic whose use has been decreasing as fewer of the American-born understand the language of their parents or grandparents. Patronage of the Mother of God Parish has continued to celebrate its liturgical ceremonies mostly in English. A school of religion has been established in the parish house for teaching religion, and hopefully for perpetuating the beautiful church hymns whose fullest spiritual impact can be appreciated only in the original church language in which they were composed.

*Byzantine Catholic Chapel in the National Shrine
of the Immaculate Conception, Washington D.C.*

The Iconostasis or icon screen separates the sanctuary from the main portion of the chapel. It has the icon of Christ the Teacher on the right and of Mary the Mother of God on the left. Between these are the "royal doors," or the entrance to the sanctuary with four Evangelists. Two "deacon's doors" are for entry of deacons and other helpers. These doors have icons of SS. Stephen and Lawrence.

ST. GREGORY OF NYSSA BYZANTINE CATHOLIC CHURCH, BELTSVILLE

St. Gregory had been functioning in Washington for two decades but the dispersal of its members into the suburbs in Virginia and Maryland led to a search for a Maryland site which would better serve the Carpatho-Ruthenians residing east of the national capital. Father Danilak, who is also administrator of the Arbutus parish, and the church members decided that Beltsville was a good central location for a metropolitan Washington congregation. A plot was purchased and services were begun in the spring of 1976 temporarily in an old structure on the premises at 12420 Old Gunpowder Road, Beltsville, while construction proceeded on the new church building.

The parish extends its coverage into the District of Columbia for those Byzantine Rite Catholics not attending the Ukrainian Byzantine Rite Catholic Church of the Holy Family at 4817 Blagden Avenue, N.W. St. Gregory had its start in Washington on February 5, 1956, when Father Edward Rosack celebrated the first Divine Liturgy for the Carpatho-Ruthenians in the auditorium of St. Patrick's Academy at 924 G Street, N.W., Washington, with 93 persons in attendance.[33] On July 15, 1960, Bishop Nicholas T. Elko of Munhall, Pa., and the parish entered into a sales contract to buy a church, hall, and rectory at 1415-1419 Gallatin Street, N.W., for the use of St. Gregory's Parish. The cost was $120,000.[34]

From donations of the faithful of the Byzantine Ruthenian Metropolitan Province, a Byzantine Catholic Chapel was erected in the largest church in the Western Hemisphere, the National Shrine of the Immaculate Conception in Washington. The Byzantine-Ruthenian Chapel was dedicated by Metropolitan Archbishop Stephen J. Kocisko on October 6, 1974, commemorating the golden jubilee of the first Byzantine-Ruthenian Diocese in the United States. Many thousands of visitors marvel at the majesty and beauty of the main mosaic icons of the Protection of the Mother of God, mosaic icons on the side walls, and paintings of icons on the *iconostasis* done by the

Mosaic in the Byzantine Catholic Chapel

The left panel depicts the religious and cultural background of Ruthenian Catholics. The Carpathians form the background. SS. Cyril and Methodius brought Christianity and Byzantine Rite to Ruthenians.

The right panel shows Byzantine-Ruthenian Catholics in the United States, the seminary in Pittsburgh, Icon of Our Lady of Perpetual Help, places of work, and Church growth.

noted Ukrainian church artist, Christine Dochwat.

ST. MICHAEL'S UKRAINIAN ORTHODOX CHURCH, BALTIMORE

The origins of St. Michael's Ukrainian Orthodox parish of Baltimore can be traced to October of 1949 when the first Holy Liturgy was celebrated in the hall of the YWCA, 26 South Broadway. The parishioners were mainly recent immigrants residing in Baltimore and also on farms as far as the Eastern Shore of Maryland. The service was conducted by Very Reverend Wasyl Bulawka, who had received permission from Metropolitan Ilarion of Canada to establish a parish. Father Bulawka, Ivan Tryhubinko, Onysym Czumak, Oleksy Fedenko, and Colonel Wolodymyr Herasymenko provided the initiative in organizing the nucleus of a parish which was formed in November 1949 under the name of St. George. In May 1950, Reverend Baker invited the Ukrainian Orthodox to hold their worship services at his church in the 200 Block North Linwood Avenue. Here the first Ukrainian Orthodox marriage ceremony took place, with Father Bulawka officiating.[35]

On the 25th of July 1950, the first general election was held, 29 persons being present. The church council which was selected consisted of Very Reverend Wasyl Bulawka, president; Colonel Wolodymyr Herasymenko, vice-president; Wolodymyr Boyko, secretary; Andrij Tretyak, treasurer; Danilo Chilyk, elder; Olesky Fedenko; Ivan Pawluk and Ivan Hrynenko, auditors. At this meeting the members voted to accept the jurisdiction of Archbishop Ivan Theodorovich of the United States. The church council on August 23, 1950, named Colonel Herasymenko as its president. The name of the parish became St. Michael's. Reverend Yakiw Kostetsky led the divine services for a number of weeks. Since near the end of September, a building at 1806 Fleet Street was being rented, with Very Reverend Andriy Ilinsky, while still working for a railroad company, agreeing to perform the pastoral duties at St. Michael's parish. In October 1950, St. George's parish ceased to exist, nearly all of its members having transferred to St. Michael's to underscore their preference for United States ecclesiastical jurisdiction. Meanwhile, Mikita Perkovets constructed an *iconostasis* for the rented location, but in July 1951 the new owner of the building, which had undergone considerable transformation for the better under parish care, gave the worshippers two days' notice to vacate. Sadly, the church belongings were transferred to the Ukrainian Home on O'Donnell Street for temporary storage.

In September of 1951 the basement facilities of the East

St. Michael's Ukrainian Orthodox Church, Baltimore, with hall and rectory on left. *U.E.A.M.*

Baltimore Street Methodist Episcopal Church were made available to the congregation for the small price of $25.00 per month. Here the parish membership grew amidst exhortations and plans for strengthening the financial base so that a permanent church could be obtained or erected.

In two years an opportune moment arrived, for on October 12, 1953, the Bolton Realty Company conveyed two lots and its buildings, subject to annual ground rents of $118.00 to St. Michael's Ukrainian Orthodox Church, Inc. for a consideration of $15,750.[36] These properties had been assigned to the Bolton Realty Company by the Baltimore Baptist Church Extension Society on August 24, 1953. At the time of purchase of the realty located at 2013-2017 and 2019 Gough Street a mortgage was issued to cover an advance of $8,500 made by the North Bond Street Bohemie Building Association No. 1 of Baltimore City, Inc. Ihor Kurinniy signed the instrument as president of the church corporation, with attorney Frank Petro as witness. Mr. Petro had offered his legal services without cost to the parish. On April 25, 1958, the mortgagee (North Bond Street Bohemie) released the mortgage "for value received," as recorded October 16, 1959.[37] Some time later, on February 9, 1973, a new loan was negotiated in the amount of $2,600 with Bond Federal Savings and Loan Association, the loan being secured by a mortgage on the church properties. The mortgage was signed by Konstantin Stryzak, president. The proceeds were used for remodeling the church hall. After payment in full on August 6, 1973, the mortgage was released.[38]

With physical structures now owned by the parish, an official entity was set up as approval was granted for the Articles of Incorporation on October 26, 1953, by the State Tax Commission of Maryland[39] Saint Michael's Ukrainian Orthodox Church, Inc., was formed by the following subscribers: Harper Lambert, 2603 Llewelyn Avenue, Baltimore; Frank Petro, 2420 East Monument Street, Baltimore; Theodore Nykula, 6618 O'Donnell Street, Baltimore; and Joseph Marmash, 7573 Westfield Road, Baltimore.

According to Article 2,

> The purposes of the corporation shall be to worship God in the faith of the Orthodox Church, to fulfill the spiritual needs of its members, to propagate the Orthodox faith, and the teachings of Jesus Christ, to cultivate by religious education and by social and welfare activities of fellowship the practice of righteousness and brotherhood in the community at large.

The officers of the corporation, as stated in the charter, are the president, first vice-president, second vice-president, secretary, and treasurer. They and six other individuals make up the trustees, all of whom are to be elected for one year at the January annual meeting. No officer or trustee may be elected for more than 3 successive terms. All trustees must be members of the congregation and the majority must be residents of Baltimore City.

Electors are those members of the congregation who have passed the 18th birthday and who are in good standing. The trustees at the time of incorporation were: Very Reverend Ilinsky, Ihor Kurinniy, Ivan Pawluk, Wolodymyr Boyko, Ivan Hrynenko, Mykola Samoyliv, Konstantin Stryzak, Danilo Chilyk, Ahrypina Czumak, Fedir Burenko, Ivan Suchomlyn, Wolodymyr Bilokin, and Kapiton Nyschuk.

Now operating as a separate unit affiliated with an American hierarchy and with adequate building space, the parishioners hopefully moved toward development of the religious community. A choir was formed, school established, and the Sisterhood of St. Sophia began functioning. Among those performing as choir directors were Nikon Procenko, Tymish Procenko, Wolodymyr Chernish, Ivan Stryzak and Mrs. Chuhaj. Serving as cantors or *dyaks* in the parish have been Nikon Procenko, Tymish Procenko, Wolodymyr Chernish, Paulina Ilinsky, Hanna Karpuk, Mrs. Chuhaj, and even Father Bulawka

Iconostasis in St. Michael's Ukrainian Orthodox Church, Baltimore.
U.E.A.M.

who was held on a ready reserve list from which he was called upon to modify his retired status. Very Reverend Bulawka was similarly drafted to carry out the priestly obligations whenever a void commanded attention to the faithful.

Many uncompensated, from a financial viewpoint, tasks were performed by the parishioners. The generosity of donors made possible physical improvements and the conduct of divine services in keeping with church requirements. In 1957 the *iconostasis* was skillfully built by Pawlo Kurriniy and Wasyl Mandrich. In 1960 icons were painted on the iconostasis, walls and ceiling by Dmytro Zacharchuk, donations for this purpose having been made by a number of members, among whom were Onysym Czumak, Wolodymyr Boyko, Wolodymyr Bilokin, and Ivan Pawluk. Nikifor and Christina Shirov paid $650 for a *plaschanitsa*, a beautiful shroud with a painting of the body of Jesus Christ, and their son-in-law and daughter, Charles M. and Natasha Flanders, contributed $2,000 for a tomb containing the body of Jesus, $350 for two metal candle holders, $140 for construction of a concrete entranceway, and $500 for two golden-framed banners used in church services or processions. Ivan Domnenko, in remembrance of his wife Anna, in 1965 purchased for the church five metal candle holders, a chalice, two priestly vestments, and one seven-candle holder at a cost totaling $2,000.

Improvements continued to be made throughout the years. In 1968, when a new roof was put on the church, a dome and cross were erected. In 1970 stained glass windows were installed, the electrical system was replaced, and the entire church was painted. The adoption in 1967 of an envelope system for obtaining revenue not only provided a means of recording and verifying each donor's payments but also a way of increasing contributions. And in the same year new by-laws for the parish were drawn and approval received from the Metropolitan Council.[40]

Very Reverend Andriy Ilinsky, who since September 1950 had been pastor while also holding outside employment, for health reasons could no longer remain in

Heads of the church council 1949-1971: Ostap Samoyluk, Dr. George Krywolap, Ihor Kurinniy, Oleksander Korotunov, Yeremiy Chechulin, Konstantin Stryzak, Ivan Hrynenko. Not shown: Col. Herasymenko, Ivan Zachepilo, Wasyl Makuha, Wasyl Melnyk, Ivan Tryhubinko.

Baltimore. By the time of his departure for the drier climate of Arizona on September 1, 1965, the parish had gained in spiritual tone and had developed the physical muscle to carry out its mission in appropriate facilities. Very Reverend Wasyl Umanetz followed as pastor, remaining nine years. Very Reverend Wasyl Bulawka was then induced to change his semi-retired status and lead the liturgical and other services for the flock. On November 28, 1976, Reverend Wolodymyr Chuhaj was transferred from Whaleysville on the Eastern Shore to assume the pastorship of St. Michael's in Baltimore. Mrs. Chuhaj performs as cantor and choir leader.

First Greek Orthodox Church in America, Holy Trinity, New Orleans, founded 1865, of which Reverend Agapius Honcharenko, a Ukrainian, was the first Pastor. **The Orthodox Observer, Oct. 1965**

For many years the spiritual leader of the Ukrainian Orthodox Church of U.S.A. was Metropolitan John Theodorovich, who died May 3, 1971. Selected to succeed him as Metropolitan was Archbishop Mstyslav S. Skrypnyk. Included in the Metropolitan *Rada* or Council in addition to the four members of the Sobor of Bishops are fourteen members of the clergy and laity. Belonging to this governing body is Dr. George Krywolap, a member of St. Michael's parish.[41] A former lay member of the Council from the parish is Anatole Bulawka. The parish officer staff for 1977 consists of Mykola Chechulin, president; Mykola Kibitz, vice-president; John Havrilenkowsky, treasurer; Wolodymyr Boyko, secretary; Mykola Bilokin, financial secretary; and Mykola Samoyliv, controller.

Members of St. Michael's Ukrainian Orthodox parish are proud of the contributions made to America of a Ukrainian Orthodox priest, Andrew Onufrievych Honcharenko, better known as Agapius Honcharenko. Father Honcharenko was born on August 19, 1832, and came to the United States January 1, 1865. He officiated at the first Greek Orthodox Divine Liturgy in the United States on January 6, 1865, at the Greek Consulate at 47 Exchange Place in New York City. With Father Honcharenko as celebrant, the first public service was at Trinity Church (Episcopal) on 26th Street, New York City, on March 2, 1865. But on April 15, 1865, Reverend Honcharenko conducted Divine Service at St. Paul's Church in New Orleans for the newly-founded Eastern Orthodox Church of the Holy Trinity. Father Honcharenko had blessed the cornerstone of Holy Trinity on April 1 and was named the first pastor of the first Greek Orthodox Church in the United States.[42]

Reverend Honcharenko then went to California, started and edited *The Alaska Herald* and became the champion of the early Ukrainian Kozak settlers as well as of the Indians and Eskimos in Alaska. This outcast from imperial Russian rule, undeterred by the influence of the Czars which extended into America's churches and which impeded his ministry, became a stellar defender of religious liberty and human rights as a pioneer in the western part of the United States.

HOLY TRINITY UKRAINIAN ORTHODOX CHURCH, WHALEYSVILLE

The Articles of Incorporation of Trustees of Holy Trinity Ukrainian Orthodox Church of the United States were signed by 15 trustees on March 10, 1958, as follows: Anthony Beryk, minister, Andriy Androsov, Iwan Bilous, Yakiw Bilous, Iwan Gnidenko, Mykola Harasymenko, Konstantyn Holowko, Maksym Holubycky, Stephen Katinsky, Nicolai Kunycia, Hryhoriy Proskurnia, Maksym Semeniw, Stephen Sisak, Anton Schumeyko, Mykola Taran, Mychaylo Welitschko. These trustees were elected at a general meeting held on March 2, 1958.[43]

According to Article 2 not less than 4 nor more than 15 trustees shall be selected. In Article 7 they were given full power to purchase from New Castle Presbytery property known as Eden Presbyterian Church in Whaleysville. The purchase was made at a cost of $1,000. Ukrainian farm laborers had been living on the Eastern Shore since 1950, they having come as displaced persons from Germany, where most of them had been enslaved during the war. About 30 families, including some Byelorussians, were of the Orthodox faith. Today many of them have their own farms, usually concentrating on poultry production but also with animals such as bees, ducks, pigs, and cows which are seldom seen on the specialized farms common to the Eastern Shore.

On March 27, 1962, the already elongated official corporate name was amended to: Trustees of the Holy Trinity Ukrainian Orthodox Church of the United States of America, at Whaleysville, Worcester County, Maryland. The Trustees were given the responsibility of choosing from among their number the president of the corporation whose term was for one year. The charter, as amended, also provides the religious corporation "shall maintain spiritual, doctrinal, and religious affiliation with the Consistory of the Ukrainian Orthodox Church of the

United States of America, which now maintains its Headquarters at South Bound Brook, N.J...."⁴⁴

This rural parish, not unlike parishes of other denominations, has had difficulty in retaining a resident priest. The last pastor with a number of years of service was Reverend Wolodymyr Chuhay who was at Holy Trinity from April 1973 to November 28, 1976, when he was transferred to Baltimore. Prior to this the congregation was also served by Fathers Petro Budniy and Wasyl Bulawka.

Holy Trinity Ukrainian Orthodox Church, Whaleysville.

U.E.A.M.

HOLY TRINITY RUSSIAN ORTHODOX CHURCH, BALTIMORE

The leading communicant group of Holy Trinity throughout its existence since February 1919 is Ukrainian, many of whom are, or are descendents of, Ukrainians, from such Austro-Hungarian areas as Galicia (Halichina),

Carpatho-Ukraine (Carpatho-Rus or Ruthenia), and Bukovina. These geographical regions only recently came under Russian rule as the result of World War II. Ukrainians, or Rusins, as many Western Ukrainians call themselves because of the ancient Ukrainian name of Rus as centered in its capital city of Kiev, came to the Baltimore area as Greek Catholics or Uniates recognizing the authority of the Holy Father, but with their own traditional worship and laws and a hierarchy severely restricted by Latin-oriented Rome. The *Ea Semper* decree of June 14, 1907, required the Ruthenian priests to be celibate, forbade them to give the sacrament of confirmation, and put them under the jurisdiction of the Apostolic Delegate.[45] In effect, Ukrainian Greek Catholics in America were denied access to their own priests, for in Europe the supply of single priests was very small. Ukrainians were also cut off from their bishops in Galicia and Carpatho-Ukraine. Under these conditions, with a growing Ukrainian population, the Russian czar and his missionary-minded Orthodox Church could pose as rescuers of the worshipper's traditional rites and ceremonies and protector against "Latinization" while providing a ready flow of quickly-trained and consecrated priests for a return to the true faith — Orthodoxy. According to *Orthodox America*, an estimated 90,000 Uniates "due to the promulgation and attempted enforcement of the *Ea Semper* decree" returned to the Orthodox Church. During the period 1907-14, "Archbishop Platon received 72 largely Carpatho-Russian Uniate parishes into the fold, and during Archbishop Evdokim's (1914 - 17) administration, 35 new parishes, consisting in many cases of former Uniates, and 30 Uniate parishes were added."[46]

Holy Trinity Russian Orthodox Church, at 1725 East Fairmount Avenue, is in the same general area as St. Michael's Ukrainian Catholic Church from which parish many of its original members came. It is not affiliated with the Orthodox Church in America, instead accepting the authority of the Patriarch of Moscow. His representative, Metropolitan John of New York, a Soviet citizen who came to the United States 4 years before, visited the parish February 12, 1967, where he led the Divine Liturgy. Metropolitan John's archdiocese at that time numbered 40,000 communicants spread over the United States and the Aleutian Islands.[47] At the present time the jurisdiction contains 38 churches in the United States with Vicar Bishop Ierenei of the Patriarch of Moscow in charge. The Cathedral of St. Nicholas at 15 E. 97th Street, New York, is under their control.

The Russian Orthodox Greek Catholic Church of America, lately referred to as the Orthodox Church in America, led by Metropolitan Archbishop Ireney (John Bekish) of New York, is a much larger body which since 1919 has been de facto self-governing but with spiritual ties to Moscow. On April 10, 1970, the Patriarch of Moscow signed the agreement granting autocephaly, "to be independent and self-governing with the right of electing her own Primate and all her bishops" but with the obligation to "firmly and inalterably preserve the divine dogmas, being guided in her life by the sacred Canons of the Holy Orthodox Catholic Church of Christ..."[48] which laws presumably are issued and explained under the guidance of the Patriarch of Moscow. St. Andrew the Apostle Russian Orthodox Church, located at Lombard and Chester Streets, is within the jurisdiction of Metropolitan Ireney.

Holy Trinity Parish, now with about 130 families as members, was spread over 24 different postal zones, yet according to a Great Russian from Kazan there were only a few true Russians in Baltimore. Holy Trinity Church was built during the Civil War and was then known as the Turner Station Methodist Church. When bought by the Holy Trinity parishioners, the building was a Lutheran church. In its earlier years, the parish had a full program of activities, with a 3-day evening school, choir rehearsals and performances, and club and social meetings and events.[49] Now the Russian or Church Slavonic language is used only part of the time in the Holy Liturgy, English assuming greater importance in a congregation where only a small percentage of worshippers understands any Slavic language. The Ukrainian and Byelorussian background of the majority of parishioners may have speeded the conversion to English rather than the acceptance of and learning of Russian, a language they did not understand.

Holy Trinity's Gospel Book, which was brought to Baltimore prior to chartering of the church and which was particularly cherished by the parish members, came from Ukraine's ancient (11th century) Monastery of the Caves in Kiev. This Slavonic Gospel Book, measuring 2 feet by 1½ feet by 4 inches in thickness and weighing about 35 pounds, is decorated in gold plate and religious scenes in inset enameled panels, according to Father Mark Odell who termed it "absolutely irreplaceable" when it was stolen in August of 1976.[50]

ST. ANDREW THE APOSTLE
RUSSIAN ORTHODOX CHURCH, BALTIMORE

St. Andrew the Apostle was founded by former parishioners of Holy Trinity who wished to be united with the parishes composing the Russian Orthodox Greek Catholic Church of America. Holy Trinity at that time was zealously guarding its independence, not recognizing the authority of any diocese, or of Moscow's "Living Church" as headed by the Patriarch[51], but subservient to civil authorities who in fact treated religion as the opiate of the people. To obtain the benefits of higher leadership and guidance, Metropolitan Theophilus of New York was asked to accept the newly-organized group under his jurisdiction. This was done in 1940. The Metropolitan (Theodore Nicholaevich Pashkovsky) was born in the Province of Kiev, Ukraine, attended Kiev Theological Seminary Preparatory School and fulfilled the requirements of the Kiev Lavra Monastery.[52]

Divine services were first held at Holy Resurrection Episcopal Church, Fayette and Linwood Avenue. Early in 1941 the unused Alnutt Methodist Church on Chester and Lombard Streets was purchased. Divine Liturgy commenced here on February 16, 1941, but the consecration services were not held until June 29, 1941.[53] The first pastor of St. Andrew was Reverend Theodate Shevchuk, an original member of Holy Trinity and the cantor, who was ordained just prior to his appointment.[54]

The parish rectory at 3107 Berkshire Road, a number of miles away from the church, was acquired in July 1964. After major renovations of the church and hall were completed in December 1969, a disastrous fire destroyed the interior and hall on February 15, 1970. Liturgical services were transferred to a rented building, a Baptist Church on South Broadway, where the parish functioned until October 1971. From October 1971 through May 1972, services were held in the parish hall. Construction proceeded on the burned church so that in June 1972 Divine Liturgy resumed in a sparkling new house of worship. The Easter Service on Sunday, April 29, 1973, was celebrated with the ornate iconostasis, or icon screen, in place.

St. Andrew Parish has served as a stepping stone for two priests who became bishops in the Orthodox Church: Archbishop Kiprian (Boris Pavlovich Borisevich) of Philadelphia and Pennsylvania, and Bishop Amvrossy of Pittsburgh and West Virginia. Archbishop Kiprian was born in the Kholm section of Ukraine and received his training in the Volynian Theological Seminary in Ukraine from which he graduated in 1925. He was pastor in Baltimore from 1953 to 1959.[55]

THE MOSCOW CONNECTION

In 1967 Maryland newspapers confirmed serious problems which affiliation with or recognition of the Patriarch of Moscow imposes on United States churches. The correspondent of the *Baltimore Sun* on November 14, 1967, wrote from New Windsor, Md.:

* * *

> While a high official of the Russian Orthodox church discussed his visit to the United States in search of peace, a small group of American churchmen picketed half a block away — protesting against his trip and calling him an agent for the Soviet Government.
>
> Metropolitcan Nikodim, chairman of the Department of External Affairs of the Russian Orthodox Church, was visiting the Church of the Brethren service center here as part of a three-week stay in the United States. . . .

Representatives of the American Council of Christian Churches picketed nearby while Nikodim spoke at an afternoon press conference. A spokesman for the group characterized Nikodim and members of his delegation as "agents and spies who are here talking under a false facade."

The *Carroll County Times* of November 16, 1967 contained the following:

* * *

Bearded, robed, 38-year-old Metropolitan Nikodim,. . .held a press conference in the New Windsor Center and said (through an interpreter): "I am not a Communist, I am not an apologist for Communism."

Leading a dozen protesting pickets, Rev. Donald McKnight, pastor of the Dublin (Harford County) Evangelical Methodist Church and State president of the American Council of Christian Churches, said: "We believe that the true Christians in Russia have been persecuted and driven underground. Those attempting to escape have been shot at the Berlin Wall while these leaders (Metropolitan Nikodim and two Russian Orthodox laymen in his party) fly in expensive jets with the approval of the Communist regime.

* * *

The visit by the Metropolitan, described as "the Russian Orthodox prelate most widely known outside the Soviet Union," was a sequel to a tour of the U.S.S.R. by a Brethren team last month, Reverend Kinsel said. The Russians observed relief processing work and Brethren Volunteer Service training the New Windsor Center and were guests at a dinner.

"There is no persecution of religion in the U.S.S.R.," Metropolitan Nikodim said at the press conference. . . .

SLAVIC CHURCH OF CHRIST, BALTIMORE

This congregation in the southeastern section of Baltimore was organized in 1960. The individual members are of various national origins, about half being Ukrainian. The minister, Adam J. Korenczuk, is of Ukrainian descent, coming from the area known as Polisia. Services are conducted in four different languages: Russian, Ukrainian, Polish, and English. In keeping with its tradition of uniting all Christians, the schedule of services on a sign in front of the churches proclaims "All are welcome."

The church building, located at 516 South East Avenue, was bought in 1972. Services were first held at 211 South

Slavic Church of Christ, South East Avenue and Fleet Street
U.E.A.M

Broadway, but in September 1961 there were shifted to the 5 South Broadway property which had been acquired. The congregation, as do 2000 other Christian churches, relies on the New Testament and the *Declaration and Address* of 1809 of Thomas Campbell in which denominationalism is deplored and all Christians are invited to participate in the communion service.[56]

UKRAINIANS AS MEMBERS OF OTHER CHURCHES AND DENOMINATIONS

Like members of other nationalities Ukrainians identify themselves with churches in which they are a minority. Many Ukrainian Catholics are "unofficial" members of Latin Rite congregations, although they may be active and accepted as regular parishioners. The *Code of Canon Law* forbids transfers to the Latin Rite except under special rules and requirements. The aim is the same as it was two centuries before, the "preservation and not the destruction of your Rite," wrote Pope Benedict XIV to Metropolitan Athanasis Sheptitsky.[57] The Second Vatican

Council, which was solemnly closed on December 8, 1965, in its "Decree on Eastern Catholic Churches" declared:

> All clerics and those aspiring to sacred orders should be well instructed in various rites and especially in the principles which are involved in interritual questions. As part of their catechetical education, the laity, too, should be taught about these rites and their rules.
>
> Finally, each and every Catholic ... should everywhere retain his proper rite, cherish it, and observe it to the best of his ability.[58]

In 1894, Pope Leo XIII in his *Orientalium Dignitas* stated:

> Neither the baptism performed of necessity by a priest of another rite, nor the confessions made to a priest of another rite, nor Holy Communions, nor extreme Unction can create a change to go over to another rite. Not even a steady practice of such a different rite regardless of how long it may be can entitle anyone to change his rite.[59]

Ukrainians have also moved into Protestant denominations, such as Episcopal, Methodist, Seventh Day Adventist, Jehovah's Witnesses, Baptist, and Lutheran within the state of Maryland. A group of Mennonites who had settled in the Kherson region of Ukraine at the end of the 18th and beginning of the 19th centuries came into the United States at the end of the 19th century, settling in Butler County, Kansas. From this location some found their way back eastward, establishing farms along the Nanticoke River on the Eastern Shore of Maryland.[60]

NOTES TO CHAPTER SEVEN

[1] Rev. Clement C. Englert, CSSR, *Eastern Catholics*, New York, Paulist Press, 1940, p. 17.

[2] Englert, p. 20.

[3] Englert, p. 22.

[4] Rev. Yaroslav Shust, *For the Patriarchate*, Philadelphia, June 1975.

[5] "Ukrainians in US," *Slavonic Encyclopedia*, New York, Philosophical Library, 1949, p. 1331.

[6] Although Christianity came to Ukraine through Byzantium, the Byzantine Rite did not originate in the City of Byzantium. Liturgists are in general agreement that the Byzantine Rite originated in Antioch in Syria, the most renowned center of Christianity in the Apostolic Era. See *The Byzantine Divine Liturgy*, by Meletius Michael Solovey, trans. by Demetrius Emil Wysochansky, Washington, D.C., Catholic University of America Press, 1970, p. 44.

[7] James F. Coughlin, K.C., *Ukrainians, Their Rite, History and Religious Destiny*, Toronto, 1945, pp. 18-21.

[8] Rev. Michael Schudlo, *Ukrainian Catholics*, Yorkton, Sask., The Redeemer's Voice, 1951, p. 42.

[9] S.C.L. Liber 2739, folio 322 and S.C.L. Liber 2739, folio 321, Land Records Office, Baltimore City.

[10] "Russians in US," *Slavonic Encyclopedia*, p. 1099.

[11] "Uniates," *Slavonic Encyclopedia*, p. 1334.

[12] Mr. Surmach, "First Ukrainian Bookstore in America," *Calendar of Providence for 1948*, Philadelphia, America, p. 151.

[13] The census of 1910 listed in the Austro-Hungarian Empire 3,998,872 Ruthenians, making up 7.79% of the population. Ruthenians numbered 3,518,854 or 12.58% of the people in Austria and 464,270 or 2.50% of the people in Hungary Proper. See "Austria-Hungary," *The New International Yearbook for the Year 1918*, New York, Dodd, Mead and Co., 1919, p. 63.

[14] Liber 1128, folio 262; Liber 1134, folio 62; Liber 2543, folio 27, Baltimore County.

[15] Bishop Michael J. Dudick, *Eastern Catholic Life*, Passaic, N.J., March 2, 1975.

[16] Peter Marudas, "St. Michael's Ukrainian Catholic Church Has Unique Rome-Eastern Role," *Baltimore Sun*, May 4, 1963.

[17] A. Dragan, *Our Ukrainian Cardinal*, Jersey City, Svoboda Press, 1966.

[18] Ukrainian Catholic Youth League pamphlet, New York, undated.

[19] *Golden Jubilee, SS. Peter and Paul Ukrainian Catholic Church*, Baltimore, 1963, p. 36.

[20] During the depression years, Russian communism was propagandizing workers in the United States, arousing them against capitalism and infiltrating many organizations.

[21] Wasyl Halich, *Ukrainians in the United States*, Chicago, University of Chicago Press, 1937, p. 106.

[22] Constance J. Tarasar, ed., *The Orthodox Church in America*, Syosset, N.Y., 1975, p. 177.

[23] *Golden Jubilee 1920-1970*, St. Basil's Ukrainian Catholic Church, Chesapeake City, Md., 1970, p.11.

[24] *Golden Jubilee 1920-1970*, p. 12.

[25] Fr. Joseph Denischuk, CSSR, *Ukrainian Catholic Shrine of the Holy Family*, Washngton, Ex-Speed-Ite Service, Inc., 1975, pp. 27, 28.

[26] *16th Annual Convention*, Washington, Ukrainian Catholic Youth League, 1954.

[27] Fr. Joseph Denischuk, pp. 54-62.

[28] Ukrainian Congress Committee pamphlet, *40th Anniversary of the Man-Made Famine (1932-1933)*, New York, 1973.

[29] Fr. Joseph Denischuk, pp. 91, 92.

[30] Fr. Joseph Denischuk, p. 56.

[31] *Souvenir Book Commemorating the Solemn Dedication of the Patronage Mother of God Byzantine Catholic Church*, Baltimore, 1973, pp. 18-20.

[32] *Souvenir Book*, pp. 42, 43.

[33] Fr. Joseph Denischuk, p. 45.

[34] Fr. Joseph Denischuk, p. 60.

[35] Mykola Samoyliv, *Short Outline History of the Ukrainian Orthodox Church St. Archangel Michael*, Baltimore, 1971, p. 4 (in Ukrainian).

[36] M.L.P. 9332, folio 376, Land Records Office, Baltimore City.

[37] M.L.P. 9332, folio 381, Land Records Office, Baltimore City.

[38] R.H.B. 3052, folio 341, Land Records Office, Baltimore City.

[39] Liber 439, folio 241, State Tax Commission of Maryland, Baltimore.

[40] Mykola Samoyliv, p. 26.

[41] *Ukrainian Orthodox Calendar 1976*, South Bound Brook, N.J., Ukrainian Orthodox Church of the USA, 1976, p. 56.

[42] Theodore Luciw, *Father Agapius Honcharenko*, Ukrainian Congress Committee of America, NY, 1970, pp. 36-40.

[43] F73-170, March 1958, State Tax Commission of Maryland, Baltimore.

[44] F295-407, March 27, 1962, State Tax Commission of Maryland, Baltimore.

[45] Constance J. Tarasar, ed., p. 47.

[46] Constance J. Tarasar, ed., p. 127.

[47] Harold D. Piper. "Russian Community Loyal to Churches," *Baltimore Sun*, Feb. 13, 1967, p. B1.

[48] Constance J. Tarasar, ed., p. 279.

[49] Harold D. Piper.

[50] "Religious articles reported stolen," *Baltimore Sun*, Aug. 22, 1976, p. A18.

[51] Constance J. Tarasar, ed., p. 218.

[52] Constance J. Tarasar, ed., p. 200.

[53] *2nd Annual Multi-Ethnic Festival*, Baltimore, Polish Heritage Assn. of Md., Inc., May 23, 1976, p. 9.

[54] Constance J. Tarasar, ed., p. 218.

[55] Constance J. Tarasar, ed., p. 226.

[56] Winthrop S. Hudson, *Religion in America*, New York, Charles Scribner's Sons, 2nd ed., 1973, p. 125.

[57] Rev. Michael Schudlo, p. 91.

[58] Walter M. Abbot, S.J., ed., *The Documents of Vatican II*, New York, Guild Press, 1966, p. 375.

[59] Rev. Michael Schudlo, pp. 93, 94.

[60] Dieter Cunz, *The Maryland Germans*, Princeton, N.J., Princeton University Press, 1948, p. 417.

Chapter Eight
Slavic Studies in Maryland
Paul Fenchak

Whether a Marylander is travelling in his auto on Pulaski Highway, Moravia Road or the Augustine Herman Highway headed for Bohemia Manor, Moscow (Md.), or Gallitzin (Pa.), or whether she is praying to St. John Nepomucene Neumann at either St. Wenceslaus or St. Stanislaus Church, or whether he is spending an evening at Memorial Stadium bemoaning or praising the decision of Umpire Nestor Chylak as he calls Bobby Grich out on a close play at home plate, or whether she is listening to a lecture about Jan Komensky (Comenius) in Ruzicka Hall at Loyola College, or working in the Bata Shoe Factory in Belcamp — Slavic history and culture are very much with him or her in the state of Maryland.

To what extent the Marylander understands and appreciates Slavic contributions to Maryland is another consideration, yet educators of the state have been charged with the following *Bylaw* 325.1 (adopted July 29, 1970) of the Maryland State Board of Education: "All public schools shall include in their programs of studies, either as part of current curricular offerings or as separate courses, appropriate instruction for developing understanding and appreciation of ethnic and cultural minorities." Whether Slavic-Americans are to be fully included in the term 'minorities' as used in Maryland has not been altogether clear. Though the term is often used, it is seldom defined, but one definition/application gleaned in a letter of June 27, 1975, from the Maryland Department of Economic and Community Development to the writer is as follows:

> Minority business enterprise means a business enterprise that is owned or controlled by one or more socially or economically disadvantaged persons. Such disadvantage may arise from cultural, racial, chronic economic circumstances or background or other similar cause. Such persons include, but are not limited to Blacks, Puerto Ricans, Spanish-speaking Americans, American Indians, and Orientals.

At Memorial Stadium baseball scorecard vendors blare out, "You can't tell the players without a scorecard!" Important questions preliminary to investigation of facets about the status of Slavic studies in Maryland are, Who has been keeping the scorecard for the equal distribution of materials, time, personnel, and finances for studies about Slavic-Americans in the public schools of Maryland? How scientifically qualified are the scorekeepers? Have educators worked with community organizations to enhance their understandings and appreciations of Maryland's Slavic peoples? These are questions of Accountability, a term often used by officials of the State Department of Education and its affiliates to mean something like "educational measurement."[1]

As the commonality of American goals and ideals is always subject to review and due recognition, prudence would include analyses of the loyalties and contributions of our nation's *ca.* 35,000,000 Slavic citizens. In the continuing American cultural revolution it is of the moment in the Bicentennial era to remember that more people died in industrial accidents in America than in fighting the Revolutionary War and in conquering the wilderness. The cemeteries of Maryland record many a Slavic hero of labor who gave all he had to build America industrially or militarily.

To belabor unsavory descriptions of Slavs in American historical literature would be to dignify the diatribes that sound like those rendered against Blacks, Jews, Orientals, Indians, and others. Suffice it is for this review to categorically state that an abundance of anti-Slavic literature existed prior to the outbreak of World War I in 1914, at which time immigration from Slavic as well as other lands dropped to practically nothing; and, that after the end of the war the tirades continued, as shown in the words of Samuel P. Orth in 1920:

> According to the estimates given by Emily G. Balch, between four and six million persons of Slavic descent are now dwelling among us, and their fecundity is amazing. Equally amazing is the indifference of the Government and of Americans generally to the menace involved in the increasing numbers of these inveterate aliens to institutions that are fundamentally American.[2]

The aforementioned indifference of the Government was not to continue — Did it exist? — and in 1921 additional restrictions were plainly applied to reduce the immigration of Slavs, among others, to America.

Institutions that are fundamentally American were helped in construction by such persons as the Bohemian Augustine Herman who worked eight to ten years completing his map, "Virginia and Maryland," starting in 1660.[3] Laborers at the Jamestown, Virginia, Settlement included peoples considered as Poles, Slovaks, Ukrainians, Byelorussians, et al. Professor George J. Prpic in a thoroughly researched book, *The Croatian Immigrants in America*, presents the possibility of Croatian sailors having landed in Virginia in the sixteenth century and he cites some of the ideas of Louis Adamic and Joseph S. Roucek about the possibility of the Indian name "Croatan" being a variant of "Croatian."[4]

General Casimir Pulaski, father of the American cavalry, was forced by Russian oppression to leave Poland. After serving with the cavalry he organized the Pulaski Legion, a detachment of primarily foreign-born soldiers, in 1778. The banner of the Pulaski Legion, constructed by the Moravian Sisters of Bethlehem, Pennsylvania, is now in the care of the Maryland Historical Society, Baltimore.[5]

Xenophobia, the distrust of strangers because of the fear that they pose a threat to the culture of the natives, appeared in Maryland in 1666 when it was the first state to pass a naturalization law under which the privilege of becoming citizens was limited to foreign-born Protestants.[6]

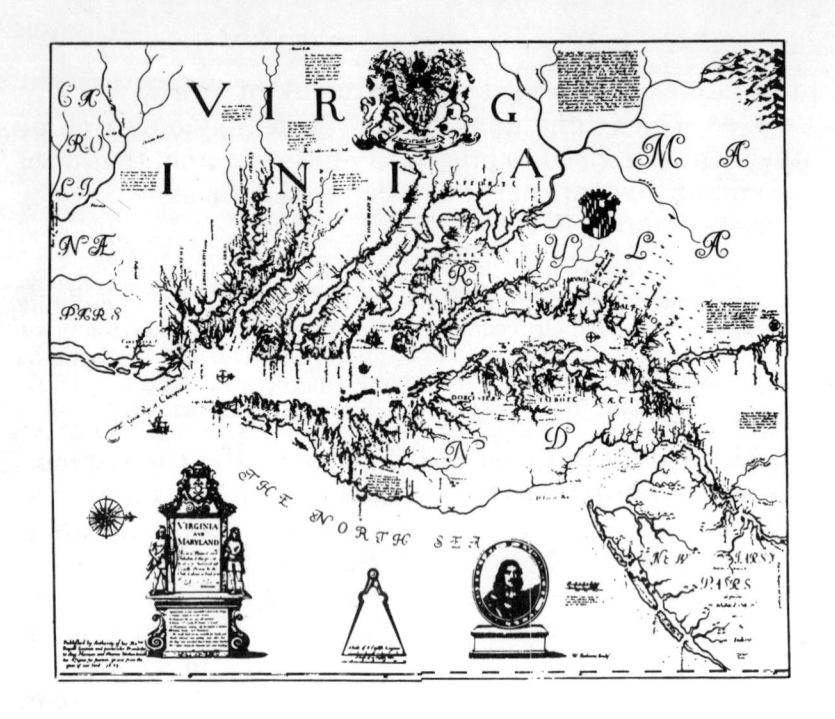

The first map of Virginia and Maryland was completed ca. *1670 by Augustine Herman, a Czech, whose estate,* Bohemia Manor, *is in Cecil County along the Bohemia River.*
Texas Education Agency, Czechoslovakia: Information Minimum

To fear immigrants is not to analyze their character judiciously. For example, the police records of Scranton, Pennsylvania, for 1931 indicate that there were only two arrests of Ukrainians of that city out of an estimated 12,000-15,000 population.[7] The record remains consistently good in Scranton and all indications suggest that the record is similarly good in Baltimore and in all of Maryland.

H. L. MENCKEN AND SLAVIC LANGUAGES

Before revising *The American Language*, Henry L. Mencken of Baltimore harbored nativist-like views about some of Baltimore's Slavic peoples. In an article, "The Last Gasp," on November 1, 1920, Mencken, in opposing the construction of a huge oil refinery for Highlandtown, wrote as follows:

It will convert a whole section of the new city into one vast stench; it will ruin a vast tract for all other purposes; worse, it will bring in a horde of low-grade laborers and so diminish the general social and intellectual level of the town, already low enough, God knows. You and I will be taxed to pay cops to club and murder those wild Slovaks and Slovenes and to pay firemen to put out the weekly fire at the refinery, and to pave streets to reach it...[8]

Although his original (1919) edition was very weak about Slavic languages, H. L Mencken must be credited with having completed extensive research with the following Slavic nationality groups in compiling the 1936 version of *The American Language*: Czechs, Slovaks, Russians, Serbs, Ukrainians, Croatians, and Poles. In the chapter about Polish influences on the American language Mencken acknowledged his indebtedness to Adam Bartosz, editor of *Jednosc-Polonia*, published in Baltimore, for his depictions of Polish-American language patterns.

ADAM S. GREGORIUS (1879-1962), long-time leader of Polish-Americans in Maryland, who in 1913 founded a literary journal, Miesiecznik Polski (Polish Monthly), *in Baltimore.*

A Slavic scholar who often exchanged ideas with H. L. Mencken was Adam S. Gregorius, a Polish-American attorney who founded three savings and loan organizations in Baltimore, and who was the prime mover in building the Pulaski Monument in Patterson Park, Baltimore. Attorney Gregorius, an accomplished linguist, in exchanges with Mencken published in *The Sun* in the 1920's, criticized Mencken with being poorly versed in and oblivious to the moral tenets of many readers. To Mr. Gregorius, Mencken was too braggadocian.

Although Emil Revyuk, editor of the Ukrainian daily *Svoboda* (*Liberty*), Jersey City, who advised Mencken extensively, tried very pointedly to eliminate Mencken's misconceptions regarding western European parlance about Ukrainians, Mencken did not completely clarify distinctions between the Ukrainian and Russian languages in his 1936 edition of *The American Language*: "Ukrainian, or Little Russian, differs enough from Great Russian for a speaker of the one to find the other very difficult." In a three-page letter to Mencken on February 25, 1936, Revyuk commented:

> Ukrainian cannot be said to be identical with Russian, virtually or otherwise. As the Russians construe the matter, the Little Russian and the Great Russian are dialects of a "pan-Russian language," which has only as much existence as e.g. the Teutonic language, or the Romance language...[9]

Vladimir Geeza, editor of *Nove Zhyttia* (*The New Life*), Olyphant, Pennsylvania, also was in communication with Mencken. In response to a question from Mencken: Does the Ukrainian spoken in this country take in any considerable amount of American words?, Geeza replied:

> Yes, a good percentage, and they are inflected according to the Ukrainian system. For instance I will make an example of a few words, although not originally American words, nevertheless, words of the English language spoken in this country. Note the close resemblance in the first two columns:
>
> | English | English-Ukrainized | Ukrainian |
> |---|---|---|
> | revolution | rewolucia | powstannia |
> | department | departament | widdil |
> | depression | depressia | prihnoblennia |
> | president | prezident | predsidatel |
>
> Those words appear in the columns of the Ukrainian publications day after day and many others can be picked out again and again...[10]

Ukrainians born and raised in America will certainly recall some of the usage cited below from a section reprinted from *The American Language*. Mencken expressed indebtedness to Emil Revyuk for[11]

The Ukrainian in America makes a copious use of English loan-words. Some of them are the names of things with which he was unfamiliar at home, and others are words that he must use in his daily traffic with Americans. Usually, he tries to bring these loans into harmony with the Ukrainian inflectional system. Thus, he forces most loan-nouns to take on grammatical gender. Those that he feels to be feminine he outfits with the Ukrainian feminine ending, *-a*, e.g., *dreska* (dress), *vinda* (window), *hala* (hall), *grocernya* (grocery store), *buchernya* (butcher's store), *strita* (street), *pikcha* (picture). *Mechka* is the match which makes a fire but match in the meaning of contest of skill is a masculine noun *mech*. Some nouns are felt to be plural and are outfitted with plural endings. Thus *furniture* becomes *fornichi*, which is equivalent to "pieces of furniture," *pinatsy* is a Ukrainian adaptation of *peanuts*, and *shusy* of *shoes*, and *Shkrenty* is the plural form of the name of the city of Scranton. *Kendi* (candy), is declined like a plural noun because its ending is the typical plural ending of Ukrainian nouns, and it reminds the Ukrainian of his name for *candy*, the plural *tsukorky*. *Blubery* (blueberries), is also plural.

The adjective must be recast also to denote by its ending the number and gender. For this reason the Ukrainian does not use many English adjectives, for they do not lend themselves easily to such changes. He has adopted, however, the following: *faytersky* (of fighting character), *bomersky* (of the character of a bum), *gengstersky* (like a gangster), *sylkovy* (made of silk), *volnatovy* (made of walnut), *bosuyuchy* or *bosivsky* (bossing, domineering). Adopted verbs, too, require a great deal of dressing up to fit them for use in the Ukrainian language, e.g., *bosuvaty* (to boss), *klinuvaty* (to clean), *ponchuvaty* (to punch), *laykuvaty* (to like), *trubluvaty* (to trouble), *baderuvaty* (to bother), *bostuvaty* (to bust), *shapuvaty* (to shop), *stykuvaty* (to stick), *faytuvatysya* (to fight with), *ringuvaty* (to ring), *swimuvaty* (to swim), *peyntuvaty* (to paint), *bonduvaty* (to bond), *bayluvaty* (to bail) and *djompaty* (to jump). *Parkuvaty karu* is the common American Ukrainian for to park the car.

The collection of letters by Slavic scholars in the Mencken Room of the Pratt Central Library, Baltimore, represents a thorough input into *bona fide* ethnic studies in America, which, when coupled with the twenty-six non-Slavic groups discussed in *The American Language*, may well represent the best over-all piece of ethnic scholarship ever completed in Maryland. Of importance to linguistic analyses in understanding ethnics is the fact that language touches the hearts and souls of immigrants and their descendants much more rapidly than some of the tools employed today by human relations specialists who are primarily grounded in the behavioral sciences. The Mencken collection contains letters from ethnic groups on subjects other than linguistic analyses. Among such letters can be found an analysis of Franklin D. Roosevelt's management of World War II written by Alexander de Sushko of the Ukrainian Academy of Sciences of America, Chicago, on August 29, 1946.

SVOBODA

LARGEST AND OLDEST UKRAINIAN DAILY
Published by
UKRAINIAN NATIONAL ASSOCIATION, INC.
81-83 Grand Street.   Jersey City, N.J.

Telephone: BErgen 4-0237

February 25, 1936

Mr. H.L. Mencken
704 Cathedral Street
Baltimore, Maryland

My dear Mr. Mencken:

I am sending you here the galleyproofs of the Ukrainian section of your book you sent me for corrections. I noted the few errors I found in them and hope you will understand the signs I used for correcting.

The Ukrainian section I find prefaced by statements which need some corrections as to facts. May I call your attention to these?

It is stated that Ukrainian, or Little Russian, is virtually identical with Great Russian, but the Ukrainians in the United States for political reasons are anti-Russian and so keep aloof from the other Russians.

Ukrainian cannot be said to be identical with Great Russian, virtually or otherwise. As the Russians construe the matter, the Little Russian and the Great Russian are dialects of a "pan-Russian-language", which has only as much existence as e.g. the Teutonic language, or the Romance language. The literary language which was developed out of the Great Russian dialects they call the Russian language, and the literary language which developed out of the "Little Russian" dialects, they call the Ukrainian language (Academician Aleksey A. Shakhmatov: An Outline of the Hisotry of the Little Russian (Ukrainian) language).

The theory as if the Ukrainians used the Ukrainian for political reasons has been exploded long ago (in March, 1905) by the Imperial Russian Academy of Sciences, in St. Petersburg, when the council of imperial ministers requested the Academy to give their opinion on the restrictions of the Ukrainian printed word. The Academy in its opinion exposed this theory of the identity of the Ukrainian and the Russian language as a convenient pseudo-scientific theory of the Russian administrators hostile to the development of the Ukrainian nationality.

This is the first page of the three-page letter written to H. L. Mencken in many exchanges by Emil Revyuk, editor of Svoboda.

U.E.A.M. Collection

282

PUBLIC LIBRARIES

Students rely upon community libraries for obtaining materials about the manifold ethnic groups of Maryland. An examination of a special folder compiled by the Young Adult Services Librarians, Baltimore County Library, 1974, reveals the not a single book about Slavic-Americans was listed among 53 titles cited in the folder, "Awakening Minorities." Strangely, not a single title was cited for Italians, also numerous in Baltimore County, nor was a title listed for Greeks, who in recent years have seen two of their kin serve as County Executives, viz., Spiro Agnew and Theodore Venetoulis. Mr. Venetoulis is quoted in "Ethnic Community Statement by the Honorable Theodore G. Venetoulis, Baltimore County Executive, February 7, 1975":

> Baltimore County can be truly great, the best in this nation, only if it allows and encourages all its citizens to play full roles in education, business, government, and the entire spectrum of community life.
>
> Thus I pledge as County Executive to help make your full participation possible. It is too important to be overlooked, too important to us all to be denied.

Michael Novak rather prophetically in 1971 analyzed some of the problems in regards to ethnics in Baltimore County in his book, *The Rise of the Unmeltable Ethnics*. Despite urgings by the County Executive and the Association for the Study of Nationalities (USSR and Eastern Europe), Inc., library holdings about Slavs and other East Europeans in the Baltimore County Public Library system can best be described as weak. What chance would a scholar have of finding materials about the baseball team from the Slovak Club in Dundalk that won the County League championship in 1939? Could he find anything about the Orthodox religious adherents, or an article about the dedication of the Patronage of the Mother of God Byzantine Catholic Church in Arbutus on October 7, 1973?

The Enoch Pratt Central Library has a superior collection of holdings about all Slavic groups in the fields of

ENOCH PRATT FREE LIBRARY
BOOKS IN UKRAINIAN Added in 1952

Dear Mr. Sushko:

      Thank you so much for the lists of books in Ukrainian and about the Ukraine, which I found on my desk when I returned from a brief vacation.

      As you know, the Library is very anxious to build up its Ukrainian collection, and we greatly appreciate your interest and help in this direction. We hope that it will be possible for us to buy a considerable number of the books on these lists.

      The acquisition of the books and the preparation for circulation takes a great deal of time, but we shall be glad to get in touch with you when some of them are available for borrowing.

                        Sincerely yours,

                        Dorothy A. Nicodemus, Head
                        Circulation Department

Byrchak, Volodymyr	Vasyl'ko Rostyslavych. 2v.	1923	AU.B9V3
Chaikovs'kyi, Andrii	Kozats'ka pomsta	1947	AU.C4K6
	Na ukhodakh	1947	AU.C4N2
Dragomanova, Oksana	Potoi bik svitu	1951	AU.D7P6
Dudko, Fedir	Chortoryi	1946	AU.D8C4
	Strybozha vnuka	1948	AU.D8S8
	Vilna	1947	AU.D8V5
	Zametil'	1948	AU.D8Z3
Fedir, Igor	Syn Ukrainy	1946	AU.F4S9
Franko, Ivan	Zakhar Berkut	1950	AU.F7Z3
Galan, Anatol'	Paxoshchi	1951	AU.G3P3
Gogol, N. V.	Nich proty Rizdva	1945	AU.G6N5
	Strashna pomsta	1952	AU.G6S8
Gzhyts'kyi, Volodymyr	Chorne ozero (kara-kol). 2v.in 1	1948	AU.G9C4
Kashchenko, Andriian	Bortsi za pravdu	1947	AU.K3B6
	Kost' Gordienko	1948	AU.K3K6
	Pid Korsunem	1947	AU.K3P5
	U zapali borot'by	1947	AU.K3U2
	Z Dnipra na Dunai	1948	AU.K3Z2
	Zruinovane gnizdo	1947	AU.K327
Koroleva, Natalena	Legendy Starokyivs'ki	1943	AUT.K6L4
Lepkyi, Bogdan	Krutizh	1947	AU.L4K7
Mukerji, D. G.	Prygody khorobrovo goluva	1947	AU.M8P7
Nechui-Levyts'kyi, Ivan	Mykola Dzheria	1948	AU.N4M9
Os'machka, Teodosii	Poet	194-?	AUC. O 8P6
Radych, Vasyl'	Maksym Zalizniak	1952	AU.R3M3
Shevchenko, Taras	Avtohraf Shevchenka 1860 roku	1951	AUD.S4A9
Slavutych, IAr	Pravdonostsi	1948	AUC.S5P7
Staryts'kyi, Mykhailo	Karmeliuk	1948	AU.S8K3
Svydnyts'kyi, Anatol'	Liuborats'ki	19--?	AU.S9L5
Tsukanova, Mariia	Buzkovyi tsvit	1951	AU.T8B8
Tys, Iuriy	Symfoniia zemli	1951	AU.T9S9

The Enoch Pratt Free Library serves Slavic readers well.

history, art, folklore, literature, languages, etc. Books exist for all Slavic languages.

Of particular value to the secondary school student is the Maryland Room, now directed by Dr. Morgan Pritchett, where vertical files containing clippings from Maryland and national papers, copies of Slavic programs, brochures, etc., are available for most Slavic groups. Some clippings date back as far as 1894, e.g., a lengthy article of that year from the *Baltimore Herald* entitled, "The Poles' Great Day — Centennial of Poland's Constitution Next Thursday — to Honor Kosciusko." The history of the Czech's St. Wenceslaus Church is also recounted in articles referring to the establishment of the Church in 1870. The Query File in the Maryland Room is most helpful in researching about Slavic groups as it leads from specific to general classifications. This cross reference file also includes small articles, notices, etc., that are affixed to 3 x 5 file cards. Also included in the Maryland Room are several papers about Slavic communities in Maryland that were written at Towson State College by the students of Professors Jean Scarpaci and Hlib S. Hayuk.

THE STATE COLLEGES

An examination of descriptions of courses about ethnic studies, minorities studies, multi-cultural studies, etc., as printed in the catalogues of the state colleges (The University of Maryland not included), suggests that methodologies, not researched studies about existing cultural groups in the state, are of the essence in preparing teachers for the public schools of Maryland, as witness

> St. Mary's College of Maryland: 247. MINORITIES (4). Theoretical and empirical approaches to the study of dominant group-minority group relations from a cross-cultural perspective. An institutional analysis of racism and ethnic discrimination in an on-going society will be made.
>
> Salisbury State College: 314. RACIAL AND CULTURAL MINORITIES. 3 hours credit. A study of ethnic differences that produce prejudices, stereotypes, and discrimination, and the social processes employed by dominant and minority groups.
>
> Bowie State College: 80.310. ETHNIC RELATIONS IN THE UNITED STATES. 3 credits. A socio-cultural approach to the

understanding of race and ethnic relations. An analysis of the various ethnic groups and the problems of assimilation. Emphasis on the black man in the American culture. This course is an analysis of the problems and techniques of group relations. Emphasis is also directed to the in-group.

Many course descriptions at the other state colleges are similar, with none of the state colleges citing the word Slavic or listing a particular Slavic group. The closest is

Towson State University: 33.241 INTRODUCTION TO COMPARATIVE ETHNIC STUDIES (3). The course will focus on Baltimore's ethnic groups as a microcosm of American society, and will examine the interaction of ethnic communities (Black, Jewish, Italian, Greek, Eastern-European, Irish, and others) in Baltimore. The interdisciplinary approach will use the talents of social scientists, community representatives, and public school personnel as consultants and guest lecturers.

In the judgment of the reviewer the Comparative Ethnic Studies program at Towson State rates as the best of the state colleges, and it might be the best in the state. Much work has already been done by students in the program and the thirteen faculty members represent a group with strong training. Prof. Hlib S. Hayuk, Geography, a native of Ukraine, commands Slavic languages in addition to having specialization in the geography of Eastern Europe and an accomplished linguist-sociologist, Dr. George Kranzler, is a native of Galicia who understands Slavic peoples well. He is also a Rabbi and has written profusely.

The addition of a course, History of Slavic-Americans, would bolster Towson's list of courses such as Oral History, Ethnic Communities of Baltimore, History of Black Americans, The Immigrant in American History, Ethnic-American Literature, et al.

None of the courses in dancing mentioned Slavic dances — hopak, mazurka, polka, et al. — nor was there any mention in descriptions of art courses of the art forms of Slavic peoples. To what extent the culinary arts of Slavs are included in courses in home economic is unknown, as is the coverage of Slavic musical instruments and styles.

THE PUBLIC SCHOOLS

New interest for studying about Euro-Americans is being developed by the Maryland State Department of Education under the direction of Dr. James Addy, Specialist in Social Studies of the State Department of Education. In past years, Slavic (Ukrainian, Polish, Slovak, and Byelorussian), along with Lithuanian scholars met with former State Superintendent James A. Sensenbaugh to suggest areas wherein improvement was needed in curricular materials. A start was made for improvement of such studies in the two-volume set prepared for Maryland teachers, *New Perspectives in Intergroup Education* (1975) and at a subsequent meeting requested by both the Ukrainian Education Association of Maryland and the Polish Heritage Association of Maryland, representatives of the State Department on June 22, 1977, evidenced an interest in providing good coverage of East European-Americans, among others, in Maryland schools. Some attention to Slavic-Americans in Maryland appeared in a series of fifteen films produced by the Division of Instructional Television, entitled, "Maryland..."

Representatives from Slavic communities desire that curricular materials include aspects that would relate to moral values, to considerations of mental health, and to the importance of character formation. Underlying these and other interests are issues of justice and equity as indicated in questions posed by the writer at the second annual conference, "Slavic Americans in Maryland: Current Ethnic Issues," held at Loyola College, Baltimore, on March 20, 1976.[12]

From the meeting of June 22, 1977, representatives of Slavic communities feel a hope of the State's filling some of the gaps of the past in addition to seeking better analyses in the future. Two officers of the Ukrainian Education Association, Paul Fenchak, President, and Stephen Basarab, Secretary, attended the meeting along with Stanislaw Mostwin, President of the Polish Heritage Association of Maryland and Dr. Danuta S. Mostwin, professor of social work at Catholic University of America; and Ellen Bohachick Fenchak, Slovak representative. Representing the Department of Education were Dr. James Addy, Specialist in Social Studies; Dr. Loretta Webb, Director of Office Program Management, Division of Instruction; and Mrs. Floretta Mackenzie, Assistant Deputy Superintendent and advisor of Project Basic. Further meetings have been scheduled.

Maryland's problems in the realm of textbooks used in public schools are often similar to those of other states: frequent omissions (or only peripheral analyses) of Slavic-Americans, inaccuracies about linguistic and religious aspects, biased statements against particular Slavic groups or Slavs generally, some imbalanced Soviet interpretations, and the like.

During the years of 1973-1974 and 1974-1975 an elective social studies course, Eastern Europe and the Soviet Union, was taught at Pikesville High School by the writer. The course offered analyses of all peoples of Eastern Europe — Baltics, Slavs, Albanians, Finno-Ugrics, Rumanians, et al. — yet with limited promotion, the course did not continue because of insufficient registration. Some of the students of this course have since advanced their interests in Eastern Europe by pursuing college courses. Various East European specialists addressed the classes.

In 1973-74 a mini-course in the Czech language was offered at Ridgely Junior High School, Lutherville. The six-week (non-credit) course was taught by Mrs. Harold Gentes, who reported that parents of the students were pleased that their Czech and Slovak heritages were being recognized. No other such programs are known at the Division of Foreign Languages.

According to Ann Beusch, Specialist in Foreign Languages, Maryland State Department of Education, the only Slavic language being taught for credit in the public schools is Russian (13 schools).

SLAVIC SCHOOLS

Slovaks, Czechs, Ukrainians, Poles, and Russians have conducted either "Saturday" or regular parochial or community schools at various times since the groups

The late Slovak author Joseph Pauco is shown explaining East European history at Pikesville Senior High School.

U.E.A.M. Collection

arrived in Maryland beginning in about 1870. Other groups, such as Serbs, Croatians, Bulgarians, and Byelorussians, have traditionally identified more closely with schools and other organizations located within the District of Columbia.

Frequently clergymen served as instructors of schools operated by Slavic groups, but all communities have had dedicated lay instructors, too, who contributed generously of their time and linguistic talents. At present schools are known to be operated by Ukrainians, Poles, Czechs, and Russians.

The United States Defense Language Institute, with an extensive library at Ft. George G. Meade, Maryland, offers instruction in many Slavic languages through the media of tapes and manuals. Many Ukrainians and other Slavs have served as language specialists in the United States Department of Defense.

Lydia Czumak, President of the Ukrainian Women's Organization, Junior Division, presides at an exhibit at Lutherville Elementary School during a multi-ethnic program sponsored by the Y.W.C.A. in 1976.

It is common for Slavic, as other, groups, to either operate or assist colleges that perpetuate their cultures. Alliance College has served Polish-Americans in Cambridge Springs, Pennsylvania, since 1912, specializing in the liberal arts. Slovaks are closely connected with St. Vincent's College, Latrobe, Pennsylvania, while Czechs maintain St. Procopious College, Lisle, Illinois. Serbian influences are deeply rooted at Duquesne University in Pittsburgh as are Croatian. These several citations of Slavic-oriented colleges are merely a casual listing and the naming of such schools could continue extensively, particularly if Catholic, Orthodox, and Protestant seminaries were to be included.

Manor Junior College, Jenkintown, Pennsylvania, typifies the type of endeavor that Slavic groups promote to perpetuate their histories and traditions. The catalog of that institution states the following under the section captioned "History:"

One of the classroom buildings of Manor Junior College, Jenkintown, Pennsylvania.

Manor Junior College

Manor Junior College evolved from the plans, initiated in 1947, to establish a women's liberal arts college in the Jenkintown and Fox Chase areas of Philadelphia, and to provide a collegiate center in the United States for the study of Ukrainian language and culture.

Established in 1959 as a two-year college, Manor Junior College is a church-related non-profit women's college, under private control and directed by the Order of Sisters of Saint Basil the Great...[13]

An increasing number of state and private universities now conduct Slavic divisions or departments. Indiana University, Ohio State, Portland State, California (Pa.) State, Pennsylvania State University and Harvard, Yale, and Columbia are among the schools having extensive programs. Specialized institutes such as the Institute of Soviet and East European Studies of John Carroll University, founded and directed by a Ukrainian emigre scholar, Dr. Michael S. Pap, have increased substantially in recent years and have contributed much to the upgrading of the education of teachers.

The Harvard University Ukrainian Research Institute,

Ukrainians come from many states and countries to study at the Harvard University Ukrainian Summer Institute.

directed by Professor Omeljan Pritsak, was founded in the late 1960's through the generosity of many Ukrainian-American donors. Offering courses, symposia, and seminars in Ukrainian language, history, literature, etc., the Institute now has a Ukrainian studies Center and also operates an extensive summer school program, which in 1977 included 180 students, 10 of which were from Maryland. The extensive collection of Ukrainian materials is housed primarily in the Widener Memorial Library and the Houghton Rare Books and Manuscript Library. Some of the rare books were printed in Lviv, Ukraine, in 1574.[14] A very extensive Ukrainian collection is also held by the University of Minnesota.

In 1957 Prof. Clarence A. Manning of Columbia University published a very useful survey, *A History of Slavic Studies in the United States,* in which he related the academic endeavors of many Slavists in American education. Manning, of English ancestry, was introduced to Slavic studies by Rev. Dr. Onuphrey T. Kowalsky, a

Ukrainian Catholic priest with whom he had attended Columbia University. The writer recalls how in the 1940's and 1950's Prof. Manning would visit Rev. Kowalsky at St. Mary's Ukrainian Catholic Church in Ramey, Pennsylvania, and would lecture to the community.

Manning's book exhibits a fondness for an alumnus of Johns Hopkins University, Prof. John Dyneley Prince, who took his doctorate at Johns Hopkins in Semitic and later turned to Slavic, mastering nearly all the languages.[15] For years, Prince directed Slavic studies at Columbia University.

Dr. George Vernadsky, son of the first president of the Ukrainian Academy of Sciences in Kiev, taught Russian history at Johns Hopkins University in the late 1940's, having also taught at Columbia, Stanford, and Yale. Professor Vernadsky arrived in the United States in 1927.

As former President Ford's statement about the abundance of freedom in Eastern Europe is being buried by President Carter's concern for human rights, a book published by The Johns Hopkins University Press in 1967 looms to have increased use by Sovietologists. The anthology, *Soviet Political Thought — An Anthology — 1917-1961*, was selected, translated, and edited by Michael Jaworskyj, a native of western Ukraine who came to the United States in 1950 after having studied economics and political science at the University of Munich. For years a resident of Baltimore, he took his doctorate at Johns Hopkins and is now on the staff of Hunter College in New York.

"THE UKRAINIAN EXPERIENCE" AT WESTERN MARYLAND COLLEGE

During the January term of 1977 a novel three-credit course was offered at Western Maryland College entitled The Ukrainian Experience. Taught by Prof. Wasyl Palijczuk, head of the art department at the college, the course exposed thirteen students to extensive analyses of Ukrainian life-styles in the American sociology, as well as providing insights into European aspects of Ukrainian life.

Western Maryland College

Let it be known that

Linda Frailey

has successfully completed all requirements in

The Ukrainian Experience

January Term Course and is therefore awarded this Diploma as a reminder of his or her experience. We urge that all Ukrainians accept her as an honorary Ukrainian from this day on.

January 28, 1977

President

*Wasyl Palijczuk
Associate Professor
Art Department Head*

Students at Western Maryland College received this Diploma to indicate completion of The Ukrainian Experience.

U.E.A.M. Collection

Prof. Palijczuk employed numerous Ukrainian individuals to enhance his coverage of Ukrainian art, language, history, musicology, egg decorating, community life, etc. A focal point of the course was the fact that all students spent several days living with Ukrainian families. The course culminated on January 28 when all students joined with parents and other Ukrainian participants in enjoying a Ukrainian Feast, which they prepared under the direction of Mrs. S. Lasijczuk. Having already passed their final examinations, the students received Diplomas indicating successful completion of The Ukrainian Experience. Student appreciation for the intensive efforts of Prof. Palijczuk was shown when they presented the two volume set, *Ukraine: A Concise Encyclopedia*, to the college librarian as a remembrance of their having participated in The Ukrainian Experience.

"SLAVIC-AMERICANS IN MARYLAND: CURRENT ETHNIC ISSUES"

Since 1975 the Ukrainian Education Association of Maryland and the Polish Heritage Association of Maryland have joined in sponsoring a yearly conference, "Slavic-Americans in Maryland: Current Ethnic Issues." Chaired jointly by the presidents of the two organizations, Paul Fenchak and Stanislaw E. Mostwin, the conferences have had as their purpose: "To delineate areas of research that will provide better knowledge of life and problems of Slavic ethnic groups in Maryland/ United States; and to identify courses of action needed for accomplishments."

Participants in the conferences have included Dr. Walter Dushnyck, Ukrainian Congress Committee of America; Dr. Jozef A. Mikus (Slovak), Georgian Court College; Dr. Vitaut Kipel (Byelorussian), New York Public Library; Dr. Thaddeus V. Gromada (Polish), Jersey City State College; Dr. Danuta Mostwin (Polish), Catholic University of America; Prof. Hlib S. Hayuk (Ukrainian), Towson State University; Paul Fenchak; Walter Melianovich, Byelorussian Institute of Arts and Sciences; Peter N. Marudas, Office of Senator Paul S. Sarbanes; Prof. Michael Novak (Slovak), Syracuse University and author of *The Rise of the Unmeltable Ethnics*; Dr. Eugene Kusielewicz (Polish), Kosciuscko Foundation; Earl Arnett, Baltimore *Sunpapers*; Janet Covington, WMAR-TV; Hon. Barbara Mikulski, U.S. House of Representatives, among others.

Stanislaw Mostwin, President of the Polish Heritage Association of Maryland, sees the Slavic conferences as being very edifying to the communities. "We are breaking the silence," he stated, "and are beginning to more fully understand our mutual interests. By reducing the feeling of insecurity, a constructive impact on identity development has followed. All of this leads to a heightened sense of achieving in America. By confronting scholars in other communities, we discover the economical potential of a great human market wherein our challenge is to gain psychologically and materially."[16]

ST. MARY'S SEMINARY, BALTIMORE

The number of students for the priesthood of Slavic ancestry at St. Mary's Catholic Seminary in Baltimore has been legion. In some cases Slavs of the Orthodox faith have also studied at St. Mary's as part-time students if not for entire theological programs. According to Fr. Vincent Eaton, Archivist of St. Mary's Seminary, the Poles have likely had the most seminarians with the result that during a number of years the Polish language was taught at St. Mary's and specialists in Polish studies have been in residence at the institution. Likewise, many Czechs and Slovaks have completed ecclesiatical studies there along with smaller numbers of Croatians and Slovenians.[17] The history of Ukrainian students at St. Mary's has been covered in Chapter Seven of this book. A smaller, but very historic seminary, Mt. St. Mary's in Emmitsburg, Maryland, possesses a surprisingly large number of books about Slavic peoples in its library. Other seminaries in Maryland likewise own some very valuable materials for Slavic researchers, as do the archives of various orders of sisters.

CONCLUSION

Slavs must ever remember that America offers latitude for actions and initiatives not enjoyed in many European areas. As is always the scholar's task, histories smacking of parochialism need to be replaced with those of the unimpassioned likes of Oskar Halecki, Ihor Sevchenko, or Hans Kohn. Tenuous claims made in a frenzy to gain 'recognition' need to perish like the Obri. Pride in Slavic origin is not as important as effectiveness in one's community. In 1973 and 1974 the Ukrainian Education Association of Maryland sponsored a booth at the state conventions of the Maryland State Teachers' Association. Interest in Ukrainian history and culture was very high among the teachers and thousands of materials were disseminated. Here in the marketplace at the Civic Center in Baltimore, with the Ukrainians being possibly the first cultural group in Maryland to take their cause to the

teachers, the need for improvement of teaching about Slavs was clearly reflected by types of questions asked by educators and moreso by the content of the educational materials exhibited by publishers. At times the writer suspects that Emperor Nero must have been the first curriculum planner, with the word *curriculum* being of Latin vintage. Who else could have so slavishly imprinted some of the discriminatory traditions that continue in American texts — with the Slavs north of the Danube often being labelled "Barbarians" during studies of the Roman Empire?

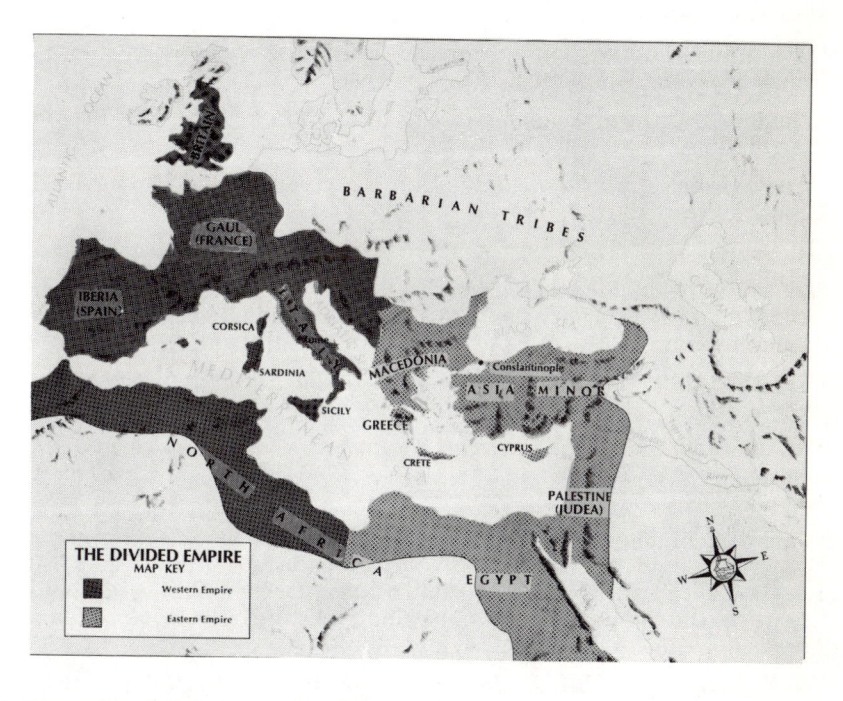

THE MAGIC BLUE DANUBE — *In many school texts, as reflected by this map, Slavs north or east of the Danube are still labelled "Barbarians," even as Indians, Blacks, and Orientals were. How civilized were westerners who sold Slavs into captivity?*

NOTES TO CHAPTER EIGHT

[1] For a study of library holdings of fifteen schools in eight states see Paul Fenchak, "Teaching about 'The United States of Russia' in Our High Schools," *Ukrainian Quarterly*, Vol. XXVII, No. 4, Winter, 1971, pp. 397-405. Books about East European peoples have not been adequately available in secondary schools.

[2] Samuel P. Orth, *Our Foreigners — A Chronicle of Americans in the Making*, New Haven, Yale University Press, 1920, p. 174.

[3] M. Norma Svejda, "Augustine Herman of Bohemia Manor," in *The Czechoslovak Contribution to World Culture*, The Hague, Czechoslovak Society of Arts and Sciences in America, 1964, p. 503.

[4] George J. Prpic, *The Croatian Immigrants in America*, New York, Philosophical Library, 1971, pp. 27-28.

[5] Miecislaus Haiman, *Polish Past in America — 1608-1865*, Chicago, Polish Museum of America, 1974, pp. 36-38.

[6] Thomas J. Curran, *Xenophobia and Immigration, 1820-1930*, Boston, Twayne Publishers, 1975, p. 13.

[7] Wasyl Halich, *Ukrainians in the United States*, Chicago, University of Chicago Press, 1937, p. 39.

[8] H. L. Mencken, "The Last Gasp," Baltimore *Sun*, November 1, 1920.

[9] Letter to H. L. Mencken from Emil Revyuk, Editor of Ukrainian *Svoboda*, dated February 25, 1936. This letter and others are on file in Mencken Room of Enoch Pratt Free Library, Baltimore.

[10] Letter to H. L. Mencken from Vladimir Geeza, Editor of *Nove Zhyttia*, June 3, 1935.

[11] H. L. Mencken, *The American Language — An Inquiry into the Development of English in the United States*, New York, Alfred A. Knopf, 1937, p. 664.

[12] See p. 2 of paper presented by Paul Fenchak at Second Annual Conference, "Slavic-Americans in Maryland: Current Ethnic Issues," at Loyola College on March 20, 1976, entitled "Current Status of Slavic Studies in the Public Schools of Maryland." Printed in *Jednota Annual Furdek — 1976*, Vol. XVI, Jan. 1977, pp. 211-221.

[13] College catalog of Manor Junior College, Jenkintown, Penna., 1972-1974, p. 5.

[14] Vladimir Wertsman, *The Ukrainians in America, 1609-1975*, Dobbs Ferry, Oceana Publications, 1976, pp. 110-114.

[15] Clarence A. Manning, *History of Slavic Studies in the United States*, Milwaukee, Marquette University Press, 1957, p. 31.

[16] Interview with Stanislaw Mostwin, Towson, Maryland, on December 20, 1976.

[17] Interview with Rev. Vincent Eaton, Archivist, St. Mary's Seminary, Baltimore, by Wolodymyr Sushko and Paul Fenchak on January 31, 1976.

Chapter Nine
Ukrainian Heritage Schools
Wolodymyr C. Sushko

In learning about the complex mosaic that is the United States, the ethnic schools have a special place. Ethnic schools were and are still today very much a part of Ukrainian life in this country and state. But they are not unique to Ukrainians. Poles, Czechs, Lithuanians, Italians and many other groups share similar educational experiences. For example, the Augustine Herman School was in operation in Baltimore in the Czech neighborhood from 1905 until 1960. At peak years about 105 students attended this school.[1] Today, at least 175 people are given the opportunity to learn Polish in the three schools that offer Polish language courses in the Baltimore metropolitan area.[2] Among the Baltimore Lithuanian community, which numbers about 750 families, many continue to send their children to their parish school in order to learn and appreciate the language of their forefathers. Similar episodes repeat themselves in every other ethnic group also. The reader may rightfully ask the question, why the establishment of ethnic schools? Perhaps the history and development of Ukrainian heritage schools may offer analysis in answering the question. But let us look first at the background and philosophy that led to the establishment of ethnic schools.

BACKGROUND

The driving force behind the ethnic schools has always been a desire and determination on the part of the leaders of American ethnics to keep their communities aware of their cultural heritages.

Indeed, there was much to be preserved within each ethnic group on the new continent. Each immigrant group brought to America a rich reserve of the culture of its land. Relating to the various immigrant cultures, Carl Wittke quotes Horace M. Kallen in calling the United States "a young country with old memories" . . . "Even the lowliest Old World peasant came from a land where the churches are centuries old, full of richly-carved chancels, altar-pieces, pulpits, sculpture, wood carvings, beautifully embroidered vestments, and walls hung with the paintings of old masters. In the songs and dances of their folk festivals, in their love of flowers and the beauties of the forest, in the elaborately embroidered bodice of a peasant girl, many centuries of Old World culture are revealed" . . . , says Carl Wittke.[3]

In the past, little attention was focused on and even less use was made of America's cultural reservoir. As a result, scholars today agree that too little is known about America's cultural diversity. "No major intellectual task has been so neglected as the development of a theory of cultural pluralism," says Earl Arnett of the Baltimore Sun, quoting Michael Novak, a noted scholar on ethnics, "the cultural histories of approximately one-half of our population are largely unknown. Teachers in our schools do not know the cultural histories of those they teach. The descendants of immigrants, because of their names or appearances or unknown backgrounds are . . . given a self-image of intellectual inferiority, assigned a lower scale of aspiration."[4]

In too many cases the foreign-born quickly shed all traces of the former selves and the traditions they brought with them to this country. No doubt, the methology of the melting pot, fostered by the host society, often speeded up this process, making many of these foreign-born ashamed and embarrassed by their own cultural heritage. Cultural diversity, the very foundation of this unique creation recognized all over the world as American democracy, was in danger of vanishing from the American scene.

It is against such a background that ethnic schools came to existence in the United States. In many ways these schools helped to remove the self-image of inferiority among American ethnics.

PHILOSOPHY

The basic goal of ethnic schools was to preserve the community's own unique culture. By gaining an understanding and love of their own cultural heritage, the children of immigrant parents hoped to keep solidarity with their own ethnic community and to perpetuate the interests of that community. In their ethnic schools they learned who they were and where they came from. But there is still another deeper philosophy behind the ethnic schools. By gaining an understanding and love of their own cultural heritage, the young American ethnics acquired a better understanding and respect for the cultural assets of other ethnic groups in America. Knowledge of their own culture implanted in them a self-pride and helped dispel a feeling of inferiority as compared with other societies.

Still another positive force behind the establishment of ethnic schools was that by learning about their ancestral language students became fluent in other language at an early age; this fact has often encouraged them in learning additional languages in their public schools. Being immersed in the studies of their ancestral land, students have opportunities in sharing their experiences with children of other ethnic groups. In sum, these experiences enriched and broadened the educational horizons young American ethnics were receiving in their regular day-time schools. Here, truly, private education supplemented the public curriculum rather than the one eliminating the other.

Ethnic heritage schools were usually conducted in the afternoons and on Saturdays. Hence, they often became known as "Saturday Schools."

EARLY UKRAINIAN SCHOOLS IN AMERICA

America's oldest Ukrainian school was organized in 1893 in Shamokin, Pennsylvania, by a Ukrainian priest, Iwan Konstankewych. One year later, similar schools were established in other areas of Pennsylvania, such as Shenandoah, Ramey, Altoona, Mount Carmel, Pittsburgh, Olyphant, Wilkes-Barre. Schools were also established in Minneapolis, Minnesota, Jersey City, New Jersey, and in other cities. By 1920 schools were rooted in many Ukrainian-American communities. In Maryland the first Ukrainian school was organized in Baltimore in 1916.

The retention of the Ukrainian language among the immigrants and their children became the cornerstone of all efforts of Ukrainian-American leaders. Through the language media they hoped to hold the immigrants and their children together. This need was very critical because Ukrainian immigrants from the period 1870-1914 were frequently illiterates from economically poor western territories of Ukraine, often without a clearly used national identity. The immigration figures for 1900 indicate that Ukrainians, then called "Ruthenians," were 49% illiterate, putting them on the lower end of the literacy scale among the Slavic groups, though better than southern Italians, Syrians and Portugese.[5] As such they sometime became victims of more aggressive Slavic groups with whom they lived and worked. Therefore, a need existed to organize Ukrainian schools for individual and community betterment.

The pioneering work in promoting Ukrainian schools was done by the Ukrainian National Association, a fraternal organization with its headquarters in Jersey City, and its Ukrainian language newspaper "Svoboda." The yellowing pages of early issues of "Svoboda" bear witness to these efforts. An editorial titled "We Need Schools" in the fifth issue in 1894 called on parents to organize Ukrainian schools in their communities. In the twenty-first issue of June 4 of the same year there is an appeal addressed to young Ukrainian-Americans:

> ... Young Kozaks! Let us not permit ourselves to become an object of jokes by outsiders! ... Prove to yourselves that you can do it. ... Attend the Ukrainian school. ...

Later another appeal in the forty-fifth issue reminded parents to speak in Ukrainian with their children at home so that they would know that they are of Ukrainian descent.[6]

The Ukrainian immigrants in America could not count on much professional help from the old country. Often the best the old country could do was to give encouragement. Perhaps a letter written by Iwan Hrymalo from Lviv in Ukraine to "Svoboda" in Jersey City in 1896, illustrates the situation:

> ... Develop your own intelligentsia. Send your children to English-speaking schools so thay can learn everything they teach there, but in addition, organize Ukrainian schools where they can learn about their own heritage. ... Do not expect the old country to send you its intellectuals. ... We need them here ... .[7]

And so the course was charted for the Ukrainian community in America.

A BRIEF LOOK AT THE DEVELOPMENT OF EDUCATION

From the beginning the majority of Ukrainian schools were parochial schools. Classes were usually conducted by the priest, the church cantor, or nuns wherever these were available. The educational program consisted of classes in the Ukrainian language, history, geography, culture and music. One of the staunch supporters of Ukrainian heritage schools was Soter Ortynsky, the first Ukrainian Catholic Bishop in the United States. "We squabble about nothing," said the Bishop in an appeal which he issued preceeding an educational meeting he called to Philadelphia for September 15, 1909, concluding, "those who do not have their own schools are like a blind beggar."[8] Bishop Ortynsky issued a directive to establish Ukrainian schools in each parish. As a result, practically all schools were put under the guidance of the Church.

Ukrainian heritage schools were always considered by

their organizers to be supplementary to public schools. They were intended to serve primarily one purpose: to teach the Ukrainian heritage. This view finds backing in Emily Balch's book, *Our Slavic Fellow Citizens*. In a chapter "A Polish Criticism of Church Schools" Emily Balch quotes a Ruthenian (Ukrainian) priest saying, "They have most confidence in parochial schools, but as supplementary to the public schools, not as a substitute."[9]

The pioneering work of the Ukrainian National Association in the field of education did not cease when heritage schools came under the direction of the Church. This Association continued its efforts to insure that heritage schools would serve the purposes for which they were intended. Over the years several successful attempts were made to improve the professional level of those schools. Education in many early schools was on an elementary level. Classes were held mostly in church halls or basements, children of all ages were grouped together, and there was no coordinated curriculum. Need for improvements was much on the order of the day. At the instigation of the Ukrainian National Association a School Fund was established in 1912 to which each member paid three cents per month. An Educational Commission was created, and it tried to improve teaching methods through a series of seminars and teacher conferences. An informative children's magazine was also published during this period.

The outbreak of World War I momentarily slowed down educational activities to be resumed again in 1922 under the leadership of a new body called United Ukrainian Associations in America. One of the greatest improvements made was a coordinated curriculum for all schools, parochial and secular alike. School programs in each school had to be approved first by the Educational Commission before they could be used in the school. The administration of each school was put under the control of parents committees and local organizations in each community. This administrative body was called "Ridna Shkola" (Native School). All Ukrainian language teachers had to be certified by the Educational Commission, and they were subject to the rules and regulations of this Commission. The Commission itself

*Samples of Textbooks used in 1930's in Baltimore.
U.E.A.M. Collection*

was renamed Administration of Ridna Shkola in America. New improved textbooks were printed. Thanks to the above measures, the Ukrainian heritage schools had reached new heights in the 1920's and 1930's in many communities throughout the United States. However, World War II brought another slow-down in the education process.

The arrival of new immigrants after World War II gave new impetus to Ukrainian heritage schools. Today there are two kinds of schools, parochial and non-denominational schools. Most classes continue to be held on weekends, usually on Saturdays. Instructional programs include Ukrainian language and literature, history and geography of Ukraine, Ukrainian culture and religion. All subjects are taught in the Ukrainian language. In addition to Saturday parochial schools, the Ukrainian Catholic Church operates sixty-six all-day elementary schools, eight high schools and two college-level institutions.[10] The Ukrainian language is taught in these schools as a subject. The parochial Saturday schools continue under the direction of churches. Most non-denominational schools are under the supervision of the Educational Council of the Ukrainian Congress Committee of America (UCCA). Some schools are under local sponsorship of Ridna Shkola associations or youth organizations such as SUMA (Ukrainian Youth Association of America) and others, but they all remain within the framework of the Educational Council of UCCA.

EARLY SCHOOL AT ST. MICHAEL'S IN BALTIMORE

Maryland's oldest Ukrainian school was organized in 1916 by the Reverend Constantyn Kurylo who was the third Ukrainian Catholic pastor in Baltimore. This school was under the auspices of the St. Michael's Ukrainian Catholic Church, and it consisted of one room located in a building at 524 South Wolfe Street next to the church. During his stay in Baltimore from 1914 to 1916 Reverend Kurylo was on the staff at St. Mary's Theological Seminary. The cantor at the Ukrainian church in Baltimore at this time was John

Boyko. He learned to be a cantor in the old country before coming to America in 1912. Boyko readily accepted an offer to leave New York and come to serve the Baltimore community. Since he was knowledgeable in Ukrainian culture, he became the instructor, teaching from 1916 until 1929. Joe Marmash, a student at this Ukrainian heritage school in the early 1920's, recalls that "our school consisted of 25-27 students. We started in one class. Each year we would progress to a higher grade. We were taught only reading and writing. Classes were held three nights a week, after regular public school hours. On Saturday mornings we were taught cathechism. During the second year of Ukrainian schooling we were taught singing . . . and on Sundays we sang the responses to the Divine Liturgy. Some of the students would take part in Ukrainian plays which were produced once a year."[11] This Ukrainian school ended for many with the receiving of First Holy Communion. Besides teaching, in the early 1920's John Boyko formed a school orchestra. His orchestra played before Bishop Constantyn Bohachevsky of Philadelphia during his canonical visit of the Ukrainian faithful in Baltimore in 1924.

THE "RIDNA SHKOLA" SCHOOL IN EAST BALTIMORE

An event took place in 1929, which had a significant effect on the further development of Ukrainian education in Baltimore during the 1930's. Following the example of other communities where education was put in the hands of the recently formed Administration of Ridna Shkola (Native School) in America, on January 27, 1929, a group of interested Ukrainians met at the hall of St. Michael's Ukrainian Catholic Church and elected a progressive school committee, with Joseph Prymak as the president. The other members were Andriy Peltz, secretary, Theodore Nykula, assistant secretary, Theodore Kaszak, treasurer, and Theodore Zacharchuk and Theodore Poliszuk as advisors. This Committee took over the authority for operating the school and school finances. The school became known as Ridna Shkola. At its second meeting on February 23, 1929, the Committee adopted a constitution and the by-laws by which the school was to be governed (Appendix I).

John Boyko continued to teach for about one more year but because of conflicts between his regular job and many church-related duties, he stepped aside as a teacher in 1929. Reverend Mychajlo Koltucky, the pastor at St. Michael's at that time, agreed to teach at the school. In his work he was assisted by his wife. Approximately 40 children attended the school at that time. In 1931 Reverend Koltucky left Baltimore for another assignment. Soon after his departure, disputes occurred over who should control the school — the parents' committee or the church. To avoid further conflicts, the school committee decided to move the school. A space was rented at 3303 O'Donnell Street and the school was transferred to this location.

The school committee was able to secure a teacher from Detroit, Michigan, by the name of Joseph Swobodjan, a good educator, who taught reading, writing, history, and geography. In addition, he possessed an excellent knowledge of music and became director of the Ukrainian National Choir in Baltimore. The school operated for one year at the new location. When the Ukrainian National Home was established at 3101 O'Donnell Street in 1932, the school moved to this Home and occupied the second floor of the building. About 80 children were enrolled at this school in the 1930's. Part-time teachers in those years were Andriy Peltz and Theodore Lucyshyn, each of whom taught for about one year. The Ridna Shkola existed until 1940. In the meantime, the Ukrainian language sessions continued at St. Michael's during the 1930's, but as years progressed they were getting smaller and more irregular. Sister Monica of the St. Basil Order was in charge of the school, while Sister Sebastiana was a teacher.

The Boys and Girls Clubs which existed in the 1930's at the Ukrainian National Home were closely affiliated with the Ridna Shkola. These clubs actually were branches of the Ukrainian Youth League of North America (UYLNA),

Members of the Girls' Club in Baltimore in the 1930's. Second from left is Magda Semenkiw who was runner-up in a beauty contest at the Ukrainian Pavillion of the Chicago World's Fair in 1933.

Mr. Theodore Nykula

one of the largest Ukrainian youth organizations in the United States at that time. Students of Ridna Shkola were active members of these clubs.

Other educational activity included the Ukrainian folk dancing lessons given in 1932 by Wasyl Avramenko, a teacher and dancer of great renown of Ukrainian historic and folk dances. Avramenko-trained dancers of Baltimore performed on many occasions throughout the thirties before the local Ukrainian community and general Baltimore audiences.

World War II involved many young men in military service, so the school as well as the rich social life of the thirties at the Ukrainian National Home came to a standstill during the war.

HERITAGE CLASSES AT CHESAPEAKE CITY

Ukrainian heritage education was also of concern to Ukrainian settlers in Chesapeake City, Cecil County. Religious and cultural instructions were given by Sisters Monica and Ihnatija of the Order of St. Basil. One-hour sessions were held each evening during the school year at St. Basil's church hall, and they consisted of Ukrainian reading, writing, religion, and history of the Ukrainian Church. During 1945-1950, approximately 42 children attended the classes. The school was closed in 1950, but reopened again in 1964. In 1967 instruction was again discontinued because of a shortage of nuns as teachers. Sister Ihnatija tried to reactivate the school again in 1972 and taught once a week for one year. At present, there is no regular Ukrainian school in Chesapeake City.[12]

Many Ukrainian settlers in Chesapeake City could not read nor write in English. To help them, Mary Wasylczuk Hrabec, a daughter of Ukrainian pioneers in Chesapeake City and a graduate of Johns Hopkins University, held classes in the English language during the New Deal era. These adult education evening classes were held at the St. Basil's church hall.

SCHOOLS IN THE UKRAINIAN COMMUNITY OF WASHINGTON, D.C.

The establishment of a Ukrainian school in Washington, D.C., dates back to 1950. In September of that year, the first effort was made in forming such a school at the home of Theodosius Diachok at 926 Sheppard Street, N.W. The school was known as *Ridna Shkola* (Native School). Fourteen children attended school during that year. The teachers were Theodosia Kichorowsky, Josaphat Pachowsky, Emilia Procinsky, and Stephania Diachok.[13] In 1952, the school relocated to the parish house of the Holy Family Ukrainian Catholic Church at 3419 12th Street, N.E., where pastor Monsignor Wolodymyr Pylypec held Ukrainian language classes every Tuesday from 7:30 to

9:00 in the evening. In 1954, a Parents' School Committee was formed, with Emilia Procinsky as its chairwoman.

After the departure of Father Pylypec in 1955, the school continued to be associated with the Holy Family Catholic Parish. Between 1957 and 1965 the supervision of the instructional program was in the hands of Professor Wolodymyr Wowchko-Kulchycky. Additional staff members included Father Theodosius Danusiar who became pastor of Holy Family Church in 1956, and Dr. Peter Oryshkewych, Myroslawa Zalucky, Ostap Zyniuk, and Iryna Stawnychy. The classes were held on Saturday mornings. Dr. Wasyl Siokalo was the chairman of the new Parents' School Committee. Subjects taught were catechism, the Ukrainian Byzantine rite, and Ukrainian language, history, and geography. In addition to these subjects, a children's rhythmic ensemble was started in 1957 under the direction of Father T. Danusiar, assisted by Olha Sushko-Nakonechny, who also directed a choir composed of students attending the Ukrainian school.

To make the Ukrainian heritage studies available to the whole community — Catholics and Orthodox — the Ukrainian Association of Washington, D.C., organized a new school in 1963 which replaced the former church school. This effort represented the spirit and purpose for which this organization was created in 1950, namely, to unite the work of both Ukrainian Catholics and Orthodox to strengthen the Ukrainian community of Washington and its suburbs. The school became known as the School of Ukrainian Studies. It found wide support among Ukrainians.

Dr. Peter Oryshkewych, who became principal, supervised the school for 11 years. In addition to Dr. Oryshkewych, the teaching staff included Anastasia Prystay, Halyna Warwariw and Maria Kobi. Three classes were conducted during the first year. The classes were initially held at St. Andrew's Ukrainian Orthodox Church located at 4812 16th Street, N.W. In 1967 the school was relocated to Forest Grove Elementary School of the Montgomery County Public School System in Silver

Paying tribute to the Taras Shevchenko monument in the Nation's Capital is the Metropolitan Washington, D.C., area School of Ukrainian Studies from Silver Spring, Maryland, Year 1975.

Mr. Bohdan Yasinsky

Spring, Maryland. From the initial three classes of 1963, the school was expanded to include kindergarten, regular grades 1 through 11 and a class for English-speaking children. A total of 112 students were enrolled during the 1972-73 school year. The teaching staff in the same year consisted of fifteen teachers, including priests from both Ukrainian Catholic and Orthodox parishes. Instructors were Bohdan Yasinsky, Olha Kurylas, Petro Krul, Reverend Stephen Shawel CSSR, Dr. Peter Oryshkewych, Reverend Petro Budny, Warwara Dibert, Olha Masnyk, Iryna Yasinsky, Yaroslawa Francuzhenko, Natalka Zacharchenko, Halya Bula, Uljana Sosj, and Dr. Myroslaw Serbyn.[14] In 1974, Dr. Peter Oryshkewych stepped down as the school principal. His duties were assumed by Bohdan Yasinsky.

A special achievement of the School of Ukrainian Studies was the accreditation for out-of-school program in Ukrainian, which was granted to this school in 1973 by the Montgomery County Public School System. This

A group picture including the teaching staff and pupils of the School of Ukrainian Studies, school year 1972-73.
Dr. Peter Oryshkewych

accreditation applies to students who are enrolled in Grades 9, 10, 11, or 12 in Montgomery County Public Schools. Credit earned at the Ukrainian School is honored as foreign language elective credit toward graduation from high school. Several considerations led to this decision, as Richard E. Wagner of the Montgomery Public Schools informed Dr. Peter Oryshkewych of the Ukrainian School:

> ...First, the emphasis of the Ukrainian School is largely on language as a medium of instruction in grammar, literature, history, and geography, and as such is comparable to the approach we are offering in our advanced language program in the larger high schools of Montgomery County. In addition, the visit of one of our staff members to your program makes it clear that the school is well organized and the students evidence a real seriousness of purpose in the program. The Ukrainian School schedule meets the requirements of the Maryland State Board of Education in reference to clock hours of instruction as related to credit...[15]

The Montgomery County School System was soon followed by the Howard and Prince George's Counties which also granted a similar credit arrangement to those students of the School of Ukrainian Studies who were enrolled in their respective county schools. Thus, the Ukrainian School in Montgomery County became the first Slavic school in Maryland where students received credit for studying a Slavic language — Ukrainian. Previously, programs for earning language credit existed only for the study of Hebrew and Greek in Maryland.

UKRAINIAN STUDIES IN BALTIMORE

One of the first concerns of new Ukrainian immigrants who settled in the Baltimore area in the post-World War II years was to have schools where their children could learn the language and traditions of their nation. The only school they found here in the late 1940's was the St. Michael's Ukrainian Catholic Church School. Classes were conducted by two nuns. The educational level of the curriculum was somewhat limited and provided only basic teaching in reading, writing, and religion. The new immigrants were all literate, many of them professionally trained. Among them there were Catholics as well as

Baltimore Ukrainian school children visiting the Taras Shevchenko monument in Washington, D.C., Year 1966.

U.E.A.M. Collection

Orthodox. This diversity placed new demands and challenges on the existing school system.

Traditionally, the church was always and continues to be the center of existence of each ethnic group. Being the case with Ukrainians, the already existing parochial school at St. Michael's in East Baltimore was revived. Similar new schools were founded at SS. Peter and Paul Ukrainian Catholic Church in Curtis Bay and at St. Michael's Ukrainian Orthodox Church organized in the early 1950's and also located in East Baltimore. Still another group of concerned Ukrainians looked beyond their religious affiliations, and wanted both Ukrainian Catholics and Orthodox united as one homogenous ethnic community in Baltimore; consequently a fourth, non-denominational, school was organized. Today after 26 years, this fourth school alone is still in operation, and it shows signs of being the kind of heritage school acceptable to all Ukrainian-Americans regardless of their religious ties.

For the record, it is in order to describe each of these four schools as they functioned in Baltimore between 1950 and 1974.

ST. MICHAEL'S UKRAINIAN CATHOLIC SCHOOL

The two nuns who taught Ukrainian prior to 1951 left Baltimore in this year for another assignment. Before they departed they were assisted in their teaching by one of the new immigrants — Olha Yachno and soon by another, Olha Diwnycz. In 1953 the teaching ranks were supplemented by Maria Charchalis. She and Olha Diwnycz ran the school until about 1955. In this work they were assisted by Anna Stelmach, Oksana Yuzeniw and Iwanna Maciurak. Practically, all of them had their own children enrolled in this school at that time. It is, therefore, a wonder that in spite of being working mothers and maintaining homes after working hours, they were willing to donate their time each Saturday morning to teach Ukrainian. In the beginning the school offered only elementary level courses but with time, as classes advanced, the courses of secondary level were added.

In 1955 further changes took place. The new pastor, Monsignor Petro Melnyczuk, secured new teachers — Iwan Seniuta, who replaced John Boyko as cantor, and Petro and Wolodymyra Wojtowycz. In addition, Wolodymyr Sushko taught geography at the secondary level in the mid-1960's. A Parents' Committee usually assisted the pastor in administering the school. Bohdan Chapelsky, Wolodymyr Sushko, and Dr. Nicholas Kohut, among others, chaired these committees at various times. The school prospered during those two decades.

The enrollment in the late 1950's exceeded 100 pupils. Each year students presented theatrical plays, such as those depicting the traditional visit of St. Nicholas. These cultural events, no doubt, contributed to a better understanding of their heritage. After Iwan Seniuta died in 1966, his vacancy was filled with Arcady

Children during a school play at St. Michael's Church Hall in early 1960's.

Mrs. Olha Sushko

Iwaskiw who remained until 1970. The last two teachers were Lubow Rad and Maria Stith.

In the early 1970's apathy and other factors reduced the school's earlier momentum. This became especially evident after the Wojtowycz couple ceased to teach in 1972 because of other commitments. The school's overall level and attendance rapidly declined. Some students transferred to other Ukrainian schools. In the spring of 1974, the pupil attendance dropped to about 10. The school ceased function in 1974.

ST. MICHAEL'S UKRAINIAN ORTHODOX CHURCH SCHOOL

This school opened in 1953, and operated for 13 years. Classes were limited to the first five grades at the elementary level, and were held on Saturday mornings under rather crowded conditions in a small church hall at 2018 Gough Street adjoining the church. The average yearly enrollment was approximately 20 children. Courses were taught by Reverend Andriy Ilinsky, the pastor, Borys Zelynsky, and Maria Iwashchenko. Additionally, other instructors included Dr. Yurij Krywolap, Raya Zelynsky, Oksana Kalynowsky, Oleh Bulawka and Evhen Cherewko.

The school closed in 1966.

SS. PETER AND PAUL CHURCH SCHOOL

The beginnings of this school go back to the pre-World War II years when nuns who were assigned to St. Michael's parish in Baltimore commuted to Curtis Bay to teach reading and writing in Ukrainian and religion. This instruction stopped with the outbreak of World War II. The teaching effort was resumed by Reverend Wasyl Solowij after he became the first resident pastor for Ukrainians in Curtis Bay in 1950. However, the first program of separate classes did not start until 1958 when a new immigrant-teacher, Olha Kozak, took charge of the school. It was an elementary school having five grades. The average enrollment was about 25 pupils during the 1960's. When the Kozak family moved to Washington, D.C., in 1960, Maria Choma took over the school. She ran the school until 1965 and was succeeded in that year by Petro and Wolodymyra Wojtowycz. The Wojtowycz couple taught until 1974. In the early 1970's, they were assisted by another teacher, Marusia Zozulak. Miss Zozulak continued to run the school until it was discontinued in 1975.

SCHOOL OF UKRAINIAN SCIENCES U.C.C.A.

This school was established in 1950. Initially it was sponsored by the local League of Ukrainian Mothers and a Parents' Committee headed by Antin Traska, who was responsible for administrative matters. It was known as Ukrainian Supplementary School, U.M.L. (Ukrainian Mothers' League). Olena Kurylas administered the curriculum for this school.

In 1952 the school came under the tutelage of the Ukrainian Congress Committee of America. In that year Semen Mychajlyshyn, a former high school teacher in Ukraine, took charge of this school. He officiated until 1955, when he was replaced by Borys Zelynsky. The present principal of the school is Mychajlo Choma, who has held this position since 1958. He also teaches Ukrainian literature, as well as language and history courses. He is

School of Ukrainian Sciences U.C.C.A. Picture showing teaching staff and pupils in native costumes, taken in 1953.

Mr. Semen Mychajlyshyn

certified by the State of Maryland as qualified to teach Ukrainian subjects. Another teacher accredited by the State of Maryland, working with Choma since 1969, is Wolodymyr Sushko. Since 1973, he has also served as assistant principal with functions relating to certification and accreditation of the school by state and local school authorities. In the sequence of this school's history, several other instructors spent various periods of time teaching here. They were Reverend Andriy Ilinsky, Sophia Mychajlyshyn, Oksana Kalynowsky, Lida Czumak, Petro Wojtowycz, Reverend Yurij Markewycz, Monsignor Petro Melnyczuk, Lidia Lemishka, and, especially, Maria Choma who taught here uniteruptedly from 1952 until 1970.

The school offers courses of a secondary level. Initially they were from the 6th grade up, and later on were concentrated at a high school level, grades 9 through 12. Admission is dependent on successful completion of the lower grades in Ukrainian studies. The average enrollment

Students preparing school work at the YWCA Center where regular school sessions were held ca. late 1950's.
   U.E.A.M. Collection

was approximately 21 students in the secondary grades. Subjects studied in the school are of advanced level, and include language, literature, culture, geography, history, and religion. The culminating point of the successful completion of the secondary school besides the 12th grade report card was and is a final examination called *Matura*. This examination is held before a board of educators who are appointed by the Educational Council of U.C.C.A. The graduating class of 1975 was the first class in the history of this school to have completed their program with such a *matura*. Upon successful completion of written and oral examinations, a total of 12 graduates were awarded diplomas which were issued by the Educational Council of U.C.C.A.

The school had a long and interesting history. First lessons in 1950-51 were given in a rented hall at Gough and Castle in East Baltimore. In 1951 the school moved to the YWCA at 26 South Broadway to be moved a year later, after this Center closed, to the hall of the Ukrainian Orthodox Church at 2020 Gough Street. It remained here until 1956. Between 1956 and 1970, classes were held in two rented rooms at the International Center, Y.W.C.A., at 16 South Patterson Park Avenue. It is worthy of mention that throughout the 1960's this friendly center hosted many

Graduating Class of the School of Ukrainian Sciences, U.C.C.A., in 1975.
U.E.A.M. Collection

Ukrainian cultural and other civic affairs. The School of Ukrainian Sciences operated here until the Center closed in December of 1970. Since that year instruction was held at the Ukrainian Self-Reliance Association Building at 239 South Broadway. Studies currently are held on each Saturday during the school year between 9:00 a.m. and 2:00 p.m.

Throughout its existence the school enjoyed much support from its Parent Committees. Worthy of mention is Emanuel Prytula who served on the committee since 1952. He was succeeded by Lidia Lemishka in 1968. The present committee chairman is Theodore Chay, who has served in this function since 1970.

The School of Ukrainian Sciences has been the first Slavic school in Maryland to be certified by the State as a non-public tutoring school offering instruction in the Ukrainian language and culture. Certificate of Approval No. 1876 was issued to this effect on May 21, 1974, by James C. Sensenbaugh, State Superintendent of Schools. The school also became accredited by the Baltimore City and Anne Arundel County school systems, and as a result, secondary level students enrolled in this Ukrainian school and schools in their respective school systems, now receive one high school language credit per year for their Ukrainian study (Appendices II, III). Credits are recorded in accordance with arrangements made by the Foreign Language Office of the Baltimore City Public Schools with the School of Ukrainian Sciences (Appendix IV). Credits earned at the Ukrainian school are also accepted by all major Catholic high schools in the area, such as Calvert Hall, Seton, Mercy, Archbishop Curley, and the Institute of Notre Dame.

The above achievement was possible through positive efforts of recognized authorities. Jeannette H. Rock. Specialist in Accreditation of Non-public Schools for the Maryland Department of Education, visited the Ukrainian school. She wrote to Wolodymyr Sushko of this school:

> ... They are dedicated to high standards of scholarship ... Learning is regarded as having intrinsic as well as practical values — a refreshing approach in this day when so much stress is placed on the career orientation of education ... One visiting ... is impressed with the program. ...[16]

> Maryland State Department of Education
>
> ## CERTIFICATE OF APPROVAL
>
> No. 1876
>
> **Be it known** That, pursuant to Chapter 489 of the Acts of 1947, as amended, of the Laws of the State of Maryland, approval is hereby granted to the Parents Committee of the School of Ukrainian Sciences U.C.C.A. (Ukrainian Congress Committee of America) in Baltimore, Maryland to operate a tutoring school offering instruction in the Ukrainian language and culture
>
> located at 239 S. Broadway, Baltimore, Maryland 21231
>
> as a nonpublic school or educational institution to be known as School of Ukrainian Sciences U.C.C.A. in Baltimore, Maryland
>
> This approval is valid unless and until declared null and void or revoked by the State Superiniendent of Schools in the manner prescribed by law.
>
> In witness whereof, for and on behalf of the State Department of Education, I have hereunto set my hand and affixed the seal of the State Board of Education, Maryland, this __21st__ day of __May__, 19 __74__
>
> State Superintendent of Schools

These sentiments are further echoed by many other authorities...

> ... We are indeed proud that our students are pursuing studies in their ancestral language. I feel that they should be encouraged and we should recognize their efforts....

says Father David M. Stopyra, Principal of Archbishop Curley High School in Baltimore.[17] Still another, William J. Gerardi, Principal of Baltimore Polytechnic Institute, wrote to each of the parents of his students who studied at the Ukrainian school in 1975:

... This grade has been entered in his permanent record at Poly and will be part of his transcript when he applies for admission to a college or a job. May I congratulate both you and your son for not only doing excellent work in his Ukrainian studies, but also for continuing an interest in the culture, language, and history of the Ukraine....[18]

The School of Ukrainian Sciences shows all signs of future growth and expansion. Today, children whose parents, in their concern for preserving the Ukrainian culture 26 years ago, were sending them to Ukrainian Saturday schools have now become parents with children of their own. They are determined to pass the rich cultural heritage of their ancestral homeland to their own children. A group of them, spearheaded by Irena Traska, organized in the fall of 1975 an elementary and junior level school under the auspices of the U.C.C.A. School of Ukrainian Sciences. A total of 47 children were enrolled in these two levels in 1975. A kindergarten class and grades 1,3,6, and 7 are taught in that school on Saturdays in rented classrooms of Hampstead Hill Elementary School in East Baltimore. The initial teacher force included Irena Traska, Maria

School of Ukrainian Sciences in Baltimore. Grade 11 in session at the Self-Reliance Association Building, Year 1975. **U.E.A.M. Collection**

Zozulak, Maria Stith, Wolodymyra Wojtowycz, Petro Wojtowych, and Monsignor Petro Melnyczuk. New teachers were added for the 1976-77 school year. They are Genia Sidlak, Nina Chychulyn, Laryssa Salamacha and Martha Tatchyn. In addition, a Parents' Committee was organized, with Taras Charchalis as the president.

School children and parents enjoying a picnic at Patapsco State Park, October 10, 1976.

U.E.A.M. Collection

LOOKING TO THE FUTURE

Given aggressive, knowledgeable and fully professional leadership, countless ethnic schools may evolve into desired bastions of what America really is — a mosaic of various cultures. Thomas D. Troy, Coordinator of Foreign Languages, Baltimore City Public Schools, put it this way:

> ...As you know, for a long time I have been interested in the promotion of various ethnic language programs, either formally in the Baltimore City Public Schools or in neighborhood situations such as your own Ukrainian school. For too long ethnic languages in this country have been subdued, and immigrants have felt the need to learn English and their own language as a subculture. A person's language is fundamental to him in all of his relationships with his fellow man. If we are to really understand other people and

United States Senator-Elect Paul Sarbanes visiting the Ukrainian Saturday School at Hampstead Elementary School in Baltimore on May 1, 1976.

Mrs. Lydia Czumak

other countries, we must make every effort to understand the fundamental ingredient, which is language. With this in mind, I am happy to say that such ethnic language groups are experiencing success in the Baltimore area. As you know, your own Ukrainian education is progressing. . . .[19]

It is often the second language that awakens an awareness in the use and abuse of one's own mother tongue. As a matter of fact, their bi-lingual and bi-cultural training gives young American ethnics an extra advantage over their peers in American schools. But there is also something more to this; at a time when the population of citizens of a foreign tongue in the United States increases daily, we must have ability to communicate with them effectively...But not only with them...Today's world is shrinking rapidly, and the world's citizens become more and more dependent on each other...Recently Dr. James A. Sensenbaugh, Maryland State Superintendent of Schools, had the opportunity to visit schools in England, Sweden, and Poland. In Poland he saw a school in which all classes were taught in English. He stated:

> ...my belief that there are numerous common problems which could be served by common educational projects among nations... Yes, we have differences of culture...and a great many other differences. But we have something more important in common — common occupancy on one small planet whose problems of survival are inextricably interdependent. One response to that big problem is international education.[20]

Without a doubt, ethnic schools provide the opportunity to increase the effectiveness of communication in one's own language and, thus, they contribute to the international education about which Dr. Sensenbaugh is talking.

APPENDIX I*

CONSTITUTION AND BY-LAWS OF THE UKRAINIAN NATIONAL SCHOOL IN BALTIMORE, MARYLAND

The Ukrainian National School was formed and put in effect after a mass meeting on February 23, 1929.

CONSTITUTION AND BY-LAWS

1. Name of the School:
   Ukrainian National School of Baltimore, Maryland.
2. Object of the School:
   To educate our children in reading, writing, history, geography and national songs of their parents native land.
3. Committee:
   The Committee is composed of a body of seven men who are elected by the members of the school at annual yearly meetings.
4. Opening of the Meeting:
   With a prayer or a song.
5. Regulations of the School:
   a. The teacher is given full charge of the children during schooling hours.
   b. In case of any faults on the teacher's part, the school committee shall call a meeting to that effect.
   c. The schooling days are Monday, Tuesdays, Wednesdays, and Thursdays. Friday is set for one hour of catechism and one hour of singing practice or any training for plays or concerts given by the school.
6. Schooling Hours:
   a. Two hours each day from five to seven o'clock in the evening.
   b. School season begins and ends same as that of the public schools.

*Original in possession of Mr. Joseph Marmash in Baltimore, Maryland.

7. Closing of the School Session:
   a. All children should pass their examinations successfully.
   b. To hold an exhibition of their work and how they are taught.
8. Funds:
   a. The funds of the school are donated by the members of the school monthly.
   b. Concerts, balls, picnics and entertainments held by the school.
   c. Contributions from friends and other parties.
9. No adult is to be admitted to the school during its session unless it is on very important business.
10. Duties of the President:
    a. To call the meetings and to preside the meetings.
    b. To look after all the materials and needs necessary to run the school successfully.
11. Duties of the Secretary:
    a. To take minutes of the meetings.
    b. Also to have the names and addresses of the members of the Ukrainian National School.
    c. To have a book of incomes and expenses.
    d. At the end of the year he shall prepare and make a report of his accounts and expenses to the members at the meeting.
12. Duties of the Treasurer:
    a. He shall receive all money of the Ukrainian National School.
    b. He shall not pay out any expenses unless he has the consent of the rest of the Committee.
    c. He shall not carry no more than twenty five dollars, $25.00, on himself; if he has more, to deposit it in the bank immediately.
    d. At the end of the year he shall prepare and make a report of his accounts and expenses to the members at the meeting.

13. Auditing Committee:
    a. Body of three men and a Vice-president.
    b. They shall check the books of the President, Treasurer and Secretary at least twice a year.
    c. To report to the Assembly any officer who is unfit to perform the duties of his office.
    d. To take interest in all school activities and also to carry out all the duties assigned to them.
14. Duties of the Parents:
    a. To send their children to school regularly.
    b. To pay their tuitions monthly, which is one dollar, $1.00.
    c. To assist the School Committee in running the school properly.
    d. In case a parent by any means cannot pay his tuitions regularly, to give a reason why to the school committee.
15. Duties of the Teacher:
    a. To run the school properly.
    b. To have a list of all of his school children.
    c. Any school needs should be brought up to school committee.
    d. In case the teacher is unable to teach school at any time, he shall notify the children one day ahead.
16. Faults:
    Any trouble between the parents, children, or the teacher shall be settled with the Committee.
17. Limitation:
    Every Ukrainian of Baltimore regardless of his ways and actions in civic life can send his children to school as long as he obeys the Constitution and By-Laws of the Ukrainian National School.
18. Meetings:
    All meetings to be held the last Sunday of the month at 1:00 P.M. o'clock.
19. Dissolution of the School:
    In case of dissolution of the school for any cause what-

ever, the funds, its treasury and its property shall be applied for the education of Ukrainian children in Baltimore, Maryland.

APPENDIX II

children are... Baltimore City Public Schools
Three East Twenty-Fifth Street • Baltimore, Maryland 21218

Office of the Superintendent

December 14, 1973

Mr. Woldymyr C. Sushko
School of Ukrainian Sciences, U.C.C.A.
126 N. Lakewood Avenue
Baltimore, Maryland 21224

Dear Mr. Sushko:

As indicated to you in my letter of November 27th, Mr. Thomas Troy was asked to visit the School of Ukrainian Sciences. Mr. Troy was very impressed with the quality of your program.

Based upon this visit and an examination of other materials submitted by you in support of your request that students jointly enrolled in your school and the schools of Baltimore City receive credit for their language study, it is my decision that this request should be granted. Consequently, students enrolled in the Baltimore City Public Schools who have completed your specialized language program will received credit for such study.

It should be brought to your attention, however, that the Department of Education will reserve the right to deny credit to any student completing this program who does not seem to possess the skill and knowledge implied by such completion. The program offered by your school will be reviewed each year by the department in order to insure that the granting of credit continues to be warranted.

Please feel free to contact me concerning this matter if and when necessary.

Sincerely,

Roland N. Patterson
Superintendent

/pvg
CC: Dr. Vernon S. Vavrina
    Dr. Rebecca E. Carroll
    Mr. Thomas D. Troy

APPENDIX III

ANNE ARUNDEL COUNTY PUBLIC SCHOOLS

27 Chinquapin Round Road
Annapolis, Maryland 21401
Telephone: 301-268-7511

June 3, 1974

Mr. Wolodymyr C. Sushko
126 North Lakewood Avenue
Baltimore, Maryland 21224

Dear Mr. Sushko:

In line with your requests for the granting of a foreign language credit to Anne Arundel County Public Schools students, grades 9-12, who have studied the Ukrainian language at the Ukrainian School in Baltimore, it is our decision that such credit be granted. This conclusion is based upon the accreditation of the Ukrainian School of Sciences by the Maryland State Department of Education and positive reports on the quality of the program offered at the school by recognized authorities.

Thus, such credit will be granted this school year to Taras Lukianczuk, senior at Brooklyn Park High School, and Taras Wojtowycz, senior at Glen Burnie High School, based upon an evaluation of their records by school authorities. Copies of these students' transcripts should also be sent to Mrs. Virginia S. Ballard, Coordinator of Foreign Languages, Anne Arundel County Public Schools, 27 Chinquapin Round Road, Annapolis, Maryland 21401.

Please let us know if you have further questions.

Sincerely,

Edward J. Anderson
Superintendent of Schools

EJA:ek

cc: Dr. Hendrickson
    Mr. Jackson
    Mrs. Frantum
    Mrs. Ballard

BOARD OF EDUCATION:
G. George Asaki, president, F. Carroll Smith, vice-president, Dr. Delores C. Hunt, Col. Raymond C. Smith, Charles G. Truffer, John B. Wright, Mrs. S. Edwin Zimmerman

APPENDIX IV

FROM	NAME & TITLE	Paul L. Vance, Deputy Superintendent	CITY of BALTIMORE
	AGENCY NAME & ADDRESS	Executive Matters East Wing - 3 East 25th Street - 21218	**MEMO**
	SUBJECT	FOR YOUR REVIEW AND APPROVAL	

TO: Regional Superintendents

DATE: February 4, 1974

The arrangements made with the School of Ukrainian Sciences to record grades received are as follows:-

1. The requirement for admission to the school is that a student must have completed the 8th grade in a recognized school of Ukrainian studies.

2. No credit is to be given below the 9th grade.

3. At the conclusion of the school year a list of students who have successfully completed the program at the School of Ukrainian Sciences will be sent to the Office of the Coordinator of Foreign Languages, Baltimore City Public Schools.

4. The list which is submitted will include:
   a. the name of the student in full.
   b. the grade which the student has completed - 9, 10, 11 or 12.
   c. the student's date of birth.
   d. the student's home address.
   e. the name of the Baltimore City Public School which the student attends regularly.
   f. an average of the grades achieved in the Ukrainian School's program during the school year for which credit is being requested (e.g., 9, 10, 11, or 12).

5. The list then, will be broken down according to the Baltimore City Public Schools which the students attend daily. This will be done in the Foreign Language Office.

6. The proper Regional Superintendent and school principal will be notified as to the grade which the student is to receive.

APPROVED   Regional Superintendents - 2/5/74

Regional Superintendents   Page 2   February 4, 1975

7. The Baltimore City Public School which the student attends regularly will report the grade on the student report card and on the white permanent record card a Foreign Language-Ukrainian grade. The grade recording should be made in compliance with the normal method of recording grades at the local school level.

    The manner of reporting by the School of Ukrainian Sciences is as follows: -

             A - Excellent   S - Pass
             B - Good   F - Fail
             C - Fair

8. The School of Ukrainian Sciences must submit the list of grades to the Office of Foreign Language Coordinator no later than May 15, to allow time for processing all grades, including those for graduating seniors.

PLV/rj

NOTES TO CHAPTER NINE

[1] Statement by Anthony Cihlar, Baltimore, Maryland, personal interview, July 21, 1976.

[2] Letter from Marie T. Giza, Baltimore, Maryland, to the author, October 19, 1975.

[3] Carl Wittke, *We Who Built America, The Saga of the Immigrant*, New York, 1939, p. XIV.

[4] Earl Arnett, "Ethnics: Who Is One's Own Kind?" *The Sun*, Baltimore, August 28, 1974, p. B6.

[5] Emily Greene Balch, *Our Slavic Fellow Citizens*, New York, 1910, p.141.

[6] Dr. Luke Myshuha (Editor), *Jubilee Book of the Ukrainian National Association in Commemoration of the Fortieth Anniversary of Its Existence*, Jersey City, N.J., 1936, pp.325-326.

[7] See 6 - *Jubilee Book*, pp. 327-328.

[8] See 6 - *Jubilee Book*, p. 334.

[9] See 5 - *Our Slavic Fellow Citizens*, p. 478.

[10] Volodymyr Kubijovyc (Editor), *Ukrainians Abroad*, Offprint from Ukraine: A Concise Encyclopaedia, Toronto, 1971, p. 46.

[11] Written information received by the author from Joseph Marmash, Baltimore, Maryland, October 11, 1975.

[12] Statement by Sister Augustina of Convent of St. Basil the Great, Chesapeake City, Maryland, in a personal interview, December 30, 1975.

[13] Fr. Joseph Denischuk, C.SS.R., *Ukrainian Catholic Shrine of the Holy Family, Washington, D.C. - Chronicle*, 1975, pp. 32, 39, 49, 51, 65, 83.

[14] Letter from Dr. Peter Oryshkewych to the author, September 1, 1976.

[15] Letter from Richard E. Wagner, Associate Superintendent for Instructional and Pupil Services, Montgomery County Public Schools, to Dr. Peter Oryshkewych, College Park Woods, Maryland, April 10, 1973.

[16] Letter from Jeannette H. Rock, Specialist in Accreditation of Nonpublic Schools, Maryland State Department of Education, to the author, May 7, 1976.

[17] Letter from Fr. David M. Stopyra O.F.M. Conv., Principal, Archbishop Curley High School, to the author, January 11, 1974.

[18] Letters from William J. Gerardi, Principal, Baltimore Polytechnic Institute, to Parents of Zenon Waclawiw, D2, Myron Waclawiw, Ae1, Roman Zaryk, Ks4, Adrian Rad, D4, Zenon Sushko, N3, June 25, 1975.

[19] Letter from Thomas D. Troy, Coordinator, Office of Foreign Languages, Baltimore City Public Schools, to the author, March 30, 1976.

[20] Dr. James A. Sensenbaugh, "A Point of View," *Public Education in Maryland Newsletter*, Vol. XXIV, No. 8, June 1976, p. 3.

Chapter Ten
Ukrainian Student Life in Maryland
Areta Kupchyk

Ukrainian students were attending Maryland colleges and universities since the first Ukrainian migration to Maryland around the turn of the century. Unfortunately, no record of activities of Ukrainian student groups or organizations exists from those times. Nevertheless, the fact that children of the hard-working pioneer parents who barely could speak English were going to college points to the vitality of early Ukrainian communities in the state.

Mary Wasylczuk Hrabec of Chesapeake City in Cecil County records that in the 1930's and 1940's at least 39 students from this town's little Ukrainian community were enrolled in colleges and universities throughout Pennsylvania, Delaware, New Jersey, and Maryland. One, a Michael Pacanowsky, was a student at Harvard University. Out of these 39 students, fifteen completed college in Maryland. The schools which they attended here ranged from Western Maryland College to Salisbury State College, with University of Maryland accounting for 6 students. Mary Hrabec herself completed the Johns Hopkins University in Baltimore.[1]

A similar trend existed in the early Ukrainian community of Baltimore. Many parents sent their children to college because they wanted them to have an easier life than their own. Among those who recognized the value of education were the Joseph Prymak and Alex Zuk families. Two Prymak daughters, Helen and Constance, graduated in Liberal Arts while the third, Mary, became a graduate nurse. The two Zuk sons, William and Myron, also graduated — the first in Architecture and the second in Industrial Engineering.

There were Ukrainian students in almost every institution of higher learning in Baltimore at those times. One of these training centers, St. Mary's Seminary, deserves special mention. The files of this institution, which is of university rank, point to an important role St. Mary's had in the early part of this century in the education of Ukrainian-Americans for the priesthood.[2] In 1917 at least 19 Ukrainian, or as they were then called, "Ruthenian" students were enrolled in theology studies at this university. The gates of this institution were again wide open to Ukrainians during World War II, when due to war events they could not study at the Ukrainian Seminary in Rome, Italy. In the 1940-1941 school year there was a total of 21 Ukrainian Catholic students registered at St. Mary's Seminary in Baltimore.[3]

Very little record of community activities on the part of Ukrainian students of those years exists. In the archives of St. Mary's Seminary for the years 1917-1918, one finds mention that Ukrainian students were permitted to assist at church services in the Ukrainian community of Baltimore during the Easter Holy Week and on Christmas Day. Still in another place, we read that upon the request of the parishioners, one student, a Roman Kachmarsky, was permitted in 1918 to spend a few days in the parish in order to settle up the accounts of the church in the absence of the regular priest at that time.[4]

It was not until after World War II that a systematic record of Ukrainian student life could be found in Maryland. This was a time when many new immigrants, the former World War II refugees from Ukraine, became settled in Maryland. Most of them were educated people who wanted their children to get a college education. October 1955 marked the inception of the Ukrainian Student *Hromada* (Association) of Baltimore. Almost 50 students joined the *Hromada* in that year. With the support of many Ukrainians from the community, especially

Yaroslaw Shaviak and Osyp Zinkewych, student activism was set into energetic motion. Shortly thereafter, the *Hromada* joined the Federation of Ukrainian Student Organizations of America (SUSTA), which had been formed two years earlier.

The Ukrainian Student *Hromada* of Baltimore cited their purpose to be the perpetuation of Ukrainian culture and language as well as the advancement of the Ukrainian community in general. The student group sponsored numerous conferences, lectures, and meetings. Deserving special mention are the annual student symposia which were held in Baltimore jointly with Ukrainian Student Associations of Washington, D.C. and Philadelphia, Pennsylvania, in the late 1950's and early 1960's, and where various Ukrainian issues were discussed. There were

November, 1958. The Second Annual Student Symposium in Baltimore.
U.E.A.M. Collection

a total of five symposia. The first symposium was held in 1957, and from the ten speakers, four were from Maryland. They were Lydia Czumak, Vira Sushko, Oksana Pisetzky and Osyp Zinkewych. The proceedings of this symposium were published by the Student *Hromada* of Baltimore in a separate book titled *Ukraine in the Second World War*. Since then this book has been used for references by many young researchers.[5]

In 1961, through the efforts of the *Hromada*, the Mayor of Baltimore, Harold Grady, proclaimed January 29, "Ukrainian Student Day," in commemoration of the heroic battle of the three hundred Ukrainian students who on

January 29, 1918, at Kruty laid down their young lives in an attempt to hamper the march of the Russian Red Army against the capital of free Ukraine, Kiev. Baltimore was among the first cities in the country to officially make such a proclamation. In 1963, the Governor of Maryland, J. Millard Tawes, issued a similar proclamation in the state.

January, 1957. A group of students of Baltimore honoring the Spirit of Kruty, Ukraine, where 300 Ukrainian students died on January 29, 1918. From left: Y. Czumak, Vira Sushko, Lydia Czumak, Osyp Zinkewych, M. Pylypczuk, Martha Pisetzky, George Ilinsky.
U.E.A.M. Collection

Since then the Baltimore students have held annual observances either alone or jointly with other youth organizations in commemoration of this event, drawing their inspiration from the gallant deed of the Krutian student heroes.

In 1956, the Baltimore students also formed a Ukrainian dance troupe that survived over a decade and during this time performed at various college and university campuses around the state. Their other activities involved displays of Ukrainian culture and craftsmanship, such as ceramics, embroidery, and artwork. Art students, Wasyl Palijczuk, Orest Poliszczuk and George M. Kotyk added much to the success of these events in those times. The last student also did much of the graphic work for the *Hromada*. Still other students ventured attempts at poetry. One of them was Taras I. Charchalis, a student of engineering at the University of Maryland and member of the Baltimore *Hromada* in the 1950's. One of his poems titled "A Thought" was published by the National Poetry Association in their 1956 edition of Annual Anthologies of College Poetry.[6]

In 1957, at the Third National Conference of the Federation of Ukrainian Student Organizations of America, the Ukrainian Studies Chair Fund was officially brought into existence. There was a compelling need for such a studies fund at the time to counter the ignorance and falsehoods propagated in American institutions, particularly those which were perpetuating the myth of a "Russian Society" exclusively in the vast and diverse Soviet Union. The Baltimore student group immediately put itself in support of the drive to promote such a studies fund. Lupa Kupchyk and Nadia Bendiuk launched a campaign to collect funds. In 1962, with the aid of Jaroslaw G. Sushko from the community, they raised almost $2,000 in donations and over $1,000 in pledges for the Ukrainian Studies Chair Fund.[7] As a result of their work and the cooperative assistance of students throughout the country, the Ukrainian people and all Americans are being served by a Ukrainian Studies Department at Harvard University.

The high level of activity for which the Baltimore *Hromada* was known in the late 1950's and the 1960's, receded in the 1970's. But Ukrainian students in Baltimore continue as a viable force in the community.

During the past five years, each year, they have participated in the annual Ukrainian Festival usually held in September in the downtown section of the city. In November of 1975 on the occasion of America's Bicentennial, the 200th birthday of the Marine Corps and the 100th anniversary of the settlement of Ukrainians in America, the Student *Hromada* sponsored jointly with the U.S. Marine Corps the "Liberty Tree" planting in Patterson Park in Baltimore. On this occasion, Ukrainians could recall Samuel Jaskilka of Ukrainian lineage and the present Assistant Commandant of the U.S. Marine Corps who has the rank of a four-star General. The Ukrainian scouting organization PLAST and the Ukrainian-American youth organization SUMA participated in that tree-planting ceremony. In his letter to Lydia M. Sushko, the chairperson of the *Hromada* in that year, Mayor William Donald Schaefer of Baltimore praised this contribution of the Ukrainian community to the City of Baltimore and the Nation's Bicentennial.[8] Also, the Maryland Bicentennial Commission issued on this occasion to the Student *Hromada* official recognition of their participation in the Marine Corps Bicentennial Tree Planting program.

The support of the Harvard Ukrainian Studies Fund continues to be one of the main goals of the Ukrainian student group in Baltimore. In 1972, the students again raised over $2,000 in donations for this Fund.

The most recent project of the Student *Hromada* is a scholarship fund. The fund, established in 1976 under Areta Kupchyk, chairperson on the *Hromada* in that year, intends to offer $600 to Ukrainian students attending local post-secondary institutions. The first scholarship will be awarded in June 1977.

With the exception of Yaroslaw Shaviak who helped to organize the *Hromada* in 1955 and chaired it for one year, the leadership of the organization was in the hands of the students. The following chairpersons served during this time: Oksana Pisetzky, Orest Hanas, Mykhaylo Pylypczuk, Taras Charchalis, Bohdan Yurchyshyn, Maria Sidlak, Orest Poliszczuk, Andrij Chornodolsky, Andrij Tatchyn, Martha Tatchyn, Oleh Choma, Oksana Lasijczuk, Lydia M. Sushko, Areta Kupchyk. Two of them, Andrij Chornodolsky and Taras Charchalis, were also active in the Ukrainian student movement on national and international levels, the first serving as president of SUSTA (Federation of Ukrainian Student Organizations of America) and CeSUS (Central Union of Ukrainian Students), and the second as vice-president of academic affairs of SUSTA.

Without question, today's Ukrainian student values the importance of a college education. Ukrainian students can be seen at almost every post-secondary institution in Maryland. Such institutions as Johns Hopkins University, Towson State University, University of Maryland — Baltimore City, — Baltimore County, and — College Park Campuses, Loyola College, Frostburg State College, Morgan State University, Western Maryland College, the Peabody Institute of Music, and the Maryland Institute of Art are attended by Ukrainians. One need not omit the United States Naval Academy at Annapolis. John M.

November 23, 1975. The "Liberty Tree" Planting in Patterson Park, Baltimore. Above: Presentation of Colors — U.S. Marine Corps — Student Hromada *— PLAST — SUMA.* **U.E.A.M. Collection**
Below: *Planting of the Tree. From left: Danylo Blaszkiw of SUMA; USMC Capt. William Kerr, 4th Engineer Battalion; Lydia Sushko, Student* Hromada, *Martha Tatchyn, PLAST; Baltimore City Council President Walter Orlinsky.* **The News American**

Shmorhun of West Friendship, Maryland, is currently a proud Midshipman First Class at this institution. Another Ukrainian Marylander who graduated from this Academy in the early 1970's was John G. Kohut from Baltimore.

In existence, along with the *Hromada*, were a number of Ukrainian student clubs. In 1958, a Ukrainian Student Club was formed at the University of Maryland — College

Ukrainian Students' Club, University of Maryland, College Park, Year 1959 — First Row: *George Ilinsky, Maria Macuk, Theodore Caryk, Arne P. Hansen, advisor, Tatjana N. Chapelsky, Orest J. Hanas.* Second Row: *Orest I. Diachok, Wasyl Palijczuk, Mychailo Fedenko, John I. Korz.*
University of Maryland, The 1960 Terrapin

Park. The Club's twenty or so members were recognized at the University for their outstanding performance in intercollegiate sports, predominantly soccer. The Club sponsored, each year, an exhibition in the library on Ukrainian culture and history.[9] In 1976, Towson State University approved the formation of a Ukrainian Student Club on the campus. Towson presently has the largest

Ukrainian student enrollment in Baltimore, with the University of Maryland at College Park having the largest enrollment in the state.

Painting the picture of Ukrainian student life, though, cannot be complete without including the students' social life. In this aspect, Ukrainian students are very similar to any other college students in the country. Some students could not survive without a party, a dance, and a movie. But there are activities that distinguish the Ukrainian student. Foremost is the Ukrainian *zabava*; that is a Ukrainian ball. Ukrainians, traditionally, are enthusiastic dancers, but students, particularly, "stamp a mean foot."

HAVING FUN — *Not all dance rehearsals are serious. Mrs. Choma giggles a little as her students learn their Ukrainian heritage through folk dance.*

Baltimore Sunpapers

Ukrainian students are also enthusiastic athletes, if not on field, then in the audience. Their favorite sports include soccer, ice hockey, volleyball, skiing, and a wide range of water sports. Early in the year 1975, Baltimore's first Ukrainian hockey team was formed, joining the Baltimore Hockey Association in the following year, and ranking in first place during the entire season.

Finally, the annual "Easter picnic" should be mentioned. Ukrainian students in Baltimore have institutionalized Easter into a day of "food and fun." Every Easter Sunday, for the past ten years, has been celebrated by students with games and sports, and by simply enjoying each other's company. On this day of Resurrection, they emerge renewed in body and spirit.

NOTES TO CHAPTER TEN

[1] Letter from Mrs. Mary Hrabec, Chesapeake City, Maryland, to Mr. Wolodymyr C. Sushko, Baltimore, Maryland, January 6, 1976.

[2] Joint interview by Messrs. Paul Fenchak and Wolodymyr C. Sushko with Reverend Vincent G. Eaton, Archivist, St. Mary's Seminary College, Catonsville, Maryland, January 31, 1976.

[3] Catalogue of St. Mary's Seminary 1940-1941, June 1941, E. J. Horan & Co., Baltimore, pp. 41-50.

[4] Letter from Very Reverend Edward R. Dyer, D.D., President, St. Mary's Seminary, Baltimore, Maryland, to Very Reverend Peter Poniatishin, D.D., Administrator, St. John's Church, 295 Hunterdon Street, Newark, N.J., January 7, 1918.

[5] Federation of Ukrainian Student Organizations of America (SUSTA), *Ukrainian Students in U.S.A., 10th Anniversary Book of SUSTA*, Baltimore-New York, 1963, p. 62 (in Ukrainian).

[6] National Poetry Association - Dennis Hartman, Secretary, *AMERICA SINGS — 1956 ANTHOLOGY OF COLLEGE POETRY*, 3210 Selby Avenue, Los Angeles, California, p. 18.

[7] See 5, p. 64.

[8] Letter from William Donald Schaefer, Mayor of Baltimore, to Lydia M. Sushko, Chairperson, Ukrainian Student *Hromada*, December 2, 1975.

[9] C. Stuart Callison, Editor-in-Chief, *University of Maryland The 1960 Terrapin*, Vol. 59, College Park, Maryland, 1960, p. 125.

Chapter Eleven
Ukrainian Foods Becoming a Part Of Maryland Traditions
Lydia M. Sushko

Foods are probably one of the most effective transmitters of customs and traditions to this country. They link sons and daughters here with their cousins abroad. Many of the dishes brought by various immigrants over the years found their way into the American cuisine. Today American cookery is a mosaic of foods from all over the world. Some interesting foods come from Ukraine.

BACKGROUND

Ukrainian foods in Europe have always been the product of Ukrainian soil and rivers. From days immemorial Ukraine was known for its rich humus soil. Agriculture and the breeding of livestock and poultry were central factors in Ukrainian life for centuries. Archeological excavations reveal that over 3,000 years ago Ukrainians cultivated wheat, barley and millet and used various meats and plants as sources of their food.[1]

Vegetables, breads and starched foods were the basic and most widely used Ukrainian edibles. And they are so today. In addition to these foods, Ukrainian aristocratic families spared no effort in developing several other specialties to suit their palates. Among them are such delicacies as pashtet, boned, stuffed chicken, or stuffed chicken breasts.[2] Chicken, Kiev Style, is one of these specialties, sold in many American supermarkets today.[3]

Some Ukrainian foods are curiously like popular American dishes. Corn is one of them. Ukraine is one of the few areas in Europe in which corn on the cob is appreciated.[4] Corn is the principal part of the diet in the Carpathian Mountain strip of Ukraine. Corn bread or *malay* and corn mush or *kulesha* are popular among the Ukrainian highlanders. The other dishes which resemble American cooking are Ukrainian recipes for turkey with bread stuffing or with apples and raisins. According to Barbara Norman, they read exactly like the American.[5]

POPULAR UKRAINIAN DISHES

Most popular Ukrainian dishes are made of cereals and flour pastes. Among these are bread and bread pastries, followed by soups and salads. The meat and poultry products complete the list of Ukrainian contributions to culinary arts.

CEREALS AND FLOUR PASTES

The most widely known of this group are dumplings or *varenyky*, stuffed cabbage leaves or *holubtsi*, *kasha* which is a cooked or baked cereal, and egg noodles or *lokshyna*. The last food is also known as *klusky* (*kluski*) in some westernmost Ukrainian territories which border Poland but this fact does not make it lose its Ukrainian identity. Many of these foods still constitute the main dishes of many Ukrainian homes in Maryland. There is hardly a family that does not make *varenyky*, *holubtsi*, or *kasha*. Being rather inexpensive and time-saving dishes, they can be prepared in advance and refrigerated and reheated.

Lokshyna or home-made noodles used to be popular among Ukrainians in this country, being easy to prepare. Many Ukrainian home-steaders in Canada still prefer to make their own *lokshyna* instead of buying the commercially made noodles.[6] In this country *lokshyna* or *klusky* are slowly disappearing, and the easily available macaronis and spaghettis of Italian make take their place in the Ukrainian kitchen. Nevertheless, one still may find *kluski* being sold in many stores in Maryland, such as Food-A-Rama.

Varenyky are made of a soft dough and filling, most commonly cottage cheese. The other favorite filling is sauerkraut. In some territories of Galicia in western Ukraine *varenyky* are called *pyrohy* and some immigrants from these territories continue to call them by this name in Maryland. Actually, *pyrohy* (*pirohi*) in the Ukrainian cuisine are baked or fried dumplings made of dough, with various fillings, and mostly used as soup accompaniments. *Varenyky* (from word *varyty* — to cook) are cooked in water and usually served with sour cream. They are often browned with buttered bread crumbs. At Christmas time Ukrainians make a special kind of very tiny *varenyky* which are called *vushka* because their shape resembles tiny ears. *Vushka* are usually filled with mushrooms and served as a soup accompaniment to clear borshch at Christmas Eve Supper.

Holubtsi (*holupki*) are cabbage leaf rolls filled with rice or buckwheat or a combination of meat or potato mixture. They may be cooked with or without a liquid, depending on the nature of the filling.

Kasha is to a Ukrainian what oatmeal is to a Scotsman.[7] It is a cereal usually of buckwheat groats baked or cooked. It also may be used as stuffing for meat, poultry

Kluski *and* kasha *have their place on shelves in stores in Maryland.*
Food-A-Rama, Baltimore, Md.

and *holubtsi*. Baked buckwheat *kasha*, specked with fried sliced bacon and served with buttermilk, is one of the foremost meals of the Ukrainian people. It also occupies an important place in the dietary habits of Ukrainians.

BREAD AND BREAD PASTRIES

Bread has always been the holiest of all foods to Ukrainians. The beautiful Ukrainian custom of greeting honored guests with bread and salt is still very popular with Ukrainians in Maryland.

Some traditional Ukrainian breads merit mentioning. One of them is *koroway* — a specially prepared wedding cake bread. The *koroway* custom is observed at many Ukrainian wedding receptions in Maryland. It is a very large bread baked from wheat flour and richly ornamented with symbolic dough ornaments and decorated with greenery. The other bread is *kolach*. This bread is associated with customs at Christmas. *Kolach* is composed of three round braided loaves, one placed atop another, with a candle inserted into the top one. The name comes from the word *kolo* — circle, which is a symbol of prosperity. *Kolach* is a traditional table decoration at the Ukrainian Christmas Eve supper. Traditionally, there are twelve dishes at the Christmas Eve supper, and they are without meat, milk, and eggs. A real challenge to the cook! One of these twelve meals is *kutya*, a very symbolic and ancient dish prepared from cooked wheat, poppy seeds and chopped nuts. *Kutya* like *kolach* symbolizes prosperity. *Paska*, another traditional bread, is a rich, round Easter bread covered with dough ornaments, among which the Christian cross is the central motif. *Paska* is always taken to church on Easter morning together with other foods to be blessed by the priest. A traditional Ukrainian Easter dessert is cheese *paska* usually prepared in the form of a pyramid or block.[8] Another traditional Easter fare is *babka* or *baba*. It is a rich yeast-raised cake bread, usually baked in a tall cylindrical pan. The word *babka* or *baba* means woman. Some believe that this ancient culinary tradition originated in prehistoric times when Ukrainian communities were

A typical Christmas Eve Table at a Ukrainian home in Maryland. The main decoration is the Kolach.

Mrs. Irena Sushko

ruled by women. *Baba* may have been an essential feature of religious rituals performed by women priestesses and connected with the fertility of the soil.[9] Other popular bread pastries at Christmas or any other occasion are *makivnyk* (poppy seed roll) and *horikhivnyk* (bars with filling of almonds, walnuts and other ingredients). Griddle cakes (*nalysnyky*) are another popular year-round dish. They are thin rolled cakes with a filling of cottage cheese, cabbage, potatoes, or crushed fruit. Ukrainian Jews popularized this pastry in America though they used the Russian name *blintzi* (*blintzes*).

SOUPS AND SOUP ACCOMPANIMENTS

Soup is an essential part of the Ukrainian menu. Of a variety of soups *borshch* (*borsch, borscht*) is the most popular. It is a hearty soup, Ukraine's greatest contribution to soup making.[10] *Borshch* can be served hot or cold. Ukrainians have several varieties of *borshch*, depending on season or locality, some using more cabbage, others more beets, with or without meat, but all seasoned to taste and perfectly delicious. A cookbook published in Kyiv (Kiev) in Ukraine in 1960, lists 22 popular variations of *borshch*.[11] Meatless *borshch* is a traditional Christmas Eve dish in Ukrainian homes. The other popular variation is sorrel *borshch* or *schav*. *Schav* is a Ukrainian name for sorrel — a small plant with tender sour leaves growing wild in Ukraine.

Marylanders can buy borshch *and* schav *at their local stores.*
Food-A-Rama, Baltimore, Md.

The *borshch*-making custom spread from Ukraine into the adjoining lands, including Russia.[12] It became popular among Poles, Russians, Slovaks, et al. Jewish immigrants who came to this country from the former Tsarist Russian Empire brought this Ukrainian dish to America although often under its Russian label. *Borshch* — the red beet soup and *schav* — the sorrel borshch are popular dishes in America. They are sold in many American supermarkets.

Nearly everyone likes some sort of accompaniment with his soup. Ukrainians have a variety of accompaniments of which the most popular are *pyrohy* and *pyrizhky*. The difference between the two is only in size, with *pyrizhky* being small pieces of dough while *pyrih* (or *pyrohy* in plural) can be the size of a rectangular pie later on cut into squares. *Pyrizhky* are fried or baked dumplings made of yeast dough or pastry dough. The fillings are innumerable, which can be meat, liver, cabbage, sauerkraut, mushrooms or cottage cheese.

An additional soup accessory is a fried or baked dumpling or patty called *knysh (knish)*. Historically *knysh* is a baked cake made of wheat dough without filling. It is one of the oldest kind among Ukrainian traditional pastry. As is the case with most foods, it underwent variations, and *knysh* as retailed now in Maryland is a roll of dough with a filling of chopped meat, mashed potatoes, *kasha* and other ingredients.

SALADS

A rich agricultural land, Ukraine has always produced an abundance of vegetables. This has abetted the creation of many salads. One of these is the "Ukrainian Salad," the name under which it is known in the United States. In 1975 this salad received praiseworthy attention from the Associated Press. Its ingredients are sauerkraut, red apples, onions and lettuce, seasoned with sugar and caraway seeds. The Ukrainian Salad is very refreshing because it isn't as sweet as the kraut salads and relishes now in vogue. "A most unusual salad" was the honor given by the Associated Press.[13]

Andrij Chornodolsky presides over Governor's Club dinners. Ukrainian foods are among the specialties offered.

Baltimore Sunpapers

MEATS

Meat cookery was especially well-developed among the urban and aristocratic classes in Ukraine. Of various meat specialties from Ukraine perhaps the most widely known in the United States is "Chicken Kiev," named after Kiev (Keiv, Kyiv), the capital city of Ukraine. Chicken is one of those few dishes in the world for which there are no ethnic nor religious prescriptions as compared to beef or pork.[14] Each country has added to chicken its own imprint in combining it with its native foods to make distinctive dishes. The Ukrainian "chicken, Kiev style" is a luxurious and very butter-rich dish. The Governor's Club Restaurant in Baltimore where it is served describes it as "breast of chicken stuffed with garlic, butter, chopped mushrooms, lightly covered with fresh bread crumbs and served on a hot platter."[15] Another famous Maryland restaurant, Danny's

Restaurant in Baltimore, also lists chicken Kiev on its regular menu, as do many other restaurants.

CREDIT TO UKRAINIAN JEWS

Important in introducing Ukrainian food to the American continent were the Ukrainian Jews. In their travels since the Dispersion many centuries ago Jews have gathered from each land where they lived the best countries offered. According to Jewish culinary experts, what is usually designated as "Jewish Cookery" is a preparation of dishes peculiar to the Jewish people supplemented by the most delectable, and often the most economical, dishes from the best of each nation in which the Jewish people have lived.[16] Thus from Ukraine came *borshch*, *knyshi* (*knishes*), *pyrizhky* (*piroshki*), *schav*, *varenyky* (*vareniki*), *kasha* (buckwheat groats), *nalysnyky* (*blintzes*), and other dishes. Some of these foods underwent the necessary variations in accordance with prevailing tastes and the availability of seasonings in the new place of living but this fact does not make these foods lose their Ukrainian identity. Some of these foods like *knyshi* (*knishes*) and

Knyshi *(Knishes)* — *a favored local sandwich in Baltimore.*
**Weiss Delicatessen Store,
Baltimore, Md.**

nalysnyky (blintzes) are today popular dishes in many Jewish-run restaurants in Maryland and are sold in mobile food trucks.

FUND RAISING AND CONTEST

Likewise, the Ukrainian immigrants themselves as they became more numerous in the United States and Maryland, began to popularize their food in their new neighborhoods. *Varenyky* (also called *pyrohy*), *holubtsi* and bread pastries became a convenient source of additional income to Ukrainian parishes and other organizations. One may find these dishes being sold on a regular

Fund Raising: Pyrohy *on sale at SS. Peter and Paul Ukrainian Catholic Church in Curtis Bay, Md.*
U.E.A.M. Collection

basis, usually on weekends, at Ukrainian church halls in East Baltimore, Chesapeake City, or Curtis Bay. *Paska* (sweet bread), *kolachi*, homemade noodles, *holupki* (stuffed cabbage) and other ethnic specialties are available at the annual Christmas bazaars held at the Byzantine Catholic Church of the Patronage of the Mother of God in Arbutus, Baltimore. They are offered along with beef barbecue, hot dogs and the usual cakes, pies and cookies.[17] Ukrainian ethnic food traditions supply one of the focal attractions of Ukrainian festivals held early in September in downtown Baltimore. To non-Ukrainian Americans these foods are a savory and pleasant surprise.

Ukrainians are not only limiting themselves to their own dishes. They readily supplement them with specialties typical to their new place of living, seafood being one of these specialties. Crabmeat, oysters, clams, etc., are today familiar dishes in Ukrainian homes in Maryland and other states.

Some Ukrainians are the proud inventors of their own recipes which help to refine the American ways of cooking. Ann Humenchuk Dubas of Deptford, New Jersey, is one of them. Creative cookery is her hobby. She experimented with a fish and oyster combination because her family liked shellfish, but not fish. The result was a dish which combined oysters with fish fillets. Her invention was such a success with her family that she sent it to the 1973 Philadelphia Oyster Cooking Contest where she won 1st prize. This contest was sponsored by the Seafood Marketing Authority of the Department of Economic and Community Development of the State of Maryland.[18] Ann Dubas is also a prizewinner in a baking contest, a competition for cookie recipes and an asparagus recipe contest.

Ukrainian homemakers like Ann Dubas and many others are proud to have their share in refining the American cuisine — a cuisine where the Old Country traditions intermix with the New World dishes.

NOTES TO CHAPTER ELEVEN

[1] L. Denysenko and A. Pylnen'kyj (Editors), *Ukrainian Dishes* (in Ukrainian). State Publishing Office of Technological Literature of the UkSSR, Kyjiv, 1960, pp. 3-4.

[2] Savella Stechishin, *Traditional Ukrainian Cookery*, Trident Press Ltd., Winnipeg, Canada, 1957, p. 123.

[3] Statement by Norman Leikach, Manager, Food-A-Rama Supermarkets, Baltimore, Maryland, personal interview, October 31, 1976.

[4] Barbara Norman, *The Russian Cookbook*, Bantham Books, Inc., New York, N.Y. 10019, 1970, p. 9.

[5] See 4: p. 9.

[6] See 2: p. 195.

[7] See 2: p. 225.

[8] Winifred E. Bautz, "Course in Ukrainian Egg Dyeing Coming to YWCA," *The Evening Sun*, March 24, 1976, p. C1; contains recipe in English.

[9] See 2: p. 323.

[10] Atherton & Patman, "Borsch, Ukrainian Borsch," *The Philadelphia Inquirer*, August 14, 1969; contains recipe in English.

[11] See 1: p. 9.

[12] See 1: pp. 89-100.

[13] *The Evening Sun*, Baltimore, November 24, 1975, "Ukrainian Salad," P. C1; contains recipe of this most unusual salad.

[14] Virginia Roeder, "Chicken Still Versatile and Economical Entree," *The Evening Sun*, Baltimore, June 16, 1976, p. D17.

[15] *Menu List*, The Governor's Club, 1123 North Eutaw Street, Baltimore, Maryland.

[16] Anne London and Bertha Kahn Bishov, *The Complete American Jewish Cookbook*, World Publishing, New York, 1971, p. VII.

[17] *The News American*, Baltimore, December 8, 1976, "Eat Ethnic Foods At Byzantine Holiday Bazaar," p. D1; contains recipes.

[18] *The Philadelphia Inquirer*, Philadelphia, Pennsylvania, October 31, 1973, "Oysters Combined With Fish Fillets Won Her First Prize in the Contest," p. 11-D; contains original recipe for Bay Country Oyster and Fish Dish.

Chapter Twelve
Pysanky: Ukrainian Easter Eggs
Sophia Mychajlyshyn

A decorated Easter egg holds one of the first places in Ukrainian folk art. It is called *pysanka* ("written egg"), stemming from the Ukrainian word *pysaty* — to write. People of many countries decorate eggs at Easter but few of these surpass the Ukrainian *pysanky* for the beauty of their color and intricate design.

The custom of decorating Easter eggs has been handed down from mother to daughter through generations in Ukraine, and it has developed to a kind of competition where one always strives for greater perfection and beauty. The art of achieving this goal has always been until today a well-kept "secret" of each family. The Ukrainian immigrants brought this art with them to their new places of settlement. Today Ukrainian Easter eggs draw the fascination of casual observers in every corner of the world. The Ukrainian Easter egg decorating became the universal art, and many non-Ukrainians pursue this art as a hobby. An article in *National Geographic Magazine*, April, 1972, remains a collector's item for many Americans who appreciate this colorful Ukrainian art. It includes brief instructions for painting eggs as well as excellent color reproductions.[1]

The tradition of decorating Easter eggs is as old as the Ukrainian people. The origin of this art is very ancient, and it goes back to the earliest pagan times. Archeological excavations in Ukraine show that this art was practised a long time before the Christian era. To ancient Ukrainians the egg was a symbol of the rebirth of nature after a long and cold winter. Being in itself the embodiment of the life principle, the egg symbolized the reawakening of the earth to a new life with the coming of spring. Therefore, a decorated egg was used in sun worship festivals. Many design symbols of today's Easter eggs originated in distant times. Designs may be geometric or may exhibit plant or animal motifs. Each design has a meaning. As an example, a simple circle or the one embellished with other lines represents the sun and it stands for good fortune; the star signifies purity, life, the giver of light, beauty, elegance, and perfection; a swastika symbolizes happiness, good fortune, and good will; a triangle represents air, water, and fire; simple lines represent the thread of life or eternity; wavy lines depict harmony and motion; the pine tree stands for strength and eternal life; the horse denotes prosperity and speed; a rooster tells of good fortune to come, and hens symbolize fertility.[2]

With the formal recognition of Christianity in Ukraine in 988 A.D., the pagan symbols were absorbed by the new religion. The symbols acquired new meaning. The star is now the symbol of Christ's birth while the triangle represents the trinity. New symbols of Christian origin were added, such as various crosses or fish. Dots of color represented Mary's tears. The egg itself embraced new meaning. It ceased to symbolize the rebirth of nature, and instead, became the symbol of the Resurrection with its promise of a better life. Thus, a decorated Easter egg now represented man's rebirth. It became a medium through which an expression of joy can be made. Today, while examining a *pysanka*, one sees a blend of both pagan and Christian symbols.

LEGENDS ABOUT ORIGIN OF PYSANKA

The new Christian ceremonies commemorating the Resurrection of Christ gave impetus to many legends about the origin of the first decorated *pysanka*. Several legends are associated with the Blessed Virgin. One tells how the Virgin Mary filled her apron with eggs and went to Pontius Pilate to plead for her son. As she dropped to her knees, her apron fell open and to the astonishment of all, beautifully designed eggs rolled out.

A Hutzul legend from the Carpathian Mountains in Ukraine tells how the Virgin Mary took eggs to the soldiers at the foot of the cross. As she wept, tears fell on the eggs, staining them with brilliant colors.

There is also a story about the son of a poor farmer who was taking a basket of eggs to sell. On his way to the market he saw an angry group of people hurling insults at a pathetic man trying to carry a heavy cross. Without hesitation he dropped his basket and went to help the man. When he returned to the basket, the eggs had been transformed to beautiful *pysanky*.

Yet another legend has to do with world peace. As long as people decorate *pysanky*, peace will prevail and the world has a chance to survive.

TWO TYPES OF EASTER EGGS

There are two types of Easter eggs: the *krashanka* (*kraska* meaning color) and the *pysanka* (*pysaty* meaning to write). The krashanka is a hard boiled egg which is dyed only in one color without any decoration. This type of egg is eaten or used to play games on Easter morning. The pysanka is a raw egg which is decorated and dyed in many different colors. The best pysanky are taken on Easter Sunday morning to the church with other food to be blessed by the priest. The blessed *pysanka* is believed to contain great powers as a talisman. It is credited with powers of healing, guarding health, preserving beauty, winning and strengthening love. The *pysanka* is usually exchanged with friends, taken to graveside services at Easter time. Bowlsful of *pysanky* are displayed in Ukrainian homes in prominent places, insuring protection against lightning and fire.

Beautiful Ukrainian Easter Eggs.

U.E.A.M. Collection

THE TECHNIQUE OF DECORATING

The process of decorating a *pysanka* is similar to batik. In ancient times the dyes were made from berries, dried plants, and roots and bark. Of course, today commercially made powder dyes are used.

The materials used in creating a *pysanka* are
1. Some natural, unbleached beeswax.
2. A candle to melt the wax.
3. A *kistka* — instrument used to draw designs.
4. Powder dyes.

The *kistka* is made by wrapping a small piece of thin flexible metal lengthwise around a stick to form a pin-point opening at the lower end. The powder dyes are dissolved with hot water and then cooled.

In order to decorate the egg, heated wax is applied with the *kistka* to the areas which are to remain white. When the basic design is completed, the egg is dipped into the lightest color dye (e.g. yellow). The whole egg is now yellow. Whatever part of the design is to remain yellow is now covered with beeswax. The egg is next dipped into the next lightest color. This process is continued as the egg is dyed in orange, red, green, etc. The more complicated the design, the more colors are used. When the design is completed the egg is placed into the darkest desired color, usually violet or black. The final step is to remove the accumulated wax. This is done by placing the finished eggs into a warm oven long enough to melt the wax. Or the wax can be removed by holding the egg over a gas flame and wiping off the wax with a soft cloth or tissue. Now the eggs are ready for Easter!

PYSANKA TRADITION IN MARYLAND

Easter eggs are an important part of Ukrainian heritage in Maryland. There is hardly a Ukrainian home where one would not find Easter eggs. The finest examples are saved from year to year. The shells are protected by a coat of clear shellac and the raw contents with years dry out to become a powder. Easter eggs are usually preserved as ornaments in a living room cabinet.

One of the first to popularize Ukrainian Easter eggs in Baltimore was Anastasia Marmash. In the 1930's, she organized a group of girls to teach them how to color Easter eggs in the Ukrainian manner. One of the girls was Helen Pise. Instructions were held at the Ukrainian-American Citizens' Club at the corner of O'Donnell Street and Ellwood Avenue. The reporter Lee McCardell visited them on April 22, 1938:

> ...Their workroom is the stage of the hall on the first floor of the home. Here they gather around a large table with half a dozen pots of dye, two or three thick candles and a basket or two of fresh, raw eggs, specially selected by Mrs. Marmash...First efforts of the egg-dyers were often too cockeyed to pass inspection...the pupil would take another egg, start all over again. Every once in a while somebody dropped an egg undergoing tedious treatment. That was the end of that *pysanka*. But the girls stuck to it, getting so deeply into the spirit as to show up for work one evening wearing Ukrainian National costumes...[3]

In 1933 on Easter Monday the Baltimore Avramenko dance group consisting of young boys and girls was invited to an egg-rolling party at the White House in Washington, D.C. This beautiful custom was held during Franklin D. Roosevelt's presidency, and the White House lawn on

Dressed in a Ukrainian dress, Helen Pise starts new design on a fresh egg.
Baltimore Sunpapers

Easter Monday was a place of joy for children. A bus load of Ukrainian Children went from Baltimore to Washington, D.C., that year. Most of them were enrolled in the V. Avramenko dance courses which were held in Baltimore in those years. They not only participated in the traditional American egg-rolling party but also performed for Eleanor Roosevelt the beautiful Ukrainian folk dances on a platform specially built for that purpose on the White House lawn.[4]

The art of painting Ukrainian Easter eggs reached a new level when immigrants arrived after World War II. Initiative to popularize the art was given by Helen Garvin who in 1953 was head of the International Center of the Y.W.C.A. in Baltimore. She asked the writer, who had arrived in Baltimore in 1949, to teach egg painting techniques in pre-Easter classes held at the Baltimore Y.W.C.A. Since 1953 the writer has taught this course each spring, classes being held at the International Center, 128

Sophia Mychajlyshyn with the funnel-shaped pens, beeswax and jars of dye she uses in decorating Easter eggs in the Ukrainian fashion.
Baltimore Sunpapers

West Franklin Street, or at the branch located at 16 South Patterson Park Avenue.

Some of the writer's background was recapped by Winifred E. Bautz in the Baltimore *Evening Sun* in 1976:

>...My father was a man of many talents... He was a teacher, a violinist, and an artist. He was such a perfectionist at decorating our Easter eggs, I was afraid to try. I didn't until much later...[5]

Throughout the years, various churches and organizations have sponsored classes. In Maryland thousands of non-Ukrainians have learned this ancient Ukrainian art and have adopted it as a part of their Easter tradition. Many collectors have purchased eggs from the writer. Her work can be found in the Museum Shop of the Baltimore Museum of Art and in the Hagerstown Museum of Art. It was a pleasure to have lectured to the art teachers of Baltimore County Schools.

Among non-Ukrainian artists who paint eggs in the

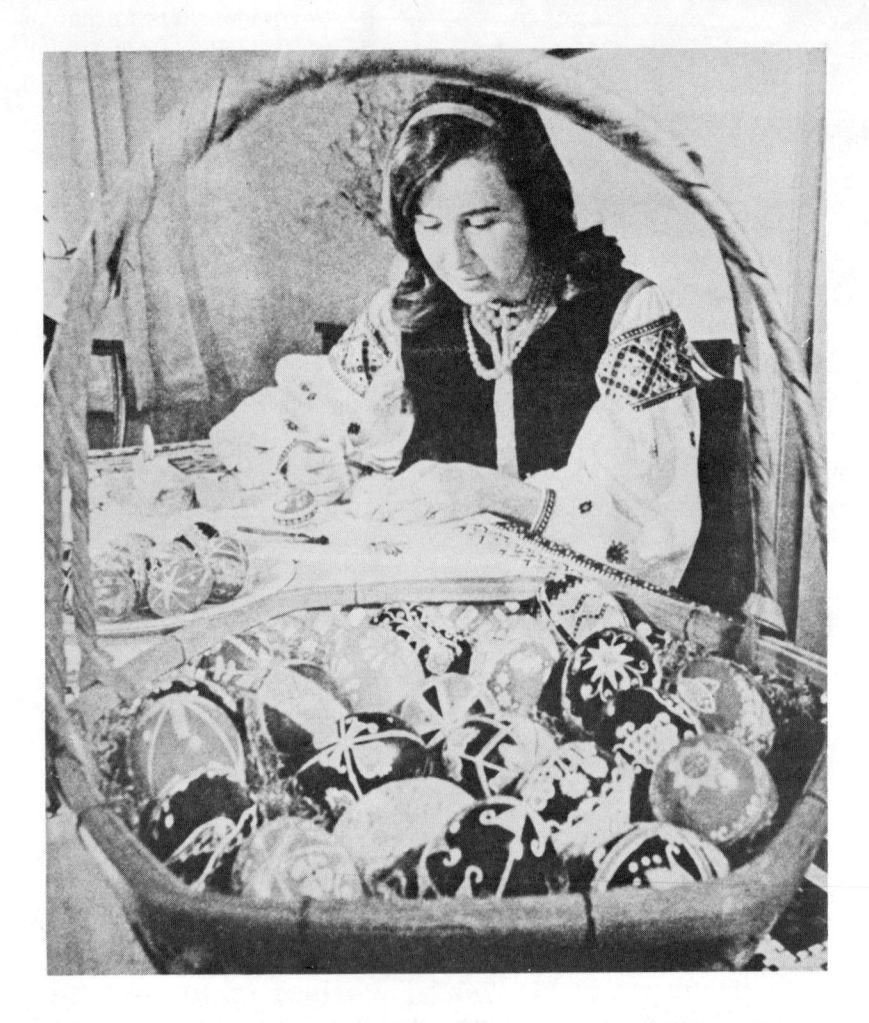

Tania Mychajlyshyn is a Michelangelo when it comes to the ancient art of decorating Easter eggs.
Baltimore News American Magazine

Ukrainian style are John C. and Audrey T. Howard of Baltimore. Their love for this art goes back a little more than five years ago when they started decorating eggs for their own satisfaction. "There is so much to share in your heritage...," says Audrey Howard. "It really binds you in family and community." Today John Howard actually makes a living from *pysanky*. He regularly goes to art shows in Maryland and adjoining states, giving demonstrations and selling *pysanky*. "There is a great interest for Ukrainian Easter eggs," he says softly. "This spring I will demonstrate this art at the Catholic University in Washington, D.C., in the pre-Lenten time. I have been already invited."[6]

Today many daughters of families like those of Anastasia Marmash or Sophia Mychajlyshyn continue this beautiful tradition. Girls enrolled in youth organizations such as PLAST, a Ukrainian scouting organization, or SUMA, a Ukrainian American Youth Organization, sponsor egg decorating projects at Easter time. Many talented artists are developing such as, Halyna Mudryj of Curtis Bay, Georgianna Kostak of Woodlawn, Luba Chornodolsky of Hamilton, and others. "I don't want the tradition to die, so I continue to make them," says Georgianna Kostak.[7] "It is not really as hard as it looks to make those unbelievable, lacy-looking designs," says 23-year old Tania Mychajlyshyn.[8] Tania learned this art from her mother when she was 11 years old. All these efforts promise that this ancient Ukrainian art will continue to make its input on the culture of America and of the world.

central office bulletin

A WEEKLY PUBLICATION OF THE SOCIAL SECURITY ADMINISTRATION

VOL. XII   MARCH 24, 1975   NO. 12

Decorating eggs is a family tradition

BDPer Georgianna Kostak has been carrying on a family tradition of elaborately decorating raw eggs for Easter since she was a child. To find out more about her techniques for creating delicate designs like the ones shown, turn to page 3.

NOTES TO CHAPTER TWELVE

[1] Robert Paul Jordan, "Easter Greetings from the Ukrainians," *National Geographic Magazine*, Vol. 141, No. 4, April 1972, pp. 557-563.

[2] Bob and Charlotte Bruce, "Symbolism of "Pysanka" Attracts All," article in April, 1976, edition of the *American Agriculturist*, reprinted in *Svoboda*, The Ukrainian Weekly, New Jersey, May 1, 1976, p. 2.

[3] Lee McCardell, "Ukrainians Still Dyeing Their Eggs for Easter," *The Sunpapers*, Baltimore, Maryland, April 22, 1938.

[4] Statements by Theodore Nykula and Joseph Marmash, interview by Wolodymyr C. Sushko, October 19, 1976.

[5] Winifred E. Bautz, "Course in Ukrainian Egg Dying Coming to YWCA," *The Evening Sun*, Baltimore, Maryland, March 24, 1976, p. C1.

[6] Statements by John C. and Audrey T. Howard, Baltimore, Maryland, interview by Wolodymyr C. Sushko, November 22, 1976.

[7] "Elaborate Easter Eggs Take 2 to 5 Hours To Decorate," an article in *Central Office Bulletin*, A Weekly Publication of the Social Security Administration, March 24, 1975, p. 3.

[8] J. Williams Joynes, "Michelangelos of the Kitchen," *Maryland Living, The News American Magazine*, Baltimore, Maryland, April 7, 1968.

Chapter Thirteen
Ukrainian Arts and Artists in Maryland
Wasyl Palijczuk

INTRODUCTION

Last year at a lecture-demonstration on oil painting to a mixed Ukrainian and general American public, the writer made the statement that there is no such thing as Ukrainian art — just good or bad art. This shocked the Ukrainian-Americans present and rightly so. The statement was deliberately made to point out that the writer is a product of an American educational background talking only about the so-called "Fine Arts" such as painting, sculpture, and graphics. This follows the normal philosophy on art in the U.S.A., where for many years the arts were separated into the Fine Arts and the Crafts. It is only in recent years that American museums and galleries started to accept photography, quilts, toys, and other folk arts as being worthy of their wall space. This about-face was inevitable, especially since America has arrived at the Bicentennial era.

All along Americans have been neglecting that which made the country great and which built its character. There is now an appreciation for Indians and their cultural, philosophical, and agricultural contributions. Our cowboys are, as the Indians, the dying species which one can only begin to appreciate when they become less numerous or approach extinction. Neglect of all but the few dominating ethnic groups has long been practiced. Only recently has our nation more fully awakened to the fact that the rest of the ethnic groups, such as Blacks, Indians, Greeks, Poles, Ukrainians, Chinese, Chicanos, and many others, have done their share to build this country.

At the present time there are more serious private collectors, not to mention the public museums and businesses, for anything that has to do with Early American life, such as toys, tools, utensils, quilts, Indian jewelry, blankets, artifacts, as well as paintings and sculpture with Indian, cowboy, western wilderness, or any other subjects that portray early American life. This definite life style has produced a characteristic art that expresses the time, struggle, and the geographical and philosophical difference of American art from the rest of the world. It is true that many people of various religious, cultural, and racial backgrounds have combined with the natives and through hard work and richness of this land developed a generally distinct American character in art and life style.

Applying similar philosophy to Ukrainian art, it is discerned that because of the movement of many racial and ethnic peoples since the beginning of time, the Ukrainian character has been developed into a set pattern pertaining to life in general and art in particular. Since the Ukrainian art now specified as Crafts was and is produced by amateur and professional artists for decoration of their homes, churches, and selves, it is of the utilitarian type such as embroidery, tool making, weaving, basketry and pottery, and the building of houses and churches. This obviously develops characteristic styles with the combination of various influences and time. No doubt exists that this type of art is Ukrainian in character mainly because it has been practiced on Ukrainian soil by its people. The only problem of nationality will be encountered in paintings and sculpture of old portraits and landscapes. The items that are different are the faces, clothing and racial type, it being very difficult to see the difference between the artistic quality of an old portrait of a Ukrainian Hetman, Bohdan Khmelnitsky, and a portrait of an American pilgrim. This is what was meant when it was stated that there is only good or bad art, disregarding the nationality. Simply the fact that a native artist paints the western wilderness or the New York skyline does not necessarily make that painting an American painting or American art. Anybody can paint George Washington or Taras Shevchenko but the painting does not automatically become an American or Ukrainian painting. The art work should be judged only on its artistic quality of line, value, color, composition, and any other artistic merit such as originality and style of the artist.

When discussing Ukrainian visual art, consideration must be given all the arts, such as basket weaving, ceramics, embroidery, weaving Kilems, wood carving, Easter egg decoration, jewelry, tools and weapons, architecture, the fine arts such as painting and sculpture and any other crafts that have been produced by Ukrainian people. In this chapter the writer will discuss a few of the major crafts that are still practiced by Ukrainians here in North America and by those in the Soviet Ukraine.

HISTORICAL BACKGROUND

According to research done on Ukrainian art a long tradition goes back to the late Paleolithic period. With additional research the time may be extended farther into the past, basing guesses on the fact that the steppes of Ukraine were well-travelled crossroads for traders between the North, South, East and West for many millenia. Because of this movement of people and the impermanence of most materials used, many things have been destroyed by plunder, fire, or the ravage of time. In the beginning Ukrainians must have produced such tools and weapons that would be necessary for their survival and protection from the elements and their enemies. Those early tools were very primitive and undecorated. But later they started to scratch or paint geometric designs for aesthetic, or more likely, religious reasons. They also carved idols of bone in the form of women with decorated lines in the geometric style. Later the ceramics, weapons, and especially personal jewelry became extremely sophisticated and showed definite Greek as well as other eastern influences; in fact, many objects were produced by Greek artisans for the Scythian tribal chieftains and their women. Americans had a chance to see some very good examples when the Soviet Union had a travelling exhibit of Scythian Gold in Washington, D.C., and later in New York. Many, if not all of the gold objects on display were discovered on Ukrainian soil and were dated from the 8th century B.C. The Scythian artifacts were usually decorated in wild animal motifs and showed relation to the Persian arts.

IKONS

In 988 A.D. Ukrainians by the order of Prince Volodymyr the Great, who was influenced by Constantinople, were led into the Dnipro River to be baptized into Eastern Christianity. After that Baptism, church construction took a most important priority and the church gained control over the arts and became the regulator of the lives of the people. This set the stage for the beginning of ikon painting. The best ikons on walls and on wood panels were done for the churches or for private homes of the wealthy. This old tradition of keeping holy pictures in homes and especially in churches goes back to the Kiev dynasty. Since Kiev was the political and religious center for the whole region which is now Central Ukraine, it obviously possessed the oldest and most beautiful churches full of marvelous frescoes and ikons. Unfortunately, most of the old churches have been accidentally or purposely destroyed by the Russians as a way of Russifying the Ukraine. So, whenever Ukrainians emigrated voluntarily or forcefully, they either brought their ikons with them or had new ones painted after they settled in their new country. This is true here in the United States and Canada where Ukrainians have settled from 1610 to the present, but especially after the 1870's. Ikons can be found in private homes in Maryland or in all Ukrainian churches as mentioned in Chapter Seven of this book.

Typical ikons take the rectangular or circular shape. The background is flat and in the best ikons painted or inlaid in gold. This symbolizes the eternal other-

Among Maryland's best, these figures in the iconostasis at SS. Peter and Paul Ukrainian Catholic Church were completed by a woman artist, Christine Dochwat.   *Roman Hankewycz*

worldliness of the subjects. It shows that it is not an ordinary human but the depiction of a holy person or spirit of a saint. The most popular subjects are the Virgin with Christ Child, Christ, Apostles (most popular, Peter and Paul), Archangels, Boris and Hlib and other local saints and church fathers. The majority of ikons are painted in frescoes on walls or in tempera or oil, mostly on wood panels, but there are some very good examples of mosaics every bit as good in color and design as the best of early Christian works of Italy and Greece.

CERAMICS

In ceramics the Tripillian pattern (2500-2000 B.C.) was one of the most beautiful in design, color combination and shape. The designs were swirling lines with some animal forms painted in red, white, and black. The color, motif, design and artistic quality of the Kiev, Poltava, and Podillya areas bear a remarkable similarity to the patterns of ancient Greece, and the pottery is contemporary with the oldest Greek art, especially that of Crete.

There are basically five main periods in Ukrainian ceramics: the geometric, Tripillian, the Kievan state, the Hetman state, and the Ukrainian Baroque of the 17th

Hutzul motifs show on ceramic plates by Slava Lasijczuk.

W. Palijczuk

century. Most of the past and present designs are based on one of the five basic periods or styles. The Hutzul ceramics are distinguished in that they use only the colors yellow, green, and red on white. Geometric lines are also combined with animals, birds, and human forms. The writer has seen similar subjects used on old Turkish ceramics but not the color combination.

In Baltimore, four women who practice this art are Mrs. Luba Rad, Mrs. Eugenia Czorniak, Mrs. Olga Hanas, and Mrs. Slava Lasijczuk. All of them are primarily self-taught. Therefore, tradition plays a more important role than does pure originality. For this reason colors and designs that have been used for centuries can still be found in use today. The Hutzul and Tripillian colors and designs are the most popular with them. They rely on commercial sources to acquire the unfinished ceramic forms such as vases, plates, pitchers, etc. Refinishing the forms, they paint designs and glaze and then have them fired by a commercial ceramic shop. Since identical commercially produced forms made

This plate by Halia Bula shows a Hutzul motif.

Halia Bula

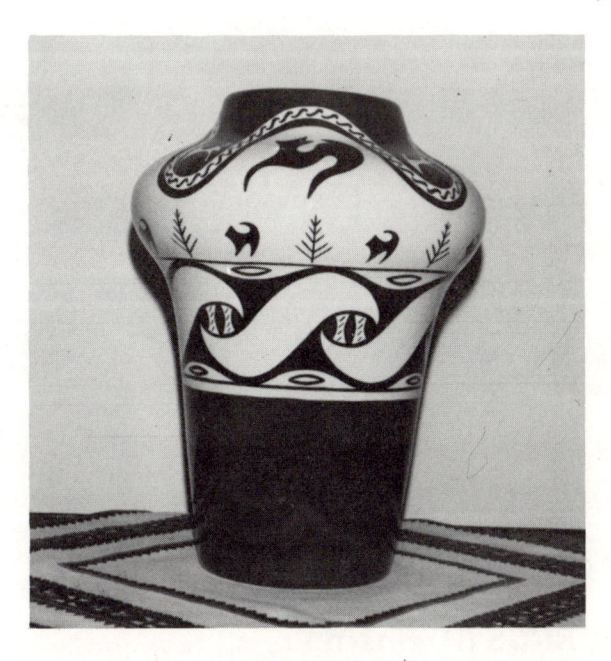

A Tripillian motif shows on this ceramic vase by Halia Bula.

Halia Bula

from the same molds are used and since they also employ the same traditional designs and colors, the only distinctions that can be made between their works is their individual craftsmanship. Most of them present the finished objects as gifts to friends and relatives or decorate their own homes with them.

Mrs. Halia Tereszczuk-Bula of Rockville became interested in ceramics about ten years ago. This led her to taking college courses at Montgomery Community College and the University of Maryland (B.S.). Now a technical illustrator by profession, she creates all her own ceramic forms. She makes free hand and wheel thrown forms and also casts, using commercial molds. Using the Trypillian, Hutzul, and other folk motifs, she is conscientious of the need for keeping the interest in Ukrainian ceramics going. She often lectures to young audiences, hopeful of developing appreciation for Ukrainian traditions. She exhibits and sells her works at Ukrainian festivals and fairs.

Combination wheel and hand built ceramic by Halia Bula.

Halia Bula

EASTER EGGS (PYSANKY)

As Chapter Twelve examined the subject of Ukrainian decorated eggs, comments in this chapter will be minimal. In addition to the use of eggs as gifts, the writer remembers as a youth of about seven in Ukraine how village children would gather on Easter morning around the church to challenge each other to a trial. Youngsters would approach each other with just the end of a *pysanka* visible in a hand. The object was to test the strength of a cooked egg against that of his opponent. One child would hold his egg while the other would take one of his and tap it with a quick motion against his foe's. Whoever had an egg that cracked lost it to the owner of the uncracked one. The test involved both ends of the eggs. While being a mirthful experience, the heartache some children endured if they lost all their *pysanky* is still remembered. The victor not only got the glory but a full stomach. It is also said that if a girl gives a specially beautifully decorated *pysanka* to a young man, the act in time may lead to engagement and marriage.

The writer feels that the young artist mentioned in Chapter Twelve, Halyna Mudrey, is no ordinary *pysanky* decorator, but a genuine artist whose creations possess the finest line and most intricate designs. Her feeling for line, color, and design result in the most beautiful and harmonious *pysanky*, based on not only traditional symbols but also showing inventions of her own. Halyna has been persuaded by the author to sign her *pysanky*, which compare favorably with those of the best of the artists in the United States and Canada. Presently a student at Maryland Institute College of Art in Baltimore, it is her generation that has so much to do to teach others so that this old Ukrainian art form will not disappear.

EMBROIDERY

One of the oldest crafts practiced by Ukrainian women is embroidery. Few, if any, men ever get involved with embroidery. As Easter egg decoration, it is an art handed down from mother to daughter. It is possible for an expert to identify a piece of work with a general region of Ukraine or to a specific village or family that used the particular design for a while. Because of personal likes and differences it is possible to assign a piece of embroidery work to a particular woman or family even here in America. This means that

Costumes from various regions of Ukraine were exhibited by Maryland Ukrainians at the 1976 Ukrainian Festival, Baltimore.

some like a certain motif or color combination better than another. To some extent this is now true in America but here less attention is paid to where the design comes from than is given to its coloration, symbols, and intricacy of design. Regardless of the region of origin, the colors are usually very limited and more of the monochromatic variety rather than a full rainbow of colors. Embroidery is popularly used on men's shirts, women's blouses, pillows, scarves, and towels — especially the type wrapped around icons or other holy pictures to help decorate them or show their importance. Towels were also used to "confirm a marriage and to line coffins at funerals." Decoration on women's blouses are concentrated on the sleeves and usually are more ornate than that of men's shirts. Among other objects seen embroidered are a bride's wedding crown, a ring pillow for a wedding ceremony, and hand embroidered draperies, such as those which adorned the apartment of the late Ukrainian priest, Rev. E. Wesolowsky of Baltimore.

Clerical vestments are also embroidered. Such

embroidery is often completed by devout women of a parish who contribute time and love into making vestments which are worn only on very special holy days or on festive occasions. A feature article, "Vestments Preserve Ukrainian Needlework," appeared in the Baltimore *Catholic Review* on February 14, 1975.

Sodality ladies at St. Michael's Ukrainian Catholic Church, directed by Mrs. Pauline Schneider and Mrs. Luba Rad, completed the vestments above for Msgr. Petro Melnyczuk in 1975.

Catholic Review *photo*

Basically the Western Ukrainians used geometric designs while the central Ukrainian motifs were mostly floral. A great variety of stitches is used now as was done in the past. Galicians used the Nyz (low) stitchery and the cross-stitch which seems most popular now. It is believed that the cross-stitch is not traditional Ukrainian, but that it was introduced from France or Germany sometime in the 1800's. The most characteristic stitching in the region of Poltava is the open work white on white stitch. In Kiev, Chernikiv and Volhyn the so-called colored thread has been used extensively. Rev. Leo Dorosz, retired, of Curtis Bay, owns an extensive collection of rare works of embroidery from Ukraine.

KILEMS

While embroidery and to some extent Easter egg decoration is done by women, it is recorded that some of the best kilems produced in Ukraine were done by men, many of whom were shepherds. Kilems are woven on large, sometimes room-size, looms. This is definitely one of the most difficult and time-consuming art forms. The ancient tradition is believed to be Eastern by the writer. Some of the motifs resemble Greek and Turkish types and others can be traced even farther southeast.

Photo of a kilem owned by Mrs. J. Chmilewsky.

W. Palijczuk

Kilems, woven tapestry rugs, used as coverings for floors, walls, seats, and sometimes used as blankets or table cloths, are mentioned in history as far back as the Kievan period. The art of Kilem weaving could have been passed on from any one of the nomadic peoples, such as, the Pecheniks, Polovtsi, Scythians, or Turks.

The characteristic ornamentation of the Poltava area is the use of plant life (Central Asia and Persian influence), while that of Galicia is generally more geometric. Because of the proximity of Bessarabia and Turkey, it is possible that geometric designs originated in either of those two areas. As an artist, the writer is always amazed by the similarity of Ukrainian Kilems, especially the geometric-patterned ones, to the blankets produced by Indians in western United States and in South America. There is also similarity in the decoration of Indian pottery and clothing to the works of early Ukrainian tribes.

The similarity does not stop here. The author's most vivid and amazing discovery was when in the middle of the jungle of Yucatan in 1962 he came upon homes that were constructed and decorated very similarly to those wherein he was born and lived until 1942. The Indian homes were not only laid out identically in plan, but also had white-washed outside walls with a blue line on the bottom, and thatched roofs very much like houses in certain regions of Ukraine. The thatch was not of wheat as in Ukraine, but of jungle grass.

A number of good examples of Kilems can be found in Maryland but unfortunately this appears to be one of the dying art forms for Ukrainians here. In Soviet Ukraine the art is still continued regularly but the quality is definitely on the wane. Colors seem to be too strong and wild and designs have too much Russian influence.

WOOD

Wood has been used for the building of houses and churches, for household utensils and art objects. Wooden constructions of typical Ukrainian design are very few in the United States (none are known in Maryland). In Ukraine, however, wood was one of the main materials from which most early churches and houses were constructed. Some churches (especially those in the Carpathian Mountains) were constructed entirely of wood, including the *ikonostases*, the altars, door casings and church furniture such as chairs and benches. In homes wood decorations were used on doorways, entrances, balconies, windows, and sometimes on ceilings and eaves.

Besides the obvious tools for home use such as spoons, knives, and plates, wood was used to produce such decorative objects as jewelry boxes, Easter eggs, ornately inlaid and carved plates, cups, carved pictures, musical instruments, dowry chests, and furniture.

The Hutzuls of the Carpathians and the residents of the Dnipro River region were the best developed wood carvers. The Hutzuls were particularly good in incrustation (inlaying of wires, mother of pearl, ivory, or beads, and using different colored woods), engraving and burning designs into wooden objects.

Traditions of woodworking continue in Maryland where such men as Oleksa Sidlak and Wasyl Wernyj have been very productive. Mr. Sidlak, born in Bazer, Ukraine, worked as a furniture and wagon maker there and from 1944 to 1949 he began to make carved and inlaid wood objects while living in Germany. He followed by making boxes of various sizes and shapes, lamps, and other art objects. Skilled in inlaying with different woods, metals, or bones, he also mastered the art of burnishing, and carving. He produced small carved figures and female busts which he painted and polished. In Maryland, he made his living designing and making custom-made furniture. Mr. Sidlak died in August of 1976.

Mr. Wasyl Wernyj, born in Markiwce, Ukraine, spent 1944-49 in Germany where he studied under a Ukrainian master wood worker. Now employed by the Domino Sugar Company in Baltimore, he uses wood working as a hobby and has been teaching various wood working techniques at the Ukrainian Youth Association Hall. He has exhibited his art work in local schools and at festivals, fairs, etc.

For some, wood working provides a livelihood, as those who manufacture or restore items, but for most it is only a hobby. For Ukrainians in Maryland engaged in agriculture, wood working serves very practical functions in providing handles for Austrian scythes, rakes for gathering hay, storage bins for grains and vegetables, handles for hammers, etc. In the area of Chesapeake City after 1912, many talents from western Ukraine were employed in building homes, barns, fences, and even the community's church.

The boxes in top photo fit into each other. Designs of Ukrainian landscapes were burned into the tops. The lower box shows the art of incrustation. All works were by Oleksa Sidlak.

Wasyl Palijczuk

PAINTING AND SCULPTURE

Because of the foreign domination of Ukraine for many centuries, most of the better known Ukrainian artists studied and practiced in St. Petersburg, Moscow, Warsaw, Vienna, or other foreign cities and became known as Russians, Poles, etc. Some of this misrepresentation continues in America, two good examples being the artists Lois Nevelson and Alexander Archipenko, world-renowned sculptors.

Lois Nevelson was born in Odessa (about 350 miles from Russian soil). Descriptions often cite her as being born in Odessa, Russia, thereby making her a Russian. Odessa,

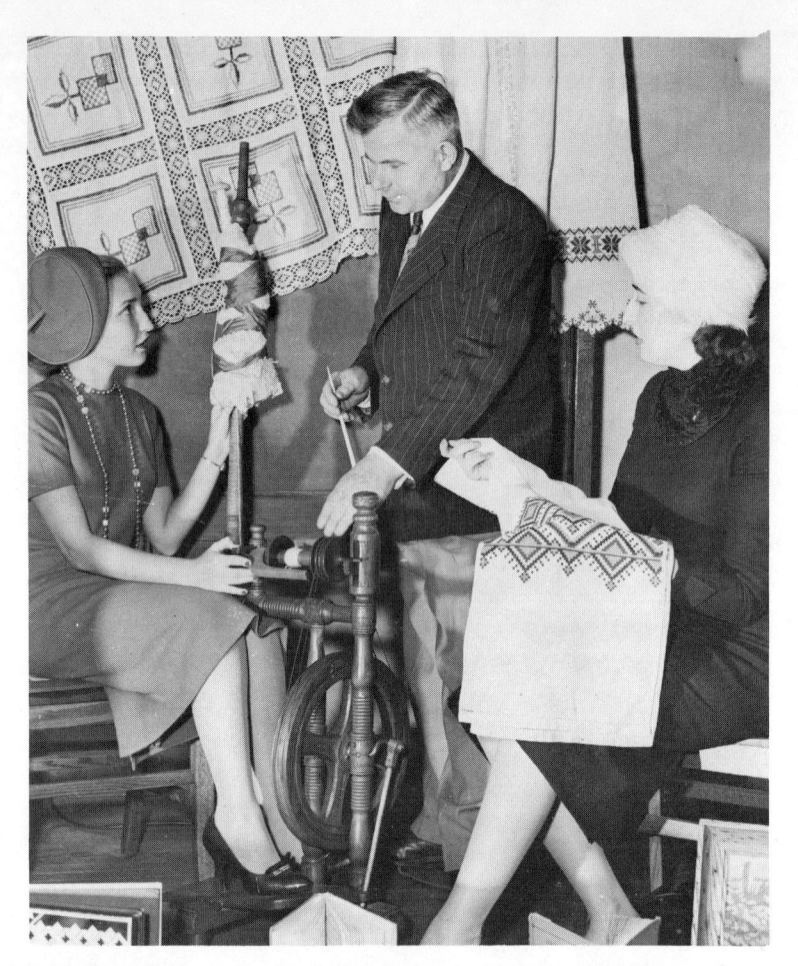

Oleksa Sidlak demonstrating his handmade spinning wheel at a crafts exhibit in 1955.

Ukraine, became the sister city of Baltimore in 1975.

Alexander Archipenko, born in Kiev in 1887, is another Ukrainian often referred to as a Russian. Archipenko emigrated to France from Ukraine and later lived in Germany before coming to the United States. The "ko" ending in Archipenko is a typical Ukrainian ending and his birthplace of Kiev was a powerful city-state many years before Moscow came into existence. Soviet sources classify Archipenko as Ukrainian. It is therefore frustrating to the writer to visit a museum or read in books or see references in

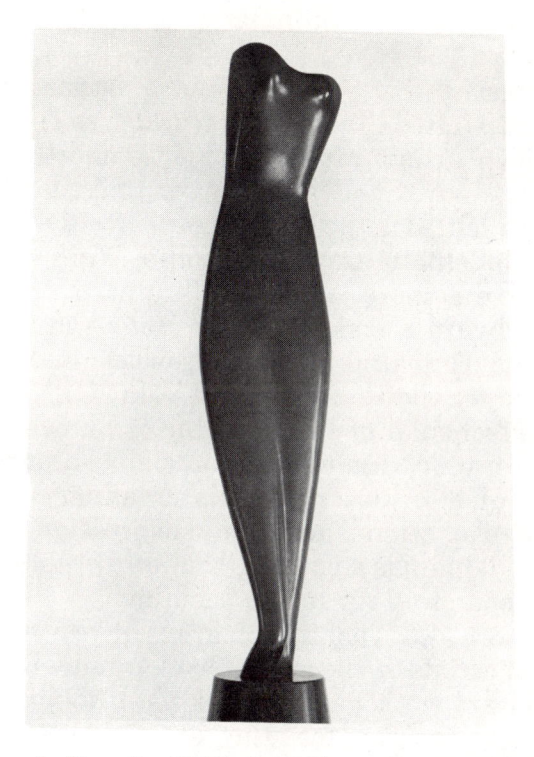

"Hollywood Torso" (1936) by Alexander Archipenko is in the Wurtzburger Collection at the Baltimore Museum of Art. Archipenko lectured on art and creativeness at the Baltimore Museum of Art in 1950.
Baltimore Museum of Art

magazines or newspapers to the effect that this great sculptor was Russian instead of Ukrainian.

Archipenko was influenced by the works of G. Brague and P. Picasso. He searched for new materials and ways to express his ideas into three dimensional forms. His experimentatins and inventive mind caused him to venture into the abstract sculpture, where he investigated spatial sculpture, concave modulation, and the relief sculpto-paintings.

The greatest influx of Ukrainian artists entered Canada and the United States after World War II. Most of the better known artists are from older generations who studied in Kiev, Lviv, St. Petersburg, or in centers in the west. They have settled in the large American cities, such as New York, Philadelphia, Detroit, Toronto, Winnipeg, etc.

Several of the more popular Ukrainian artists in America are Edward Kozak, Nicholas Butovych, Michael Moroz, Lubomyr Hutsaliuk, O. Teodorowycz, B. Mukhyn, C. Milonadis, Mychajlo R. Urban, and Yakiv Hnizdowsky. Peter Kapschutschenko of Philadelphia is known for his figurines in ceramic, including porcelain, bronze and various other plastic materials. His creations are very ethnic and full of emotional action and expression. Andrey Maday of Philadelphia is a young Ukrainian graphic artist whose talents bode well for future acclaim.

The Baltimore and Washington areas have attracted a good number of artists of Ukrainian background. Some are artists who do art work part time or as a hobby. Adam Markowski, who works for the state of Maryland, Department of Assessment and Taxation, paints still life and landscapes in his spare time. His mother, Mrs. Karolyna Markowski, seventy-eight years of age, is also an artist, having studied at the Vienna Academy and painted while still living in Ukraine. Mrs. Markowski arrived in Baltimore in 1951 and has resided in that city continuously. Her favorite subjects for painting are still life, which she paints in oil.

The same as Adam Markowski, Theodore Kuzmiw of Baltimore was born in Lviv, Ukraine. He came to New York in 1950 and commenced studies at the Delehanty Institute

The top is a lithograph, "Horse and Rider" (1960 series) by Dr. M. Kushnir, and the bottom is a woodcut re: mythology (1965).

School of Art and Drafting from which he received a diploma in 1954. In 1964 he received a diploma from the Art Instructor School (correspondence) in Illustrating and

Related Arts. Presently a technical illustrator and draftsman-designer for the Koppers Corporation of Baltimore, he designs book covers, program illustrations, and posters in addition to painting in oils and decorating stage backdrops. Since 1951 he has taught at the Ukrainian Youth Association in Baltimore.

Dr. Harion Kalynewych resides in Silver Spring, Maryland, with his wife Donna (Havrishchuk) and daughter Olha. His training in art was obtained in Lviv, Vienna, and at the University of Maryland. His doctorate is in agriculture and he works in the National Agricultural Library. He paints landscapes and still life in oil and acrylic.

Dr. Mychajlo Kushnir was born on August 23, 1887, in Stanyslaviv, Ukraine. He studied art at the Vienna Art Academy and at the Munich Art Academy. Additional studies were at the Ukrainian Underground University in Lviv. In 1950 he received the doctor of philosophy degree from the University of Heidelberg. A captain in the Ukrainian Halytska Armiia in 1918-1919, he was wounded in the fight for Ukrainian freedom. A member of the Shevchenko Scientific Society, he has written seven books and numerous articles on art, culture, and politics in the Ukrainian, German, and English languages. His linguistic mastery also includes Polish, French, and Italian. He and his wife Sophia (Sydoryk) reside in Silver Spring where he is a graphic artist and a political analyst.

A former physician in Baltimore, Jaroslaw Chmilewsky, was intensely interested in archaeology and art. He painted landscapes and some still life. His widow Joanna and daughter Marika (Ulanowicz) still reside in Maryland, where Marika is a musician and a teacher.

In Chesapeake City, Mrs. Mary Hrabec, whose beautiful home faces the northern extremity of Chesapeake Bay where ships can be seen traversing the Chesapeake and Delaware Canal, has maintained an avid interest in art. An alumna of Johns Hopkins University, she paints in several media and has an extensive collection of various items of art.

"Orfika" (Orpheus), a woodcut, rendered by Dr. Michael Kushnir in 1927.

Shown above are four advertising designs created by George M. Kotyk, a specialist in the graphic arts.

Of Ukrainian artists who earn their livelihoods in the field of art four stand out. These professionals are George M. Kotyk, Orest Poliszczuk, Mrs. Halia Bula (see Ceramics) and Wasyl Palijczuk. Commentaries about these artists follow.

George M. Kotyk was born on October 21, 1934, in Lviv, Ukraine. He arrived in America in 1949 after spending several years in Germany. Mr. Kotyk attended the Johns Hopkins University and the Maryland Institute College of Art, from which he received a B.F.A. degree as an Advertising Graphics Major. He does some free lance commercial art, his main job being with the Imperial Packaging Company where he is the Art Director and Department Head. He specializes in all phases of

Works of Orest Poliszczuk: Top left, "Circular Dance" (oil); right, "Bandura Stillife" (oil); bottom, "Church, Family, and Community" (painted steel).
Orest Poliszczuk

packaging design. He lives in Baltimore with his wife Maria (Hanas) and two sons, Bohdan and Marko.

Orest Poliszczuk was born in Lviv, Ukraine, on January 7 (Christmas Day), 1942. He immigrated to the United States in 1949 and has resided continuously in the Baltimore area. In 1966 he received his B.A. in art from the University of Maryland and two years later received an M.A. from the same school. Since 1969 he has been teaching sculpture and drawing at Montgomery College, Rockville, Maryland, as an assistant professor.

Orest went through a few styles until he reached his present style of painting. His preference is for rounded forms. He usually starts with a square canvas or paper on which he places a circle. In this circle he does most of his creation. The roundness of the circle he repeats in his subject whether it may be a still life, landscape, or figurative. Designs are well organized into a uniform and pleasing composition. Hard edges separate one area or object from the other. Composition and color harmony form an original and beautiful work of art. All these steps combine to make Orest a modern and definitely Ukrainian artist.

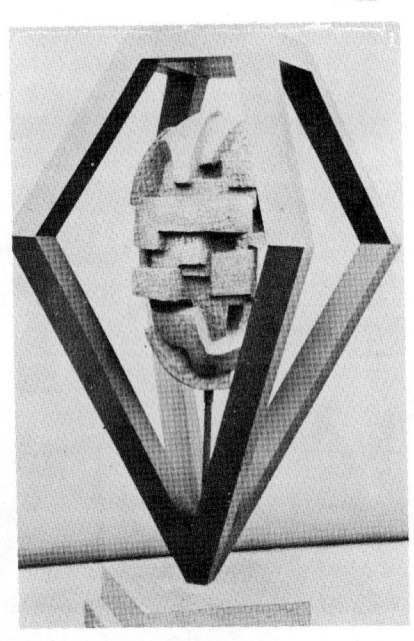

Sculpture by Orest Poliszczuk, "Diamond Forms," in cast stone, plastic, and aluminum.

Orest Poliszczuk has exhibited extensively throughout Maryland as well as in New York, Washington, and Philadelphia. Works of his were included in over 30 group shows and he has also had many one man shows, some as far away as San Francisco, Detroit, Chicago, New York, and Cleveland. He is the recipient of several sculpture commissions in the Maryland area and national awards. In 1966 he was awarded second prize in a National Collegiate Sculpture Competition for a piece now on permanent exhibition in the Garden of Patriots in Cape Coral, Florida. He also won second prize for sculpture in the National Young Sculptors Competition in Bryant Park, New York City. The artist is a member of the Maryland Branch of Artists Equity Association, having served as vice president for two years. He belongs to the Southern Sculptors Association.

His wife is the former Marika Sidlak and they live with their daughter Lisa in Columbia, Maryland, where their large modern house is loaded with Orest's paintings and sculpture pieces. Most of the walls are decorated with hand painted murals.

Wasyl Palijczuk was born in Tuczypy, Ukraine, 1934. In 1942 he was taken to Germany and eight years later he arrived in Baltimore. After graduation from high school he entered the United States Air Force for four years, attaining the rank of staff sargeant and also serving as head draftsman and illustrator. After military service he studied at the University of Maryland (B.A., 1961, and M.A., 1963). After two years as a fellow in the Rinehart School of Sculpture he was awarded a M.F.A. degree and the Henry Walters European Travel Award of $1,500. He has travelled in Europe, Mexico, Canada, and has crossed the United States four times, last in the summer of 1975. Since 1961 he has held various teaching positions. Presently he is Associate Professor of Art and Art Department Head at Western Maryland College where he began instructing in January, 1967. He continues to teach adult classes at the Baltimore Museum of Art where he has lectured since 1965.

In June 1975 he married Oksana L. Lasijczuk. They live in Baltimore. Their twin daughters, Ksenia and Natalka, were born on September 30, 1976.

Wasyl Palijczuk is primarily a painter (oil and watercolor) and a sculptor in wood, stone, bronze casting, and some steel and various build-up methods. His style constantly changes, but in all his phases one can always recognize some forms or subject matter. His sculptures are organic and figurative. The winner of numerous local and national prizes, his works are represented in about 200 private and public collections.

In 1975, Wasyl completed a mural (11' x 18') entitled "U.S.A./200" for Elderdice Hall, Western Maryland College, with the assistance of three of his students

Wasyl Palijczuk's "Humanity in Harmony" (steel) inspires many at Taylor Manor Hospital, Ellicott City, Md. **Wasyl Palijczuk**

majoring in art. Last year he installed a ten foot steel sculpture piece, "The Welcome," on the same campus.

In August, 1976, Taylor Manor Hospital, Ellicott City, Maryland, held the unvieling of Wasyl's major outdoor sculpture piece, "Humanity in Harmony." The sculpture piece was commissioned by Dr. and Mrs. Irving Taylor who on the occasion of the unveiling sponsored a banquet attended by about two hundred guests. The sculpture is a group of three ten foot steel figures which have their hands

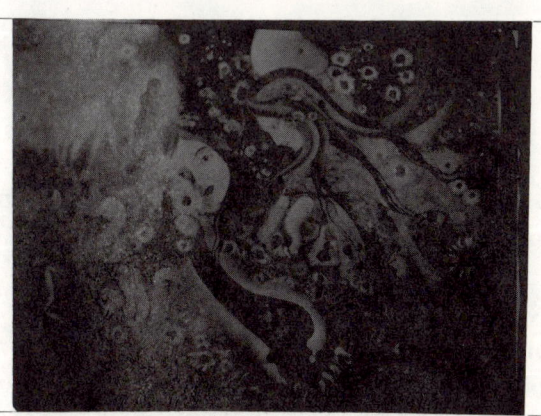

Works of Wasyl Palijczuk: Top, "The Visit" (oil); bottom, "Dreaming in My Garden" (oil).

Mr & Mrs A. Handler

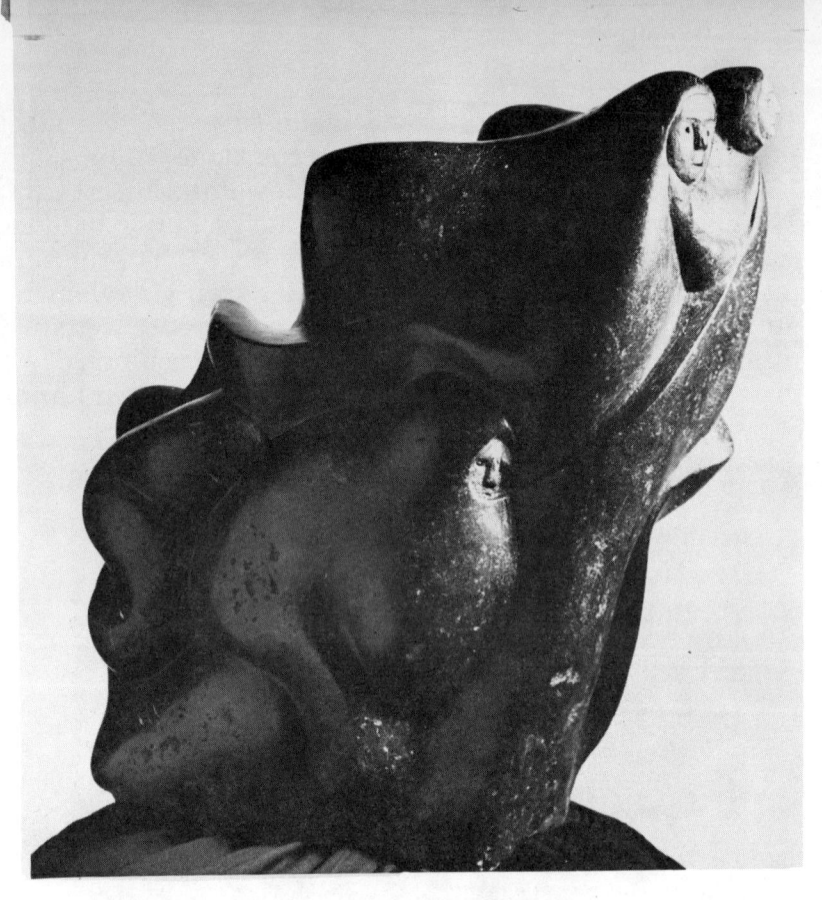

"Just What They Can Carry" by Wasyl Palijczuk *(soapstone).*
Studio Wasyl

up holding on to each other and forming a circle as in a dance. This work was fabricated and installed by the Dynamech Corporation of Finksburg, Maryland.

Wasyl is a member of the Artists Equity Association (Maryland Branch), the Ukrainian Education Association of Maryland, Inc., and the Ukrainian-American Association of University Professors.

CONCLUSION

It should be clear to the reader of this chapter that this is not a scientific dissertation. Instead, the goal was to present an outline of the major visual arts of Ukrainians who settled on American soil, with emphasis on developments in Maryland.

The writer apologizes for omissions which could easily occur in the complex American mosaic and respectfully requests written data that would be helpful in developing a more extensive treatment of Ukrainian endeavors in Maryland.

It was necessary to abbreviate so the writer knowingly skipped many stitches in the embroidery section and also did not discuss all the other ceramic styles or sectional differences that exist in Ukraine and which are practiced here in America. More background and other art facts were given about the few Ukrainian-Americans who make a living from art. They are the people who are most involved in art and who by their works of art, teaching, or art demonstrations, exemplify Ukrainian art most to the general American public. This is not to reduce the importance which other artists have played in keeping Ukrainian identities.

If it were not for the arts, literature, traditions, costumes, political activity, and to a large extent, the Ukrainian Orthodox and Ukrainian Catholic Churches, 50 million Ukrainians would be lost today without any nationalistic identity.

BIBLIOGRAPHY FOR CHAPTER THIRTEEN

Archipenko, Alexander, and fifty art historians, *Archipenko — Fifty Creative Years — 1908-1958*, New York, Tekhne Publications, 1960. (Introduction by Sviatoslav Hordynsky).

Halich, Wasyl, *Ukrainians in the United States*, Chicago, University of Chicago Press, 1937. (Reprinted by Arno Press in 1970.)

Istoria Ukraiinskoho Mystetzwa (6 volumes in Ukrainian), Kiev, Zowten, 1966.

Kubijovyc, Volodymyr (Ed.), *Ukraine: A Concise Encyclopedia* (2 vols.), Toronto, University of Toronto Press, 1971.

Kuropas, Myron B., *The Ukrainians in America*, Minneapolis, Lerner Publications, 1972.

Mitz, Anne (Ed.), *Ukrainian Arts*, New York, Ukrainian Youth League of North America, Inc., 1955.

Shtohryn, Dmytro M. (Ed.), *Ukrainians in North America — A Biographical Directory...*, Champaign, Association for the Advancement of Ukrainian Studies, 1975.

A journal that contains excellent reproductions of Ukrainian works of art is *Forum — A Ukrainian Review*, a quarterly edited by Andrew Gregorovich. *Forum* is published by the Ukrainian Workingmen's Association, 440 Wyoming Avenue, Scranton, Penna. 18501.

Chapter Fourteen
Contributions to Maryland

MILITARY SERVICES

America's battle heroes have come from all corners of the earth, for this is a land of many peoples. Among the fighters for independence assuredly were those of Ukrainian descent, since Ukrainian-sounding names appear on records of troops engaged in the Revolutionary War. Such names also occur in Civil War rosters, but proof of national origin has not been determined.[1]

Brigadier General John Basil Turchin, born in the Don Region of the Russian Empire and considering himself Kozak, fought in the Crimean War. Coming to the United States in 1856, General Turchin was noted for training of troops and his daring during maneuvers with the Union forces. He distinguished himself as commander of a brigade at the Battles of Bowling Green, Huntsville, Chickamauga, and Missionary Ridge in March 1862, April 1862, September 1863 and November 1863.[2] For a time he commanded Union soldiers in Baltimore. Because of illness he resigned from military service on October 4, 1864. He wrote an extensive history of the Battle of Chicamauga, *Noted Battles for the Union during the Civil War in the United States of America, 1861-65: Chicamauga,* published in Chicago in 1888. Turchin is buried in Anna in southern Illinois, not far from where he helped establish a Slavic community called Radom along the Illinois Central Railroad.

Private Michael Kozub is shown at Camp McClellan, Alabama, during World War I.

Maryland Ukrainians were in American military forces during World Wars I and II, the Korean War and the Vietnamese War. Assigned to the 29th Division, 110th Machine Gun Battalion, Company C, during World War I was Michael Kozub of Baltimore. Protecting the United States-Mexican border while with the U.S. Cavalry was George Podhorniak, a native of Volynia and resident of Baltimore. He joined the Cavalry in June 1917 and was discharged from the 11th Field Artillery Battalion in May 1920. Zachary Prodanchuk, a shipbuilder from Curtis Bay, was inducted June 12, 1918, and discharged April 22, 1919, at Camp Meade, serving with the 6th Division, U.S. Army.

The roll of honor (a partial listing) at St. Michael's Ukrainian Catholic Church in Baltimore contains 93 members of the parish as having served their country in World War II, while the one at SS. Peter and Paul Ukrainian Catholic Church of Curtis Bay lists 45 service personnel. In Chesapeake City names of 90 parishioners of St. Basil's Ukrainian Catholic Church are shown as having been in the military forces during World War II. One of them, Sgt. Walter Basalyga, was killed in the Battle of the

In 1945 Ukrainian American veterans of World War II met again in front of St. Michael's Ukrainian Catholic Church, Baltimore.

Bulge in Europe. A Baltimore infantryman, Nicholas Blama, was captured by the Germans in their early drives during the same offensive in December 1944 as a member of the 99th Division. He was one of 52 out of 2,000 prisoners in his camp to survive captivity. A combat medic (surgical technician) with the 17th Infantry Regiment of the 70th Division, George Prodanchuk of Baltimore took part in the operations in Southern France, Saar Valley and the final breakthroughs into Germany.

In North Africa, Sicily and Italy with the 21st Aviation Engineers as a demolition specialist immobilizing mines and bombs was John Shulka of Baltimore who was in the service from October 1941 to October 1945. Landing in Northern France and battling eastward with the 769th Ordnance Company of the 69th Division was Bohdan Maksymchuk of Hyattsville. When his first sergeant became a casualty Bohdan became acting first sergeant, continuing his unit's light maintenance functions. To the south Technical Sergeant Michael Ewanciw of Rockville touched African shores near Oran, Algeria in May 1943 with the 10th Port of Embarkation (Mobile) after which he took part in unloading and loading troops, equipment and supplies in Arzew, Algeria, and Bizerte, Tunisia, for the invasion of Sicily. Set up in Palermo in July 1943, T.Sgt. Ewanciw as part of the 10th Port performed manpower and materiel functions for the Sicilian, South Italian, Corsican and Anzio operations. Similar duties were carried out in Naples in June–August 1944 for the Southern France onslaught and in Leghorn from September for the Northern Italian campaigns. William Rybak, a civil engineer residing in Forest Heights, was a very agile combat engineer. Receiving a battle field commission and attaining the rank of colonel, he geared his construction units to quick repair and erection tasks so as to facilitate troops movements and hot pursuit of the enemy in battles in North Africa, Sicily, Italy, and Southern France. In the South Pacific shooting at the enemy from aircraft of the U.S. 13th Air Force was gunner Harry Kany. After a long series of campaigns, three wounds and continuous bouts with malaria, Sgt. Kany returned 39 months later to the restful shores of the Chesapeake Bay.

With the United States naval forces in World War II were two Baltimoreans, Michael Peltz and Theodore Shulka, who were rescued from the seas after their ships had been sunk by enemy actions. Seaman First Class Shulka was on the U.S.S. Helena, a cruiser which had survived the attack at Pearl Harbor, when it was engaged in the Battle of Kula Gulf in the Solomon Islands and was struck by 3 Japanese topedoes on July 6, 1943.[3] Rescued from the same waters was bandsman Peter Lisko of Annapolis who was at Pearl Harbor during the Japanese attack of December 7, 1941. Lieutenant William Zuk, while on Saipan, the stepping stone for the attacks planned against mainland Japan, because of his knowledge of Japanese was put in charge of Japanese prisoners of war. Joseph Kozub of Abington and a naval pilot operated from carrier forces in the Pacific. Half way around the world, supporting the D Day invasions at Normandy, was Michael Peltz, first class gunners mate, who was wounded on June 6, 1974, while on the sinking mine sweeper *U.S.S. Osprey*.

Captain Theodore Woronka, who served as a Navy officer in this global war, is Deputy Group Commander of a Naval Reserve Group at Fort McHenry.

Major Theodore Switty of Essex came to Ft. Meade as an enlisted man of the 44th Infantry Division, then graduated from the Chemical Warfare School at Edgewood in the first officer class in 1942. He remained in chemical warfare in 1943 and 1944, serving in New Guinea, after which he transferred to Air Corps Intelligence. In 1945 in Berlin he was responsible for interzonal travel in the four military zones. Commended in 1961 while in Germany for having demonstrated expert competency in the intelligence field, Major Switty from 1962 to 1966 acted as an instructor at the Intelligence School, Ft. Holabird. He is the recipient of the Legion of Merit.

Lt. Col. Theodore Kalakuka, born in New Jersey and a 1927 graduate of West Point, served under General MacArthur as part of the United States Air Force Far East during the Japanese conquests of the Philippines. He died while a prisoner of war on Luzon on October 31, 1942. Among his awards were the Distinguished Service Medal and 3 Silver Stars. Prior to his wartime service, Lt. Col. Kalakuka was in the Washington area in the Quartermaster Corps. He is remembered in the Ukrainian community for his skill and daring on the Hains Point polo field, recalling his Kozak forebears who galloped in battle on the Ukrainian steppes.

Brigadier General Stephen Malevich of Pittsburgh, who before going to the Philippines in July of 1941 assisted in the development of goverment war projects in Baltimore, is another Ukrainian who took part in the Bataan Death March. Surviving four years of Japanese prisoner-of-war treatment, General Malevich remained in the Army until 1964, part of the time assuming duties at Fort Meade and installations near Washington. An engineer, Gen. Malevich's units made possible troop retreats as they repaired or rebuilt bridges and roads when General MacArthur decided to keep American soldiers on the Islands. Gen. Malevich died in March 1969 and was buried in Arlington National Cemetery.

Major General Peter G. Olenchuk entered the Army as an enlisted man in 1943, fighting in North Africa, India, and Burma during World War II. Commissioned a second lieutenant in 1945 in the Army Chemical Corps, he was stationed at the Army Chemical Center in various capacities until 1950. From 1953 to 1955 General Olenchuk was executive officer at Ft. Detrick, to which installation he returned in September 1966 to become commanding officer. General Olenchuk had many important assignments while based in Washington or vicinity. Graduating with honors from the Army Command and General Staff College in 1959, he was on the Army General Staff as Deputy Chief, Chemical Biological Division, until 1962. In August 1964 he was an Army member of the plans and policy directorate of the joint chiefs of staff. Named Deputy Commander of the U.S. Army Munitions Command in February 1969, he became in February 1970 the chief of the U.S. Army Ammunition Procurement and Supply Agency.[4]

Brigadier General Bohdan Danyliw has been at Andrews Air Force Base in Maryland since June 1971 when he was appointed Deputy Staff Judge Advocate of the Air Force Systems Command. In May 1973 he was promoted to Staff Judge Advocate, with the rank of Brigadier General. General Danyliw came to the Washington area in 1946

Brigadier General Bohdan Danyliw, Staff Judge Advocate, Air Force Systems Command, is shown above.
U.S. Air Force photo

when he entered Catholic University. After graduation he enrolled in the Georgetown University Law School, completing his studies in February 1952. He also served in the Office of Special Investigations at Bolling Air Force Base in the District of Columbia in 1951.[5]

Captain Dan T. Radzykewycz attended Sykesville High School and received degrees from the University of Maryland in 1964 and 1966. Commissioned a lieutenant in June 1964 through the ROTC, he was assigned to a project evaluating the effectiveness of airpower in Southeast Asia and to editing a series of studies and monographs about the war. In August 1975 he was given the duties of a speech writer for the Secretary of the Air Force.

Assigned to the 352nd Civil Affairs Command, U.S. Army Reserves, Riverdale, was Colonel Lev Dobriansky, who retired in 1976. Colonel Dobriansky, professor of economics at Georgetown University and a leading American authority on Eastern Europe and the Soviet Union, has lectured frequently at various war colleges and institutes and testified at many congressional hearings. He has written books and many articles striving to alert and prepare America and the free world to meet the dangers posed by the rigidly-controlled ideological and military power sources in Moscow. A reserve officer with the 97th Army Command in Jessup is Lt. Colonel Ihor Masnyk of Potomac. In the Transportation Corps as a reserve officer was Lt. Colonel John Telencio of Towson. He had been assigned to the 1176th U.S. Army Outport of Curtis Bay prior to his departure for Michigan at the end of 1976. Captain Yuriy Woloshyn of Prince Georges County functions as a legal officer while carrying out reserve duties in a unit of the Army Judge Advocate General's Office.

Hlib S. Hyuk of Timonium, a former inhabitant of German displaced persons camps, was the chief area coordinator for Vietnam refugees at Indiantown Gap, Pa., in 1976. The Civil Affairs Section of the U.S. Army Reserves, entrusted with the tasks of housing, training and settling over 17,000 South Vietnamese, called on Major Hayuk, a professor of geography and environmental planning, to help solve the many problems caused by the aftermath of a war from which the United States withdrew. His active duty included two years with the 3rd Infantry Division in Europe in 1962-1964.

A refugee of another era, Major Hlib S. Hayuk in 1975 assisted Vietnamese refugees at Ft. Indiantown Gap, Penna.

U.S. Army photo

Taras Nowosiwsky, ranking as a colonel since June 12, 1973, and now a resident of Rockville but a native of Ukraine, is a medical officer with service in the 24th Infantry Division in Europe and the Headquarters, U.S. Army Vietnam. Specializing in preventive medicine, this graduate of Harvard Medical School (1958) and the Master of Public Health Program of Johns Hopkins University (1962), has taught preventive medicine and health care at a number of universities and Army schools and has written on health topics which he has researched during his military assignments. Colonel Nowosiwsky since 1971 has been in the Washington area as Deputy Director, Division of Preventive Medicine, Walter Reed Army Institute of Research, then Director of this Division (June 1973-1976), followed by appointment in July 1976 as Consultant in Occupational Medicine and Deputy Chief, Health and Environment Division, Office of the Surgeon General. In September 1977 Colonel Nowosiwsky was made Chief, Health and Environment Division, with Army-wide responsibility. He was awarded the Legion of Merit in 1971 and the Meritorious Service Medal in 1976.[6]

Colonel Orest Hawryluk, whose military service began May 5, 1955, returned to Maryland upon completion of a tour of duty with the 1st Armored Division in Germany. After many teaching, research and command assignments in preventive medicine, Colonel Hawryluk is now in the Surgeon General's Office in the Pentagon.

Among the Ukrainians who have graduated from the U.S. Naval Academy in Annapolis are John G. Kohut and John M. Shmorhun of Maryland. Lt. Kohut, trained in chemistry and engineering and Russian area subjects, is now stationed in Newport, Rhode Island, at the Anti-Submarine Warfare Officer School as an instructor and administrative officer. Ensign Shmorhun, with a major in Russian area studies, graduated in June 1977 and is now undergoing training in nuclear power plant theory and technology in Florida.

At the second Battle of Fort McHenry on July 4, 1975, witnessed by over 75,000 persons (including President Ford), were the Baltimore Independent Artillerists who are dedicated to promoting "history, truth and patriotism." They provide authentic cannon and mortar fire in their demonstration battles of the War of 1812. Commanded and organized by Michael P. Zacharko and containing from 18 to 70 members since its beginning, these Artillerists have spawned 17 other groups. The members, among whom is Joseph P. Zacharko II, have performed in their authentic uniforms at many locations throughout Maryland.[7]

The mobile life of an "Army brat" did not deter Joan Michel Ehrgott from becoming an honors graduate of the University of Maryland and from becoming Miss Maryland of 1971. Daughter of Brigadier General Herbert and Maria (Lewkovich) Ehrgott of Avondale, Md., Joan took first place in both the talent and swim suit contest.[8]

A tough leatherneck, whose parents Michael and Ella and brothers and sister came to Baltimore in the 1940's, is Walter Panchison. Joining the Marines on November 20, 1939, he rose rapidly to master sergeant and became a naval flight pilot. In February 1944 he was commissioned a second lieutenant, then fought in the Pacific with the Marine fighter squadrons. Twice he flew in Korea, then was an exchange pilot with the British Royal Air Force and the Royal Dutch Air Force. He commanded a number of squadrons and served in various divisions and departments, terminating his 30 year career as a colonel and Chief of the Plans and Operations Division for the Marine Corps Landing Force Development Center at Quantico, Va. His son, Captain Walter Scott Panchison, was a Marine Corps pilot for 10 years before leaving the service.[9]

Col. Walter Panchison, U.S. Marines

On June 12, 1977, at 2:30 P.M., General Samuel Jaskilka, Assistant Commandant of the United States Marine Corps and National Honorary Chairman, National Flag Week, was the leading speaker at the opening of National Flag Week ceremonies honoring the 200th birthday of the flag. Standing at Constellation Plaza overlooking the beautiful inner harbor in Baltimore, General Jaskilka praised the Marines for their patriotism and daily recognition of the American Flag and recalled how he had to correct Ambassador Dobrynin of the Soviet

Union at College Park during the USSR-US Field Meeting in August 1976. When asked, he told the ambassador that the name Jaskilka was of Ukrainian origin. To which Dobrynin replied that the Ukrainians and the Russians were the same. "That's not what my mother had taught me," retorted General Jaskilka in the vigorous manner typical of a Marine who still runs 10 miles without breaking into a sweat. He agreed with Dobrynin that the U.S. Marines were great fighters, but reminded him that the Ukrainian Kozaks were also famous for their military valor and exploits. The four-star general left no doubt in Dobrynin's mind of America's will to fight nor of his Kozak warrior ancestry.

John Malko, General Samuel Jaskilka, and Stephen Basarab (l. to r.) gather at end of Flag Day Ceremonies in Baltimore on June 12, 1977.
U.S. Marine Corps photo

UNITED UKRAINIAN WAR VETERANS IN AMERICA

Among the new immigrants are many veterans of the Ukrainian wars. Like their counterparts, the Ukrainian-

American veterans formed brotherhoods and associations of their own. Their central organization is called the United Ukrainian War Veterans in America, or as it is abbreviated in Ukrainian, ObWUA.

The membership of this group consists of two generations of veterans, the older one being associated with the Ukrainian Liberation War from the World War I period and the younger generation consisting of soldiers of various military formations which fought for the independence of Ukraine in World War II. Posts are located in all major Ukrainian settlements in the United States. The Baltimore post was established on September 27, 1958, the initiative coming from Pavlo Talan, a former colonel in the Army of the Ukrainian National Republic in 1917-1920. Commanding the newly-formed post of 12 veterans was Major Pavlo Kalynowsky.

The Ukrainian War Veterans of Baltimore are active in the social and cultural life of their ethnic community. On October 13, 1968, on the recommendation of Dr. Andriy Rastawecky a specially-designed banner was acquired for use at national celebrations and other appropriate public appearances and ceremonies. The post commander then was Ostap Charchalis.

Baltimore United Ukrainian War Veterans at Banner Dedication Ceremonies in 1968.

At one time the Baltimore post had 40 members, but the current membership is down to 22. One of the more prominent older members is General Peter Samutyn who served in the Army of the Ukrainian National Republic in 1917-1920. In 1975 he was the commander of the Baltimore post. On the same executive board were Dr. Nicolas Lasijczuk, Mykola Turyk, Michael Comishak and Zenowij Goy.

SPORTS

By Paul Fenchak

Dr. John E. Bodnar, Associate Historian of the Pennsylvania Historical and Museum Commission and editor of the book *The Ethnic Experience in Pennsylvania*, believes that Ukrainians and other immigrant groups became intensively involved in sports in order to gain recognition or status in America.[10] Others think that opportunities for economic advancement prompted extensive Ukrainian participation in sports. Whatever the reasons, Ukrainians have enjoyed success in professional, collegiate, scholastic, and amateur sports in America, often excelling in games that were unknown to their European-born ancestors.

Baseball

One impressive story comes from the small coal mining community of Yatesboro (population about 1700) in western Pennsylvania. Yatesboro was the birthplace in 1919 of two Ukrainian Americans who became major league baseball players: Steve Souchock (New York Yankees, Detroit Tigers and Chicago White Sox) and Mike Goliat (Philadelphia Phillies). The Yatesboro story could be repeated often, if not always on major league terms, then on minor league, collegiate, or semi-pro levels.

Performance in major league baseball yields good financial returns. For a family to have a father-son combination of major league performers is an uncommon attainment, yet such success came to the Tresh family of Hazleton, Pennsylvania. Mike "Iron Man" Tresh entered the major leagues in 1938 as a catcher for the Chicago White

Father Mike Tresh and son Tom Tresh talk at Yankee Stadium before the start of a game during the 1962 World Series. Tom was American League rookie of the year in 1962.

Philip J. Sarno, Hazleton, Pa.

HARRY DORISH, who pitched for the Orioles in 1955 and 1956, is shown getting ready for the 1956 season at the Orioles' spring training camp
Baltimore News American

Sox and the scrappy, alert receiver played in the majors until 1949 when he concluded his career with the Cleveland Indians. The nickname of "Iron Man" came to Mike Tresh during the season of 1945 when he caught every game played by the White Sox. After his playing career, Mike Tresh was a talent scout. His son Tom, born in 1938, broke into the majors with the New York Yankees in 1961 as a shortstop and outfielder, enjoying outstanding success in 1962 when he was named rookie of the year in the American League by both the *Sporting News* and the Baseball Writers' Association. Tragically it was in Baltimore later that shortstop Tom Tresh collided with a Yankee outfielder and so injured himself that his career began to go down hill immediately. He ended his major league career with the Detroit Tigers in 1969.

A Ukrainian who pitched for the Baltimore Orioles in 1955 and 1956 was Harry Dorish of Swoyersville, Pennsylvania. He had previously pitched for the Boston Red Sox, St. Louis Browns, and Chicago White Sox. Also a good fielder and hitter, Dorish, primarily a relief pitcher, was often switched to third base from the mound for a batter or two and then sent to the mound again by Manager Paul Richards of the White Sox. This was Richards' way of inserting left handed relievers when desired and then returning to the reliable right hander Dorish.

Aside from the Yatesboro story of Souchock and Goliat, the Tresh father-son performances, and the versatility of Harry Dorish, Ukrainians in major league baseball have included Mike(Guzelak) Gazella (New York Yankees, infielder), Danny Kravitz (Pittsburgh Pirates, catcher), Greg Terletsky (St. Louis Cardinals, pitcher) and Nestor Chylak, presently senior umpire in the American league. There have been many other performers in both the American and National Leagues whose names suggest Ukrainian heritage, but good research is presently unavailable. The annals of minor league records abound with Ukrainian players, some of whom changed their names to accommodate fans and sports writers.

Football

In football Ukrainians have made significant contributions. Bronislaw (Bronko) Nagurski came off a farm in International Falls, Minnesota, the son of Ukrainian immigrant parents, to become one of the greatest players in the history of collegiate and professional football and "The Bronk" was fittingly inducted into the Professional Football Hall of Fame in Canton, Ohio, in 1963 after having earlier been admitted to the Helms Foundation Hall of Fame and the National Football Foundation Hall of Fame. Grantland Rice in *The Tumult and the Shouting* commented as follows about Nagurski:

BRONISLAW (BRONKO) NAGURSKI *whose first name in Slavic languages means "Defender of Glory" has been recognized on most All-American college and professional teams. Here as a fullback for the Chicago Bears he talks with a spectator before a game in 1935.*
Baltimore News American

> A great many coaches, including Bernie Bierman, name Bronko Nagurski as the greatest player of all time. He was a star end, a star tackle and a crushing fullback who could pass. I believe 11 Nagurskis could beat 11 Granges or 11 Thorpes. Bronko weighed 228 pounds and he was fast and quick [11]

Immigrant groups have tended to make all kinds of tenuous claims in order to gain recognition in America. Bronko Nagurski has been claimed by Lithuanian, Polish, and other nationality groups. Nagurski was born on November 3, 1908, in Rainy River, Ontario, sixty miles from International Falls, Minnesota. Doc Spears, who coached Nagurski in college, relates how he discovered Nagurski:

> "I was driving past a farm," said Doc, "when I noticed this big, strong, farm boy plowing in a field — without a horse. I stopped to ask directions. The boy pointed — with the plow. That's how I found Bronko Nagurski."[12]

Ukrainian immigrants often lived in difficult economic circumstances and the account by Coach Spears reflects realism of the type observed among various immigrant groups. How Ukrainian Nagurski is — in the fact of his having been claimed by various other groups — can best be answered by Bronko himself as indicated in a letter to the writer on January 2, 1976: "I am Ukrainian and I speak the language well." In similar vein the baseball player Steve Souchock, now an instructor in the New York Yankee organization, wrote on December 14, 1976, "I am proud to be Ukrainian." After the height of his professional career with the Chicago Bears, Bronko Nagurski turned to wrestling and appeared in Baltimore at the 104th Regiment Armory in the late 1930's. Joe Marmash and John Malko of the Ukrainian community visited with Nagurski who was pleased to talk in Ukrainian with them. He obliged Baltimore with a victory.

Ukrainian participants in college football are so numerous that a book might be devoted to the subject. At the University of Maryland fullback and place kicker Dick Bielski, son of a Ukrainian mother (Stella Kuchtiak) and a Polish father, was an All-American in 1954 during the heyday of Coach Jim Tatum. He played tight end for the Philadelphia Eagles from 1955 to 1959 and was with both Dallas and Baltimore until concluding his playing career in 1963. Bielski joined the Colt coaching staff in 1964 and moved to the Redskins in 1973. In February, 1977, he returned to his native Baltimore as Colt coach of receivers.[13] His son Randy has been a football standout at Towson State University where his educated toe helped him to be Towson's leading scorer during a most successful season in 1976. Randy's older brother Ricky has been the starting fullback on the same team at Towson State, where both are majoring in business administration.

Sam Havrilak joined the Baltimore Colts in 1969 after rewriting most of the school, game, and career records for offense at Bucknell University in Pennsylvania, where he was born in 1947 in the steel town of Monessen. It was from Monessen in the 1920's that about 30 Ukrainian families moved to Baltimore in search of better employment. A versatile back, Havrilak saw service in rushing, receiving, and passing for the Colts and often served in clutch

Dick Bielski

Sam Havrilak
Baltimore Colts Photos

situations to pull the Colts through when other key players had suffered injuries. His biggest year for the Colts was 1972 when the Ukrainian athlete started all 14 games, making 33 catches for 571 yards and four touchdowns, including a 62-yarder. He also carried 12 times for 72 yards and two more touchdowns.[14] Today it is Dr. Sam Havrilak, who having been graduated from the University of Maryland Dental School, maintains an office on Eastern Avenue in the heart of ethnic East Baltimore.

Soccer

What baseball and football were to the earliest generations of American born Ukrainians, soccer became to those who located in or were born in America after the second world war.

By 1951 interest in soccer in the Baltimore area had built to such a level that Ukrainians playing for other teams decided to organize their own Dnipro Soccer Club. The primary organizer of the Dnipro Soccer Club was Marion Wenger, who was also a player on the early teams. In July of 1952 an official organizational meeting was held

FIRST DNIPRO TEAM, 1951-1952. Front, left to right: J. Czumak, W. Rodzikewycz, M. Wenger, M. Hrynczyschyn, M. Kaschewka, J. Harnez, I. Nischzuk. Back: P. Wojtowycz, S. Kurylas, J. Werner, M. Caryk, S. Kupchyk, R. Rudynskyj, S. Lazarko.

at the Ukrainian Citizens Club and a constitution was prepared for the Ukrainian American Sports Club — Dnipro. A roster of 12 players, most of whom had played soccer in Europe, was established and the team commenced to play in the Baltimore Unlimited Soccer League from 1952 to 1968. In the developmental years the team was always in contention for championships, often finishing in second or third place.

According to the constitution players had to be of Ukrainian ancestry. Monthly business meetings were held. Among the active committee members in the early years were Dr. Stephan Kurylas, president; Theodore Chay, treasurer; Lev Podolak, secretary; Petro Wojtowycz and Dr. T. Kurycki, managers; Mykola Turyk, equipment manager. Among players who gained high respect in Baltimore soccer circles were Marion Kaschewka, a high scoring lineman; Michailo Hrynchyschyn, goalie; Marion Wenger, fullback; Jurko Czumak, halfback; and Steve Kupchyk, who had played in Ukraine for a team called *Russalka* in Zolachiw. In 1957 Dnipro competed in the Arnold Cup Tournament in Washington, D.C., and won the cup in competition among 25 teams from Maryland and the District of Columbia.

In 1959 the original constitution was revised and Dnipro experienced a complete reorganization. While building a Junior Program initiated by Marion Wenger in 1958, adult soccer was discontinued in the years 1958-61 in order to build for the future. Petro Wojtowycz coached the Youth team (ages 10-12) and many Ukrainians participated. Ostap Stelmach was president of the Youth Program.

DNIPRO JUNIOR TEAM, Back, left to right: Coach Rick Matuszak, Bill Burdyck, Paul Wenger, Brian Rannie, Cary Callinan, Paul Dlabich, Ken Wisniewski, Rich Rohde. Front: Jim Lountouro, Jeff Kokosinski, John Rockstroh, Pete Wenger, Matt Rockstroh, Mike Manning.

In 1961 the adult program was resumed with the following officers: Walter Boyko, president; Michael Comishak, treasurer; Bohdan Wasyl, vice president; Nick Czechulin, information officer; Nick Bilokin, secretary; Nick Kondratenko, equipment manager; Alex Hanas, financial seretary; and Marion Wenger, general manager.

In 1968 Dnipro entered the Maryland Major Soccer League and displayed great progress in Baltimore's highest

Pictured above is the 1968-1969 Dnipro Soccer team, the first to play in the Maryland Major Soccer League.

The 1970-71 Dnipro Soccer Club was undefeated (12-0) and established more records in Maryland soccer competition than any other team in the history of soccer in Maryland.

soccer league by finishing in the first division. From this point the success of Dnipro is legendary in Baltimore's soccer annals. In 1970-71 the team won 12 games and lost none in the Maryland Major Soccer League ranking as the area champion of the Maryland-District of Columbia Soccer Association and also being the Baltimore-District of Columbia area national champions. As fate goes, Dnipro lost the regional championship to the Ukrainian Soccer Club of Philadelphia in the finals, 1-0. Trophies garnered during the 1970-71 season included the National Amateur Cup and two Maryland cups, the Rowland and the Stewart.

League championships by Dnipro followed in 1971-72 and 1972-73 and the succeeding three years evidenced second place finishes.

In 1976 Marion Wenger withdrew from the position of general manager of Dnipro and he was replaced by Bohdan Oleksiuk, while remaining as a consultant to the team. Prospects for the team appear promising as another Youth Program was begun in 1973-74.

The Youth team won league championships in both 1975-76 and 1976-77. In 1975-76 Youth titles included the League, State Cup, and National Regionals, while the following year city and state titles were won. The Dnipro Adult team finished third in 1976-77 and bodes to be strong under the tutelage of Bohdan Oleksiuk.

Dnipro plays its games at Patterson Park, Baltimore, on Sunday afternoons. Some games have drawn as many as 2,000 spectators.

In recognition of Dnipro's outstanding contributions to soccer the Maryland Major Soccer League two years ago organized the Dnipro Tournament in appreciation for what is now the oldest soccer club in the area of Baltimore. Tournament officials meet monthly at the Ukrainian Citizens Club, whose facilities are now operated by Dnipro. Bohdan Oleksiuk was chairman of the 1976-77 Dnipro Tournament which involved teams in the second division on down.

Last year 39 teams participated in the League in 5 divisions, involving 15-16 players per team ad playing 20 games every Sunday.

DNIPRO SOCCER STARS

Marion Wenger

Danilo Kupchyk

Walter Krywolako

Nykola Schkirka

WALTER BOYKO and MICHAEL COMISHAK, second and third from left, officers of Dnipro, are shown at a soccer banquet opening the 1970 season of Verkhovna (N.Y.), the resort facility of the Ukrainian Workingmen's Association

Among the Dnipro products who have earned varsity positions at various colleges are John Zarubajko, Maryland; Danilo Kupchyk, an All-American fullback at Maryland; John Fedarcyk, Community College of Baltimore and Loyola College; Tony Kondratenko, goalie, Maryland; Walter Krywolako, University of Baltimore; Nykola Schkirka, Maryland; and Taras Charchalis, Maryland.

Dnipro Ice Hockey Club

In October of 1976 a group of young Ukrainian Americans, perhaps inspired by the prominence of Ukrainians in professional hockey circles, decided to organize a hockey team and to participate in the Baltimore Hockey Association. Selecting Orest Hanas as manager and the same Orest Hanas and George Zelinsky as co-captains, the team requested and received financial assistance from the Dnipro Soccer Club. The Ukrainian Women's League also provided financial assistance while the players purchased their own equipment other than jerseys which were bought by Dnipro Soccer Club.

The Dnipro Hockey team got off to a torrid start in the Baltimore Hockey Association by winning the first seven games and going from there to compile a season record of 11 victories, 3 defeats, and 2 ties in winning the league championship in their initial season.

Manager Orest Hanas' team, composed mostly of students but assisted by others such as a city policeman, played their games at Northwest Ice Rink where practice sessions were also held on Fridays. To provide for expenses at the rink the team sold gold athletic shirts marked "Dnipro Ice Hockey" in blue lettering. Money was also earned by holding a Cassino Night at the Ukrainian Citizens Club.

Such activities developed an excellent *esprit de corps* among the members of the team: Orest Hanas, George Zelinsky, Andrew Hanas, Alex Lawrence, Roman Kostrubiak, Roman Stelmach, John Lye, John Gunn, Mike Carroll, David Hess, Julian Baum, Tim Toppen, Arcady Zinkewych, Milton Pniewski, Ted Wozniak, Zenon Sushko, and Warren Shepherd.

The Dnipro Hockey Team, champions of the Baltimore Hockey Association in 1977, is shown at a banquet and trophy presentation held at the Ukrainian Citizens Club.

Mike Carroll who compiled 45 goals and 38 assists for a total of 83 points was the top scorer in the league. John Gunn's 16 goals and 19 assists (35 points) was second highest for Dnipro.

To direct the team in 1977-78 competition Orest Hanas remains as manager and team captain and Alex Lawrence has been named assistant captain as Dnipro vies for another championship.

Conclusion

Ukrainian participation in lacrosse, basketball, tennis and in other sports not already mentioned has occurred primarily at the secondary school and sandlot levels and would be overly extensive if reviewed along with scholastic activity in football, baseball, and soccer. Participation would include numerous areas throughout the state with such mention as Peter Waclawsky's being one of the stalwarts of a championship soccer team for Chesapeake City High School in the early 1930's to Eugene Shmorhun's being named the scholar-athlete of the year in 1974 for his accomplishments in academics and football at Glenelg

Of the 17 players pictured on the Pioneer Baseball team in Madera, Penna., in 1939 only 3 live in the mining area today. The majority of the players are of Ukrainian heritage. Their records of organization and self-support are registered in the Baseball Hall of Fame, Cooperstown, N.Y. Two of the Ukrainians live in Baltimore now, and others have close relatives in Maryland.

Lewis Swistock

High School in Howard County. Eugene's honors included a $2,500 scholarship from the Quarterback Club of Baltimore.

Throughout the state Ukrainian participation in semi-pro sports has been shown by performances of such all around players in Baltimore softball as Milt Nikula, a yearly hitting and pitching leader in the 1940's and 1950's.

No mention of sports in the Land of Pleasant Living would be complete without mention of horse racing. Marie Kozub Herold, a daughter of Ukrainian immigrants, brought good acclaim to Ukrainians as owner and part-time trainer of Kozub King, a horse that won the Penn National race in 1974. She has owned race horses for many

Marie Kozub Herold of Abington is shown admiring champion namesake after Kozub King won the Penn National in 1974.

years at her home in Abington.

    The role of sports in the movement of Americans is shown in the life of Dr. Sam Havrilak, son of a Ukrainian foundry worker in Monessen, Pennsylvania. Through participation in college and professional football he was able to complete dental studies in Maryland and to provide the state now with professional services. The story is often repeated in similar ways, whether the names be Braase, Unitas, Tabacheck, Sandusky, Micheloson, or Moore.

* * *

LITERATURE

Traditional Ukrainian literature has often been compared to French literature because of the inflected and poetic styles of expression. Though Ukrainian literature has been read and appreciated extensively in Maryland, writers in the Ukrainian language have not been numerous. Probably the most productive of those who wrote in Ukrainian was Dr. Julian Radzykewycz, a physician whose degree in medicine was earned at Charles University, Prague, in 1927. After arriving in Maryland in 1949, Dr. Radzykewycz became head of the tuberculosis section of Springfield State Hospital, Sykesville. An author of primarily historical novels, his books included *Polkovnik (Colonel) Danylo Nechay, Polumba (Flame), and Lupuloyi Skarby (Treasures)*. At the time of his death in 1968 he left unprinted a novel about Captain John Smith, who had travelled through Ukraine in escaping.

As in most ethnic literature, poems and stories telling of a longing for the home land exist. Such tender poems are found in *Svitlo (Light) Magazine* written by Irena Waclawiw of Baltimore.

Freedom and resurrection are popular themes among noted Ukrainian writers such as Taras Shevchenko, Lesyia Ukrainka, and Ivan Franko. Roman Orest Tatchyn, a native of Baltimore and presently a doctoral candidate at Stanford University, recently completed a translation into English of Ivan Franko's lengthy poem, "Pansky Zarty" (The Noble's Joke), in which the oppressive and ignominious nature of owners of serfs is revealed during the time prior to the liberation of serfs in the Austro-Hungarian Empire in the mid-1800's. The entire poem is being published by the Shevchenko Scientific Society, a Ukrainian research group. An excerpt of Tatchyn's translation showing callousness and hope follows

CANTO XVIII FROM "PANSKY ZARTY"

Our Easter! God above-no doubting,
That ne'er in hist'ry might be found
An Easter happier or better!
From daybreak: bustling, clamor, shouting,
Into an anthill turned the town,
Aswarm with people. All together,
As one attended Mass. And when
"Chrystos voskrehse",(¹) throbbing, faded,
Then ev'ry voice with sobbing grated—
From which the church reverbed again.

It seemed that countless years we'd waited,
And fin'lly triumphed, fin'lly made it,
To see Him rise-unfettered men/
And in our hearts we felt arise
A lightness and a joy so splendid,
That each of us, it seemed, was ready
To all the firmament and skies
To sing and shout: "Our evil's ended!"
Both friend and foe were freely shaking,
Embraces, kisses, giving, taking,
And all the while the bells could burst!
And here the youths, like drunks behaving,
Cavort around and scream, dispersed,
"There's no more Master, no more slaving!
We're free, we're free, we all are free!"
And th' little kids, their elders eyeing,
Themselves go on carousing, crying,
Like darting quail-chicks o'er the lea.

And when the holy service ended,
Toward the graveyard did we stir;
'N as many hundreds as we were,—
To ground each one of us descended,
And thence, in ringing chorus, blended
That great inimitable hymn,
"Tehbeh, o Hospodeh, khvalym!"(²)
With thunder's roar went forward leaping
The lofty words' revered vibration,
But th' ending of the cantillation
Was smothered with unfettered weeping! . . .

(¹) "Christ is arisen", Ukrainian Easter hymn.
(²) Laudamus te.

Ukrainians from Maryland have produced a number of works in English, often of a scientific nature.

Dr. William Zuk, Dean of the College of Architecture of the University of Virginia, is author of *Concepts of Structure* (Van Nostrand-Reinhold, 1963) and he collaborated with Roger H. Clark in writing *Kinetic Architecture* (Von Nostrand-Reinhold, 1970). Dr. Zuk's family resides in Baltimore where he completed his master's degree at Johns Hopkins University. Professor Volodymyr Bohun-Chudyniv, now retired from the faculty of Morgan State University in Baltimore, published numerous mathematical treatises and papers, with a large amount of his work having been completed in Europe prior to his arrival here.

A talented young Ukrainian economist who has published extensively is Dr. J. Robert Malko of Baltimore whose Doctorate in economics is from Purdue University (1972). After he earned his baccalaureate degree from Loyola College in Baltimore, Dr. Malko was an assistant professor of economics at Illinois Wesleyan University from 1970 to 1974 and additionally he taught at Illinois State University (Normal, Illinois) and at the University of Wisconsin. He has served on many regulatory and advisory commissions and has served as a consultant for governmental units. He is now chief staff economist for the Wisconsin Public Service Commission.

Roman O. Tatchyn   J. Robert Malko

An important book for the analysis of the Soviet political system was compiled and edited by Michael Jaworskyj, *Soviet Political Thought — An Anthology — 1916-1961* (Johns Hopkins University Press, 1967). Dr. of works in English, often of a scientific nature.

ACTION

Dedicated to greater personal committment . . . . for God and Country

Too often we seek justice for just us.

Vol. 11 No. 3   LEAGUE OF UKRAINIAN CATHOLICS   MAY-AUG 1976

38TH ANNUAL CONVENTION

SO. ANTHRACITE COUNCIL

P.O. BOX C — McADOO, PA 18237

Mount Airy Lodge   MT. POCONO, PA.

OCTOBER 15, 16, 17, and 18th

The League of Ukrainian Catholics' Action, edited by Harry V. Makar, is published in Ellicott City, Maryland.

NEWS FROM UKRAINE
Information About the Current Struggle For National Independence and Human Rights

Vol. 2, No. 2   WINTER 1973

Strikes, Riots in Ukraine

RIOTS IN DNIPRODZERZHINSK. On June 25, over 10,000 people rioted for two days in Dniprodzerzhinsk, a city in East central Ukraine with a population of over 270,000. According to reports reaching the West, the rioters, many of whom consisted of women and children, stormed the KGB (State Security) and MVD (Ministry of Internal Affairs) buildings and inflicted great damage upon them. All political documents, passport registrations, and private files of citizens were destroyed by the rioting populace. Several rooms in the building were burned, windows were broken, doors were ripped off their hinges, and portraits of Brezhnev, Lenin and other party functionaries were torn down and mutilated. The rioters then proceeded to another building which housed Party and Komsomol (Youth League) offices and destroyed many documents. KGB and militia units were called to the scene and opened fire on the populace. Estimates of the dead and injured range from 7 dead and 80 injured to scores

Unrest In Ukraine

June: Riots break out on June 25 in Dniprodzerzhinsk in east central Ukraine after KGB arrests several youths. Thousands of persons participate, KGB headquarters are demolished, 10 people are killed, scores arrested.

September: Workers go on strike in Dnipropetrivsk. demand better living standards. 5 persons are reported killed, many wounded. At the end of September strikes, riots and demonstrations break out in several cities in Ukraine, sparked by demands for better working conditions and living standards. Several persons are reportedly killed by KGB troops.

Before Gulag Archipelago. News from Ukraine *told from Maryland of Soviet atrocities before Solzhenitsyn's famous book.*

432

Michael Kushnir of Riverdale, Maryland, who is also an artist, published extensively in the fields of political science and philosophy. Among the educators of Maryland Paul Fenchak has published in *The Ukrainian Quarterly, Slovakia, Furdek,* and *The International Migration Review.* Hlib S. Hayuk has written in the field of geography in *The Ukrainian Quarterly* and other publications. Jaroslaw Shaviak has served as a co-editor of a Ukrainian language publication, *The Ukrainian Journalist* (Newark, New Jersey).

Throughout the years Ukrainian clergymen in Maryland have contributed regularly with books, articles in journals, and newspaper accounts. A recently published book that is well-recognized among Eastern rite scholars was written by Monsignor Walter Paska, pastor of SS. Peter and Paul Ukrainian Catholic Church, Curtis Bay. The book, *Sources of Particular Law for the Ukrainian Catholic Church in the United States,* was published by the Catholic University Press in 1975. Monsignor Petro Melnyczuk, recently retired pastor of St. Michael's Ukrainian Catholic Church, published several books on theological and historical subjects and is now completeing a biography of Bishop Hryhorii Khomyshyn of Stanislaviv who died in a Kiev prison in 1945.

The successor to Msgr. Melnyczuk at St. Michael's, Rev. Ivan Dornic has edited a nationwide newspaper, *Ethnic American News,* since he established the paper in Pittsburgh, Pennsylvania, in 1972. The paper now published in Baltimore, closely reviews Slavic culture in the new world. Fr. Dornic taught Slavic languages and numerous courses in ethnic studies at the University of Pittsburgh.

POLITICS AND GOVERNMENT

The Dypsky family of Southeast Baltimore is one of the most active politically in the State of Maryland. Beginning with Philip and going to Cornell, the youngest, the Dypsky brothers have given the citizens a voting choice outside the usual machine-supported political candidates. In the years 1947, 1951 and 1971 Philip ran for councilman, Baltimore City, in unsuccessful campaigns notable for their appeals to voters to assert their views through an unfettered candidate independent of the well-oiled Democratic party organizations. Although himself a loser, he fanned the spark of political activism in the family which eventually led to the victories of Raymond to the House of Delegates and Cornell to the Senate of Maryland.

The Canton Eagle built by Philip Dypsky at age 15.

Philip C. Dypsky's background reads like that of the All-American Boy, with endless energy and boundless curiosity. He built a hang glider, then an airplane and a 12 foot rowboat which he used to board ships in the harbor so he could sell newspapers to supplement the income of a large family. Soon a sailplane was constructed by him and his cronies, it passing the licensing requirements of the Department of Commerce and flying out of Curtis-Wright Airport. Next came a 26-foot boat, designed for travel to South America. But this prospect was put aside as Philip landed a job at the Glenn L. Martin factory as an airplane mechanic in 1931. By 1943 he had become War Production Board Coordinator for the Army Division at Martin, after having studied Industrial Engineering at night at Johns Hopkins University. With the decline of Glenn L. Martin in the Baltimore area, Philip turned to the real estate business, and in 1953 opened the Ebb Tide Motel which he had built in Ocean City.

But the love of political action lured him back to Baltimore where he now runs a real estate business and operates a tavern. He and his brothers and sister, whose father Julius was born in East Galicia in the village of Nova Witkova and who was one of the original members of St. Michael's Ukrainian Greek Catholic Church when it was built in 1913, and whose mother Catherine, was born on the Eastern Shore, have weathered many a torrid campaign. Raymond A., in his down-to-earth, home-spun way, campaigned to victory as the majority choice for the House of Delegates in 1966, 1970, and 1974. He calls himself a public servant — not a politician. And the voters like his ideas of service, for they have kept him in office for over 10 years.

Cornell won the Democratic primary for the Maryland Senate in the 47th District in the year 1974, this nomination being tantamount to election to office since no other party candidate filed in the primary. In his first term as a state senator, teamed with his brother Raymond, Cornell fought the powerful interests in behalf of the small businessmen and workers.

One of the leaders of the most powerful political

Philip Dypsky, master of ceremonies during War Heroes Welcome at Glenn L. Martin Co.

Martin Photo

organizations in East Baltimore is Joseph A. Staszak, who is part Ukrainian. For many years he was an influential political figure in the Democratic Party of Maryland. He served in the Baltimore City council and from 1967 through 1974 he was a senator in Annapolis. After his retirement from the Senate, he was appointed to the Baltimore City Liquor Board.

Carl J. Yarema of Sparks on September 10, 1974, won the Democratic Party nomination in Subdistrict 5B of Baltimore County for the House of Delegates. In the general election, he lost to the Republican nominee in this generally rural section of Baltimore County. Carl's father,

John, is a prominent business man and farmer from Maryland Line who at one time ran for membership in the County Council.

Mary W. Hrabec of Chesapeake City, Cecil County, has campaigned for a position on the State Central Committee of the Democratic Pary and for the Cecil County Council.

In John G. Shmorhun of West Friendship, Ukrainians and members of other ethnic groups belonging to the Republican Party have a capable leader who in 1972 was Nationalities Chairman, Maryland Committee for the Re-election of the President. Since then he has performed similar functions in other Republican campaigns. He has also been chairman of the Ukrainian American Republican Club of Maryland.

Myron B. Kuropas, Special Assistant for Ethnic Affairs for President Ford, is a resident of Maryland. He serves on the staff of Senator Dole as legislative assistant with responsibility for liaison with the Commission on Security and Cooperation in Europe which monitors the Helsinki Accord.

The Ukrainian-American Democratic Club of Maryland, with its headquarters in Baltimore, has been issue-oriented in its appeals to the Ukrainian voters. Radicals and their supporters are rejected and a high order of preparedness and patriotism with a sense of justice toward all peoples are stressed. In the 1976 elections Ukrainian as well as English language appeals were addressed to Ukrainian voters.

Ukrainians serve on at least two governmental commissions in Maryland. Hlib S. Hayuk of Timonium is a member of the Maryland Bicentennial Commission while Mrs. Sophie Zadoretzky of Accokeek is president of the Prince George's County Library Board. Constantine Warvariv of Montgomery County since January 1974 has been the United States deputy delegate to the United Nations Educational, Scientific and Cultural Organization in Paris. A State Department employee since 1963, Mr. Warvariv won a merit award in November 1971.

For many years Ukrainian organizations and individuals have called for religious freedom, human rights extensions, and self-determination for all peoples. The Ukrainian Congress Committee of America, Maryland Branch, has been the leader in stressing the ideals traditional to America's laws and ways of life which have brought honor and greatness to its people. As a foreign policy guide, Maryland Ukrainians feel that all Americans must heed the ideas extracted below:

> The Helsinki Agreement, in upholding basic individual rights, reveals the fundamental principles under which justice must be distributed. The repressions and sufferings imposed on the citizens of Ukraine, Lithuania, and other Russian-dominated areas of Eastern Europe and Asia can be mitigated when America extends respect for its great ideals beyond patriotic recitations into the active portfolio of instructions which emanate from every member of America's government and from every representative of America's business, labor, cultural, and religious institutions.
>
> When Soviet leaders recognize that Americans proudly proclaim their ideals in all of their exchanges, transactions, negotiations and conferences, and do not by their silence or condescending politeness come as cowering and cringing creatures as they have for many ignoble and insensitive years, the stature of America will rise and with it hope for all mankind. Only then will the United States be truly qualified to be a leader of the free world and of those who would be free.

UKRAINIAN MUSIC INSTITUTE

The Ukrainian Music Institute was established in the United States by post World War II immigrants, many of them having had training in music while others were also qualified as teachers of music. They aimed for the rapid development of the musical abilities of Ukrainians so that their musical culture could continue and grow. It was hoped that through musical performances and compositions Ukrainians would be more generally accepted in the United States as a talented people and respected as a worthy contributor to a young nation's growing cultural assets.

Professor Roman Sawytsky, piano virtuoso, assembled a group of Ukrainian music teachers to form The Ukrainian Music Institute (UMI) on August 29, 1952. He was convinced that only Ukrainian schools could train Ukrainian youth to perceive and understand Ukrainian music sufficiently to guarantee its creative development and spread among the people. Professor Sawytsky organized branches of UMI in various cities in the United States, with 60 teachers and over 500 students.

UMI was incorporated on September 2, 1966, with New York City having the central offices. The program at UMI extends from 8 to 10 years, the student having the option of continuing for 2 more years in concert training. Mid-year and year-end examinations are given at each branch, with supervision by instructors from the central office. Instruction is carried on in the Ukrainian language, but students are also acquainted with English language terms. Training is primarily of Ukrainian youth, although significant numbers of non-Ukrainian young people are also enrolled.

The Baltimore branch of UMI was established on September 19, 1954. A meeting of parents was held with Professor Sawytsky in charge of organizing the branch. Professor Lidia Shaviak, a pianist and professional teacher, was appointed director. She has continued to this day in this position and also as teacher of piano and musical theory.

In its 8th school year (1961-62), UMI-Baltimore expanded to include classes in violin. Prof. Yaroslav Labka, a violinist and director of UMI in Trenton, N.J., traveled weekly to St. Michael's Ukrainian Catholic Church hall where he taught violin playing and gave lectures in theory. He did this for 7 years, to 1967-68, when he became seriously ill and had to discontinue his instructions.

In the school year 1964-65, Olenka Gerdan-Zaklynska of the UMI staff, started teaching ballet and dancing. But at the year end, June 6, 1965, somewhat over 10 students remained in her class. These courses were then discontinued.

Beginning with the school year 1959-60, UMI-Baltimore joined the National Guild of Piano Teachers. In the following 6 years, 55 UMI students who competed in Guild contests received commendations and awards for their performances. By taking part in these auditions the music of Ukrainian composers received wider recognition among diverse listeners while many teachers became acquainted with important Ukrainian musical numbers.

Besides training students in the fundamentals of music and in Ukrainian repertoires, UMI-Baltimore has produced two teachers of music. Other students of UMI have joined local Ukrainian orchestras or other ensembles.

Registration is held at the end of the school year. At this time the public is invited to hear the performance of the outgoing students in a program of Ukrainian and miscellaneous music. This demonstration of talent, the outcome of serious study and application and adherence to the discipline and devoted training of qualified teachers, has received the acclaim of the Ukrainian community which waits with high expectancy for each year's presentations.

The students of UMI have become a part of the cultural and patriotic programs given frequently by the Ukrainian community. Significant were the presentations of March 16, 1958 and December 2, 1962. In the former, local students, reinforced by a like number from New York and Philadelphia, gave a concert so outstanding as to leave an indelible impression of the competency of the participants. In the second, or Mykola Lysenko concert in honor of the Father of Ukrainian National Music, the artistic qualities of the compositions and the renditions vibrated through the very soul of each listener as he moved onto or longed for that plateau of greatest happiness atop the cool, forested Carpathians where the clouds of eternity refresh and free the human spirit.

PROFESSIONS, BUSINESS, AND INDUSTRY

Ukrainians of Maryland have been engaged in a wide variety of occupations, trades, and professions. In 1920 a survey made by Theodore Nykula of 46 individuals or families that had come to Baltimore disclosed that there were among the members 4 grocery store owners, a shoe maker, a barber, a hotel manager, a stevedore, 2 packinghouse workers, a slaughterhouse worker, 5 tailors, 11 copper plant workers, 2 Bethlehem Steel laborers, 11 Baltimore and Ohio Railroad employees, and 6 general laborers. A booklet announcing a concert for March 29, 1931, by the choir of St. Michael's Ukrainian Catholic Church contained business advertisements showing that in the Baltimore area were a tailor, a theater operator, 9 grocers, a pressing and cleaning establishment, a window cleaner, 3 confectioners, 3 barbers, a roofing and spouting installer and repairman, 2 cannery owners, and a hotel and restaurant proprietor. The employment categories of Ukrainians have gradually broadened so that from the initial factory, railroad, and shipyard labor they have gone into the trades as electricians, plumbers, carpenters, etc. and into distribution, sales, financial, clerical and office and other white collar jobs, and into the multitude of professional and governmental occupations.

Among the earliest business enterprises were taverns, for already in 1898 the Baltimore City Directory listed Simon Gregorowicz (a native of Kiev) in this activity. In 1893 he was shown as a tailor. Another immigrant, Sawery Kwoka, who came to Baltimore in the 1890's also ran a tavern, first at Ann and Aliceanna Street then at 2306-2308 Boston Street in Canton until the prohibition amendment made many beverage sales illegal. Sawery Kwoka obtained the land for St. Michael's Ukrainian Greek Catholic Church and was one of the organizers of the parish. Alexander Shandrowski who came to Baltimore in 1907 operated a shoe repair shop in Curtis Bay and also made shoes and boots for military personnel at a shop near the entrance to Fort Holabird. Later he bought a sand and gravel deposit where he made and sold concrete blocks. In addition, he acquired and sold real estate.

One of the leading Ukrainian business men in Maryland, John Yarema, arrived in Baltimore in 1930 from Michigan. His parents came from the village of Hludno,

Man-made lake is to right of swimming pool. L to R: Theodore Nykula, Casimir Jarema, Stephen Basarab, John Yarema, Mrs. Yarema and their daughter. **U.E.A.M.**

near Dynow, in a westernmost area of Ukrainian population in Galicia. Like his father who spearheaded the arrival of over 100 persons from his Ukrainian homeland to Boyne Falls, Michigan, John Yarema led many of his country men out of the laboring ranks into the operation of business proprietorships. After working in a grocery and meat market, John opened his own store in 1933 at 500 S. Macon Street in Highlandtown. Successful here, in 1938 he added a bowling alley in Towson, then the Midway Diner near Parkton. In 1945 he acquired his present business, the Maryland Line Inn, on York Road near the Pennsylvania line, after which he sold his Highlandtown store and the Midway Diner. In the meantime he had gone into farming near Hereford, then Maryland Line where he built Yarema's Lake and facilities for outdoor (and indoor) recreation, celebrations or festivals and where he set out a section for cross country motor cycle racing. This self-grounded airplane pilot who spoke only Ukrainian until the age of 9 years has extended a helping hand to many other persons, going beyond his own relatives whom he assisted to become business operators. His son Carl is a retail beverage distributor, active in Baltimore County politics and in educational matters, having been president of the Parent Teachers Association.

Casimir Jarema, brother of John Yarema, began a grocery and meat market in South Baltimore in 1936 which is still family-operated by his son Casimir at 1600 E. Clement Street. In 1956 Casimir acquired 20-mile House on Hanover Pike in Arcadia from his brother Albert. This old, historical tavern was a favorite stopover and resting point for farmers bringing produce to Baltimore City. Also on Hanover Pike is his automobile service station which is now managed by another son.

Members of another Ukrainian family, the Zacharkos, were prominent in Baltimore area retailing the first half of this century. They included grocery owners Philimon, Joseph and Michael Zacharko. Perhaps stocking the shelves of these stores were the products of the Stec & Kozub Cannery Company of Abingdon whose organizers were Frank Stec and Michael Kozub. Michael Kozub, Jr., of

Casimir Jarema, proprietor of 20-Mile House, historic tavern and inn on Hanover Road near Upperco.

Abington provides fresh meat for inhabitants of the locality from his slaughterhouse.

Fasanko Motors in downtown College Park from the early 1930's until the mid 1950's conducted a new car dealership and repair shop for Pontiac and General Motors cars. Selling new Pontiac automobiles and parts, used cars and trucks, and repair services in Annapolis is Menke's Car Store, a large dealership operated by Fred and Mary Ann (Kalowsky) Menke. Repair garages operated by Ukrainians are found in various parts of Maryland, including the Eastern Shore, Cecil County and Montgomery County. Restoring the fresh and shiny look to automobiles at the Chase Street Car Wash in downtown Baltimore are the employees of Emil O. Derey who had been an attorney in Western Ukraine. Alexander Shandrowsky, whose grandfather made walking a joy, assures the smooth movement of ocean-going ships by overseeing the functioning of their engines and complex machinery. He is a marine engineering graduate of the Calhoon MEBA Engineering School of Baltimore.

The Marenka Stainless Steel Corporation of Laurel and at other sites during its formative years has had a background of over 30 years in the fabrication and installation of stainless steel equipment in hotels, restaurants, factories, etc. And building dens to large modern school structures are companies (Zadmer Enterprises and Merando, Inc.) organized and headed by Walter Zadoretzky of Accokeek who has been in the engineering and construction business in the area since 1946. Doing business in Chesapeake City is the Hotra Construction Company, Inc.

Engaged in land surveying and engineering work for over 25 years, Alexander P. Ratych of Baltimore established his own company, APR Associates, Inc., in 1960. He is registered in the states of Maryland and Pennsylvania and has offices in Elkton and Baltimore specializing in design of roads, utilities, subdivision planning and surveying. Employing a large staff offering civil engineering and surveying services to a rapidly-growing and developing region is Leon A. Podolak and Associates of Westminster.

A Ukrainian architect, Alexander S. Timoshenko, did much of his work in later years in and near Maryland. He aided in the restoration of Lafayette Square in front of the White House in 1965, the construction of the D.C. Court of Claims building and the science building at the Naval Academy in Annapolis. In 1968 he was placed in charge of design and supervision of the Washington metropolitan subway system, part of which is already functioning. A former president of the Ukrainian Engineers Society, he organized a branch in Washington.[15]

Basil V. Nakonechny, a navel architect and senior research analyst, leads a technical group at the Naval Ship Research and Development Center in Bethesda, where he has been since 1957 and has received numerous awards. He obtained his doctorate in engineering at Catholic University. Pursuing the architectural profession with offices at 823 Park Avenue in Baltimore is John V. Markowski of Baltimore. Employed as an architect is Eugene Ratych of Long Green. Theodosius Diachok of

Takoma Park submits plans and designs for highway beautification to his superiors in the District of Columbia Highway Department.

Oles Lomacky, a structural research engineer who received his doctorate in science from Georgetown University, is employed at the Naval Research and Development Center. He resides in Silver Spring.

The National Aeronautics and Space Administration (NASA) has a Ukrainian electronic engineer, John Y. Sos, from Silver Spring who on November 9, 1972, received the Exceptional Service Medal for monitoring the technical design, development, and fabrication of the highly complex NASA Data Processing Facility at Goddard and contributing to the success of the first Earth Resources Technology Satellite. He is head of the Image Processing Branch.[16] At the same Goddard Space Flight Center, working as a mechanical engineer since 1970, is Volodymyr Werchniak of Annapolis. He has written papers in the field of fracture mechanics, fatigue, and residual stresses. A research associate and physicist at Goddard, Theodor Kostiuk, who received a doctorate of philosophy from Syracuse University, resides in Greenbelt.

Michael I. Yarymovych, until May 1977 Assistant Administrator of the Energy Research and Development Administration, was formerly chief scientific advisor in the Air Force and Director of the Advisory Group for Aerospace Research and Development, a NATO unit. He recieved his doctorate in engineering science from Columbia University in 1960. The Washington Academy of Sciences chose Dr. Yarymovych in 1964 as the outstanding young engineer for Washington. He came to the area in 1962 when he joined the National Aeronautics and Space Administration (NASA) to become Acting Director of Manned Earth Orbital Mission Studies.[17]

Vitaliy Garber succeeded Dr. Yarymovych as Assistant Administrator for Field Operations at the Energy Research and Development Administration. He is responsible for ERDA field resources, including all laboratories, and their efficient functioning through the establishment of effective strategy, policy and procedures.

Previous to this assignment, Dr. Garber headed the Army's research programs from the Pentagon.[18]

The Smithsonian Institute has on its staff specialists of unusual types, one of whom, Eugene Jarosewych of Silver Spring, studies the chemistry of meteorites, lunar samples, minerals, and rocks. He has been at the Smithsonian since 1964. Orest Ihor Diachok, Ph.D., a graduate of the University of Maryland and Georgetown University, researches and writes reports on the oceans as a staff member of the Naval Oceanographic Office. Harry Makar of Ellicott City, with the U.S. Bureau of Mines since 1965, is a supervising metallurgist in charge of research recovery work aimed at salvaging materials for reuse and preventing polution while protecting the environment for better living. He graduated from Carnegie-Mellon University.

With the Voice of America in Washington from 1955 to 1973 was a former political exile, Petro V. Odarchenko, who was sent to Alma Ata, Kazakhstan in 1930, and arrested and sent to Uralsk, Kazakhstan for 3 years in 1934. Afterwards he taught at various schools and universities in the Soviet Union, Poland, Austria, and Germany. This prolific writer on literary themes, including many articles about Lesia Ukrainka and Taras Shevchenko, now lives in Takoma Park.[19] A radio production specialist serving with the Voice of America, Stefan Maksymjuk of Takoma Park, is also a collector of Ukrainian records and author of articles on Ukrainian folk songs and ballads.

Creating a large variety of illustrations as chief illustrator at Koppers Company in Baltimore is the well-known painter, music and stage director, artist and illustrated film producer, Theodore Kuzmiw. He has drawn cartoons for and produced color films, such as "Katerina," "Suffering Mother," "Daughter of Ukraine," and "On a Sunday Morning She Dug Herbaceous Roots." These films have been accepted for use as teaching mediums for Ukrainian youth.

Michael Dankewych of Bethesda, recipient of the doctorate in philosophy from Georgetown University in Russian Area Studies in 1969, is employed as a technical information specialist in the Army Topographic Command.

Dr. Michael T. Boretsky, the senior economic policy advisor to the Secretary of Commerce, was awarded the Gold Medal in October 1971 for his economic policy contributions. He has written extensively on world trade and comparative technology, analyzing the deteriorating United States position and emphasizing particularly an area where the United States traditionally enjoyed a large surplus, that of technology-intensive goods.[20] Valentine Zabijaka of Silver Spring has been a statistician with the Unites States Census Bureau, economist with the Department of Agriculture and with the Department of Comerce. He is co-author of *Agriculture in the United States and the Soviet Union* and editor of *World Agricultural Studies*.[21]

In charge of production at Mrs. Filbert's, makers of margarine, mayonnaise, and other food products, is Alexander W. Traska, an engineer from Ellicott City. An industrial managment graduate of the University of Maryland, Myron Zuk of Baltimore is employed by Bethlehem Steel as an industrial engineer. Here, too, is Taras Charchalis, an engineer and inventor who added efficiency and quality to nail production by the invention of a nail segregator, a machine which separates nails of various sizes as well as other small objects. The patent, No. 3,670,884, was registered in June 1972.

Chief chemist and leader of the Research and Development Division at Cello Chemical Company and the recipient of a number of U.S. patents is Osyp Zinkewych of Ellicott City. He is also noted as a writer on Ukrainian political subjects and human rights, having authored *Svitlychny and Dziuba: Ukrainian Writers Under Fire*, *From a Generation of Innovators* (Ukrainian), and *Ukrainian Olympic Champions*.

A renowned chemist and educator from New Jersey, Joseph Daniel Stett was senior chemist in research and development in titanium pigments at the American Zirconium Corporation, Baltimore, during 1941-1942. Since then he has been professor of metallurgy at Rutgers

University; chairman, Department of Mechanical Engineering 1949-61; chairman, Department of Chemical Engineering, 1961-66; professor of Chemical Engineering and Director of the Graduate Program 1966-73. He is the author of publications on pigments, powder metallurgy and gas cleaning equipment for air pollution abatement and wrote the chapter on the Ukrainian language in the *Ukrainian National Association Jubilee Book, 1934.*[22]

Responsible for imparting the correct body, aroma, and taste to the beers at Carling National Breweries in Baltimore is Roman Herasymowycz, an expert brewmaster

John and Luba Rad in their Southeast Baltimore home displaying some of the articles marketed at the Columbia arts and crafts sale Nov. 21-Dec. 30, 1976.

> ## CRAFTSMANSHIP AWARD
>
> THIS IS TO CERTIFY
> THAT THE BUILDING CONGRESS & EXCHANGE
> OF BALTIMORE
> IN RECOGNITION OF EXCEPTIONAL CRAFTSMANSHIP
> SHOWN IN THE
>
> BANK TELLERS' AND BACK COUNTER, CHECK DESKS,
> HANDRAIL, AND LOGO ON WALL
>
> OF THE
>
> OAKLAND MILLS BRANCH OFFICE, COLUMBIA, MD.
> FIRST NATIONAL BANK OF MARYLAND
>
> MAKES THIS AWARD TO
>
> BOHDAN WOJTOWYCZ
>
> EMPLOYED BY
> DISPLAY CENTER, INC.
> 1970

Recognition given a Ukrainian craftsman, Bohdan Wojtowycz of Glen Burnie

who trained in Belgium in this rare specialty and who now is director of brewing.

Not only must Ukrainian art and crafts be produced by competent persons, but there should be distribution and rewards in money through appropriate outlets to sustain the creative workers. Sales are made in Baltimore at the Slovo Ukrainian Bookstore at 1828 Fleet Street operated by Clemens Babiak, by Emmanuel Prytula at the Self-reliance Federal Credit Union building at 239 South Broadway, at bazaars and events held at St. Michael's Ukrainian Catholic Church hall at 524 South Wolfe Street and at the Ukrainian Youth Home at 2301 Eastern Avenue. Ukrainian-crafted products are also sold at the annual

Ukrainian Festival, the Baltimore City Fair, and at special marketing projects such as that at Columbia Mall sponsored by "Ethnic'ly Yours" of Southeast Baltimore.

Ukrainian woodworkers and craftsmen have received recognition for their skills from formal outside statements and presentations. Bohdan Wojtowycz received a "Craftsmanship Award" from the Building Congress and Exchange of Baltimore. Turning out decorative items of many kinds out of metal, Julian Tymm of Hyattsville in this way continues his decades of experience, first as a machinist in the Navy, then in the Washington Navy Yard.

A strong contingent of Ukrainians is employed at the Library of Congress. This may be attributed to their educational qualifications and language abilities for many of them know 2 or 3 languages other than Ukrainian and English. Before his death on December 26, 1976, Ivan Dubrowsky of Silver Spring, a graduate mechanical engineer, performed as a cataloger. He is credited by American Ukrainians with the initiative and drive for the successful completion of the magnificent monument to Taras Shevchenko in Washington.[23]

Iryna (Matussevych) Fatiadi, former language instructor in Montgomery County schools and from Takoma Park, is also a cataloger. Theodosia Kichorowsky of Adelphi imparts knowledge from the Rare Books Division. A staff specialist at the Slavic Central European Division is Basil Nadraga of Silver Spring. Bohdan M. Skaskiw of Adelphi directs a cataloging unit. Bohdan Yasinsky of Silver Spring works as an assistant officer in the Preservation and Microfilming Unit.

Outside of Washington Bohdan I. Kohutiak of Mt. Rainier has been dispensing librarian services in Prince Georges County since 1967 at Marlboro, Bladensburg, and Bowie.

Significant numbers of Ukrainian farmers have settled on the Eastern Shore, particularly after World War II. Most of them specialize in raising poultry, some attaining production figures of 70,000-80,000 broilers yearly. At the upper end of the Eastern Shore in Cecil County is the Losten dairy farm and dairy, a major supplier of milk products in

The Losten Dairy and Farm at Chesapeake City
U.E.A.M. by Judy Fenchak

region. In the northern part of Baltimore County near Maryland Line are the farm lands of John Yarema, growing the grasses and grains typical of this uneven but rich terrain. Farther to the west in Howard County is the beef cattle and general farm of John Shmorhun. And not many miles from there are the bee hives of John Romanik who in his spare time tends 24 colonies of bees, each colony capable of producing 100 pounds of honey. At Abington is the horse farm of Marie Kozub Herold. The Herold farm has bred and trained horses which have raced on Maryland and other tracks.

Scattered throughout the state are other tillers of the soil and specialists concerned with animal and plant growth. In Sykesville is Michael Senkiw, an agronomist of over 25 years of Maryland experience, engaged in landscaping and production of different varieties of grasses or hybrids through cross-breeding. Searching for a cure for blackspot disease of roses is a federal government scientist, Dr. Peter Semeniuk, of the Agricultural Research Service in Beltsville. With the Service for 25 years, this native of Baltimore believes blackspot disease resistant roses are within sight. Already he has found genes of promise that eventually can become part of budwood which will be grafted on roses to produce resistant buds.[24]

Protecting the health of farm and other animals as well as of human beings are veterinarians working in the Washington area: Eugene Gill of Silver Spring who is with the Animal and Plant Health Inspection Service of the U. S. Department of Agriculture; J. N. Geleta of College Park; and Roman Baranowsky of Hyattsville, a veterinary medicine officer with the Bureau of Medicine of the Food and Drug Administration.

Maintaining and beautifying the landscape at the Baltimore City Public Schools, as well as promoting the educational processes with their nature study centers are Wolodymyr and Jaroslaw Sushko of Baltimore. Wolodymyr, a forester, is in charge of maintenance and improvements on all the city school grounds. Yaroslaw, a horticulturist within the same department, grows and transplants the seedlings, flowers, and ornamental plants which radiate the mysteries of nature to form an environment conducive to better learning. He received a Blue and Silver Award from the Mayor's BALTIMORE IS BEST COMMITTEE in December 1976.

As owner of a general law office at 2420 E. Monument Street in Baltimore, Frank Petro has for many decades given legal and business advice to the Ukrainian people and their organizations. An experienced lawyer and active in the Republican party, William M. Manko has offices in Reisterstown. His grandparents were among the organizers of the first Ukrainian Greek Catholic Church in the United States, which edifice is located in Shenandoah, Pennsylvania.

More recent members of the bar in Baltimore are Ronald J. Kwoka with offices at 10 Light Street, Roman Choma of Curtis Bay, and John G. Kruchko of the Mercantile Building who specializes in management labor law.

Serving clients for over 10 years in Elkton is Paul Podolak who is also assistant state's attorney for Cecil County. Zenon Nizankowsky who previously practiced law in Ukraine 1931-39, Poland 1940-41, U. S. Occupation Zone of Germany 1945-1949, and worked for a title insurance company before acquiring his American license, qualified as a member of the District of Columbia bar in 1956. He then became a senior specialist in European law in the Library of Congress and consultant to the Congress and other government agencies in Washington.[25] After World War II Stephen Kistulentz was a licensed lawyer in the Washington area, but later transferred to Pennsylvania. Michael Waris, Jr., of Bethesda has been practicing law with emphasis on the tax aspects in offices on Connecticut Avenue in Washington. A certificated lawyer and instructor in Ukraine, George Starosolsky has been employed in the Library of Congress where he has led the translating section of the Congressional Record Service.

The teaching professions have absorbed many Ukrainians probably because of the large number and dispersion of job openings which occur yearly in a variety of fields. The many subjects that can be taught offer opportunities outside the classroom — in government, industry, self-employment, etc. — so that a teacher need not be frozen within that profession. It is no wonder that in the largest universities and the smallest public and private schools are found Ukrainian teachers. Many Ukrainians are impelled to meet the challenge of the shortcomings which exist about Ukraine and its people in American periodicals, journals, and books as well as in school curricula, manuals, and instructions which often misguide or intone on the grossly inadequate or inaccurate.

At the University of Maryland School of Denistry, Dr. George N. Krywolap who holds a doctorate in microbiology is teaching aspiring dental and medical students. A

Explaining Ukrainian Studies at Harvard University and displaying publications of the Ukrainian Institute at Harvard during the Ukrainian Festival at Baltiore on August 27 and 28, 1977.

Baltimorean, William Zuk has gone to the University of Virginia in Charlottesville where he has become Director of Architectural Technology and Professor of Architecture. Teaching mathematics at Loyola College is George Mackiw of Pikesville. Irene Traska Terziev, formerly of Baltimore, taught German at Gettysburg College and at other institutions. At Hagerstown Junior College, Askold I. Skalsky instructs students in German language and literature. Retired as professor of mathematics from Morgan State University, Volodymyr B. Chudyniv was a highly-repsected mathematician in Ukraine and Poland. His wife, Anna, now deceased, was instructor of Russian and German and headed the Russian Department at Morgan State. Enlarging the geographical horizons and environmental concerns of students at Towson State University is Hlib S. Hayuk of the Department of Geography and Environmental Planning.

A prominent educator in the United States and in Ukraine,Mykola Stepanenko has also written and

and announced for the United States Information Agency, served as department chairman for Radio Liberty and as a free lance writer, taught at Syracuse, Rutgers, George Washington and Central Michigan University, being professor at the last-named institution. Since 1967 Dr. Stepanenko whose home is in Silver Spring has been Vice President of the Ukrainian National Republic Government in Exile.[26]

In secondary education the Ukrainians are well represented. Theodore Woronka at the time of his recent retirement was a principal in the Baltimore City schools. Iryna I. Fatiadi (Matussevych) taught languages in Montgomery County during 1962-65 and Daniel Kupchyk is teaching in the same county. Mrs. Davis, whose husband was a policeman, taught for many years in Prince Georges County, beginning in the 1930's. Nina Kalynowska Bangs has been a part-time teacher of Russian in Baltimore County and a librarian at Friends School. Paul Fenchak is a social science instructor in Baltimore County and also has taught at nearby junior and senior colleges. George Koneyak has instructed in the sciences but now is a guidance counselor. In his off-duty hours he serves Baltimore County teachers as treasurer of their credit union, Sebco Federal Credit Union, which currently operates at 4 locations. John J. Hmelnicky is an instructor at North Point Junior High School, and not far away at Sparrows Point High School is Stephen Letnaunchyn. John Zarubajko teaches industrial arts at Ridgely Junior High. Karen King of Grasonville is a library science teacher. A Howard county middle school teacher, John Romanik includes in his science programs laboratory work and field trips which study the bees which he grows. Teaching at Patapsco Middle School in Howard County is Mrs. Mary Lohr.

Elementary and middle school teachers are numerous and are spread throughout Maryland. Among those in and around Baltimore are Maria Zozulak, Charyn Marmash, Mrs. Richard Carico, Robert Bilakita, John Hrabowenski, Eleanor Lucyshyn (now in Cleveland), Dianne Strahotsky Keogh, Elsie A. (Harasym) Krauk, Basil Kowalenko, Sister

Evelyn Grudza of St. Joseph's School on Belair Road, John Havrilak, Irene Charchalis, and Roman Choma who is now an attorney at law.

Professionals in medical and related job fields among the Ukrainians in Maryland are relatively numerous. Nicholas Kohut of Baltimore is chief of dental services at Rosewood State Hospital. Samuel C. Havrilak, graduate of the University of Maryland Dental School and former Colt football player, now practices dentistry in Towson and in the center of the Ukrainian community in East Baltimore. In this same sector are Nicholas Lasijczuk and Nicholas Ilchyshyn. Michael Oristian has his dental office in nearby Washington, while Yaromyr Oryskewych has two offices, one in Silver Spring and the other in Waldorf. Treating dental patients at Oxon Hill is Vincent J. Zugay who trained at the University of Maryland Dental School.

Physicians in the Baltimore area include Stephen Toms and Andriy Lemishka, a general practioner, who is on the staff of Church Home and Hospital. Victor R. Hrehorovich is director of the Department of Medicine for the South Baltimore General Hospital and member of the faculty of the University of Maryland School of Medicine. A graduate of the Univeristy of Maryland Medical School who also trained at Mercy Hospital is Daniel Joseph Fall, now a specialist in internal medicine at Ann Arbor, Michigan. His sister, Evelyn, is a medical technologist in Baltimore. Tracking down the elusive causer of illness and performing research at Johns Hopkins Hospital is biologist Lydia Czumak. Practicing medicine in Silver Spring is Steven Oristian and in Salisbury on the Eastern Shore is Stephen Tymkiw who is on the staff of the Peninsula General Hospital. Associated, for many years, with Sinai Hospital in Baltimore is Dr. Dmytro Kostrubiak.

Earlier physicians in Maryland, now deceased, were Michael Zawalniak of Mt. Wilson State Hospital Center, Myron Nyzankiwsky, resident physician of Springfield Hospital Center, Yaroslaw Chmilewsky of the Henryton Hospital Center, and Julian Radzykewycz who headed the tuberculosis section of the Springfield Hospital Center.

New pharmacists filling prescriptions in Maryland are Wasyl Tymiuk of Baltimore and Martha Procinsky of

Silver Spring, and among the veteran pharmacists is Myron Dobrowolsky of Clarksville.

Many Ukrainian graduates of Maryland and other nursing schools are engaged in their professions in Maryland and elsewhere. Tessie (Matachek) Black, after graduating from Sinai Hospital in Baltimore, became Assistant Superintendent of Nursing Services at that hospital and later was in charge of all nursing services at Bon Secours Hospital. Presently she has a high administrative position in Saudi Arabia. Administrator at the Gould Convalesarium in Baltimore is Nadia Bayda Kachnowich. Others who graduated as nurses are Mary Prymak, Stephanie Rakoczy, Connie Boyko, Catherine Posko, and Miss Luckton who worked as a surgical nurse on heart operations at Johns Hopkins with the famous Dr. Blalock.

The last two White House physicians, Brigadier General Walter R. Tkach and Rear Admiral William M. Lukash, are Ukrainian-descended Americans. Dr. Tkach was assistant physician to President Eisenhower from 1953 to 1961 and physician to President Nixon from 1968 to 1974. He is the holder of the Legion of Merit, Air Medal, and the US Air Force Commendation Medal and was stationed at Andrews Air Force Base.[27] Dr. Lukash was head of Gastro-Enterology at the US Navy Hospital, Bethesda, in 1966 and 1967, White House physician and assistant physician to President Nixon 1967 to 1974, physician to President Ford 1974-1976, and now physician to President Carter.[28]

ORGANIZATIONS
Ukrainian American Citizens Club and Ukrainian National Home

The rigors of the American labor scene at the turn of the century led Ukrainians, as others, to organize mutual aid societies. Employed as laborers by oil, sugar, copper, and fertilizer processing plants, they toiled in an era when labor saving devices were unknown and as a result some incurred hernias, back ailments, and the like.

The Ukrainian Citizens Club, 3101 O'Donnell Street, Baltimore

As the new Americans began to purchase properties, with a few establishing businesses, the desire to transmit certain life styles to their children led them to establish the Ukrainian American Citizens Club and the Ukrainian National Home in East Baltimore. Organizers of the two associated groups were Peter Marmash, president; Theodore Nykula, vice president; George Ewanowicz, secretary; Andrew Peltz, financial secretary; Joseph Svobojohn, Joseph Prymak, Jacob Semenkow, John Rakochy and Theodore Nykula, cultural committee members; Joseph Prymak, Michael Krist, and Alexander Ewachiw, house committee members.

The Ukrainian American Citizens Club, Inc., and the Ukrainian National Home, Inc., were organized on February 23, 1929; the Ukrainian National Home was established on December 20, 1931. Objectives of all groups in addition to promoting traditional American values were to "participate in programs which were beneficial to the Community, City, State, and Nation in such a manner as to reflect credit upon members of the groups and upon the Ukrainian American peoples." Housed originally at 2903 O'Donnell Street in a rented store building, the groups were able by 1931 to own a corner property at 3101 O'Donnell Street, which structure became known as the Ukrainian National Home. This building was completely renovated by members, some of whom were carpenters and plumbers. Working with the investments of members, the mortgage was paid within two years and debts (interest free) were paid to members within the following two years.

It was at the Ukrainian National Home, 3101 O'Donnell Street, that extensive programs in Ukrainian language, history, geography, and culture began to be held under the aegis of instructor Andrew Peltz, the first finanical secretary. Later Joseph Svobojohn came from Detroit to be a teacher. Mr. Svobojohn organized a choir of 26 members that came to be known as the Ukrainian American Citizens Club Choir, which in addition to serving the community, presented programs for branches of the Knights of Columbus, the Peabody Conservatory of Music, and for radio station WCBM. Too, the choir often joined with the Lithuanian American community in observing Lithuanian Independence Day.

The Vasile Avramenko School of Ukrainian Dancing *taught many Ukrainian Americans the techniques of dancing in the 1930's.*

Additionally the Ukrainian National home provided facilities for instructional programs given by the Vasile Avramenko School of Ukrainian Dancing. The Baltimore dancers of the Avramenko School participated at half time for the Baltimore Colts when the first try was made to bring professional football to Baltimore. The most noteworthy invitation came to participate in egg hunting and dancing on the White House lawn in Washington.

The Ukrainian American softball team was managed by Joseph Marmash and in its first year made the state play-offs, losing in the second round. The team won the Ukrainian Eastern States championship in Philadelphia in 1939.

In the field of dramatics, with Mrs. George Ewanowicz being a leading actress, such plays as *Natalka Poltavka* were produced before overflow audiences.

Throughout the years the Ukrainian American Citizens Club aided the community in may ways — helping with the processing of naturalization papers, providing impetus for political rallies, and serving as a meeting place for developing groups such as the Ukrainian Youth League of North America. Here, too, refugees to America were aided after the throes of World War II. The Citizens Club building was utilized as temporary living quarters for displaced persons by installing cots for barracks-type accommodations.

The Citizens Club has long been a gathering place for banquets, song fests, and general socializing among several generations. Those who had an inadequate command of English could find rapport among co-linguists at the Citizens Club; and, too, they could sharpen their English there by associating with those who knew both Ukrainian and English well.

Whatever the functions, funds for programs were obtained primarily from membership dues, private donations, admissions from plays, etc., dinners prepared by associated ladies, semi-yearly dances, shore parties, Christmas carolling ventures, and from profits from the bar which was open on weekends.

During the years of the economic depression in the 1930's Ukrainian community solidarity improved because of the efforts of members of the Citizens Club. Among the leaders of the depression era were Andrew Peltz, financial secretary; George Ewanowicz, secretary; Theodore Nykula, a productive leader in program development and maintenance until today; John Malko, long-time treasurer of the organization; and Joseph Marmash, who has worked for many Ukrainian causes since his early teens. He aided many immigrants by translating American newspapers for them and by completing citizenship applications, etc. Too, he made arrangements for many cultural programs, such as, the one by the internationally known Ukrainian Chorus directed by Prof. Alexander Koshetz that appeared in Baltimore in the 1930's. In 1939 Mr. Marmash was elected president of the Ukrainian National Home and the Ukrainian American Citizens Club, a position he holds to this day. In addition to serving as parade chairman he was also chairman of the All Nations Day, a multi-ethnic event held yearly at Gwynn Oak Park in the 1940's and 1950's.

Plast: Ukrainian Scouting Organization

Plast is a Ukrainian youth organization closely connected with the principles of scouting. It was founded in 1911 in Western Ukraine and is only three years younger than the English Boy Scouts and six months younger than the Boy Scouts of America. Plast expanded the basic scouting ideals of R.S. Baden-Powell by adding Ukrainian heritage studies and arts to its program. For these additions it was restricted and finally outlawed in 1930 by the Polish government which occupied western Ukraine between the world wars. Plast is proscribed in Soviet Ukraine today.

With an influx of Ukrainians to America after World War II Ukrainian scouts began to develop organizations here. In America and in all free countries Ukrainian scouting leaders began inculcating scouts with an appreciation for historical and cultural inheritances. Plast began in the United States in the early 1950's.

The Baltimore Branch had its start in the spring of 1950 when four senior girl scouts, Chrystyna Kotyk, Olha Charchalis, Lida Chilewska, and Nadia Bilan, newly arrived with their families from Europe, formed two girl scout patrols, *Kluch Zhurawliw* (Flock of Cranes) and *Mewy* (Sea Gulls), continuing work they performed in girl scout

Members of Plast in Baltimore in 1950.
Oksana Koropeckyj

Plast participating in Scout-O-Sphere at Timonium, Maryland, in 1970.
U.E.A.M.

troops in displaced persons camps in western Europe. In the summer of 1950 two boy scout patrols, *Sokoly* (Falcons) and *Karpatski Wedmedi* (Carpathian Bears), were formed by the senior scouts Mykhajlo Cilyk and Stepan Chorpita. On September 21, 1950, the first general meeting was held and Scoutmaster Anna Mryc was elected first president. By the end of the year Baltimore Plast numbered 40 members.

The basic work of Plast is done at regular weekly meetings of patrols. Meetings are held in the Selfreliance Building and in a building of St. Michael's Ukrainian Catholic Church. Each year a Plast spring rally is held, often jointly with scouts from nearby Washington and Philadelphia. Numerous scouts participate in Plast summer camps where they obtain leadership training. Baltimore Plast scouts also participate in many cultural activities of their Ukrainian community as well as in general events in Baltimore and elsewhere in Maryland. They have won several trophies for their achievements and exhibits of folk art. In 1975 Baltimore Plast had 84 members, including Plast Birdies, a pre-school introductory patrol of seven members.

Among present leaders of Plast in Baltimore are Andrew Lemishka, M.D., Olena Pisetzky, Teofil Popowych, Petro Wojtowycz, Oksana and Mykola Koropeckyj, Nadia Zinkewych, Olha Sushko, Iljana Shaviak, and Olha Korz. Many of these leaders served for several years as elected presidents of *stanychnys*. Their proteges now serve as leaders also. In a Ukrainian tradition a *pysanka* (Ukrainian Easter egg) is a medium through which joyful greetings are extended to friends. A group of

Amy Carter

Thank you for writing to me. It's fun living in the White House, and I'm glad you are my friend.

Amy Carter

Plast members displayed friendship during the Easter season of 1977 by sending President Carter's daughter Amy a *pysanka*. A heartfelt message of appreciation was received in turn by the senders from Amy Carter.

Organization for the Defense of Four Freedoms for Ukraine, Inc.

The Organization for the Defense of Four Freedoms for Ukraine, Inc., was established in Baltimore in 1950. This branch, No. 14, of ODFFU acts in every lawful way to bring the Four Freedoms to the Ukrainian people and to further the associated concepts and procedures presented by President Franklin D. Roosevelt during a critical period of world history. In his State of the Union Message of January 6, 1941, and later embodied in the Atlantic Charter, President Roosevelt appealed for freedom of speech and expression, freedom to worship God, freedom from want, and freedom from fear everywhere in the world.

The forceful occupation of Ukraine after World War II demanded counter political and ideological forces directed by a strong, central organization composed of individuals not only informed about the enemy and its goals and tactics, but hardened by experience and direct confrontations.

Branch No. 14 was organized at a general meeting held in Curtis Bay on May 14, 1950, called by Dr. Yaroslav Bernardin of Baltimore. Selected as officers were Wolodymyr Ilnytsky, president; Ivan Matskula, vice-president; Dr. Bernadin, secretary; Lev Yuzheniw, membership director; Stepan Scherbak, financial secretary; Klym Babiak, assistant financial secretary; Oleksander Hanas, Stepan Maksymovich, and Petro Woytowycz, executive board members; and Julian Monastersky, Theodore Kolodnitsky, and Theodore Charyk, control commission members.

In its operations ODFFU has worked closely with the local branch of Ukrainian Youth in America. ODFFU's members and its choir have participated in may patriotic and cultural programs. On the governing board for 1973-77 are: Wolodymyr Stelmach, president; Theodore Kuzmiw,

Governing Board members of the Organization for the Defense of Four Freedoms for Ukraine, Inc., Baltimore Branch

vice-president; Wasyl Tymiuk, secretary; Omelan Monastersky, financial secretary; Andriy Chorney, political secretary; Adam Cizdyn, culture and education; Safron Hankewich and Mykola Turyk, controllers; Harry Wojtowycz, membership; John Hrytskiwsky, Stepan Iwashko, Bohdan Macuk, Wasyl Werney, Petro Werny, members.

The Ukrainian American Youth Association

The Ukrainian American Youth Association or SUM (*Soyuz Ukrainskoi Molodi*) is dedicated to fostering the Ukrainian heritage among its members and the American public. Another objective is to acquaint people in the free world about Ukraine's present struggle for freedom. SUM was organized in the United States in 1949 through the impetus of post-World War II immigrants with branches having been established in most larger Ukrainian communities. Headquarters of the organization are in New York City.

SUM originated in Baltimore on January 8, 1950, on which date Bohdan Wojtowycz, Theodore Caryk and Iwan Susj directed its formation. Ostap Stelmach was elected

Ukrainian American Youth Association Building, Baltimore
Judy Fenchak

first president of the Baltimore group that was officially formed on January 20. Initially the branch had 32 members in the age category of eighteen to thirty-five. In 1952 Anna Stelmach organized a division of younger members within the age bracket of seven to seventeen. Since 1956 Theodore Kuzmiw has been the leader of the younger division. About 52 members belong to the younger group. The Parents Committee, headed by Andrey Chorney and Anna Cizdyn, provides maintenance services and financial resources. During the formulative stage of the Ukrainian American Youth Association meetings were held in the hall of St. Michael's Ukrainian Catholic Church, but in 1966 SUM acquired a home of its own at 2301 Eastern Avenue, across from Patterson Park. The renovated hall has been made accessible for meetings and other functions of many other Ukrainian groups.

SUM maintains a wide spectrum of activities in Baltimore. It has a dancing unit, a mandolin ensemble, and an amateur theatrical group. Courses in ceramics and wood carving have been offered and academic programs have been sponsored. Groups from SUM have appeared before the wider Baltimore audiences at City Fairs, colleges, and public schools. The drama group stages Ukrainian plays. Young members attend SUM summer camp at Ellenville,

Members of SUM appear in this photo in 1950.
Adam Cizdyn

Baltimore group at SUM summer camp, Ellenville, New York, in 1973.
Adam Cizdyn

New York, where opportunities abound to participate in sports programs and various cultural activities.

Ukrainian American Citizens Club Women's Auxiliary

An early and productive women's organization was the Ukrainian American Citizens Club Women's Auxiliary. Their activities were very beneficial from the 1930's to the 1960's, after which time they yielded to newer groups. In addition to preparing benefit fund-raising dinners for needy families the group complemented patriotic endeavors by sponsoring banquets for returning American servicemen, etc. Presidents of the Auxiliary were Elizabeth Podhorniak, Anna Peltz, and Helen Marmash. Kathryn Evanowicz served as secretary and Julia Malko Richmond was treasurer. Among the members were Katheryn Nykula, Anna Semenkow, Alexandra Ewanowicz, Anna Smolak, Helen Malko, Mary Taras, Agnes Marmash, and Mary Semenkow.

Ukrainian National Women's League of America (UNWLA)

The largest of current Ukrainian women's groups is the Ukrainian National Women's League of America which has two branches in Baltimore, Nos. 59 and 115. The origins of UNWLA go back to 1925 when three groups in New York City (Women's Community, Women's Aid, and Ukrainian Women's League of America) formed the new central group — UNWLA — with the objectives "to organize women of Ukrainian birth and extraction throughout America and bring them into relations of mutual helpfulness, to further social, civic, cultural knowledge, domestic science, welfare work, and make combined actions possible when deemed advisable." There are now 115 branches in America with national headquarters in Philadelphia. A monthly journal, *Our Life*, is published and the organization has been a member of the National Council of Women and has participated in several conferences of the International Council of Women.

Branch 59 was founded in 1940 by Julia Maniowsky. During World War II the group sold war bonds, helped

An exhibit of a Ukrainian home at All Nations Day Festival, Baltimore, 1956. The UNWLA Branch 59 won top honors in the competition.   *U.E.A.M.*

Executive members of UNWLA Branch No. 59, Baltimore, 1967
U.E.A.M.

needy families, endeavored to increase war production, and helped in elevating national morale. After the war assistance was given to Ukrainian refugees. With the coming of refugees membership of the branch increased to

70 and activities multiplied. Presently the branch contributes financially to an elderly Ukrainian refugee woman in Germany and donates to two needy students in Brazil. Funds were raised for earthquake victims in Yugoslavia, among whom were many Ukrainians. The branch is active in cultural activities throughout Maryland, while also having directed much effort toward alleviating intolerable conditions among Ukrainian women in Soviet prisons.

In thirty-six years the presidents of Branch 59 have been Julia Maniowsky, Rosalia Ewachiw, Valentyna Luciw, Lidia Lemishka, Anna Samutyn, and Anna Stelmach. Maria Bulawka is the current president.

In 1968 a group of younger Ukrainian American women, led by Irene Traska, Marie Ulanowicz and Maria Poliszczuk, organized a Junior Section of Branch 59. In 1975 this group became Branch No. 115 of the national organization. Its current membership is 17 ladies, most of whom are professionals in education and the sciences. They combine full time work with the responsibilities of the home. One of their recent developments is the starting of a Ukrainian nursery. Another project, partly funded by the Maryland Bicentennial Commission, was the completion of a photographic display of Ukrainian life, culture, history, etc., which is presented at public functions. Lydia Czumak supervised this project. Maria O. Poliszczuk and Lydia Czumak were the first two presidents and Luba Knysh is president now.

Women's Association of the Organization for the Defense of Four Freedoms for Ukraine

In 1973 a Baltimore Branch of the Women's Association of the Organization for the Defense of Four Freedoms for Ukraine was founded. Activities of this group are weighted toward attaining freedom for Ukraine. The women hope to abet the freedom movement through such actions as peaceful demonstrations and dissemination of information about the deplorable state of human rights in Soviet Ukraine. Another field of action is to maintain the Ukrainian American Youth Association Building in

Baltimore and to materially support the youth organization. Seventeen members belonged to this organization in 1976. Maria Stelmach, one of the founders, is its president.

Selfreliance Organizations

In Baltimore there are three Selfreliance organizations, closely connected but having separate functions, viz., the Selfreliance Association of American Ukrainians, Inc., the Selfreliance Baltimore Federal Credit Union, Inc., and the Selfreliance Holding Corporation. Their primary objectives are the promotion of thrift and the promotion of home and property ownership among members while bettering Ukrainian communities.

The Selfreliance Association of American Ukrainians is the oldest of the entities. Established in 1950 through the efforts of the late Dr. Yaroslaw Chmilewsky, it is one of the many branches which came into existence in Ukrainian communities in the 1950's. With immigrants feeling a need to have centers where they could look for information and help in the face of linguistic and economic difficulties, Selfreliance organizations took root and grew in the spirit of the name.

The original Selfreliance Association was founded in New York City in 1947. By 1956 a total of 19 branches existed throughout the country. The association in New York became the national headquarters. The charter describes the Selfreliance Association as a non-partisan organization of a national, social, cultural, educational, economic, and benevolent character.

For the past 26 years the activities of the Baltimore Selfreliance Association followed the guidelines of the charter. Special attention was placed on benevolent work. Clothing, books in the Ukrainian language, and money were collected and distributed to needy Ukrainians in Maryland as well as in Brazil, Poland, Yugoslavia, et al. This was accomplished through campaigns such as People of Good Will and From Children to Children that were conducted by humanitarian workers such as Emmanuel Prytula, Ostap Charchalis, Danylo Pisetzky, Walter Hanas, Semen Poliszczuk, and Petro Wojtowycz.

FROM CHILDREN TO CHILDREN. Youngsters at the Baltimore Selfreliance prepared packages for Ukrainian children in Brazil in fall of 1956. *U.E.A.M.*

The Baltimore Selfreliance nurtured the formation of the Selfreliance Federal Credit Union. Members of Selfreliance in 1957 acquired a building located at 239 South Broadway in East Baltimore, listing the title in the name of Selfreliance Holding Corporation. The building serves as home of the three organizations. Other Ukrainian groups utilize its facilities for lectures, art displays, Ukrainian classes, and meetings. Chairman of the Selfreliance Association in 1976 was Emmanuel Prytula and Maria Charhalis was the secretary.

The Selfreliance Baltimore Credit Union was established on September 12, 1955, and it is a cooperative non-profit organization which works closely with the Selfreliance Association of American Ukrainians. Only members of the latter can belong to the Credit Union.

The charter of the Credit Union was obtained in October, 1956, in concurrence with the Federal Credit Union Act. From its beginnings in 1956 with 73 members and $1,643.58 in assets, the Credit Union has grown to 488 members and $736,257.60 in assets. The 1956 dividend was 2%; by December of 1976 it was 6.5%. "Our goal and expectation of one million dollars in assets is now not a fantasy but simply a reachable star within economic powers of a highly responsible Ukrainian community," maintains its president, Dr. Emil Derey.[31]

In serving the Ukrainian communities of Maryland and Washington, D.C., the Credit Union has granted 1,401 loans totalling more than $2,000,000. In 1974 the Credit Union earned a National Credit Union Administration Thrift Honor Award for its success in stimulating savings among small savers and for its excellent financial operations.

The firm is managed by a board of directors and by committees of members. In 1976 officers were Dr. Emil Derey, president; Stanley Stelmach, vice president; Theodore Chay, treasurer; Emmanuel Prytula, chairman of the Credit Committee; and Walter Romanowsky, chairman of the Supervisory Committee. Other officers and committee members were Walter Hanas, Anna Samutyn, Oksana Kalynowsky, Anatole Bulawka, Bohdan Macuk, Eugene Snihura, Wolodymyr Sushko, Peter Samutyn, and Wasyl Palijczuk.

Board of Directors and Committees — Baltimore Selfreliance Federal Credit Union — 1976. *Dr. Emil Derey*

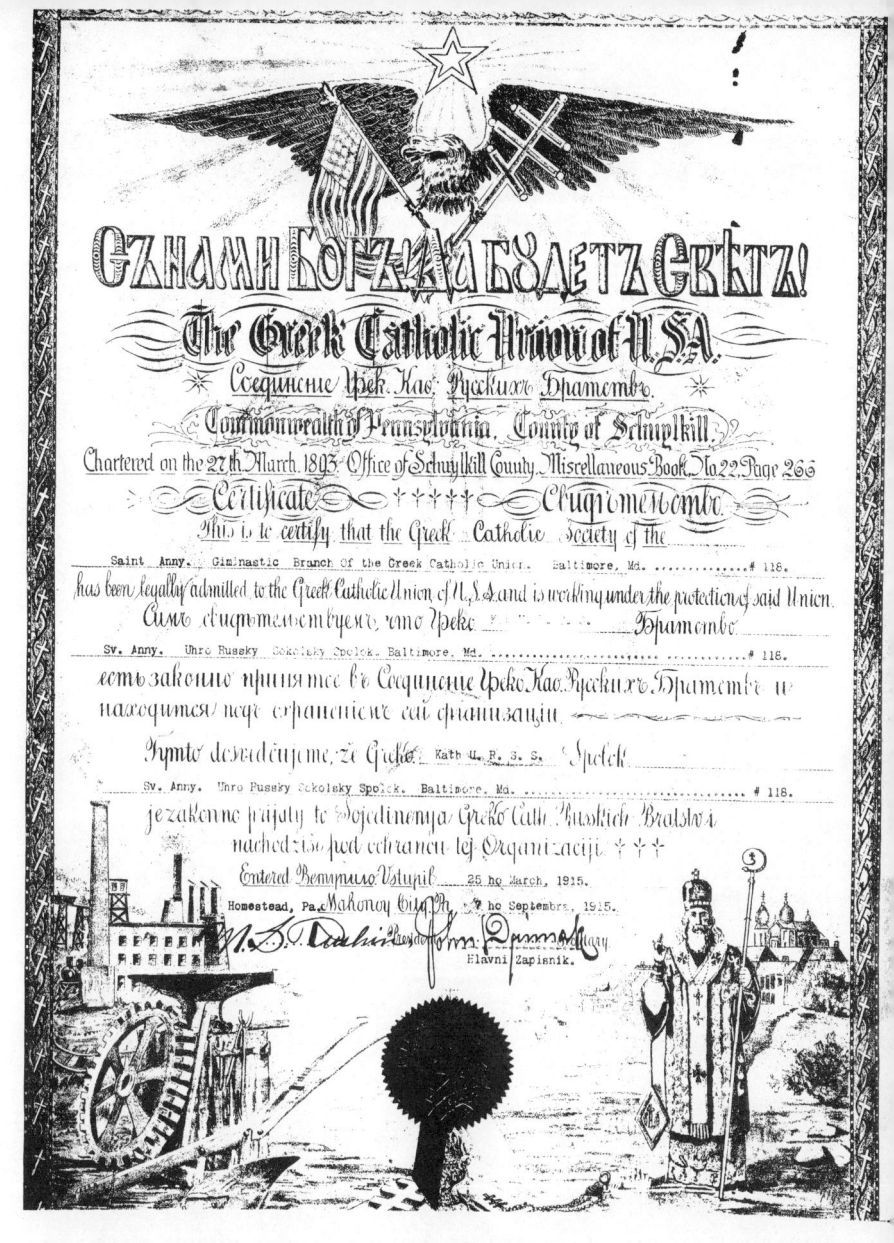

St. Anne's Sokol or Gymanstic Branch No. 118 of *Sojedinenya (Greek Catholic Union of U.S.A.)* was organized on March 25, 1915 as indicated on the certificate in possession of St. Michael's Ukrainian Catholic Church, Baltimore.

Sojedinenya (Greek Catholic Union of the U.S.A.)

The first fraternal organization of immigrants from Ukraine in America was *Sojedinenya* (Greek Catholic Union of the United States), founded in Pittsburgh in 1892.

The St. Andrew Lodge began in Baltimore in 1907 with John Batryn as president. By 1908 over 80 members belonged. For many years meetings and conferences were held in the hall of St. Michael's Ukrainian Catholic Church. After John Batryn's death his daughter, Anna R. Luckton, served *Sojedinenya* for 33 years. In 1977 the lodge's activities focus primarily on handling insurance matters though the publications of the organization, *The Greek Catholic Messenger* and a yearly *Almanac*, along with books and programs, continue to be influential in Maryland. Among the founders in Baltimore were John Warga, Makary Terpak, and Ihnaty Ladna. Today a newer Lodge No. 986 has about 56 members under President Andrew McDeshen, Jr., and Secretary-Treasurer Ed McDeshen. A lodge exists in the Beltsville area of Maryland, too.

The Ukrainian National Association

Oldest, largest, and most influential of the distinctively Ukrainian fraternal insurance groups is the Ukrainian National Association, founded in 1894 in Shamokin, Pennsylvania, and relocated in Jersey City in 1907. The Association now has a 15-story office building located in Jersey City. In recent years several leading stock brokerage firms have abandoned their Wall Street locations in favor of establishing offices in the building of the U.N.A. In 83 years this largest Ukrainian fraternal organization in the free world has enrolled 90,000 members and established 460 branches throughout twenty-nine states and seven Canadian provinces. At present $160,000,000 of insurance is in force and assets total $41,000,000.

A close affinity exists between the Ukrainian National Association and Ukrainian American activities, with the U.N.A. being a patron of cultural and religious activities — supporting heritage schools, granting scholarships, and providing loans for the construction of churches, homes, halls, etc. Since 1893 the Association has published *Svoboda* (Liberty), the oldest Ukrainian language newspaper in the free world along with the *Ukrainian*

U.N.A. Plaza. A new 15-story office building of the Ukrainian National Association, Jersey City.

U.E.A.M.

(Svoboda) Weekly in English as well as a children's journal, *Veselka (Rainbow).*

U.N.A. has also published many books in both the Ukrainian and English languages. Throughout the years the group has championed the cause of freedom for Ukraine. Financial help was often given at times of disaster, e.g., earthquakes in Yugoslavia where numerous Ukrainians live; Ukrainian war refugees; flood victims in Wilkes-Barre and Johnstown, Pennsylvania. The Association owns a splendidly developed 500-acre estate near Kerhonkson, New York, where cultural courses, sports tournaments, and children's camps are held, among other activities. The supreme officers of the U.N.A. have been outstanding Ukrainian American leaders, such as, Rev. Gregory Hrushka, the founder, Constantine Krychiv, Dmytro Kapitula, Semen Yadlowsky, Nicholas Murashko, and Dmytro Halychyn. Joseph Lesawyer is currently president of U.N.A.

In Maryland there are eight branches and 2,220

members. Six branches are in Baltimore — 3 in East Baltimore and 3 in Curtis Bay. These groups were formed between 1903 (Branch No. 81, Curtis Bay) and 1926 (Branch No. 337, East Baltimore). Some of the founders and early leaders were Josyf Kulchycky, Petro Semenkiw, Mykola Durdela, Mykhajlo Kluchka, Mykola Kapustiy, Maria Bukata, Alexander Shadrowsky, Jacob Semenkiw, Anna Wojtowych, Josyf Semenkiw, Catherine Miskiw, and Theodora Semenkiw.

The largest and most active Baltimore Branch has been No. 320, also known as the Brotherhood of the Holy Trinity. It was formed in 1912 with 24 members. Today it has 345 members. Its activities encompass financial contributions to various civic and religious organizations. After World War II over a thousand dollars was contributed to the Shevchenko Scientific Society in Sarcellas, France, and to the Ukrainian Congress Committee of America, Inc., in New York City. Also, the United Ukrainian American Relief Committee and the local Ukrainian churches and other organizations received contributions. Books on Ukraine were presented to the Enoch Pratt Free Library, the Eisenhower Library of Johns Hopkins University, and the libraries of the University of Maryland, Mt. St. Agnes

John Malko (right) and Emil Derey lead Ukrainian group at All Nations Day Festival in Baltimore in 1953.
U.E.A.M. Collection

College, Notre Dame College, Loyola College, et al. One of the productive leaders of this branch has been John Malko, secretary for 25 years and organizer of 450 members. He has been active in the Maryland-District of Columbia Fraternal Congress as an officer and has aided other local and national fraternal organizations in addition to participating in conventions. Another steady leader for the U.N.A. has been Emmanuel Prytula of Branch No. 337.

Maryland branches and their presidents and secretaries are as follow:

Branch No., Location   President, Secretary
15 - Silver Spring   Bohdan Yasinsky, Ostap Zynjuk
55 - Curtis Bay   Mykhajlo Smoljak, Adam Cizdyn
81 - Curtis Bay   Petro Zozulak, Anton Lukianczuk
148 - East Baltimore   Teresa Kolotski, Pauline Schneider
260 - Berlin   Petro Korzaniwsky, Wasyl Macuk
  (Eastern Shore)
290 - Curtis Bay   Mykhajlo Choma, Mychajlyna Evanuk
320 - East Baltimore   Theodore Chay, John Malko
337 - East Baltimore   Ostap Stelmach, Emmanuel Prytula

In 1959 all branches located in Maryland, Washington, D.C., and Virginia were grouped into a district. Present district officers are Theodore Chay, president; Ostap Zynjuk, secretary, and John Malko, treasurer.

The Ukrainian Workingmen's Association

In October, 1910, the Ukrainian Workingmen's Association was founded in Scranton, Pennsylvania. It now has 25,000 members organized in 340 branches in the United States and Canada. Publications of the U.W.A. are *Narodna Volya (The People's Will)* and a quarterly journal that is recognized for the excellence of its quality and style, *Forum: A Ukrainian Review.* The Association has regularly responded to the needs of the Ukrainian people by generously supporting causes that exhort the betterment of Ukrainians both here and abroad. It avidly supports the Ukrainian Studies Program at Harvard University, both monetarily and promotionally by providing extensive coverage of events at Harvard in *Narodna Volya.* U.W.A.

sponsors various cultural and educational events of which many occur at the Association's summer resort in Glen Spey, New York. For senior members a home for the aged is maintained.

Rev. Iwan Adran was the first president of the Ukrainian Workingmen's Association. The current president, Iwan Oleksyn, succeeded Antin Batiuk in 1973, the latter retiring after 14 years of service as president. Theodore Mynyk has had a distinguished career as secretary for 47 years while Ed Popil has been treasurer for many years.

In Maryland U.W.A. has three branches: No. 65 in Baltimore, No. 68 in Glen Burnie, and No. 76 in Silver Spring. The largest, No. 65, is known as the Taras Shevchenko Branch, was founded by Stefan Topolnick on July 16, 1911, with seven members. In 1950 it had 150 members. Officers of this branch during its history of 66 years have been Theodore Nykula, Theodore Kaszak, Andriy Peltz, and Mykola Woznyj. Theodore Nykula is serving his third term as president in his 51 years of service. Wolodymyr Boyko is secretary. The contributions of Theodore Nykula to the U.W.A. and to the Ukrainian community are too numerous to mention in organizational and promotional endeavors.

The Providence Association of the Ukrainian Catholics in America

The Providence Association of Ukrainian Catholics in America was founded in 1912 under the leadership of Soter S. Ortynsky, the first Ukrainian Bishop in the United States. Each Metropolitan of the Ukrainian Catholic Church in the United States is the Supreme Protector of the Association.

In addition to providing various types of insurance, the Association has as an aim the strengthening of the religious and national lives of Ukrainian Americans. Programs and activities are promoted through the pages of its newspaper, *America*, printed in both English and Ukrainian.

The Providence Association also contributes financial support to many Ukrainian religious and lay institutions.

Its home office is located in Philadelphia near to the Ukrainian Cathedral wherein its founder, Bishop Soter Ortynsky, is interred.

The Providence Association has two branches in Baltimore, Nos. 66 and 87. No. 66, East Baltimore, is the larger and is known as the Brotherhood of SS. Apostles Peter and Paul. It was established on June 1, 1929, by the then pastor of St. Michael's Church, Rev. Mykhajlo Koltucky. Early leaders of the group included Petro Bodnar, Julia Maniowsky and Wolodymyr Chornodolsky. The president now is Mykola Turyk and the secretary is Andriy Chornodolsky. Membership is 110.

Branch 87 is located in Curtis Bay and the present president is Theodore Caryk.

The Ukrainian National Aid Association

The home office of the Ukrainian National Aid Association is located in Pittsburgh, Pennsylvania. In existence since 1914 the Association provides insurance coverage and aids and abets Ukrainian causes both in America and abroad. Its newspaper, *Ukrainske Narodne Slovo (The Ukrainian National Word)* was started the same year as the insurance aspects and from the intensely ethnic base of Pittsburgh has helped to engender cultural, educational, and social development. Since 1966 Wolodymyr Masur has been the national president. Anany Nikonchuk is secretary.

Branch No. 156 of the U.N.A.A. in Baltimore is known as the Sisterhood of Olha Basarab and was founded in 1937 through the efforts of Antonina Semenkiw, Tekla Zachidna and Anna Chorney, with six members. Today the branch lists 45 members under the presidency of Iwan Radj. Stephen Polischuk is secretary of the Association.

The Ukrainian Medical Association of North America

The Ukrainian Medical Association of North America Maryland Branch, was begun September 10, 1959, at the initiative of Baltimore and Washington physicians. The organizational meeting provided for a committee

Members of Maryland Branch, UMANA: L to R: Mykola Lasijczuk, Joseph Wityk, Daria Kostrubiak, Stephen Tymkiw, Dmytro Kostrubiak, pres., Semen Paluch, Lydia Lemishka, Theodore Zalucky, Yaromyr Oryshkewych, Oksana, Starosolska, Stephania Baranowska, Andriy Lemishka.

Jan. 1974 Convention Bulletin

consisting of Drs. Michael Zawalniak, Yaroslaw Chmilewsky, and Andriy Lemishka to prepare for the first general election to be held on May 14, 1960. Elected then to the first board were Michael Zawalniak, president; Dmytro Kostrubiak, secretary; Yaroslaw Chmilewsky, treasurer; and Andriy Lemishka, Tatiana Antonowych, and Mykola Lasijczuk, control commissioners.

The UMANA strives to achieve a number of important goals: preserve the identity of and assist and protect Ukrainian medical professionals; provide assistance to non-English-speaking patients; publish what now is the only Ukrainian medical journal in the world; establish a special fund to aid Ukrainian medical and medicine-related students; and hold scientific conventions and discussions to advance professional competence and medical knowledge.

The membership has grown steadily, averaging 20 in recent years, and coming from Maryland, Virginia, West Virginia, and Washington, D.C. Among its members are Dr. Theodore Zalucky, professor and later chairman in the Department of Pharmacy at Howard University, and Dr. Tatiana Antonowych, assistant professor at Georgetown University.

The 10th Scientific Convention of the UMANA, held at the Hotel Statler Hilton, Washington, on May 25,26 and 27, 1974, was planned and directed by the Maryland Branch. The medical topics presented varied from "Viruses and Cancer" to the "Treatment of the Arteriosclerotic Heart by 'Diathermic Radar Rays'."

Organization for the Rebirth of Ukraine (ODWU) Inc.

ODWU had its United States beginnings in 1928 and 1929. In these years Colonel Eugene Konovalets traveled through the American Ukrainian communities calling for the formation of units to support the liberation battles being waged in the homelands by the Ukrainian Military Organization. The first to respond to these appeals were the Ukrainian centers in Ansonia and Hartford in Connecticut and Cohoes and Troy in New York. By 1931 there were 19 units in Ukrainian communities throughout the various states in America. In that year the first meeting of delegates was convened in New York, where the name Organization for the Rebirth of Ukraine was adopted and the first leader of the executive board, Hryhory Herman, was elected. In the 1930's ODWU enjoyed its greatest growth. Attracted to it were the most patriotic Ukrainian elements which strove to attain general acceptance and support among the people.

In Baltimore, operating since March 1955, is Branch No. 31, named for Colonel Ivan Bohun. Established under the initiative of Wolodymyr Romanowsky and Petro Wojtowycz, the first governing body consisted of six persons and three members of a control commission. On the executive board then were Wolodymyr Romanowsky, president; Petro Wojtowycz, secretary; and Ostap Charchalis, treasurer.

Colonel Ivan Bohun Branch from its inception has been one of the organizational members of the Maryland Branch of the Ukrainian Congress Committee of America, strongly aiding its programs. Moral guidance and leadership, as well as material assistance, are provided for attaining a free and more humane life for the Ukrainian people in their native land and for retaining and developing the national and cultural resources of Ukrainians in America. To futher these aims the governing body arranges assemblies and conferences and sends messages, memoranda and pamphlets. Yearly solicitations are conducted for obtaining the financial means to carry on these campaigns and for bringing attention of the free world to the colonial status of Ukraine's inhabitants.

The present executive board members are Petro Wojtowycz, president; Osyp Lazarko, secretary; and Oleh Bendiuk, treasurer.

The Patriarchate of the Ukrainian Catholic Church

The Society for the Promotion of the Patriarchal System in the Ukrainian Catholic Church was founded in 1965, with branches in all cities where Ukrainians are numerous. Headquarters of the organization are in Philadelphia and centers exist in other countries. In 1974 representatives convened in Washington, D.C., and formed a Ukrainian Patriarchal World Federation to coordinate joint activities.

The Baltimore Branch was formed on January 24, 1965. Rallies were held in 1969 and 1971 at which petitions were drafted to support the cause of Patriarch Josyf Slipyj. These petitions were sent to the Pope in Rome. Since 1965 the sum of $13,002 has been collected among Ukrainians in Baltimore and submitted to the Partriarchal Fund in Rome.

Petro Wojtowycz is now chairman of the Baltimore branch which includes such active members as Danylo Pisetzky, Andrew Lemishka, M.D., Emmanuel Prytula, Wolodymyr Sushko, Wasyl Tatchyn, Semen Poliszczuk, and Semen Mychajlyshyn. A unit in the area of Washington includes Dr. Roman Baranowsky, Dr. Yaroslaw Geleta, Bohdan Yasinsky, Dr. Yurij Starosolsky, Rosa Siokalo, and Dr. Antin Prockiw among its membership. Wolodymyr Procinsky is chairman for 1977.

Members of the Patriarchate of the Ukrainian Catholic Church aver that the patriarchal system of administration is typical and traditional for Eastern Churches and that from the beginning the Ukrainian Church was a Particular (*Pomisna*) Church. By the Union of Brest in 1596 separate character was guaranteed to the Ukrainian Catholic Church by the Roman pontiff. Metropolitans of Kiev-Halych had the status of Major Archbishops and enjoyed the powers of patriarchs, excepting the title. This central authority over the Ukrainian Catholic faithful ended in 1945 when the Ukrainian Catholic Church in the Soviet Union was banned by the Russian regime and all bishops, including the Major Archbishop of the metropolitan see of Kiev-Halich, Josyf Slipyj, were arrested.

After 18 years of imprisonment Metropolitan Slipyj arrived in Rome and presented his historic, particular rights. At the 46th session of Vatican Council II he opted for the establishment of a patriarchate for Ukrainian Catholics, feeling that Ukrainians without a patriarchate would succumb to assimilation and Latinization beyond the borders of Ukraine. His appeal received support in 1964 when the Decree on Catholic Eastern Churches, adopted by Vatican II, recognized that "the patriarchal office in the Eastern Churches is a traditional form of government" and indicated a desire to erect new patriarchates "where there is need." The Decree stated that all rulings of Vatican II regarding patriarchs are equally applicable to major archbishops. With impetus from Major Archbishop Slipyj the Decree on Catholic Eastern Churches went into effect in the Ukrainian Church on April 7, 1965. The movement to establish a patriarchate gained in 1969 when the Fourth Archiepiscopal Synod of Ukrainian bishops in Rome ruled to elevate the Major Archbishop of Kiev-Halych to the status of Patriarch. On October 25, 1969, a petition requested papal recognition of this elevation. Thereafter Major Archbishop Slipyj, following the procedures in other Eastern Churches, began to use the term of patriarch. At the Sixth Synod in Rome in 1973 the Ukrainian bishops accepted the Patriarchal Constitution for their Church and Patriarch Josyf I presented a copy to the Holy Father. No confirmation has been received from the Apostolic See.

With a faith as tenacious as that of the late Cardinal Mindszenty of Hungary, with whom he had developed a rapport of concern for the suffering Christians in Eastern Europe, Patriarch Joseph stated on his third visit to the United States in October, 1976, "If I were interested in personal honor and status, I would have received it from the Soviet regime without having had to pass 18 years in slave camps."[29] In reminding the world about the plight of his Church, Patriarch Josyph addressed the Vatican Council, "The Catholic Ukrainians who have sacrificed mountains of bodies and rivers of blood for their fidelity to the Apostolic See, even now are undergoing terrible persecutions, but what is worse, they are defended by no one."

Ukrainian Catholics and other Catholics endeavor to promote the efforts of their Primate in the interest of their Particular (*Pomisna*) Church. To many young Ukrainian Americans the issue of a Ukrainian patriarchate is a part of their search for cultural and religious identities.[30]

President Gerald Ford and Patriarch Josyf I meet at the White House, September 18, 1976. Bishops Ivan Prashko of Australia and Basil H. Losten (l. to r.) are also shown.

For the Patriarchate Bimonthly

The Ukrainian Congress Committee of America, Inc. — Baltimore Branch

A national organization, the Ukrainian Congress Committee of America, Inc., was founded in New York City in 1940 to unify Ukrainian endeavors throughout the land. In addition to holding national symposia, promoting Ukrainian heritage schools, informing American officials about issues pertaining to Ukrainians here and abroad, the Congress Committee has published *The Ukrainian Quarterly*, a journal of European and Asian affairs.

Earl Arnett, feature writer for the Baltimore Sun, *displays a plaque presented to him by Baltimore U.C.C.A. "in recognition of outstanding contributions in furthering understanding of the multi-cultural community in which we live." Presentation was made on January 22, 1976, the anniversary of Ukrainian independence.*

Roman Hankewycz

In the area of Baltimore the first branch of U.C.C.A. was founded in Curtis Bay through the auspices of the

Ukrainian Committee of Curtis Bay whose officers were Anton Chimiak, chairman; Dr. Yaroslav Bernadyn, vice chairman; Petro Wojtowycz, secretary; and John Mackula, chairman of the initiating committee. The Ukrainian Committee of Curtis Bay decided on January 27, 1950, to curtail its activities and created in its place a U.C.C.A. Branch. Curtis Bay's U.C.C.A. officers included Mykola Shandrowsky, chairman; Ivan Tryhubenko, vice chairman; Petro Wojtowycz, secretary; Mykola Turyk, treasurer; Dr. Yaroslav Bernadyn, director of activities; John Shandrowsky, English language secretary; Magdalina Evanuk, social services; and Volodymyr Hanas, director of events. An auditing committee consisted of John Mackula, Alex Duda, and Julian Manastyrsky. Among the activities promoted by the Curtis Bay U.C.C.A. were the holding of Shevchenko programs, providing services for refugees, and the observation of Ukrainian Independence Day.

As time passed the activities of the Curtis Bay group declined and the branch merged with the Baltimore U.C.C.A. in 1954.

The founding meeting of the Baltimore U.C.C.A. was held on September 10, 1950, at the Ukrainian National Home through the efforts of an initiating committee of Ostap Charchalis, George Shulka, Theodore Nykula, Rev. Wasyl Bulawka, Alex Zuk, and Volodymyr Kaminsky. Delegates were present from the following Ukrainian organizations: Ukrainian American Citizens Club, Ukrainian National Association, Ukrainian Workingmen's Association, Ukrainian Youth Association, Plast, Curtis Bay Branch of U.C.C.A., and United Ukrainian War Veterans of America. Julian Revay, former prime minister of the Carpatho-Ukrainian Republic, was a delegate to the meeting from U.C.C.A. headquarters in New York City.

Chairman of the founding meeting was Dr. Yaroslav Chmilewsky, while other officers were Volodymyr Kaminsky, vice chairman, and Dr. Emil Derey and Sylvester Martiuk, secretaries.

The first Baltimore Branch consisted of thirty-eight members with these officers: Joseph Marmash, chairman;

EXECUTIVE DEPARTMENT

ANNAPOLIS, MARYLAND

THEODORE R. McKELDIN
GOVERNOR

December 11, 1951

Mr. Vladimir C. Sushko
Information Officer
Ukrainian Congress Committee
of America-Baltimore Branch
2132 East Baltimore Street
Baltimore 31, Maryland

Dear Mr. Sushko:

        I wish to acknowledge receipt of your recent letter and accompanying copy of letter and story from the Ukrainian Congress Committee of America.

        I have the deepest sympathy for the people of Europe who are under the iron grip of the Soviet Union, as I so recently expressed myself in an address which was broadcast over the "Voice of America" to the people behind the iron curtain, a copy of which I am happy to enclose.

        Assuring you of my interest and support on behalf of oppressed nations, I am

        Sincerely yours,

        Governor

TRMcK/w
encl.

Governor McKeldin responded to U.C.C.A. correspondence with a copy of an address stressing religious freedom, long desired by Ukrainians.

Dr. Yaroslav Chmilewsky, first vice chairman; Theodore Nykula, second vice chairman and director of organization; Sylvester Martiuk, activities director; Iwan Tryhubenko, treasurer; Alexander Ratych, information officers; Volodymyr Kaminsky, recording secretary; John Malko, English language secretary.

    An auditing committee consisted of Paul Talan, Jacob Semenkiw, and Danilo Pisetzky while a grievance committee was made up of T. Chorniy, Dr. Emil Derey, and Ostap Charchalis.

    The following members have served as chairmen of the Baltimore Branch of U.C.C.A.: Joseph Marmash (September, 1950 - May, 1952), Theordore Chornij (May 1952 - May 1954), Dr. Emil Derey (May 1954 - May 1957), Ostap Stelmach (May 1957 - June 1959), Klemens Babiak (June 1959 - June 1960), Theodore Caryk (August 1960 -

September 1961), Dr. Emil Derey (September 1961 - May 1964), Dr. Demetrius Kostrubiak (May 1964 - October 1967), Gen. Petro Samutyn (October 1967 - February 1968), Volodymyr Chornodolsky (October 1968 - March 1973), Wasyl Tatchyn (March 1973 - November 1973), and Bohdan Salamacha (November 1973 - present).

The Ukrainian Congress Committee has helped sustain community life in addition to promoting the national interests of the people of Ukraine. An annual collection is taken for the Ukrainian National Fund, as were special collections for such activities as the building of the Shevchenko Monument in Washington and the campaign for the translation of Prof. M. Hrushevsky's *History of Ukraine* into English. Wasyl Tatchyn directed the latter campaign which raised $1,700. Cultural

A delegation from the Baltimore U.C.C.A. received a Proclamation commemorating Ukrainian independence from Ted Venetoulis, County Executive of Baltimore County in January of 1977.
Baltimore County photo

programs have included performances of the Ukrainian Bandurist Chorus in Baltimore, a vocal performance by Hanna Kolesnyk, and lecture programs featuring such accomplished scholars as Petro Stercho, Mykola Stepanenko, Ivan Kedryn-Rudnitskyj, Natalia Pasuniak, Anatol Bedrij, Julian Revay, Dmytry Halychyn, Roman Smal-Stocki, Matthew Stachiw, Lew Shankowsky, A. Dragan, Athanas Figol, and Askold Skalsky, among others. Members of the United States Congress have likewise addressed sessions.

Over the years the Baltimore Branch of U.C.C.A. has participated and led in the promotion of Captive Nations Week, a week set aside in July to recognize the desires of freedom loving peoples trapped in the Soviet system. This week was founded largely through the efforts of Prof. Lev E. Dobriansky, national chairman of the U.C.C.A. and professor of economics at Georgetown University.

In Baltimore the group participated in "I Am an American Day" parades for many years and also took part in All Nations Days held at Gwynn Oak Park. Commemorative programs recognizing manifold Ukrainian freedom fighters and national heroes have been sponsored on a regular basis with the cooperation of many groups in the community. A bulletin in Ukrainian, *Visti U.C.C.A.*, has been published periodically. The group was instrumental, under the direction of Andrij Chornodolsky, in organizing the first Ukrainian Festival at Hopkins Plaza in October of 1973, with a festival being held each year since.

The Ukrainian Education Association of Maryland, Inc.

The Ukrainian Education Association of Maryland, Inc., founded in 1972, is committed to the idea of penetrating American institutions in order to realize improved considerations for Ukrainian Americans. The group believes that the positive elements of a culturally pluralistic society will be fostered only if there is healthy interaction among the diverse groups which comprise our nation's citizenry.

Officers of the Association have remained as elected originally: Paul Fenchak, president; Hlib S. Hayuk, vice president; Stephen Basarab, secretary; John Malko, treasurer. Wasyl Tatchyn has served as membership chairman.

Specific objectives of the Association, which was incorporated on October 7, 1975, are as follows:

1. To influence course content and selection of instructional materials in schools/colleges
2. To upgrade holdings about Ukrainians in libraries
3. To promote courses in Ukrainian history/culture
4. To initaite prompt response to incorrect or inimical analyses dealing with Ukrainians
5. To activate and coordinate the optimum number of Ukrainian educational resources
6. To complete writings to influence educators, governmental officials, and the general public.

An example of the group's adherence to stated goals is the very publication of this book, *The Ukrainians of Maryland*. Rejected for funding by the U.S. Office of Education under the Schweiker Ethnic Heritage Studies Program, the Association did not yield in its determination and was later able to secure grants totalling $4,350 from the Maryland Bicentennial Commission, which coupled with a fund raising campaign directed by Treasurer John Malko, produced monies to help have the book completed.

Since the inception of the Association, some of its achievements follow: Ukrainian coverage is now given, as a result of visitations to and correspondence with the Maryland State Department of Education, in a state curriculum guide, *New Perspectives in Intergroup Education;* several feature articles about Ukrainians appeared in Baltimore newspapers and the submission of articles to ethnic publications has been sizeable; folders containing basic information about Ukrainians were distributed to libraries, schools, colleges, and governmental organizations; two conferences, "Slavic Americans in Maryland: Current Ethnic Issues," were sponsored jointly with the Polish Heritage Association of Maryland, Inc.; exhibits were sponsored and materials distributed at conventions of the Maryland State Teachers Association; exhibits were sponsored in schools, colleges, etc.; several

STATE OF MARYLAND
EXECUTIVE DEPARTMENT
ANNAPOLIS, MARYLAND 21404

MARVIN MANDEL
GOVERNOR

January 25, 1974

Mr. Paul Fenchak, Chairman
Ukrainian Education Association
of Maryland
2301 Eastern Avenue
Baltimore, Maryland 21224

Dear Mr. Fenchak:

      Governor Mandel has asked me to reply to your letter of January 22 recommending Professor Hlib S. Hayuk for appointment to the Maryland Bicentennial Commission.

      Please be assured that Professor Hayuk will be given every consideration for appointment to this Commission.

      Thank you for taking the time to inform the Governor of your interest in this matter.

Very truly yours,

Michael S. Silver
Assistant Appointments Officer

MSS:rrl

Copy of letter from office of Governor Mandel re recommendation of H. S. Hayuk by Ukrainian Education Association.

493

exhibits and programs were coordinated and jointly sponsored with other Ukrainian groups at Maryland Historical Society, Cathedral of Mary Our Queen, St. Mary's Seminary, et al.; interaction with Poles, Slovaks, Blacks, Lithuanians, Estonians, Czechs, and others has increased; members have participated in ethnic conferences at Maryland colleges; a Ukrainian language course was initiated at Essex Community College.

Hlib S. Hayuk was named to the Maryland Bicentennial Commission through initiative and promotion of the Association. Suggested for membership on the anniversary of Ukrainian Independence in 1974 (January 22), Commissioner Hayuk was appointed in the fall of 1974 and was likely the only Ukrainian in America to have been a member of a state bicentennial commission. The impetus and drive of the Ukrainian Education Association led to the expansion of considerations for all ethnic groups in Maryland as previously little, if any, consideration was given ethnic communities. After the appointment of Commissioner Hayuk, a sub-committee for Ethnics was founded by the Maryland Bicentennial Commission. This group, in essence, has become the current Maryland Ethnic Commission, chaired by John Shmorhun, a Ukrainian American.

In advocating the appointment of Hlib Hayuk the experience of years of productive activity on the Maryland scene was marshalled from community leaders such as Joseph Marmash, John Malko, Stephen Basarab, Myron Zuk, Wolodymyr Sushko, Wasyl Tatchyn, Ray Dypski, Cornell Dypski, Barbara Mikulski, and others. Strong support was collected from Byelorussians, Slovaks, Lithuanians, Latvians, Estonians, Czechs, et al. All groups, in turn, profited from the initiative of the Ukrainian Education Association.

Myron Zuk is currently directing the completion of a filmstrip about Ukrainians in Maryland for the Ukrainian Education Association. This project received a sub-grant from Towson State University, which in turn had received a grant of about $15,000 to research ethnic communities of Baltimore. Paul Fenchak was a member of the advisory

IN THE FOOTSTEPS OF POLETICKA — Hlib S. Hayuk (2nd from left) is with other members of Maryland Bicentennial Commission at a ceremony honoring George Washington, February 22, 1976, by Baltimore's Washington Monument. Petro Poleticka, another native of Ukraine, showed admiration for the Monument in his book published in Baltimore in 1826.

committee of the Towson State University project directed by Dr. Jean Scarpaci. He gathered extensive data about the European origins of Jewish American students in attendance at Pikesville High School as one phase of his research.

In compiling the book, *The Ukrainians of Maryland,* the Education Association has exhorted the greater Ukrainian community to increase its consciousness of Marylandia. Many persons assisted — writing shorter chapters, sketching a cover, taking photographs, etc. George Koneyak prepared all letters of acknowledgement and appreciation for contributions received.

By presenting this book the Ukrainian Education Association of Maryland, Inc., aspires to grow and it is hoped that interest in the Ukrainians of Maryland will also increase in this era when, as in the words of Michael Novak, "America is becoming America."

Paul Fenchak joins Greek, Italian, and Jewish scholars for a photo at Towson State University Ethnic Research Project, 1976.

NOTES TO CHAPTER 14

[1] Jaroslav J. Chyz, *The Ukrainian Immigrants in the United States,* Scranton, Pa., Ukrainian Workingmen's Association, 1940.

[2] *Civil War Times,* Vol. III, No. 5, Aug. 1961.

[3] Gilbert Cant, "Rescue In the Pacific," *Saturday Evening Post,* Jan. 29, 1944.

[4] *Ukrainian Weekly,* Jersey City, Feb. 23, 1970.

[5] *Biography,* United States Air Force, Bolling AFB, D.C., March 15, 1974.

[6] *Curriculum Vitae of Col. Taras Nowosiwsky, M.D.,* Sep. 30, 1977, and *Ukrainian Weekly,* Oct. 6, 1973.

[7] *Baltimore City Bicentennial News,* Aug.-Sep., 1975.

[8] *Ukrainian Weekly,* Aug. 14, 1971.

[9] *The Way,* Philadelphia, May 3, 1970.

[10] Interview of Dr. John E. Bodnar, Associate Historian of Pennsylvania Historical and Museum Commission, Harrisburg, by Paul Fenchak, August, 1977.

[11] Grantland Rice, *The Tumult and the Shouting — My life in Sport,* New York, A.S. Barnes and Co., 1954, p. 211.

[12] Arthur Daley, *Pro Football's Hall of Fame,* New York, Grosset and Dunlap, 1963, p. 83.

[13] Baltimore Colts, *Baltimore Colts 1977 Media Guide,* Baltimore, 1977, p. 7.

[14] Baltimore Colts, *Baltimore Colts 1973 Media Guide,* Baltimore, 1973, p. 36.

[15] *Ukrainian Weekly,* Sep. 1, 1973.

[16] *Ukrainian Weekly,* Nov. 24, 1972.

[17] *Ukrainian Weekly,* June 20, 1970, and May 15, 1977.

[18] *Ukrainian Weekly,* May 15, 1977.

[19] Dymtro M. Shtohryn, ed., *Ukrainians in North America,* Champaign, Ill., Association for the Advancement of Ukrainian Studies, 1975, p. 226.

[20] *Ukrainian Weekly,* Jan. 15, 1972.

[21] *Ukrainians in North America,* p. 372.

[22] *Ukrainians in North America,* p. 328.

[23] *Svoboda,* Jersey City, Dec. 31, 1976.

[24] Francis Rackemann, "Breakthrough In Blackspot Disease In Sight," *Baltimore Evening Sun,* Jan. 20, 1977, p. B2.

[25] *Ukrainians in North America,* p. 223.

[26] *Ukrainians in North America,* p. 327.

[27] *Ukrainians in North America,* p. 342.

[28] *Ukrainians in North America,* p. 189.

[29] "Ukraine: A Tragedy without Frontiers," *Crusade for Christian Civilization,* Vol. 7, January-February, 1977, p. 20.

[30] George A. Maloney, "Ukrainians on the March," *Catholic World,* Vol. 214, December, 1971, p. 111.

[31] Anatole Bulawka, Baltimore, an interview with Dr. Emil Derey, president of Selfreliance Baltimore Federal Credit Union, December 27, 1976.

A business owned by George Shulka, Baltimore, made and repaired shoes beginning in early 1900's **Theodore Shulka**

Walter Melianovich of Byelorussian Academy of Arts and Sciences commends Ukrainian Endeavors at Banquet sponsored by Ukrainian Congress Committee, 1976. **Myron Zuk**

Bibliography

GENERAL

Alaska Herald and Free Press (Sloboda) Newspaper, (Vols. 1-6, 1868-1874.) Reprinted. San Francisco, R. and E. Research Associates, 1968-1970.

Allen, William E., *Ukraine - A History*, New York, Russell, 1940. (Reprinted)

Amalrik, Andrei, *Will the Soviet Union Survive Until 1984?*, New York, Harper and Row, 1970

Anatoly (Kuznetsov), A., *Babi Yar*, New York, Dell Publishing Company, Inc., 1966.

Andrusyshen, C. H. and Kirkconnel, Watson (Translators), *Ukrainian Poets, 1189-1962*. Toronto, University of Toronto Press, 1963.

Armstrong, John A., *Ukrainian Nationalism*, New York, Columbia University Press, 1963.

Balaban, Victor and Hirka, Bohdan, *Ukrainians in Texas*, Huston, Publisher: Victor Balaban, 1976.

Balch, Emily, *Our Slavic Fellow Citizens*, New York, Charities Publications Committee, 1910. (Reprinted by Arno Press.) An extensive early study of many Slavic American groups.

Basarab, Stephen, Fenchak, Paul, Sushko, Wolodymyr C., et al., *The Ukrainians of Maryland*, Baltimore, Ukrainian Education Association of Maryland, Inc., 1977. This book, partially funded by the Maryland Bicentennial Commission, is the first in-depth study of any Slavic group in Maryland and contains in nearly 500 pages over 200 photos with many materials of Marylandia/Ucrainica previously unpublished.

Bilinsky, Yaroslav, *The Second Soviet Republic,* New Brunswick, Rutgers University Press, 1964.

Bird, Thomas E. and Piddubcheshen, Eva (Eds.), *Archiepiscopal and Patriarchal Autonomy—A Symposium*, New York, Fordam University, 1972.

Bloch-Halun, Marie, *Aunt America*, New York, Atheneum, 1963.

Bloch-Halun, Marie, *Marya of Clark Ave.* New York, Coward-McCann, 1957.

Bloch-Halun, Marie, *Ukrainian Folk Tales,* New York, Coward, 1964.

Bodnar, John E. (Ed.), *The Ethnic Experience in Pennsylvania,* Lewisburg, Bucknell University Press, 1973.

Brown, Francis J. and Joseph Slabey Roucek, *One America: The History, Contributions and Present Problems of Our Racial and National Minorities.* New York, Prentice Hall, 1949. (Reprinted by Negro Universities Press.)

Browne, Michael, *Ferment in the Ukraine,* New York, Praeger, 1971

Chamberlin, William H., *The Ukraine: A Submerged Nation,* New York, Macmillan Company, 1944.

Chornovil, Vyacheslav, *The Chornovil Papers,* New York, McGraw-Hill, 1968.

Chyz, Yaroslav, *The Ukrainian Immigrants in the United States,* Scranton, Pa., Ukrainian Workingman's Association, 1932.

Chyzhevsky, Dmytro, *A History of Ukrainian Literature* (Translated by D. Ferguson and D. Gorsline), Littleton, Ukrainian Academic Press, 1975.

Cousins, Norman, *The Improbable Triumvirate — John F. Kennedy, Pope John, Nikita Khrushchev,* New York, W. W. Norton and Company, 1972. Includes analyses of events leading to the release from Soviet prison of Ukrainian Archbishop Joseph Slipyi after 18 years. Cousins is editor of *Saturday Review.*

Dobriansky, Lev E., *The Vulnerable Russians,* New York, Pageant Press, 1967.

Dobriansky, Lev E., "Ukrainian Rivulets in the Stream of American Culture," *Ukrainian Quarterly. 4:55-62.* Winter, 1948.

Dragan, A., *Our Ukrainian Cardinal (Josyf Slipyj),* Jersey City, Ukrainian National Association, Inc., 1966.

Fishman, Joshua A., *Language Loyalty in the United States — The Maintenance and Perpetuation of Non-English Mother Tongues by American Ethnic and Religious Groups,* Den Hagen, Mouton, 1966. Contains a 40-page section about the Ukrainian language in America.

Franko, Ivan, *Moses and Other Works* (translated by Vera Rich and Percival Cundy), New York, Shevchenko Scientific Society, 1973.

Fr.-Chirovsky, Nicholas L., *A History of the Russian Empire* (2 vols.), New York, Philosophical Library, 1973.

Goldelman, Solomon I., *Jewish National Autonomy in Ukraine — 1917-1920,* Chicago, Ukrainian Research and Information Institute, 1968.

Grady, Joseph (Ed.), *The Immigrants' Influence on Wilson's Peace Policies,* University of Kentucky Press, 1967.

Halich, Wasyl, *The Americanization of a Ukrainian Boy*, St. Paul, University of Minnesota Press, 1975.

Halich, Wasyl, *Ukrainians in the United States*, Chicago, University of Chicago Press, 1937. (Reprinted by Arno Press within last few years.)

Hauk-Abonyi, Malvina (Ed.), *Ethni-City — A Guide to Ethnic Detroit, Vol. 2*, Detroit, Michigan Ethnic Heritage Studies Center and Wayne State University, 1976. Contains helpful information about the many Ukrainian groups of metropolitan Detroit.

Hrushevsky, Michael, *A History of Ukraine*, New York, Archon Books, 1970.

Holy Family Ukrainian Catholic Church, *Ukrainian Catholic Shrine of the Holy Family*, Washington, D.C., Holy Family Ukrainian Catholic Church, 1975. Contains much data about Ukrainians in area of Washington. Arranged chronologically.

Hryshko, Vasyl, *Experience with Russia*, New York, Ukrainian Congress Committee of America, Inc., 1956.

Jones, Lesya and Yasen, Bohdan (Eds.), *The Ukrainian Herald, Issue 6: Dissent in Ukraine* (An underground journal from Soviet Ukraine), Baltimore, Smoloskyp Publishers, 1977.

Kamenetsky, Ihor, *Hitler's Occupation of the Ukraine*, Milwaukee, Marquette University Press, 1956.

Kaye, Vladimir J., *Early Ukrainian Settlement in Canada, 1895-1900 — Dr. Joseph Oleskow's Role in the Settlement of the Canadian Northeast*, Toronto, University of Toronto Press, 1964.

Khvylovy, Mykola, *Stories from the Ukraine*, New York, Philosophical Library, 1960.

Kolasky, John, *Education in Soviet Ukraine*, Toronto, Peter Martin Associates, 1968.

Kononenko, Konstantyn, *The Ukraine and Russia: A History of the Economic Relations, 1564-1917*, Milwaukee, Marquette University Press, 1958.

Kowalsky, Onuphrey T., *Ukrainian Folk Songs: A Historical Treatise*, Boston, Stratford Company, 1925.

Kravchenko, Victor, *I Chose Freedom*, New York, Charles Scribner's, 1946.

Kuropas, Myron, *Ukrainians in America*, Minneapolis, Lerner Pub., 1972.

Luciw, Theodore, *Father Agapius Honcharenko, First Ukrainian Priest in America*, New York, Ukrainian Congress Committee of America 1970.

Luciw, Wasyl, *Ahapius Honcharenko "Alaska Man,"* by Wasyl Luciw and Theodore Luciw, Toronto, Slavia Library, 1963.

Luckyj, George S.N., *Modern Ukrainian Short Stories*, Littleton, Libraries Unlimited, 1973.

Mamchur, Stephen, "Ukrainian cultural change," in *Jubilee Book of the Ukrainian National Association* in Commemoration of the Fortieth Anniversary of Its Existence. Jersey City, N.J., Svoboda Press, 1936.

Manning, Clarence A., *History of Slavic Studies in the United States,* Milwakee, Marquette University Press, 1957.

Manning, Clarence A., *Twentieth Century Ukraine,* New York, Bookman Associates, 1951.

Manning, Clarence A., *Ukrainian Literature — Study of the Leading Authors,* Freeport, Books for Libraries Press, 1971.

Margolin, Arnold D., *From a Political Diary... Russia, The Ukraine and America, 1905-1945,* New York, Columbia University Press, 1946.

Marunchak, Mykhaylo, *The Ukrainian Canadians; a History,* Winnipeg, Historical Publications, 1970.

Mencken, Henry L., *The American Language — An Inquiry into the Development of English in the United States,* New York, Alfred A. Knopf, 1937. Includes a section about the use of English by Ukrainian Americans.

Mirchuk, I., *Ukraine and Its People,* Munich, Ukrainian Free University Press., 1949.

Mitz, Anne (Ed.), *Ukrainian Arts,* New York, Ukrainian Youth's League of North America, Inc., 1955.

Moroz, Valentyn, *Boomerang — The Works of Valentyn Moroz,* Baltimore, Smoloskyp Publishers, 1974.

Moroz, Valentyn, *Report from the Beria Reserve,* Chicago, Catarack Press, 1974.

Nagurney, Michael S., "The Teaching of Ukrainian in the United States," in *American Slavonic and East European Review.* 4: 186-194, 1944.

Nahayewsky, Isidore, *History of Ukraine,* Philadelphia, America Publishing House, c. 1960.

Osadchy, Mykhaylo, *Cataract: A Ukrainian Poet's Memoir of Repression and Resistance,* New York, Harcourt Brace Jovanovich 1976.

Pap, Michael S. (Ed.), *Ethnic Communities of Cleveland,* Cleveland, John Carroll University, 1973. Includes a chapter "The Ukrainian Community of Cleveland."

Paska, Walter, *Sources of Particular Law for the Ukrainian Catholic Church in the United States,* Washington, Catholic University of America, 1975.

Penkovskiy, Oleg, *The Penkovskiy Papers,* Garden City, Doubleday and Co., 1965.

Prychodko, Nicholas, *Good-Bye Siberia,* Markhan, Simon and Schuster, 1976.

Prychodko, Nicholas, *Stormy Road to Freedom*, New York, Vantage Press, 1968.

Raymond, Ellsworth and Martin, John Stuart, *A Picture History of Eastern Europe*, New York, Crown Publishers, Inc., 1971.

Reshetar, John, Jr., *Ukrainian Revolution, 1917-1920: A Study in Nationalism*, Princeton University Press, 1952.

Rudnyckyj, Jaroslav B., *Canadian Place Names of Ukrainian Origin*, 3rd ed., Winnipeg, Ukrainian Free Academy of Sciences, 1957.

Saciuk, Olena and Yasen, Bohdan (Eds.), *The Ukrainian Herald, Issue 7-8: Ethnocide of Ukrainians in the U.S.S.R.*, (An underground journal from Soviet Ukraine), Baltimore, Smoloskyp Publishers, 1976.

Sawczuk, Konstantyn, *The Ukraine in the United Nations Organization: A Study in Soviet Foreign Policy, 1944-1950*, New York, Columbia University Press, 1975.

Sichynsky, Volodymyr (Ed.), *Ukraine in Foreign Comments and Descriptions from VIth to XXth Century*, New York, Ukrainian Congress Committee, 1953.

Slavs in Canada — Proceedings of the First National Conference of Canadian Slavs, Editorial Committee, Yar Slavutych, Chairman. Vol. l. Edmonton, Alta., Interuniversity Committee on Canadian Slavs, 1966.

Smal-Stocki, Roman, *Captive Nations — Nationalism of the non-Russian Nations in the Soviet Union*, New York, Bookman Associates, 1960.

Smal-Stocki, Roman, *Shevchenko Meets America*, Milwaukee, Marquette University Press, 1964.

Smoloskyp Publishers, *Invisible Spirit — Art and Poetry of Ukrainian Women Political Prisoners in the U.S.S.R.*, Baltimore, Smoloskyp Publishers, 1977.

Snowyd, D., *Spirit of Ukraine*, New York, United Ukrainian Organizations, 1935.

Solovey, Meletius Michael, *The Byzantine Divine Liturgy — History and Commentary* (Translated by Demetrius E. Wysochansky), Washington, Catholic University of America Press, Inc., 1970.

Solzhenitsyn, Aleksandr I., *The Gulag Archipelago —— 1918-1956* (Translated by Thomas P. Whitney), New York, Harper and Row, Publishers, 1973. Dedicated to "all those who did not live to tell it," this book reviews many atrocities perpetrated against Ukrainians, among others.

Stechishin, Savella, *Traditional Ukrainian Cookery*, Winnipeg, Trident Press., Ltd., 1967.

Sverstiuk, Ievhen, *Clandestine Essays*, Cambridge, Harvard Ukrainian Research Institute, 1976.

Tys-Krokhmalius, Yuriy, *UPA Warfare in Ukraine*, New York, Vantage Press, 1972.

Ukrainian Bicentennial Committee of Philadelphia, *Ukrainians in Pennsylvania — A Contribution to the Growth of the Commonwealth*, Philadelphia, 1976.

Ukrainian Congress Committee of America, *The Story of the Ukrainian Congress Committee of America*, New York, Ukrainian Congress Committee of America, 1951. The story of the Ukrainian Congress Committee of America and its work on behalf of the Ukrainian cause.

Ukrainian Congress Committee of America (Maryland Branch), *Ukraine — The Achilles Heel of the Soviet Union*, Baltimore, 1959.

Ukrainian Congress Committee of America, *Ukrainian Resistance*, New York, 1949.

Ukrainian Congress Committee of America, *Ukrainians and Jews — A Symposium* (of Jewish and Ukrainian scholars), New York, 1966.

Ukrainian National Association: Its Past and Present, 1894-1964, Antin Dragan, (Ed.), New York, Ukrainian National Association, 1964.

Warzeski, Walter, *Religion and National Consciousness in the History of the Rusins of Carpatho-Ruthenia and the Byzantine Rite Pittsburgh Exarchate*, Pittsburgh, University of Pittsburgh, 1964. (Dissertation)

Wertsman, Vladimir (Ed.), *The Ukrainians in America — 1608-1975 — A Chronology and Fact Book*, Dobbs Ferry, N.Y., Oceana Publications, 1976.

Weinryb, Bernard D., *The Jews of Poland — A Social and Economic History of the Jewish Community in Poland from 1100-1800*, Philadelphia, Jewish Publication Society of America, 1973.

Wichorek, Michael, *Ukrainians in Detroit*, Detroit, privately published by the author, 1955.

Winter, Nevin O., "The Ukraine, Past and Present," *National Geographic*, Vol. 34, No. 2, August, 1918, pp. 114-128. Has 14 interesting illustrations but the article suffers from weak history and terminology.

Zernov, Nicholas, *The Ukrainians and Their Church*, London, Society for Promoting of Christian Knowledge, 1945.

REFERENCES

Allworth, Edward (Ed.), *Soviet Nationality Problems*, New York, Columbia University Press, 1971.

Attwater, Donald (Ed.), *The Christian Churches of the East: Vol. I Churches in Communion with Rome; Vol. II Churches Not in Communion with Rome*, Milwaukee, Bruce Publishing Co., 1962.

Baltimore Council for International Visitors, *Maryland, Our Maryland — An Ethnic and Cultural Directory*, Baltimore, 1975. Includes addresses and officers of 40 Ukrainian organizations throughout Maryland.

Bodnar, John E., *Ethnic History in Pennsylvania — A Selected Bibliography*, Harrisburg, Pennsylvania Historical and Museum Commission, 1974.

Conquest, Robert (Ed.), *Religion in the U.S.S.R.*, New York, Frederick A. Praeger, Publishers, 1968.

The Directory of the Ukrainian-Catholic Archieparchy of Philadelphia, Byzantine Rite, Philadelphia, Ukrainian Catholic Archieparchy of Philadelphia, 1952.

Eastern Orthodox Church. Directory of the United States 1968, San Francisco, R & E Research Associates, 1969.

Gambino, Richard, *A Guide to Ethnic Studies Programs in American Colleges, Universities and Schools*, New York, Rockefeller Foundation, 1975. Contains a useful bibliography, one section of which is "Slavic, East European, Russian."

Glushakow, A. D., *Maryland Bicentennial Jewish Book*, Baltimore, Jewish Voice Publishing Company, 1975. Written by a Ukrainian-born former merchant and labor leader who had wide experiences with Ukrainians in East Baltimore.

Goldhagen, Erich (Ed.), *Ethnic Minorities in the Soviet Union*, New York, Praeger Publishers, 1968.

Gregorovich, Andrew, *Books on Ukraine and Ukrainians*, Toronto, Stadium Research Institute, 1963. A useful multi-subject bibliography.

Horak, Stephan, *Junior Slavica — A Selected Annotated Bibliography of Books in English on Russia and Eastern Europe*, Littleton, Libraries Unlimited, Inc., 1968

Hunter, Edward, *In Many Voices*, Norman Park, Ga., Norman College, 1960. Reviews foreign language press in United States.

Jakobson, Roman, *Slavic Languages — A Condensed Survey*, New York, Columbia University Press, 1955. An excellent basic booklet to distinguish among the Slavic languages.

Kamenetsky, Ihor (Ed.), *Nationalism and Human Rights: Process of Modernization in the U.S.S.R.*, Littleton, Colo., Libraries Unlimited, Inc. 1977.

Kassof, Allen (Ed.), *Prospects for Soviet Society*, New York, Praeger Publishers, 1968.

Katz, Zev (Ed.), *Handbook of Major Soviet Nationalities*, New York, The Free Press, 1975.

Koropeckyj, I.S., *Location Problems in Soviet Industry Before World War II: The Case of the Ukraine*, Chapel Hill, The University of North Carolina Press, 1965.

Lewis, Robert A. (Ed.), *Nationality and Population Change in Russia and the USSR*, New York, Praeger Publishers, 1976.

Lydolph, Paul E., *Geography of the U.S.S.R.*, 2nd Ed., New York, John Wiley & Sons, Inc., 1970.

Peeler, Alexandra and Barnes, Mary, *The Ethnic Directory — Ethnic Organizations in Prince George's and Montgomery Counties, Maryland and Metropolitan Washington,* Brentwood, Md., Neighborhoods Uniting Project, Inc., 1976.

Potichnyj, Peter J. (Ed.), *Ukraine in the Seventies,* Mosaic Press, Oakville, Ontario, 1975.

Roucek, Joseph S. (Ed.), *The Slavonic Encyclopedia,* New York, Philosophical Library, 1949. (Reprinted by Kennekat Press.)

Shtohryn, Dmytro M., *Ukrainians in North America — A Biographical Directory of Noteworthy Men and Women of Ukrainian Origin in the United States and Canada,* Champaign, Association for the Advancement of Ukrainian Studies, 1975.

Ukraine: A Concise Encyclopedia (2 vols.) Volodymyr Kubijovych (Editor), Totonto, University of Toronto Press, 1963-71.

Weres, Roman, *Ukraine — Selected References in the English Language,* Chicago, Ukrainian Research and Information Institute, Inc., 1974. An annotated bibliography of 312 pages and nearly 2,000 entries.

Wynar, Lubomyr R., *Encyclopedic Directory of Ethnic Newspapers and Periodicals in United States,* Littleton, Colo., Libraries Unlimited, 1972.

Wynar, Lubomyr R., *Encyclopedic Directory of Ethnic Organizations in the United States,* Littleton, Libraries Unlimited, Inc., 1975.

THE UKRAINIAN PRESS IN THE UNITED STATES

In numbers Ukrainians maintain the second largest press in the United States with 73 publications in both the Ukrainian and/or the English languages. These journals and newspapers provide a continuous source of new information about Ukrainian communities. For general research only publications in English and Ukrainian and English exclusively are listed below

A. Maryland Publications in English

Action (Quarterly Bulletin of the League of Ukrainian Catholics), 1965—. Harry V. Makar, Editor, 3522 Belfont Drive, Ellicott City, Md. 41403.

News From Ukraine — Information about the Current Struggle for National Independence and Human Rights (Published quarterly by Ukrainian Division of AF-ABN), 1972—. Askold Skalsky, Editor, Box 142M22, Ijamsville, Md. 21754.

B. Publications Containing Articles in Both Ukrainian and English Languages

Ameryka (America), 1912— 817 North Franklin Street, Philadelphia, Pennsylvania 19123.

Feniks-Zhurnal Molodykh (Phoenix-Journal of Social and Political Thought), 1951—. P.O. Box 141, Riverton, New Jersey 08077.

Kryza (Crisis), 1971—. 140-142 Second Avenue, New York, New York 10003

Misionar (The Missionary), 1917—. 1825 West Lindley Avenue, Philadelphia, Pennsylvania 19141.

Narodna Volya (The People's Will), 1911—. 524 Olive Street, Scranton, Pennsylvania 18509

Nashe Zhyttia (Our Life), 1944—. 4636 North 13th Street, Philadelphia, Pennsylvania 19141

Nova Zorya (New Star), 1965—. 2203 West Chicago Avenue, Chicago, Illinois 60622

Novi Napriamy (New Directions), 1969—. 140-142 Second Avenue, New York, New York 10003

Shlakh (The Way), 1940—. 805 North Franklin Street, Philadelphia, Pennsylvania 19123

Soniashnyk (Helianthus), 1970—. Box 145 Student Center, Wayne State University, Detroit, Michigan

Svoboda. Ukrainskyi Shchodennyk (Liberty. Ukrainian Daily), 1893—. 30 Montgomery Street, Jersey City, New Jersey 07303

Ukrainske Narodne Slovo (Ukrainian National Word), 1915—. P.O. Box 1948, Pittsburgh, Pennsylvania 15230

Ukrainskyi Hospodarnyk (The Ukrainian Economist), 1954—. 47 Ellery Avenue, Irvington, New Jersey 07111

Ukrainskyi Istoryk (Ukrainian Historian), 1963—. P.O. Box 312, Kent, Ohio 44240

Ukrainskyi Pravoslavnyi Visnyk (Ukrainian Orthodox Herald), 1933—. 90-34 139th Street, Jamaica, New York 11435

Za Pravdu Pro Ukrainu. Biuleten' Ukrainskoho Publitsystychno-Naukovoho Instytutu (For the Truth About Ukraine. Bulletin of Ukrainian Research and Information Institute), 1963—. 2534 West Chicago Avenue, Chicago, Illinois 60622

C. Ukrainian Publications In English

Ameryka (America), 1912—. 817 North Franklin Street, Philadelphia, Pennsylvania 19123

Annals of the Ukrainian Academy of Arts and Sciences, 1951—. 206 West 100 Street, New York, New York 10025

Digest of the Soviet Ukrainian Press, 1956—. 875 West End Avenue, New York, New York 10025.

Forum: A Ukrainian Review, 1967—. 440 Wyoming Avenue, Scranton, Pennsylvania

Recenzija (A Review of Soviet Ukrainian Scholarly Publications), 1970—. 1737 Cambridge Street, Room 208, Cambridge, Massachusetts 02138

The Ukrainian Quarterly, 1944—. 302 West 13th Street, New York, New York 10014

The Ukrainian Weekly, 1933—. 30 Montgomery Street, Jersey City, New Jersey 07303

D. Multi-Ethnic Publications

Ethnic American News, 1972—. 524 S. Wolfe Street, Baltimore, Maryland 21231. Phone: 301-675-7557. This national paper examines cultural, religious, political, and social issues with solid treatment accorded Slavic Americans, among others. Founded in Pittsburgh, the paper moved to Baltimore with its original editor, Ivan Dornic, in October, 1977.

Nationalities Papers, 1972—. c/o Andris Skreija, Sociology, University of Nebraska at Omaha, Omaha, Nebraska 68101. This journal, published semi-annually by the Association for the Study of the Nationalities (USSR and EastEurope), Inc., is edited by Prof. Stephan M. Horak, who is chairman of the Association. East European scholars of all backgrounds contribute to the journal in disciplines of history, sociology, linguistics, demography, political science, etc.

Index

Academy of Sciences of the Ukrainian SSR, 180
Alaska Herald, 58, 261. See Also Honcharenko, Rev. Agapius
Albanians, 288
Aldridge, Ira, 150-153
Alexander II: rejection of Ukrainian language, 32; mentioned 31, 138
Alexandrof, Bishop Vladimir Vladimirof, 198-199
America, 480
American Ukrainian Society, 112-113
Andrew, St., 188
Anna, Princess, 9
Antae, 6
Anti-Semitism, 180-181
Antonovich, Volodimir, 31
Archipenko, Alexander, 386, 388
Arnett, Earl, 164-165, 166, 295, 300
Artists, Ukrainian, 388-399
Armenians, 16
Association for the Study of Nationalities (USSR and Eastern Europe). See Slavic studies
Austrians, 21, 55, 138, 140, 175
Austro-Hungarian empire: decline of, 40; formation of, 38; immigrants, attitude toward, 138, 140-141; Ukrainian areas in, 33; mentioned, 51, 52, 53, 62, 185, 201, 429. See also Ukraine
Avramenko, Vasile, 460-461
Azov sea, 1, 2

Baerlein, Henry, 38-39
Baida. See Vysnevetsky, Prince Dmytro
Balch, Emily G., 60, 277
Baltic sea, 4, 129, 169
Baltics, 288
Baltimore and Ohio Company: influence on Russian railroads, 129-130; job opportunities, 64; steamship service, 72, 141-142; mentioned, 135

Baltimore Museum of Art, 216, 365
Baltimore Ukrainian Relief Committee, 103-105
Baludiansky, Michael, 38
Bandera, Stepan, 4
Bartosz, Adam, 279
Bathory, Stephen, 15
Bazilovich, I., 38
Benedict XI, Pope, 193, 269
Berestechko, 20
Bessarabia, 42, 283
Bible, translation of, 8
Bielski, Dick 418
Black sea, 1, 2, 4, 5, 10, 13, 18, 129, 169, 188
Black, Tessie (Matachek), 458
Bodnar, John E., 413
Bogoliubsky, Andrew, 10
Bohdan, Ivan, 136
Bohachevsky, Bishop Constantine: building of seminary, 198, 235, 236, 237; League of Ukrainian Catholics, 220; of Philadelphia eparchy, 193; on calendar, 211; visit to Baltimore, 307; mentioned, 228
Bohun, Ivan, 27, 483
Boleslaw. See George II
Boleshevik Revolution, 40-42, 227
Bonsal, Stephen, 42
Boretsky, Michael T., 448
Boyars, 11, 12, 14, 36
"Bread-basket of Europe", 4
Brest, 12. See also Union of Brest
Bukovina, 33, 36, 39, 40, 42, 45, 56, 60, 264
Bulawka, Msgr. Wasyl, 254, 257-258, 259, 261, 263
Bulgaria, 7, 166
Bulgarians, 3, 7, 289
Byelorussia, 1, 12, 25, 44, 45, 172, 174
Byelorussians, 13, 17, 55, 147, 153, 176, 277, 289, 494
Byzantine Slavonic rite: com-

pared with Latin rite, 185-187; preservation of, 269, 270, 484-486; mentioned, 17, 190, 196, 216, 220, 228, 232, 250, 252. See also Eastern rite

Calendar: Julian and Gregorian, 211; mentioned, 187, 236
Campbell, Thomas, 269
Captive Nations Week, 491
Carpathian mountains, 1, 11, 37, 38, 56, 189, 348, 383
Carpatho-Rusins. See Rusins
Carpatho-Russians. See Rusins
Carpatho-Ruthenia. See Ukraine
Casimir, King of Poland, 12, 13, 15, 19, 20
Caspian sea, 7
Catherine II, 28, 149, 169
Catholic University, 236, 367
Caucasus mountains, 1
Censorship, 43
Central Rada. See Kiev
Ceramics, Ukrainian, 340, 373, 375-378
Charles XII, 25, 27
Chernivtsi, 36
Chirovsky, Nicholas, 7, 8
Chomyshyn, Bishop Hryhoriy, 214
Christianity, 7, 188, 360
Chrysostom, St. John, 250
Chuprynka, Taras, 4
Church Slavonic Language, 33. See also Language
Church Union, 17, 20
Cicognani, Amleto, Apostolic Delegate, 235, 237
Clement, St., 133, 188
Coal miners, 61, 64, 134, 137, 159
Collective farms, 43
Constantinople, 5, 8, 10, 18, 374
Cossacks. See Kozaks
Cracow, 21
Crimea, 2, 18, 20, 134
Crimean war, 29, 134, 401
Croatians, 188, 193, 279, 289, 296
Crusades, 10
Cultural diversity, 300, 301
Curtin, Jeremiah, 21
Cumans, 9-10
Customs, Ukrainian: Christmas and Easter, 350-351, 352, 356; festivals, 357
Cyril, St. See Bible, translation of
Czars, 28, 30, 261
Czechoslovakia, 42, 45, 63, 211
Czechs, 75, 189, 279, 288, 289, 290, 296, 299, 494
Daniel, King of Rus, 11
Danube river, 1, 2, 7, 11, 297
Danyliv, Bohdan, 406-407
Degler, Carl N., 51
Demyanovich, Sister Miriam Teresa, 211-212
Diet of Princes, 9
Displaced Persons Act, 100-103, 107. See also Maryland Committee for Displaced Persons
Dniester river, 10
Dnipro Ice Hockey Club, 425-426
Dnipropetrovsk, 3
Dobriansky, Adolph I., 38
Dobriansky, Lev, 407, 491
Don river, 2
Donbas, 31
Donets river, 2, 13
Donetske, 3, 31
Dorish, Harry, 416
Dornic, Rev. Ivan, 433
Doroshenko, Petro, 24
Dukhnovich, Alexander, 38
Dypsky, Cornell 434, 435
Dypsky, Philip, 434-435
Dypsky, Raymond, 434, 435

Easter eggs: and Ukrainian legends, 360-361; classes in decorating, 364-367; classification of, 361; decorating technique, 362-363; Ukrainian art form and symbolism of, 359-360, 371
Eastern rite, 3, 29, 37, 79, 105, 185, 190, 193, 220, 244, 433, 485. See also Byzantine Slavonic rite
Edelman, Jacob, 174
Education. See Ethnic studies; Schools; Slavic studies
Eisenhower, Dwight D., 146
Embroidery, Ukrainian, 379-381, 449
Emigration, reasons for, 49, 52, 60-64
Estonians, 176, 494

Ethnic studies: college course descriptions, 285-286; current concerns, 295-297; inadequate material, 283; Ukrainian and American Indian, 158-159, 161; Ukrainian and Black, 153, 155-156, 158; mentioned, 281. *See also* Schools; Slavic studies; Ukrainian Education Association of Maryland
"Eternal Alliance", 21

Famine, man-made, 43, 144
Farm labor. *See* Maryland Farm Labor Plan
Federation of Ukrainian Student Organizations of America, 339, 341. *See also Hromada*
Fedkovich, Joseph, 36
Fillmore, Millard, 140
Finno-Ugrics, 288
Fisher, H.H., 15-16
Foods, specialties of Ukraine, 218, 347-356
Fortress. *See* Sich
Forum: A Ukrainian Review, 479
France, 9
Franko, Ivan, 429

Gabro, Bishop Jaroslav, 242
Galati, *See* Romania
Galicia: as part of Austria, 33-36, 40; occupation by Russia, 39; Polish rule of, 13, 33-36, 41-42, 189; serfdom, 14-25, 37; mentioned 18, 32, 45, 56, 60, 62, 79, 140, 146, 172, 213, 263, 264 349, 383. *See also* Galicia-Volynian state
Galicia-Volynian state, 10-12
Galician diet, 33
Galician Star, 33
Galicians, 97
Galitzianers, 172
Gallitzin, Rev. Demetrius, 146-147
Garber, Vitaly, 446-447
Gedimin, Prince of Lithuania, 12
Geduminas, King of Lithuania, 147
Geeza, Vladimir, 280
General Ukrainian Council, 39-40

George I, 11
George II, 11
Germans, 15, 67, 71
Germany, 28, 44, 172, 203
Gershwin, George, 181
Glushakow, A.D., 174
Gogol. *See* Hohol
Goldeman, Solomon I., 171
Goldfaden, Abraham, 174
Goliat, Michael, 413
Goths, 6
Grady, Mayor Harold, 339-340
Grain: naming of in America, 149-150; shipment to Soviet Union, 144. *See also* Ukraine, products of
"Grand Duchy of Rus", 23
Greek Catholic: under See of Rome, 37, 264; mentioned, 39, 225.*See also* Byzantine Slavonic rite; Eastern rite
Greek Catholic Union of the U.S.A. *See Sojedinenija*
Greeks, 3, 7, 75, 283, 372
Gregorius, Adam S., 279
Grunwald, battle of, 13
Gutheim, Frederick, 135

Haidamaks, 28
Halich. *See* Galicia-Volynian state
Harvard University: Ukrainian Research Institute, 291-292, 479; Ukrainian Studies Chair Fund, 341, 343
Harvey, Catherine, 134
Havrilak, Samuel, 418-419, 428-429, 457
Hawryluk, Orest, 409
Helsinki Agreement, 438
Hertzen, Alexander, 181
Hetmans, 5, 30
Hitler, Adolph, 44, 45
Hohol, Mykola, 4
Holy Family Ukrainian Catholic Church, 113, 235-237, 239, 310, 311
Holy Name Society, 242
Holy Trinity Ukrainian Orthodox Church, 262-263
Honcharenko, Rev. Agapius, 48, 261-262

Hoverlia, Mt., 2
Hromada, 338-341, 343, 344
Hrushevsky, Michael, 4, 35, 37, 40
Hrushiv, 37
Hungarians, 53, 55, 79, 166, 188, 193
Hungary: revolution, 38-39; mentioned, 11, 12
Huns, 6, 7
Hust, 45
Hutzuls, 384

Icons: description and tradition of, 186, 187, 374-375; mentioned, 35, 244, 252, 258
Iconostasis, 187, 216, 248, 252, 254, 258, 267, 383
Ihor, Prince, 7
Ilarion, Metropolitan of Canada, 254
Ilarion, monk appointed as bishop by Yaroslav, 9
Immigrants: common concerns of American Indian and Ukrainian, 161; comparison between Negro and Slavic, 159; description of journey, 51, 71-74; distrust of, 277-278; geographical dissemination of, 121,128; numbers of, 50-51, 53, 60, 63, 71, 101, 105, 121-128, 138, 140-141, 189, 302, 441-443; occupations of, 63-63, 76-80. 93-95, 97, 113-115, 121, 134, 135, 142, 190, 222, 441-458; religious development of, 146-149,190-201. *See also* Settlements; Refugees
Institute of Soviet and East European Studies. *See* Slavic studies
International Refugee Organization, 100. *See also* Refugees
Irish, 75, 286
Italians, 71, 75, 283, 299
Ivan III, Czar, 11, 13, 15, 166
Ivancho, Bishop Daniel, 237
Ivanenko, Petro, 25

Jadviga, Queen of Poland, 13
Jagello, King of Poland, 13
Jamestown, 277
Japan, 32
Jaskilka, General Samuel, 341, 410-411
Jaworskyj, Michael, 293,431-432
Jesuits, 15
Jewish-Ukrainian relations. *See* Ukrainian-Jewish relations
Jews, Ukrainian. *See* Ukrainian Jews

Kalakuka, Theodore, 405
Kennedy, John F., 49, 242
Kharkiv, 3
Khazars, 7, 167
Khmelnitsky, Bohdan: as enemy of Polish armies, 18-23; brutality against Jews, analysis of, 168-169; compared with Cromwell, 22-23; mentioned, 4, 372
Khmelnitsky, Yuriy, 23-24
Kholm, 41, 267
Khomyshyn, Bishop Hryhoriy, 433
Khortytsia, 16
Kichko, Trofim K., 180
Kiev: as political and religious center, 8,324; capital of Ukraine and population of, 3, 188; *Central Rada,* 40; decline of, 9-10; food specialties of, 354-355; origin and name, 6,7; trade, 8; mentioned 13, 28, 29, 32, 41, 152, 164, 177, 180, 264, 266, 340, 341, 375, 381, 386, 388. *See also* Rus; Tatars
Kiev University, 137
Kievan state: decline of, 9-10; origin of, 6-7; Polish and Lithuanian rule of, 7; practice of Christianity, 188; reign of Volodimir, 8; rule of Yaroslav, 8-9; mentioned, 38, 375
Kievan Rus: *See* Kievan state
Kilems, 373, 382-383
Knights of Columbus, 221
Kocisko, Metropolitan Stephen J., 252
Konotop, 23
Koriatovich, Prince Theodore, 37
Korsun, battle of, 18
Koshetz, Alexander, 462
Kostomarov, Nicholas, 30
Kotlyarevsky, Ivan, 29. *See also* Ukraine, nationalism

Kowalsky, Rev. Onufrey, 198, 292-293
Kozak-Hetman state, 56-57
Kozaks: as warriors, 6; brutality, analysis of, 168-169; names for, 57; nationalism, 16-17; schools, importance of, 302-303; wars against Sweden, Moldavia, Muscovy, Poland, 18-29; mentioned, 411
Krai, 5. See also Ukraina
"Krevo Union", 13
Kubala, L., 22-23
Kuban river, 1
Kudirka, Simas, 177, 179
Kuntsevich, St. Josaphat, 244
Kuzmiw, Theodore, 388-390, 447, 467
Kyi, Prince, 7
Kyiv. *See* Kiev

Labor camps, 51, 64, 67
Landlords, 5, 15, 18, 20, 29, 37, 38
Landowners. *See* landlords
Language: Czech, 288; Hungarian, 39; Polish, 33, 279; Russian, 288; Slavonic, 8, 33, 36, 190, 192, 265, 279; Ukrainian, 12, 15, 29, 30, 31, 32, 33, 34, 35, 36, 39, 56, 67, 75, 76, 78, 166, 280, 292, 302, 311, 314, 322, 325-326, 494; United States Defense Language Institute, 289. *See also* Alexander II; Library of Congress
Latin rite: *Code of Canon Law* on Ukrainian Catholics, 269-270; compared with Byzantine Slavonic rite, 185-188; mentioned, 12
"Latinization", 264
Latvians, 176
League of Ukrainian Catholics, 220-222, 236
Leo II, 11
Leo XIII, Pope, 270
Library of Congress, 451,454
Lichten, Joseph L., 174
Literaturna Ukraina, 178
Lithuania: capture by Czar and Kozaks, 20; Polish influence in, 14; rule of Ukraine by, 12-13; mentioned, 100, 169, 172, 438
Lithuanian Federation, occupation of Volynia, 12
Lithuanian-Rus state, 12-13
Lithuanians, 14, 16, 97, 148, 175, 176, 299, 460, 494
Little Russia, 30, 32, 57
Little Russians, 32, 39, 60, 97
Litvaks, 172
Lodi, Peter, 38
Losten, Bishop Basil, 234, 244
Lublin, 11, 21. *See also* Union of Lublin
Lubny, 16
Luchkai-Pop, Michael, 38
Lukash, William M., 458
Lviv: capital of Western Ukraine, 3,11; literary center, 34; national revival in, 33; mentioned, 2, 18, 40, 189, 204, 216, 292, 303, 388
Lviv University, 33, 35
Lysenko, Mykola, 440

MacArthur, Douglas, 405
Magnus Dominus. *See* Clement, St.
Magyarization, 38-39
Makiyivka, 3
Malevich, Stephen, 405
Malko, J. Robert, 431
Malo-Russian. *See* Little Russia
Maniosky, Rev. Basil, 201,202-204, 206, 209, 220, 227, 494
Manor Junior College, 290-291
Manning, Clarence A., 292-293
Maps: *Distribution of Ukrainians in Baltimore*, 124; *Distribution of Ukrainians in Maryland*, 127; *Nationalities in Austria-Hungary*, 34; *Ukraine*, xvi
Margolin, Arnold M., 169, 171
Maryland Bicentennial Commission, 343, 437, 471, 492, 494
Maryland Committee for Displaced Persons, 102-103; *See also* Displaced Persons Act
Maryland Farm Labor Plan, 107-109, 114
Maryland Historical Society, 216, 277, 494
Maria Theresa, Empress, 37

513

Marxian theory, 43
Masnyk, Ihor, 407
Mazepa, Ivan, 4, 25-27, 130-131
Melnyczuk, Msgr. Petro: and Cardinal Slipy, 216-218; and ecumenism, 215-216; as Archdiocesan consultor, 213, 218; as writer, 214-215; church choir, 216; vocations, 218; mentioned, 229, 242, 316, 319, 325, 433
Mencken, H. L., 278-280
Mennonites, 270
Methodius, St. *See* Bible, translation of
Mikulski, Barbara, 295, 494
Military forces, American Ukrainian, 401-411
Moldavia, 18, 27, 36
Moldavians, 24
Mongols, 132. *See also* Tatars
Moravia, 53
Moscow, 13, 15, 20, 21, 147, 180, 385, 407
Mostwin, Stanislaw, 295
Mstyslav I, 10
Muscovy: absolutist principle, 14; division of Ukraine, 24, 25; gains from Catherine II, 28; invasion of Ukraine, 23; renamed Russia, 27; mentioned, 6, 18, 21, 57, 147, 166, 201

Nagurski, Bronislaw, 416-418
Nalivaiko, Kozak leader, 17. *See also* Kozaks
Narodna Rada, 35
Narodna Volya, 479
National Democratic Party, 35
National Shrine of the Immaculate Conception, 244, 252
Nationalism, *See* Ukraine; Shevchenko, Taras
Neuman, St. John Nepomucene, 147-148, 275
Nevelson, Lois, 385
Nicholas I, 30, 129
Nicholas, St., 204, 316
Normans. *See* Varangians
Norway, 9
Novak, Michael, 283, 295, 300, 495
Nove Zhyttia, 280

Nowosiwsky, Taras, 408-409

O'Boyle, Cardinal Patrick, 236, 240, 242
October Revolution, 227
Odessa, 3, 13, 40, 144, 145, 146, 152, 176, 177, 385, 386
Olenchuk, General Peter G., 406
Olgerd, Prince of Lithuania, 12-13
Olha, St., 8, 188, 240
Orchard Street Church, 160-161
Order of St. Basil the Great (OSBM), 206, 218, 229, 234, 238, 291, 310
Organization for the Defense of Four Freedoms for Ukraine, 465-466, 471-472
Organization for the Rebirth of Ukraine (ODWU), 483-484
Orientalium Dignitas. See Leo XII, Pope
Orlik, Philip, 27
Orthodox America, 227, 264
Orthodox Church of America, 193, 227, 264, 265
Orthodoxy, 14, 21, 29, 30, 37, 198, 264
Ortynsky, Bishop Soter Stephen, 89, 93, 192, 194, 199, 200, 223, 244, 480, 481
Orun, Rev. Zachary, 80, 190, 192, 194, 199, 200, 224, 225, 232
Osmomysl, Yaroslav, 11
Ossolinski, Chancellor of Poland, 21
Ottoman empire, 6, 36, 131

Painters. *See* Artists
Paliy, Semen, 25
Panchison, Walter, 410
Pans, 34
Paska, Msgr. Walter 433
Patriarch of Moscow, 265, 267-268
Patriarchate of the Ukrainian Catholic Church, 484-486
Patronage of the Mother of God Byzantine Catholic Church, 245, 247-248, 250, 283
Peace Conference, 42
Peasants, 5, 11, 14, 15, 16, 20, 28, 29, 31, 35, 36, 38, 40, 44, 150, 169, 181

Peremyshl, 10
Peter I, Czar, 25, 26, 27, 130, 149
Petliura, Semen, 4, 171
Plast: Ukrainian Scouting Organization, 462-465, 488
Pochayiv, 244
Podilia, 20, 24, 28, 37, 41, 375
Poland: aggression in Galicia-Volynia, 11-12; division of Ukraine, 24, 42; occupation of Volynia and Kiev, 13; partition of, 28; rule of Ukraine by, 15, 17; mentioned, 1, 2, 5, 6, 11, 12, 13, 44, 45, 63, 172, 327, 454. *See also* Polonization
Poles, 13, 15, 16, 17, 18, 20, 21, 23, 24, 28, 29, 33, 55, 71, 75, 97, 148, 189, 277, 279, 288, 296, 298, 299, 353, 372, 385, 494
Poleticka, Petro, 137-138, 495
Poliani, 6, 7
Polish Heritage Association of Maryland, 287, 295, 492
Polonization, 15, 16
Polovtsi. *See* Cumans
Poltava: battle of, 27, 30; mentioned, 375, 381, 382
Pontifical Institute for Eastern Studies, 193
Populist movement, 34, 35, 36. *See also* Ukraine, nationalism
Pospishil, Msgr. Victor, 234
Prairies, *See* Steppes
Pravda, 34
Prince, John Dyneley, 293
Providence Association of Ukrainian Catholics of America, 240, 480-481
Prpic, George J., 277
Prussia, 35
Pulaski, Casimir: monument, 279; Pulaski Legion, 277
Pushkin, Alexander, 153
Pysanky. *See* Easter eggs

Radygin, Anatole, 179-180
Radzykewycz, Julian, 429, 457
Railroads. *See* Baltimore and Ohio Company
Redemptorist Fathers, 232, 234, 242, 243-244
Redemptorist Seminary, 149

Refugees, 39, 44, 100, 101-102, 105, 121, 163, 171, 176-177, 338, 407, 461, 470, 477, 488. *See also* Emigration; Immigrants
Religious persecution, 65
Revay, Julian, 488, 491
Revyuk, Emil, 280
Rice, Grantland, 416-417
Roborecki, Bishop Andrew, 237
Romania, 1, 11, 42, 44, 63, 100
Romanians, 36, 166, 288
Roosevelt, Eleanor, 364
Roosevelt, Franklin D., 363, 465
Roxolanians, 7
Rozumowsky, Kyrylo, 28
Rurikides dynasty, 7, 11
Rus, 6, 55, 58. *See also* Kiev; Kievan state
Rus Law. *See Ruskaia Pravda*
Rusins, 55, 56, 60, 78, 97, 147, 166, 187, 191, 201, 264, 302. *See also* Ukrainians, various names for
Ruskaia Pravda, 8
Russia, 1, 2, 39, 40, 51, 57, 67, 130, 138, 164, 166
Russian Federation, 1
Russian Orthodox, 5, 56, 136, 188, 193, 217, 226, 267, 268
Russian Orthodox Church, 27
Russian Orthodox Greek Catholic Church of America. *See* Orthodox Church of America
Russians, 30, 31, 44, 55, 56, 67, 163, 166, 174, 176, 265, 268, 279, 288, 289, 353, 385
Russification: policy, 28, 29, 30, 32, 44, 45-46, 179, 374; mentioned, 36, 58
Rusyns. *See* Rusins
Ruthenia. *See* Ukraina
Ruthenians, 56, 58-59, 147, 188, 212, 252, 302

Sacred Congregation of the Eastern Churches, 193
Sahaidachny, Petro, 18
St. Andrew the Apostle Russian Orthodox Church, 266-267
St. Andrew's Ukrainian Orthodox Church, 113, 311
St. Basil's Ukrainian Catholic Church, 95, 229-234, 310, 402

St. Francis de Sales Catholic Church, 105, 117
St. Gregory of Nyssa Byzantine Catholic Church, 252-253
St. Josaphat's Ukrainian Catholic Seminary, 113, 198, 222, 232, 235, 236
St. Mary's Seminary, 146, 174, 194-199, 216, 247, 296, 306, 338, 494
St. Mary's Ukrainian Catholic Church. *See* St. Michael's Ukrainian Greek Catholic Church
St. Michael's Ukrainian Greek Catholic Church, 80, 112, 158, 191, 199-202, 206, 209, 211, 216, 218, 220, 306, 307, 314, 317, 402, 435, 439, 464, 467, 476
St. Michael's Ukrainian Orthodox Church, 253-261, 315, 317-318
St. Nicholas Monastery, 37
St. Petersburg, 28, 385, 388
St. Sophia Cathedral, 8, 9
St. Vincent de Paul Chapel, 236, 240
St. Wenceslaus Church, 285
SS. Peter and Paul Ukrainian Catholic Church, 84, 117, 201, 222-229, 315, 318, 402
Samutin, Petro, 181, 413
Savaryn, Bishop Niel, 237, 242
Scandinavians, 6
Schaefer, Mayor William Donald, 341, 343
Schmondiuk, Bishop Joseph, 240, 242
School of Ukrainian Sciences. *See* Slavic studies
School of Ukrainian Studies. *See* Slavic studies
Schools, ethnic heritage, 288-294, 299-336, 476-487. *See also* Ethnic studies; Slavic studies
Self-determination, 39-40, 41-42, 438
Selfreliance Association of American Ukrainians, 472-474
Selfreliance Baltimore Federal Credit Union, 472-474
Sembratovych, Metropolitan Sylvester, 189
Semeniuk, Peter, 453
Senyshyn, Metropolitan Ambrose, 213, 237, 240, 245
Serbia, 28
Serbs, 166, 279, 289
Serfdom, 14, 28, 30-31, 37, 44, 150, 429
Sensenbaugh, James A., 287
Seton, St. Elizabeth Ann, 211
Settlements: Baltimore, 75-87, 110, 111, 113, 123, 125, 191; Chesapeake City, 87-97, 110-111, 113, 126, 310; Curtis Bay, 75, 76, 78, 84-87, 110, 113, 125, 191, 222; Eastern Shore, 111, 114-115, 117, 126, 451; Washington, D.C., 111-113, 126, 128; Western Maryland, 97, 126; mentioned, 412. *See also* Emigration; Refugees
Sheptitsky, Metropolitan Andrew, 35, 180-181, 204, 240, 269
Shevchenko Scientific Society, 390, 429
Shevchenko, Taras: Aldridge friendship, 150, 152-153; defense of Jews, 169; monument, 242, 243, 451, 490; nationalism, 30; mentioned, 4, 34, 373, 429
Shmorhun, John G. 437, 452
Siberia, 28, 31, 57, 67
Sich, 16, 17, 28
Sienkiewicz, Henryk, 21
Silesia, 11, 15
Sister Cities International, 146
Sisters of Charity, 211
Sisters of the Third Order of St. Francis, 218
Sisters of St. Basil the Great. *See* Order of St. Basil the Great (OSBM)
Skrypnyk, Metropolitan Mstyslav S., 261
Slavic Church of Christ, 268-269
Slavic studies: American Association for the Advancement of Slavic Studies, 168; Association for the Study of Nationalities, 283; importance in education, 275-278; Institute of Soviet and

East European Studies, 291;
School of Ukrainian Sciences,
318-325; School of Ukrainian
Studies, 113, 311, 313-314;
Ukrainian Studies Institute,
341, 343; mentioned, 241
Slavonic Gospel Book, 266
Slavs. *See Antae*
Slipy, Cardinal Joseph, 89, 216-218, 242, 245, 484, 485-486
Slovakia, 1, 211
Slovaks, 75, 79, 97, 148, 188, 189, 193, 277, 279, 288, 290, 296, 353, 494
Slovenians, 296
Smal-Stotsky, Stephen, 36
Smolensk, 18
Sobiesky, Jan, 24-25
Society of SS. Cyril and Methodius, 30. *See also* Bible, translation of
Sojedinenija, 79, 206, 207, 475-476
Solzhenitsyn, Alexander, 46
Souchock, Stephen, 413, 418
Sovietization, 45
Stalin, Joseph, 44, 45
Staszak, Joseph A., 436
Stefanyk, Wasyl, 50
Stepanenko, Mykola, 455-456
Steppes, 224, 405
Stett, Joseph Daniel, 448-449
Supreme Ruthenian Council, 33
Sushko, Rev. Wasyl, 105-106, 202
Sviatoslav, reign of, 7
Svoboda, 189, 194, 280, 302, 303, 476-477
Sweden, 9, 18, 21, 326
Swedes, 21, 25

Tatars: aggression against Ukraine, 13; capture of Byelorussia and Lithuania, 20-21; destruction of Kiev, 11; mentioned, 3, 10, 12, 16, 18, 25, 29, 166. *See also* Kiev
Tatchyn, Roman Orest, 429-430
Tawes, Gov. J. Millard, 340
Telencio, John, 407
Teutonic Order, 13
The Ukrainian Quarterly, 433, 487
The Way, 235

Theodorovich, Metropolitan John, 261
Timoshenko, Alexander S., 445
Tkach, Walter R., 458
Transcarpathia. *See* Ukraine
Transylvania, 21
Treaties: of Andrusowo, 24; of Buchach, 24; of Nystadt, 27; of Pereyaslav, 20, 23; of Riga, 41; of Zboriv, 19-20
Tresh, Mike, 413, 415
Turchin, John Basil, 57-58, 401
Turkestan, 31
Turkey, 18, 21, 188
Turks, 10, 16, 18, 24, 25, 29, 382

Ukraina, 5, 58. *See also Krai*
Ukraine: areas in Austro-Hungarian empire, 33-36; as independent nation, 40; battle of Habsburgs and Transylvanians, 37; Bukovina, 36; climate of , 2-3; composition and location of, 1-2; famine, manmade, 43, 144; historical influences in, 4-6; Hungarian revolution, 38-39; Kozak era, 16-29; literary figures of, 38; Lithuanian and Polish rule of, 7, 12-16, 17; nationalism, 16, 30, 33, 34, 35, 37, 43-44, 57, 61, 67; population, 3, 30, 36; products of, 3-4, 31, 43, 347, 382, 383; Russian rule of, 29-33; Sovietization of, 45; Transcarpathian, 37-39; Union of Brest, 17; World War I, effects of, 39-46, 226; mentioned 60, 264, 408
Ukrainka, Lesyia, 429, 447
Ukrainian Academy of Sciences of America, 281. *See also* Slavic studies
Ukrainian American Citizens Club, 458-462
Ukrainian American Citizens Club Women's Auxiliary, 469, 488
Ukrainian American Democratic Club of Maryland, 437
Ukrainian American Republican Club of Maryland, 437

Ukrainian American Youth Association (SUM), 466-469
Ukrainian Catholic Youth League. *See* League of Ukrainian Catholics
Ukrainian Congress Committee of America, 110, 171, 306, 318, 438, 478, 483, 487-491
Ukrainian Dancing Club, 81, 83
Ukrainian Education Association of Maryland, 155, 158, 159, 287, 295, 296, 398, 491-496
Ukrainian Exarchate, 241-242
Ukrainian heritage schools. *See* Schools, ethnic heritage
Ukrainian-Jewish relations, 168-172, 182. *See also* Baltimore Committee for Soviet Jewry
Ukrainian Jews, 53, 55, 144, 163-183, 351, 353, 355-356
Ukrainian Medical Association of North America, 481-483
Ukrainian Music Institute, 438-440
Ukrainian National Aid Association, 481
Ukrainian National Association, 79, 85, 302, 304, 476-479, 488
Ukrainian National Choir, 81, 83, 308, 462
Ukrainian National Home, 81, 308, 309, 458-462, 488
Ukrainian National Republic, 40-41, 412, 413
Ukrainian National School, 307-309, 328-331
Ukrainian National Women's League of America, 469-471
Ukrainian Orthodox Church, 253-263, 320
Ukrainian Peoples Republic, 171
Ukrainian Radical Party, 35
Ukrainian Republic of 1917 and 1918, 58
Ukrainian Self-Reliance Federal Credit Union, 161
Ukrainian Student Association of Baltimore, 338-340, 341, 343, 344
Ukrainian Studies Institute. *See* Slavic studies
Ukrainian Women's League, 425
Ukrainian Workingmen's Association, 479-480, 488
Ukrainian Writers Congress, 179
Ukrainian Youth Center, 155, 179, 465
Ukrainian Youth League of North America, 308, 461
Ukrainians, various names for (Rusins, Ruthenians, Slovaks, Croatians, Little Russians, Hungarians), 30, 38, 39, 55, 58, 79, 97, 100, 140, 147, 153, 166, 172, 176-177, 187-188, 191, 201
Ukrainske Narodne Slovo, 481
Uniates. *See* Greek Catholic
Union of Brest, 17, 485
Union of Hadiach, 23
Union of Lublin, 14, 15. *See also* Lublin
Union of Soviet Socialist Republics, 41
United States Defense Language Institute. *See* Language
United Ukrainian Association in America, 304
United Ukrainian War Veterans in America, 411-412, 488

Valuev, Peter, 31, 32
Varangians, 8
Vatican; on patriarch, 485; on priests and marriage, 187
Venetoulis, Theodore, 283
Vernadsky, George, 293
Vienna, 24, 33, 39, 67, 385, 390
Vikings, 6, 7
Vitovt, ruler of Lithuania, 13
Voice of America, 113, 239, 447, 455-456
Volansky, Rev. Ivan, 189
Volodimir, St., 4, 8, 37, 188, 374
Volodimirko, 10
Voloshyn, Msgr. Augustine, 45
Volynia, 10-11, 13, 15, 29, 41, 402
Vyhovsky, Ivan, 23
Vysnevetsky, Prince Dmytro, 16

Warsaw, 18, 19, 21, 385
Weinryb, Bernard D., 167-169
Wertsman, Vladimir, 136, 174
Western Ukrainian National Republic. *See* Ukrainian National

Republic
Winans, Thomas, 130
Wilson, Woodrow, 42
Women's Association of the Organization for the Defense of Four Freedoms for Ukraine, 471-472
Wood, uses of in Ukraine and in Maryland, 383-384

Yarema, Carl J., 436, 443
Yarema, John, 436, 437, 442-443, 452

Yaroslav the Wise: rule of Kiev, 8-9; mentioned, 4, 62. *See also* Kiev
Yarymovych, Michael I., 446

Zaikan, Ivan, 38
Zalizniak, Maxim, 28
Zamostia, 21
Zaporizhia, 3, 130, 177
Zinkewych, Osyp, 448
Zolotny, 223
Zuk, William, 430-431, 455